THE ROUGH GUIDES

ROUGH GUIDE CREDITS

Series Editor: Mark Ellingham
Editorial: Martin Dunford, John Fisher, Jack Holland, Jonathan Buckley, Greg Ward, Richard Trillo
Production: Susanne Hillen, Kate Berens, Andy Hilliard
Typesetting: Gail Jammy

Our thanks for their help with this new edition to Chryssa in Haniá, Jackie Richardson in Sitía, Pandelis Iliakis, Alex in Haniá, Vangeli in Loutró, and Kate and Susanne in Kennington. From the first edition, continued thanks to Mark Ellingham, Tim Salmon, Marc Dubin, Martin Dunford, Jack Holland, Despina Katsirea at the NTOG, Pavlos Seliniotakis, Manolis Sgouros, Howard Potts, Aliki in Haniá, and Anne Marie Barrett and Bob Defee. Thanks for additional information to Gideon Henderson, Pete Raine, Bruce Caughey, Jerry Graham and Carol Phile. And for letters and other help – in no particular order – to Gareth Bridge, Terence Brace, Carola Scupham, Heather Gourlay and Christine Bell, Eleanor Healey, Joan and Jim Barkley, Cryss Healey, Francesca Melandri, M.J. Frost, Tony Walsh, Elspeth Barker, Caroline and David Watson, Fergus King, Tracy Austin, Freya and Paul Steele, Ken Kimber, Jeremy Pearce, Sarah Chambers, John Bunt, Margaret Stewardson, Wendy Jarvis, Beverly Myers, Sue Manning, Bert Broeckart, Malcolm Clifton, Miss P.A. Womersley, Della Reader, Philip Springthorpe, P.J. McCarthy, Mrs P. Rischmiller, Mrs J. Merz, Christine Hall, David Poyser, Dave Kail, Jan Brookes, Jane Pickering, Pauline Carroll, Maureen Eastany, Jem Eastwell, Philomena Searson, Robin Wilkinson, John Mansley, K. Mitchell, Maxine Gandy, Hilary Roberts, Keith Plant, R. Fletcher, Kay Davies, Michael and Catherine Gaum, Mrs B. Massey, Bill Badham, Denise Walden, Ms S. Graham, Tony Samuel, Elizabeth Adlam, Karl Keyte and to everyone else who wrote in.

Above all, to Stretch and to J.D. for their support and inspiration.

Reprinted July 1992 and June 1993 by Rough Guides Ltd, 1 Mercer Street, London WC2H 9QJ.
Distributed by Penguin Books Ltd, 27 Wrights Lane, London W8 5TZ.
First and second editions published 1988 and 1989 by Harrap Columbus Ltd.

Typeset in Linotron Univers and Century Old Style to an original design by Andrew Oliver.
Printed in the UK by Cox & Wyman, Reading, Berks.

Illustrations in Part One and Part Three by Ed Briant.
Basics illustration by Simon Fell. Contexts illustration by Henry Iles.

304pp. includes index

British Library Cataloguing in Publication Data
A catalogue record for this book is available from the British Library.
ISBN 1-85828-049-4 (previously published by Harrap Columbus under ISBN 0-7471-0262-7).

CRETE
THE ROUGH GUIDE

Written and researched by

JOHN FISHER

AND GEOFF GARVEY

Edited by
John Fisher

THE ROUGH GUIDES

HELP US UPDATE

We've gone to a lot of effort to ensure that this new edition of *Crete: The Rough Guide* is accurate and up-to-date. But things change fast – new bars and tavernas appear and disappear, restaurants and rooms raise prices or lower standards, sites and museums change their opening hours, extra buses are laid on. If you feel we've got it wrong or left something out, we'd like to know – any suggestions, comments or corrections would be much appreciated, in fact. If you can remember the address, the price, the time, the phone number, so much the better.

We'll credit all contributions, and send a copy of the next edition (or any other Rough Guide if you prefer) for the best letters. Please write to:

John Fisher, The Rough Guides, 1 Mercer Street, London WC2H 9QJ.

CONTENTS

Introduction vi

INTRODUCTION

Crete is a great deal more than just another Greek island. Much of the time, especially in the cities or along the developed north coast, it doesn't feel like an island at all, but a substantial land in its own right. Which of course it is – a mountainous, wealthy and at times surprisingly cosmopolitan one with a tremendous and unique history. There are two big cities, **Iráklion** and **Haniá**, a host of sizeable, historic towns, and an island culture which is uniquely Cretan: the Turks were in occupation less than a hundred years ago, and the Greek flag raised for the first time only in 1913.

Long before, Crete was distinguished as the home of Europe's earliest civilisation. It was only at the beginning of this century that the legends of King Minos, and of a Cretan society which ruled the Greek world in prehistory, were confirmed by excavations at Knossós and Festós. Yet **the Minoans** had a remarkably advanced and cultured society, at the centre of a substantial maritime trading empire, as early as 2000 BC. The artworks produced on Crete at this time are unsurpassed anywhere in the ancient world, and it seems clear, wandering through the Minoan palaces and towns, that life on Crete in those days was good. Their apparently peaceful culture survived a number of major disasters, following

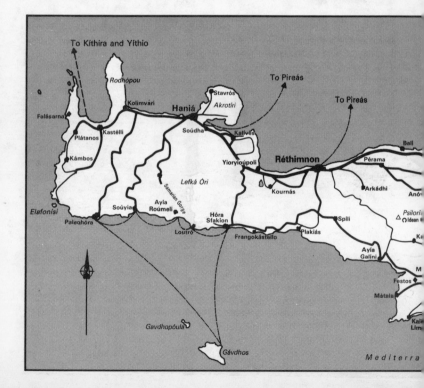

each of which the palaces were rebuilt on an even grander scale. It is only after a third that significant numbers of weapons start to appear in the ruins, probably because Mycenaean Greeks had taken control of the island. Nevertheless, for nearly 500 years, by far the longest period of peace the island has seen, Crete was home to a civilisation well ahead of its time.

The Minoans are believed to have come originally from Anatolia, and the island's position as meeting point – and strategic fulcrum – between east and west has played a crucial role in its **subsequent history**. Control passed from Greeks to Romans to Saracens, through the Byzantine Empire to Venice, and finally to Turkey for 200 years. During World War II Crete was occupied by the Germans, and gained the dubious distinction of being the first place to be successfully invaded by parachute. Each one of these diverse rulers has left some mark, and more importantly they have marked the islanders and forged for the land a personality toughened by endless struggles for independence.

Today, with a flourishing agricultural economy, Crete is one of the few Greek islands which could support itself without tourists. Nevertheless, tourism is heavily promoted, and is rapidly taking over parts of the island altogether. Along the populous **north coast**, Crete can be as sophisticated as you want it, and the northeast, in particular, can be depressingly overdeveloped. In the less known coastal reaches of the **south** it's still possible to find yourself alone, but even here places which have not yet been reached are getting harder and harder to find. By contrast, the high mountains of the interior are barely touched, and one of the

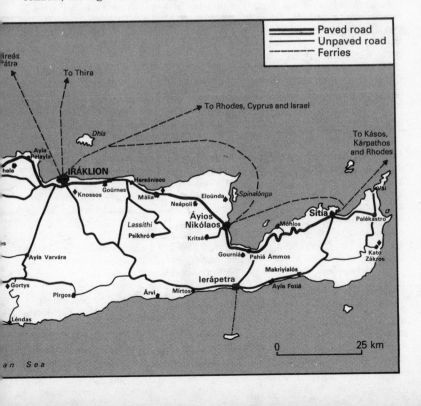

best things to do on Crete is to hire a Vespa and head for remoter villages, often only a few kilometres off some heavily beaten track.

The **mountains**, which dominate the view as you approach and make all but the shortest journey an expedition, are perhaps the most rewarding aspect of Crete. In the west, the White Mountains are snowcapped right into June, Psilorítis (Mount Ida) in the centre is higher still, and in the east the heights continue through the Dhíkti and Sitía ranges to form a continuous chain from one end of the island to the other. They make a relatively small place – Crete is about 260km long by 60km at its widest, roughly the size of Jamaica – feel much larger. There are still many places where the roads cannot reach.

Where to go

Every part of Crete has its loyal devotees and it's hard to pick out highlights – but on the whole if you want to get away from it all you should head for the ends of the island – west, towards **Haniá** and the smaller, less well-connected places along the south and west coasts, or east to **Sitía**. Wherever you're staying, though, you don't have to go far inland to escape the crowds.

Whatever you do, the first main incentive is to get away from the urban blight of **Iráklion** (Heraklion) as quickly as possible – having paid the obligatory, and rewarding, visits to the **archaeological museum** and nearby **Knossós**. The **Minoan sites** are of course one of the major attractions of Crete: as well as Knossós itself there are many other grand remains scattered around the centre of the island – **Festós** and **Ayía Triádha** in the south (with Roman **Górtys** to provide contrast) and **Mália** on the north coast. Almost wherever you go, though, you'll find some kind of reminder of this history – the town of **Gourniá** near the tourist enticements of **Áyios Nikólaos**, the palace of **Zákros** over in the far east or the lesser sites scattered around the west.

For many people, unexpected highlights also turn out to be Crete's **Venetian forts** – dominant at **Réthimnon**, magnificent at Frangokástello, and found in various stages of ruin around most of the island; the **Byzantine churches** – most famously at **Kritsá** but again to be discovered almost anywhere; and, at Réthimnon and Haniá, cluttered **old towns** full of Venetian and Turkish relics.

The mountains and valleys of the interior also deserve far more attention than they get. Only the **Lasíthi** plateau in the east and the **Samarian gorge** in the west really see large numbers of visitors, but almost anywhere you can turn off the main roads and find agricultural villages going about their daily life, and often astonishingly beautiful scenery. This is especially true in the west, where the Lefká Óri – the **White Mountains** – dramatically dominate every view, and numerous lesser gorges run parallel to the Samarian one down to the Libyan Sea. But there's lovely country behind Iráklion, too, in the foothills of the Psilorítis range, and especially on the other side of these mountains in the **Amári Valley**, easily reached from Réthimnon. The east also has its moments, in the Dhíkti range and in the spectacular cliff drive from Áyios Nikólaos to Sitía.

As for **beaches**, you'll find great ones almost anywhere on the north coast. From Iráklion to Áyios Nikólaos there's very heavy development, and most package tourists are aiming for the resort hotels here. These places can be fun if nightlife and crowds are what you're after – especially the biggest of them, like **Mália** and **Áyios Nikólaos**, which have the added advantage of being large enough to have plenty of cheap food and accommodation, plus good transport links. Mália also has sand as good as any on the island (if you can find it through the crowds), but Áyios Nikólaos really doesn't have much of a beach of its own. Further east things get quieter: **Sitía** is a place of real character, and beyond it on the east coast are a number of beautifully tranquil places – especially **Zákros** – and one which is very busy with day-trippers, **Vái**. To the west there's another tranche of development around **Réthimnon**, but the town itself is relatively unscathed, and a rather lesser cluster of apartments and smaller hotels near **Haniá**, the most attractive of the big towns. Other places at this end of the island tend to be on a smaller scale.

Along the **south coast**, resorts are far more scattered, and the mountains come straight down to the sea much of the way along. Only a handful of places are really developed – **Ierápetra**, **Ayía Galíni**, **Mátala**, **Paleohóra** – and a few more, like **Plakiás** and **Makriyialós**, on their way. But lesser spots in between, not always easy to get to, are some of the most attractive in Crete.

When to go

As the southernmost of all Greek islands, Crete has by far the longest summers: you can get a decent tan here right into October and swim at least from April until early November.

Spring is the prime time to come: in April and May the island is relatively empty of visitors, the weather clear and not overpoweringly hot, and every scene is brightened by a profusion of wild flowers.

By mid-June the rush is beginning. **July and August** are not only the hottest, the most crowded and most expensive months, they are also intermittently blighted by fierce winds and accompanying high seas, which make boat trips very uncomfortable and at their worst can mean staying indoors for a day or more at a time. The south coast is particularly prone to these.

In September the crowds gradually begin to thin out, and **autumn** can again be a great time to visit – but now the landscape looks parched and tired, and there's a feeling of things gradually winding down.

Winters are mild, but also vaguely depressing: many things are shut, it can rain sporadically, sometimes for days, and there's far less life in the streets. In the mountains it snows, even to the extent where villages can be cut off; on the south coast it's generally warmer, soothed by a breeze from Africa. You may get a week or more of really fine weather in the middle of winter; but equally you can have sudden viciously cold snaps right through into March.

	CRETE'S WEATHER				
Month	Average daytime temperature		Average water temperature		Average rainy days
	°C	°F	°C	°F	
January	12	52	15	59	14
February	12	52	15	59	11
March	14	57	16	61	8
April	17	62	17	62	6
May	21	70	20	68	3
June	23	74	23	74	1
July	25	77	24	75	0
August	26	79	25	77	0
September	25	77	24	75	2
October	21	70	23	74	6
November	18	64	19	66	8
December	14	57	17	62	12

Readings from Iráklion, roughly in the centre of the island

Crete's mystery is extremely deep. Whoever sets foot on this island senses a mysterious force branching warmly and benificently through his veins, senses his soul begin to grow.

Níkos Kazantzakís, *Report to Greco*

PART ONE

THE

BASICS

GETTING THERE

The vast majority of visitors to Crete are on some form of package tour which includes a charter flight direct to the island. This is certainly the simplest way of going about things, and even if you plan to travel independently, a seat on a charter to Iráklion is the most straightforward way to start out. But charters – the only way of getting straight to Crete – do have their drawbacks, especially if your plans don't fit neatly into their two-week straitjacket. Anyone planning a longer or looser visit will have to fly to Athens and take the ferry or a domestic flight from there. A brief guide to surviving the city is included below.

Overland travel is exhausting. It's a good 2000 miles from London to Crete, at least three days' non-stop travel, more realistically four. But if you want to take your time over the journey then driving or taking the train can be enjoyable, while the coach remains the cheapest option of all.

DIRECT TO CRETE

The only way to fly direct to Crete is with a **charter**. Direct charter flights may seem expensive, but there are no international scheduled flights, and the saving in time and hassle over travel via Athens is considerable. Be warned that there is on the whole a shortage of flights to Crete, especially to Haniá, and that if you try to book at the last minute you may be forced to go to Athens instead: **student flights** operate only into Athens.

From Britain you can get a charter to Iráklion for about £150 for a low-season night flight rising to around £260 at peak time: Haniá flights are slightly more expensive, and seats are very much harder to come by. These prices are from London, May–October. Virtually no flights operate over the winter, flights from British regional airports only in the main summer season, usually at a premium of £20–30 over the London flights.

Direct charters also operate from **Ireland** and most other **European** countries – again they'll usually be the most straightforward option, if not the cheapest.

There are, however, various **problems with charters** resulting from Greek airline regulations. These specify that a ticket must be for no less than three days and no more than four weeks and must be accompanied by an accommodation voucher for the duration of your stay (only student flights are exempt): if your ticket fails to satisfy these conditions you could be refused entry. In practice, the "accommodation voucher" has become a formality in recent years – you're given one but are not expected to use it and wouldn't be able to if you tried – but periodically the authorities tighten up, and for years have been threatening to reform this whole system. As for the time limit, a cheap flight can sometimes prove economic even if you just use the outward half – the more so if you manage to sell your return (a practice that's officially illegal but much in evidence on the notice boards of youth and student hostels).

For charters out of London you'll find the best selection of ads in the magazines *Time Out* and *LAW*; elsewhere in Britain, check the travel pages at the back of the *Observer* and other Sunday newspapers. Good sources of specifically Cretan charters include *Simply Crete* and others listed under specialist operators overleaf.

There are no international **scheduled flights** – from anywhere – direct to Crete. The best you can do is go with *Olympic*, changing planes in Athens: the cheapest official (SuperPEX) fare is over £300 from London even in the low season, rising to almost £400 at peak times. Tickets bought through "bucket shops" or consolidators may be considerably cheaper, however. All other airlines into Athens use a separate terminal some distance from the *Olympic* one, so be sure to leave

AGENCIES AND AIRLINES

STUDENT/YOUTH AGENCIES

Campus Travel, *London Student Travel*, 52 Grosvenor Gdns, London SW1W 0AG (☎071/730 3402).

STA Travel, 86 Old Brompton Rd, London SW7 3LQ (☎071/937 9921).
Both STA and Campus Travel (useful for non-students, too) have agencies throughout Britain; see their adverts at the back of the book for addresses.

SPECIALIST TOUR OPERATORS

Simply Crete, 8 Chiswick Terrace, Acton Lane, London W4 5LY (☎081/994 4462, 5226). Excellent selection of villas, small hotels and special-interest tours.

Travel Club of Upminster, Station Road, Upminster, Essex RM14 2TT (☎04022/25000). Better than average apartments and hotels.

Freelance Holidays, 40b Grove Road, Stratford upon Avon, Warks CV37 6PB (☎0789/297705). Again, concentrates on the smaller places.

Sunvil Holidays, Sunvil House, Upper Square, Old Isleworth, Middx TW7 7BJ (☎081/568 4499). Bigger company, but good choice of smaller resorts.

Explore Worldwide (RGC), 7 High Street, Aldershot, Hampshire (☎0252/319448). Offer an organised rambling tour round the White Mountains.

AIRLINES

Olympic Airways, 164/165 Piccadilly, London W1 (☎081/846 9966).

British Airways, 75 Regent St, London W1 (☎081/897 4000).

JAT, 37 Maddox St, London W1 (☎071/629 2007, 409 1544).

MALEV, 10 Vigo St, London W1 (☎071/439 0577).

Balkan, 322 Regent St, London W1 (☎071/637 7637).

Kenya Airways, 16 Conduit St, London W1 (☎071/409 0185).

IRELAND

USIT, 19/21 Austin Quay, Dublin (☎01/679 8833). Student/youth specialists with good charter deals.

Joe Walsh Tours, 8–11 Lower Baggot St, Dublin (☎01/789 555). General budget fares agent.

Aer Lingus, 59 Dawson St, Dublin (☎01/795 030). For direct flights.

---

plenty of time for the connection. For details on this and *Olympic* flights to Athens from other parts of the world, see the following sections.

If you are asked to confirm your return flight, do so. There have been problems with overbooking even on charters out of Crete.

PACKAGES

If you intend to do little more than stay in one place soaking up the sun, a **package holiday** can offer exceptional value. Any high-street travel agent can sell you a standard package to eastern Crete, but for something a bit less predictable at the west end of the island, try one of the smaller, specialist operators listed above.

TO ATHENS AND THE GREEK MAINLAND

If you plan a long stay or want to be flexible about dates, if you're trying to save every last penny, if you want to visit other islands along the way, or if you're just plain unlucky, you may well find yourself travelling to Crete via Athens.

FLIGHTS

Despite the provisos mentioned above, **charter flights** are again frequently the cheapest way of getting to Athens. Whether the saving over a direct charter is worth it is up to you – by the time you've reached Crete it's unlikely to amount to more than £20 at best – but you may be forced to go this way. Tickets to Athens are available long after all the Crete flights have sold out. If you hold out for a last-minute booking you may find that you can fly to Athens half-price but that there's nothing available to Crete at all. Charters to Athens – aim for around £150 return in season – are very widely available, the sources largely the same as those mentioned above.

Student or under-26 flights are available for considerably less, starting at just under £100 for a middle-of-the-night low-season charter, rising to about £180 for special reductions on scheduled flights. Be warned, though, that you must be a legitimate student as you may well be required to prove your credentials on boarding, especially leaving Greece. People have been denied seats for not having valid ISIC cards. *Campus Travel* have some of the best deals and also offer one-way tickets: a good way of avoiding the voucher requirement – by combining one-ways you can also stay much longer than a month. *STA Travel* have some bargains, too.

Scheduled flights offer much more flexibility, and there are occasionally some very good offers around in the off-season. *Olympic Airways* have a range of such deals from all over Europe, while *Balkan* (Bulgarian), *Malev* (Hungarian), *JAT* (Yugoslav) and *Kenya Airways* can also be relied on to provide a number of cheap seats, especially to students or those under 26.

From Australia and New Zealand

Thanks to the number of Greeks who've adopted the country, connections between Australia and Greece are good, with affordable flights most weeks from both Sydney and Melbourne. New Zealanders will usually have to go via Australia or Britain. Long-term travellers, however, are going to want to cover some of the ground in between. This works out well: Athens is a prime destination on cheap flights from India, Sri Lanka, Nepal and Thailand. *Aeroflot*, *EgyptAir* and *Bangladesh Birman* are among the cheapest Asia–Greece operators, though their flights almost always turn into wearing and elaborate relays, whose only advantage is the number of stopovers they allow.

STA Travel are usually a good bet for discount (and youth/student) flights. They have offices throughout Australia and New Zealand. Their head office addresses are:

STA, 1a Lee St, Sydney 2000 (☎02/212 1255).
STS, 10 O'Connel St, Auckland (☎09/399 191).

Try also contacting *Olympic Airways* direct: Melbourne (84 William St, 3000 Victoria; ☎03/602 5400); Sydney (44 Pitt St, NSW 2000; ☎02/251 1047).

TRAINS

The cheapest return train ticket to Greece is an **Interail** pass, valid for a month's free travel on all European railways (half-price within Britain, and reductions on certain ferries). It's a very good deal if you're planning to visit several countries, but in Greece itself you won't get much mileage out of it since the railway network is slow and limited. Once you reach Crete there are no trains at all, of course. Prices are currently £175 if

---

RAIL TICKET OFFICES

USIT/Eurotrain, *London Student Travel*, 52 Grosvenor Gardens, London SW1 0AG (☎071/730 3402).

Wasteels, 121 Wilton Road, London SW1 (☎071/834 7066).

British Rail European Travel Centre, Victoria Station, London SW1 (☎071/834 2345).

---

you're under 26, £235 for the new over-26 version: two-week passes are also available at £145 and £175.

Regular train tickets are considerably more expensive, but they do allow you two months validity, as many stops as you like on the way (along your pre-chosen route) and include all ferry crossings. Prices depend on route, but start at around £260 (£220 under-26) via Yugoslavia, £345 (£275 under-26) through Italy. Regular tickets and Interail passes can be bought from any station or travel agent; under-26 tickets are usually cheaper from a specialist like *Eurotrain* or *Wasteels*.

There are two basic **routes** to Athens, either of which takes around three and a half days with the minimum of stops on the way. The cheaper one is London–Paris–Venice–Belgrade–Athens, but the last leg of this journey, through Yugoslavia, is interminably hot and crowded. The alternative route, down through France and Italy, crossing over to Greece by ferry, is considerably more comfortable, but the ferries aren't included in the rail pass.

COACHES

Unless you're lucky enough to get a rock-bottom flight, **coaches** are going to be your cheapest form of transport between London and Athens. Again you'll find the ads in the back of *Time Out* or the Sunday newspapers, but don't necessarily take the cheapest unless you've heard something about it – many companies are short-lived, and there have been a string of accidents over the years with operators flouting the terms of their licence. The most official, reliable and expensive coach service is *Eurolines* (☎071/730 0202; tickets available from any *National Express* office), operated by *National Express* and other international companies. They charge around £100 one-way, £180 return, with small youth reductions.

The journey itself takes nearly four days with stops of about twenty minutes every five or six hours, and you'll probably spend the first few days in Greece recovering from the ordeal. But the bus will at least get you there when all other forms of cheap transport are booked solid. Copious supplies of food and drink are advised – and no illegal substances, customs checks are frequent and thorough.

DRIVING OR HITCHING

It's about 1900 miles from London to Athens – at least two days' non-stop **driving** – and there are two basic **routes** you can take: overland via Yugoslavia, or down through Italy and across to Greece on the ferry. The *AA* will – for a small fee – provide up-to-date details of routes, including any major roadworks or other likely delay, which are well worth getting hold of. They can also advise on the legal requirements for the countries you pass through: a green card from your insurer is essential, an International Driving Licence (from the *AA*) advisable, and many countries require that you carry such things as a warning triangle, fire extinguisher and assorted spare parts.

For **hitchers** there are arguments for both routes, but either way is liable to take a full week. On the Yugoslav route it's better to set out from Ostend or the Hook of Holland, thereby bypassing French indifference to hitchers and plugging straight into a major European travel vein which, if you're lucky, could get you a truck ride from Ostend all the way to Greece. On the other hand, Yugoslavia is a bad place in which to run out of lifts: it has two main highways – the coast road which is beautiful but very slow, and the central route through Zagreb and Beograd, which is fast, dull and accurately nicknamed "the death road" for the number of heavy lorries that thunder down it. The drive through Italy, while perhaps slower, is rather more pleasant and Italian trains are cheap if you're hitching and the lifts run out.

ITALY–GREECE FERRIES

On the Italian run, there are regular **ferries** from Ancona, Bari, Brindisi and Otranto to **Pátra** (at the tip of the Peloponnese) or **Igoumenítsa** (the port for Epirus in northwestern Greece); both sail via the island of **Corfu**, on which you can stop over at no extra charge if you get this specified on your ticket. It takes about nine hours from Brindisi – much the most common port of departure – to Corfu and from there it's two more hours to Igoumenítsa, ten to Pátra. The passenger

fare in peak season is around £25 to Corfu/ Igoumenítsa, £30 to Pátra, with a twenty percent reduction for students on most of the lines. These figures should include a small port tax and off-season may be considerably lower. Small cars are charged about £35–40; motorbikes around £25. If you're taking a car over in mid-season it's essential to book in advance, otherwise you may face a two- or three-day wait.

Brindisi is in many ways the best place to leave from – if only because there are far more ferries from here – and it's a reasonably interesting place to wait around. On the other hand embarkation is a chaotic nightmare. Less stressful departure points include Ancona, much further north hence less driving but a longer, more expensive ferry trip, and Bari. The cheapest ferry is run by *R-Lines* from Otranto, 70km south of Brindisi, from May to October only.

Heading for Crete, Pátra is the obvious destination: from there you can avoid Athens altogether and continue down through the Peloponnese to **Yíthio** (or less conveniently to Monemvassía or Neápoli) where you can pick up the twice-weekly ferry to Kastélli in western Crete (see "Greece to Crete", below). On the train, it's an easy run from Pátra to Athens.

In July and August only, there are ferries **direct from Italy to Crete**. *Adriatica* (British agent *Sealink Stena Line*, PO Box 29, Victoria Station, London SW1; ☎071/828 1948) run a service from Venice to Iráklion: a mini-cruise for three days (two nights) which will cost about £100 for a small car, plus almost £300 per person for cabin accommodation and all food – cabins are compulsory. *Marlines* (British agent *Viamare*, 33 Mapesbury Rd, London NW6; ☎081/452 8231) have a service from Ancona to Pátra and Iráklion (48hrs): about £80 for a small car, plus £50 per person deck class, or over £100 in a cabin.

GREECE TO CRETE

FLIGHTS

Olympic run at least seven flights a day from **Athens to Iráklion** in peak season – five daily through the winter – and four daily to **Haniá**. This may seem a lot, but in summer they are all booked well in advance. If you can get a flight, they are good value: one-way prices for night flights are £30 or less, daytime fare around £35 to Haniá, £40 to Iráklion, and the flight lasts less than an hour. Flights leave from the West terminal, for details of which see "Surviving Athens".

Fully booked or not, it can be worth trying to go **stand-by**, especially if you arrive at the airport in the middle of the night and can be first in the queue next morning. You have to purchase a ticket (credit card will do) in order to get on the stand-by list: if in the end you don't manage to fly they should give you a full refund. Once you're on the list, despite appearances, the system works pretty well – just make sure you are by the departure gate when they call out the names of the lucky few for each flight.

There are also daily flights from **Rhodes to Iráklion** (and Rhodes to Sitía), and twice weekly **from Thessaloníki**, as well as regular flights from some of the smaller islands, detailed at the end of each chapter. All of these, again, tend to be heavily booked, and the short hops are relatively expensive.

FERRIES

There are **ferries to Crete** from Pireás (the port of Athens), from Yíthio (at the tip of the Peloponnese) and from many of the Cycladic and Dodecanese islands. The vast majority of ferry traffic goes **from Pireás**. Two major lines operate on this route, *ANEK* and *Minoan*, each with a daily ferry to Iráklion and to Haniá (though *Minoan* sometimes run only one ferry to Haniá, in which case it runs on Mon, Wed, Fri and Sat). In theory the Minoan ferries leave at 6.30pm and the *ANEK* ones half an hour later, but in practice they race to be first out of the harbour and continue jostling for position all the way to Crete, where they arrive around twelve hours later (sooner in good weather). There's virtually nothing to choose between the two: both charge around £15 for a deck class passenger, £30–50 for a car. A new company, *Rethymniaki*, also offers a service from Pireás to Réthimnon, with departures Monday, Wednesday and Friday at 7.15pm, Sunday at 8am. Beware of tickets offered on any other line – these will almost certainly involve a roundabout route through the Cyclades and take twice as long.

It's an overnight journey, and a matter of opinion whether it's worth paying the extra for a berth

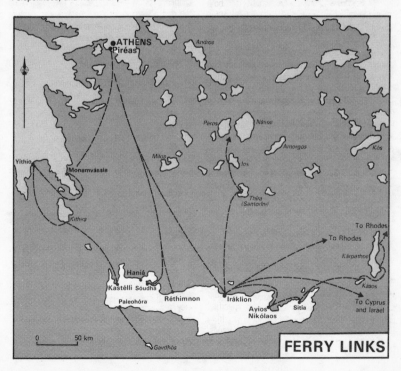

FERRY LINKS

SURVIVING ATHENS

The first time you see it, **ATHENS** is invariably a disappointment. It looks terrible from just about every approach; its air pollution is dire; and its traffic and postwar architecture a disaster. This is definitely not the city of Pericles. Nonetheless, modern Athens has excitements of its own, and if you are passing through it's well worth taking a couple of days out to see the Acropolis (inevitably) and some of the great museums – and to come to grips with some of the less obvious attractions, from the traditional "blues" music of *rembétika* clubs to a bazaar area that still feels more out of the Levant than Europe.

POINTS OF ARRIVAL

Athens **airport** – Ellenikóu – has two separate terminals: **West** which is used by *Olympic Airways* for all flights, domestic or international, and **East** which is used by everyone else. They're on opposite sides of the runway, which means you have to drive halfway round the perimeter fence to get from one to the other: *Olympic* buses connect the two regularly from around 6am to midnight if you are simply changing planes. It's about 16km in **to central Athens**, and a **taxi** should cost less than £5: but make sure that the meter is working or fix a price in advance, as new arrivals are seen as easy meat. **Buses** also run to the centre and direct to Pireás from both terminals: blue and yellow double-deckers into Síntagma Square and Omónia; yellow single-deckers to Pireás. You buy your ticket before boarding: departures for the centre every 20min 6am–midnight and from mid-May to mid-September hourly from midnight to 6am; to Pireás every 30min, 90min at night. From the west terminal there's also a faster but much more expensive *Olympic* bus (every 20min 6am–8pm).

International **trains** arrive at the Stathmós Laríssis in the northwest of the city centre: there are hotels in this area or take the yellow trolley bus (#1) immediately outside to reach Síntagma. International **buses** vary. They may take you right into the centre, they may terminate at the railway station, or they may go to the bus station at Kifisóu 100, a long way out. From here, take bus #051 to Platía Omónia. The airport express buses also serve the station and main bus stations.

THE CITY

Once you've found it, **central Athens** covers a mercifully small area. **Síntagma Square** (Platía Sintágmatos, "Constitution Square") is to all intents and purposes the city's focus, with the Greek Parliament on the upper side, banks and airline offices grouped around. Most things you'll want to see in a fleeting visit are within 20–30 minutes' walk of here: to avoid getting lost get to know too the other great square – **Omónia**, linked to Síntagma by the broad thoroughfares of Stadhíou and Panepistimíou – and the hills of the **Acropolis** and **Likavitós**. With these placed, orientation should never be too hard. The city's main **tourist office** is located inside the *National Bank of Greece* on the Stadhíou corner of Síntagma: an invaluable source of maps, timetables and general information.

Very briefly, the main areas of the city look as follows. To the northeast of Síntagma, the upmarket **Kolonáki** quarter curls around to the slopes of **Likavitós**, with a funicular to save you the final climb. To the east, behind the Parliament, the jungly **National Gardens** function as the city's chief lung and meeting place; beyond them are the 1896 **Olympic stadium** and the attractive neighbourhoods of **Pangráti** and **Mets** – two good drinking and eating options. To the southwest, lapping up to the base of the **Acropolis**, justifiably the city's pre-eminent sight, spread the ramshackle but much-commercialised lanes of **Pláka**, the surviving area of the nineteenth-century, pre-Independence, village.

Omónia (Platía Omonías, "Harmony Square") lies to the northwest, an Athenian Piccadilly Circus or Times Square. North of here is the slightly "alternative" neighbourhood of **Exárhia**, with a

or cabin. The older ferries tend to be retired veterans of the North Sea run, and designed for freezing conditions – they can be airless and thoroughly unpleasant down below on an Aegean summer night. Newer ones are efficiently air-conditioned and far more comfortable. Travelling on deck (or in the seats available to deck class passengers) can be fine – even idyllic in the right conditions – but it can also be crowded, noisy and cold. If you do go this way, embark early to claim some space. While the Aegean is usually calm and comfortable, high winds (especially in August) can sometimes make for a very queasy crossing.

Much the most useful of the other services is that from the **Peloponnese to Kastélli**. For lively concentration of bars. South of Omónia, towards **Ermóu** and **Pláka**, spreads the city's main commercial centre and market area.

As a preparation for Crete, there are a couple of Athens museums well worth visiting. Most importantly, the **National Archaeological Museum** (Patissíon 28; Tues–Sun 8am–5pm; Thíra section closes at 3pm) contains, upstairs, the brilliant **Minoan frescoes from Thíra** (Santoríni). Even more spectacular than anything which survived on Crete itself, these were also important evidence in the earthquake theory of the Minoan destruction. The Mycenaean rooms downstairs are also relevant to Crete, besides being great in their own right. The **Benáki Museum** (Koumbári 1; 8.30am–2pm; closed Tues) is wonderful on a much smaller scale and has some fascinating stuff – in Room 9 – on Venizélos and the rebellions against the Turks.

ACCOMMODATION AND FOOD

Finding **somewhere to stay** in Athens is unlikely to be a major problem except at the very height of summer – even so you can get footsore unless you phone around first. A few cheap, hostel-style places are listed below – you can book more upmarket rooms through the reservations desk by the tourist office or find full listings in the Greece *Rough Guide*. **Pláka** is the handiest area, though increasingly upmarket: *George's Guest House* (Níkis 46; ☎322 6474) is a good first try; the *XEN* (*YWCA*, Amerikís 11; ☎362 6970) an excellent safe refuge for women; *Student Inn* (Kidhathinéon 18; ☎324 4808) is central but noisy. **Exárhia**, north of Omónia, is away from the mainstream but cheap, quiet and handy for the National Archaeological Museum: *Athens Connection* (Ioulianóu 20; ☎822 4952) is one of the best "student hostels" in Athens; *Paradise Inn* (Méhonos 4; ☎524 1109) is friendly and has two subsidiaries if the main building is full. **Pireás** can also make a handy place to stay – see below. There are no **campsites** anywhere near the city centre – best is *Athens Camping*, 7km out on the road to Corinth.

Food follows the same pattern as hotels – Pláka is bursting with touristy restaurants, most very pleasantly situated but few good value; the area around Monastiráki and Omónia is cheap and characterful but rarely picturesque; the more residential areas surrounding the centre better value but less packed with alternatives. Finding *something* to eat, though, is never going to be a problem.

ON TO CRETE: PIREÁS

Leaving Athens, you'll be headed either for the airport, in which case take the buses from Síntagma outlined earlier, or for the ferries at **PIREÁS**. The easiest way to the port is on the **metro**, which has stops in Omónia and Monastiráki squares. The journey to Pireás, last stop on the line, takes about 25 minutes – trains run from 5.30am to midnight – and there's a flat fare, so you just buy a ticket and get on. Green **bus #040** from Síntagma also runs to the port; frequently in the day, hourly at night from 1 to 5am, but it's very slow. If you're travelling from Pátra, the train continues through Athens down to Pireás.

The **ferries for Crete** leave from the heart of the port, not far to the south of the metro station – simply turn left and follow the harbour round. If you've arrived by bus get someone to point you in the right direction, basically down the hill from Platía Koraí. **Ticket agents** crowd all around the harbour, and just about any will be able to sell you a ticket to Crete, but make sure it's with *ANEK*, *Minoan* or *Rethymnaki*: the two lines' main agencies have vast signs up behind where their respective ferries dock.

It's possible to **stay** in Pireás if you want to, though since most Crete ferries leave late and arrive early there's no real need: the *Hotel Acropole* (Gounari 7; ☎417 3313) is a friendly place very handy for metro, train and boats, with beds at a wide range of prices. More likely, you'll be wanting to **eat** and to buy **provisions for the trip**. Both of these are easily catered for all round the port, but best avoid the tourist traps lining Aktí Possidhónos and head inland a block or two.

most of the year this runs twice a week, setting out from Pireás and running down to Monemvassía, Neápoli, the island of Kíthira, Yíthio, back to Kíthira and across to Kastélli. On its current summer schedule, the boat leaves Yíthio late on Monday and Thursday evenings, arriving in Crete the following morning: prices are around twenty percent lower than from Pireás.

From other islands the chief services are as follows: you can get to Iráklion from the larger of the Cycladic islands (daily from Thíra) and from Rhodes; to Sitía and Áyios Nikólaos from Rhodes and the Dodecanese. There's also a weekly service to Iráklion **from Israel and Cyprus**. All of these ferries are included in the "Travel Details" at the end of each regional chapter.

RED TAPE AND VISAS

British, Australian, New Zealand, Canadian and EC nationals need only a valid passport for entry to Greece and can stay on an ordinary entry stamp for up to three months. Almost anyone else – except citizens of Eastern bloc countries – can stay for shorter periods without a visa (two months for US citizens). Canadians and Americans will, however, need visas to travel via Yugoslavia; these can be obtained at frontier posts for a small fee, or – much better –

get them gratis at a Yugoslav consulate beforehand. If you have a British Visitor's Passport you'll be issued a Yugoslav tourist card at the border.

If you want to stay longer than three months you must apply for an **extension**: the main office is the Aliens Bureau in Athens (Halkondhíli 9, off Káningos Square; open 8am–1pm), but in Crete you can apply direct to the local police and hope they are in sympathetic mood. It is advisable to do this a couple of weeks before your time runs out and also to keep all your pink bank exchange slips as confirmation that you can support yourself without working. It's also possible, although not strictly legal, to get round this law by leaving Greece for a few days every three months, thus bypassing the bureaucracy and living in the country for as long as you like on an ordinary visitor's stay. Just don't re-enter at the same border post!

If you overstay your allotted three months and then leave on your own (ie are not deported), you are fined a small amount upon exit – technically the cost of various revenue stamps to effect a retroactive extension, amounting to about 50p per month. Either this, or leaving discreetly every three months, is a lot less bother than applying for a formal extension.

COSTS, MONEY AND BANKS

Crete is no longer *really* cheap – the days of four people renting a house for a thousand or so drachmas a week are long gone – and EC membership (since 1980) has brought the familiar pattern of spiralling food prices. Still, it is remarkably inexpensive in comparison with anywhere in northern Europe, and if you're willing to cut a few corners and avoid the more overtly developed areas, you can get by on very little. Needs are simple.

COSTS

If you camp, hitch some of your transport and buy some of your own food in the shops it should be possible to manage on less than £10 a day; whilst on £15 a day you can start to live quite well. Once you've reached the island, **buses** are efficient and pretty cheap. Travelling the length of the island, from Haniá to Sitía, costs around £10 one way. You should always be able to find a basic **room** for two for less than £10 a night, sometimes half that; **campsites** cost little more than £1.50 a person or, with discretion, you can camp on your own near the beaches for free. A solid **taverna meal**, even with considerable quantities of wine, should rarely work out much above £5 a head, though if you're eating seafood in a touristy place you can more than double that.

All of the above is, of course, subject to when and where you go and with whom. You'll pay much more for the same quality room in Áyios Nikólaos or the other big resorts (if you can find one at all), and the coast and the east are generally more expensive than the west and the mountains. **Single accommodation**, too, is rare and much poorer value (you'll often have to pay the full double price). Food likewise is cheaper if shared, but even in the resorts with their inflated "international" menus, you'll usually find a market or tavernas where the locals eat. For students, an **ISIC card** offers small discounts on museum and archaeological site entry, plus some discounts on transportation.

CURRENCY AND EXCHANGE

Greek currency is the **drachma** (*Dhrahmí*), at present a little over 300 to the pound. The most common notes in circulation are those of 100, 500, 1000 and 5000 drachmas (*dhrahmés*), coins of 1, 2, 5, 10, 20 and 50drs: the drachma is theoretically subdivided into 100 *leptá*. You are officially allowed to take just 3000 drachmas (about £9) into Greece with you, so the majority of your money will have to be changed after arrival – though it's well worth having some local currency to tide you over the first few hours.

Travellers' cheques are freely importable into Greece but more than £350 in **cash** should be declared on entry to minimise hassles if you want to take it out again. Similarly, if you have any reason to believe that you'll be acquiring large quantities of drachmas – ie you will be working or selling something – declare everything on arrival and save the pink, personalised

receipts for each exchange transaction. Otherwise you can only recover up to £70 worth of drachmas on departure. Travellers' cheques are accepted at all banks and, when they're closed, at quite a number of hotels, agencies and tourist shops. If you intend to spend much time away from the bigger centres, though, you should plan to have a fair amount of currency to hand. **Eurocheques** are also honoured at Greek banks and post offices – and are probably the easiest way of all to carry your money – but they're not widely recognised by shops.

Banks on Crete are normally open Mon–Thurs 8am–2pm, Fri 8am–1.30pm. Certain branches in the tourist centres open extra hours in the evenings and Saturday mornings to change money. Generally speaking, though, Greek banks are not known for their courtesy, especially to non-Greek speakers: always take your passport with you as proof of identity and be prepared for at least one long queue – often you have to line up once to have the transaction approved and again to pick up the cash. **Commissions** can also vary considerably, even between branches of the same bank, so ask first. Remember, though, that both commission and rate will be worse if you change money at a hotel or travel agent. Two **alternatives to banks** which can be useful when you arrive in town cashless at the end of a day are **travel agents** and **official tourist offices**. The former often serve as general purpose information centres in smaller resorts and will change travellers' cheques and banknotes. Although they're likely to be trustworthy it's a good idea to have a rough idea in your mind of what the official exchange rate is. The government tourist offices are to be found in most of the major centres and usually stay open until quite late in the evening; they offer exchange facilities at a rate similar to (and sometimes better than) the banks.

Major **credit cards** are fairly widely accepted but only by the more expensive shops, hotels and restaurants: they're useful for hiring cars, for example, but no good in the cheaper tavernas or rooms places. If you run short of money, you can also get a **cash advance on a credit card**, but be warned that the minimum amount is 15,000drs (about £50): the *Emborikí Trápeza*/Commercial Bank handles *VISA*; the *Ethnikí Trápeza*/National Bank acts for *Access/Mastercard*. Some private exchange places will also give advances on credit cards, with a lower minimum, but they may charge more. Failing this, you'll have to arrange to have **money wired** from home in an emergency. Though this is theoretically very quick, you should in practice count on delays of three to six days for receipt of telexed funds. You can pick up the sum in foreign currency, or even travellers' cheques, but there are, of course, reconverting commissions and you can only do this on the day of receipt.

One useful solution – to this and to the bank queues – is a post office **giro account**. If you have one of these you will be able to draw money out at almost any post office in Crete.

HEALTH AND INSURANCE

There are no required inoculations for Greece, though it's wise to have a typhoid-cholera booster, and to ensure that you are up to date on tetanus.

The **water** is safe pretty much everywhere, despite the fact that everyone drinks the bottled stuff instead. Crete has few of the **water shortages** which bedevil smaller islands – it's only in isolated villages or resorts that have grown faster than the plumbing can cope with that you're likely to come across any problem.

More serious threats to your health have to do with overexposure and the sea. Wear a hat and drink plenty of fluids in the hot months to avoid any danger of **sunstroke**, and don't underestimate the power of even a hazy sun to **burn**.

In the sea, you may just have the bad luck to meet an armada of **jellyfish**, especially in late summer; they come in various colours and sizes including invisible and minute. Urine or ammonia lessens the sting. Less vicious but more common are **sea urchins**, which infest rocky shorelines year-round; if you are unlucky enough to step on, or graze one, a sterilised needle, scalpel and olive oil are effective for removing spines from

your anatomy. And they should be extracted, or they will fester. A pair of goggles for swimming and footwear for walking over wet rocks should help avoid both of the above. The worst maritime danger – fortunately very rare – seems to be the **weever fish**, which buries itself in tidal zone sand with just its poisonous dorsal and gill spines protruding. If you tread on one the sudden pain is unmistakably excruciating, and the venom is exceptionally potent. Consequences can range up to permanent paralysis of the affected area, so the imperative first aid is to immerse your foot in as hot water as you can stand. This degrades the toxin and relieves the swelling of joints and attendant pain.

Lesser hazards include **hayfever** – sufferers should be prepared for an earlier season than at home – and **mosquitoes** (*kounóupia*). While the latter don't carry anything worse than a vicious bite, they can be infuriating in places. The best solution is to burn pyrethrum incense coils (*spíres* or *fidhákia* in Greek), widely and cheaply available on Crete. If you're going to be staying in hotels you can also use an electrical device called a *Vape-Nat* in Greece, which activates a chemical tablet. Most hotel rooms have a two-pin plug and the appliance (and tablets) are widely available from pharmacies, for much less than they cost at home.

MEDICAL ATTENTION

For serious **medical attention** you'll find English-speaking doctors in any of the bigger towns or resorts: the tourist police (☎104) or your consulate should be able to come up with some names if you have any difficulty. For **minor complaints** it's enough to go to the local *farmakí* (chemist). Greek pharmacists are highly trained and dispense a number of medicines which in Britain can only be prescribed by a doctor. In the larger towns there'll usually be one who speaks good English. If you regularly use any **prescription drug** you should bring along a copy of the prescription together with the generic name of the drug – this will help should you need to replace it and also avoid possible problems with Customs officials*.

Homeopathic and herbal remedies are also widely available: there are homeopathic pharmacies in Iráklion and Haniá, and probably elsewhere too.

British and other EC nationals are officially entitled to **free medical care** in Greece – but this means admittance to only the lowest grade of state hospital (known as a *yenikó nosokomeío*). Basic treatment for cuts, broken bones and emergencies is given (and in practice they'll treat anyone free of charge in an emergency), but extended care, and nursing, will be virtually nonexistent; Greek families take in food and bedding for relatives so as a tourist you'll find difficulties. Rather better are the ordinary state outpatient

---

*A warning needs to be sounded about codeine, which has recently been banned in Greece. If you import any – and it is fairly common in headache drugs including Codeine, Panadeine, Veganin, Solpadeine and Codis – you just might find yourself in serious trouble. So check labels carefully.

clinics (*yatría*) attached to most hospitals and also found in rural locales; these operate on a first come first served basis so go early – usual hours are 8am–noon. To qualify for free treatment Britons will need to produce Form E111, available from post offices; without this, outpatient clinics make a small charge.

INSURANCE

Any more extended hospital treatment is very expensive, and in practice **travel insurance** is a must. Just about any travel agent, bank or insurance broker will sell you comprehensive cover to include not only medical expenses but also loss or theft of baggage: if you think you might rent a car or motorbike, make sure that it is included – the vast majority of tourist accidents in Crete involve falling off motorbikes. If you need to claim, be sure to keep all receipts, including those from the pharmacy. For claims on stolen items you need to get the loss registered at the local police station. This can occasionally be a tricky business as many officials simply won't accept that anything could be stolen on their patch, or at least don't want to take responsibility for it: be persistent and if necessary enrol the support of the local tourist police or tourist office.

INFORMATION AND MAPS

The National Tourist Organisation of Greece (*Ellinikós Organismós Tourismóu*, EOT) is the obvious first stop for information on

Crete, even though few of their impressive array of glossy pamphlets apply exclusively to the island. Go armed with specific questions you want answered, or you'll simply be given the general leaflet on Crete, which has plenty of pictures, a very small-scale map, and hardly any hard information at all. They may also have up-to-date bus and ferry timetables and prices.

The National Tourist Organisation maintains **offices** in most European capitals (though not Dublin), Australia and North America. Addresses include:

London: 4 Conduit St W1 (☎071/734 5997).

Amsterdam: Leidsestraat 13 (☎254-212).

Copenhagen: Vester Farimagsgade 3.

Stockholm: Grev Turegatan 2 (☎211-113).

Sydney: 51–57 Pitt St (☎241-1663).

On the island, there are EOT offices in Iráklion (Zanthoudhídhou 1; ☎081/222-487), Haniá (Aktí Tombázi 6; ☎0821/26-426) and Réthimnon (on the beach; ☎0831/29-148). Elsewhere there may be a municipal tourist office or a tourist police post, or local travel agencies are always helpful.

Island **maps** are available locally too, but you'll almost certainly find a better one at home. None seems to be particularly accurate when it comes to minor roads and footpaths: the *Nelles* and *Freytag & Berndt* offerings are the clearest. More detailed **hiking/topographical maps** are virtually non-existent. The 1:200,000 maps of the National Statistical Service (*Ethnikí Statistikí Ipiresía*), occasionally available in specialist shops, are so out of date as to be almost entirely worthless. The only real hope of anything better is if the Greek mountaineering magazine *Korfés* (16 Platía Ayíou Vlassíou in the Athens suburb of Aharnés; ☎246-1528) gets round to covering

Crete in its 1:50,000 series of alpine areas. More than thirty now exist and a new one is issued every other month as a centrefold in the magazine, which is sold at many newsstands. Recently production of Roman-lettered maps began, but you have to go out to the Aharnés office to get these.

The maps are extremely accurate, based as they are on the generally unavailable maps of the **Hellenic Military Geographical Service**. If you want to try your luck at obtaining those, visit the HMGS at Evelpídhon 4, north of Areos Park in Athens, Monday, Wednesday or Friday from 11.30am to 2pm only. If the officer in charge decides you have a legitimate reason to procure a map or two (not more) he will authorise your purchase, but you must sign a statement declaring that you won't sell, give away, export, photocopy or trace said map(s), under penalty of two years' imprisonment! You'd also better speak good Greek or send a Greek friend to get them for you.

GETTING AROUND

By Greek standards Crete is pretty well served for roads and transport, and the main towns and resorts along the north coast are linked by an excellent road served by a fast and frequent bus service. To get away from the crowds, though, and see a little of the real Crete, you'll want to get off the main roads – for at least some of your time you should think about hiring some transport or, better still, setting out on foot.

BUSES

Buses are the standard – indeed the only – form of public transport on Crete, covering the island remarkably fully. Along the main north coast road modern coaches run every hour or so, very fast and efficient. Off the major routes services vary: the ones used primarily by tourists – serving, for example, Omalós and Hóra Sfakíon for the Samarian Gorge, or Festós and Mátala – tend also to be modern and convenient; those that cater mainly for locals are generally older buses which run once daily as transport to market or school – in to the provincial capital very early in the morning and back out to the village around lunchtime. This means that for day trips they are little use. If you are determined, though, there are few places not accessible by bus, and if you combine the services with some hitching and/or walking you'll get about exceptionally cheaply, if not always especially quickly.

Buses on Crete are turquoisey green, and run by a consortium of companies jointly known as **KTEL**. That this is not one single company is most obvious in Iráklion where there are four distinct (and quite distant) termini serving different directions. On the whole, buses serving a given village will run from the provincial capital – Iráklion, Réthimnon, Haniá or, in the case of Lasíthi, Áyios Nikólaos or Sitía – but there are also a number of small-scale services which cross inter-provincial borders. The main routes and timings are detailed at the end of each chapter.

HITCHING

Your luck **hitching** in Crete will very much depend on where you are. The main road along the north coast is very fast if you want to travel some distance in a hurry, but its traffic pattern is also much more north European: people passing are going too fast and feeling too harassed to be bothered to stop. In rural areas hitching is great as long as you're not too bothered by time – most people will stop (the more obscure the road, the better your chance) but there may be little traffic and locals are rarely going further than the next village along.

Greece in general is also one of the safer countries for **women** travellers, but Crete now has more than its fair share of men who believe in the myth of the single foreigner as easy meat. This rarely amounts to more than infuriating harassment, helped by keeping reasonably well covered when you travel. As ever, there's a great deal of confidence in numbers – the ideal hitching team being two, one man and one woman.

Thumbing may prove the quickest form of travel if you want to take an unusual route which would otherwise involve a string of bus connections, or it may be the only way to get back from somewhere served by a once-daily bus. At its best it's a wonderful way to get to know the island, to pick up some Greek and to meet Cretans not jaundiced by too much contact with mass tourism. There's no finer way to take in the Lasíthi Plateau, for example, than from the back of a truck that looks converted from a lawnmower.

DRIVING – BIKE AND CAR HIRE

Motorised transport of your own has obvious advantages for getting to the more inaccessible areas, and especially if you want to cover a lot of ground in a hurry, but **renting** can work out very expensive.

For a small **car** you can expect to pay £100–180 a week, depending on season, and on top of that fuel at prices comparable to the rest of Europe and possibly a charge for mileage as well. Local companies are considerably cheaper than the internationally known names, and on the whole just as reliable.

All agencies will want either a credit card or a large cash deposit up front (they'll often want to keep your passport and/or driving licence as well); minimum age requirements vary from 21 to 25, and usually you need to have held a full **driving licence** for at least a year. Less scrupulous operators may not look at your licence, or may not understand it, but if anything did happen while you were driving a vehicle which you were technically not allowed to drive, the insurance would almost certainly be invalid (this applies particularly to motorbikes; most places will rent to anyone with a licence, but strictly speaking you shouldn't ride anything above 50cc unless you have a motorbike licence, group D). Make sure that the price you are paying includes **full insurance**: it's not worth the risk of not having it. And don't be too excited when you see a brochure advertising car hire for approximately half of the cost suggested – by the time tax, insurance, mileage etc has been added it will have doubled again. It's always worth bargaining and shopping around for discounts, especially out of season: a few places mentioned in the text have offered discounts to anyone carrying this book, but usually you can get one anyway.

Motorbikes, mopeds and Vespa scooters are also widely available, at prices starting at around £7 a day, £35 per week for a moped to about £12 a day, £60 a week for a 175cc trail bike. Again, the price in the ads will be about half this, exclusive of compulsory tax and insurance. The smaller bikes are ideal for pottering around for a day or two, but don't regard them as serious transport: Crete is very mountainous and the mopeds simply won't go up some of the steeper hills even with only one person aboard. Be sure not to run beyond the range of your petrol tank, either, as they're not designed for long-distance travel and there are few filling stations outside the towns. For serious exploration, or to venture into the mountains, you really need a motorbike or a powerful Vespa – the latter is cheaper but much more dangerous. Whatever you hire, make sure you check it thoroughly before riding off, since many are only cosmetically repaired and if you break down it's your responsibility to return the machine. It's worth taking the phone number of whoever hires them to you in case they do give out miles from anywhere.

Although motorbikes are enormous fun to ride around, you need to take more than usual care: there's an alarming number of **accidents** each year (many fatal) among visitors and locals because simple safety procedures are not followed. It's only too easy to come to grief on a potholed road or steep dirt track – especially at night. Two tips: never rent a bike which you feel you can't handle, and use a helmet. The latter will probably be the one item that saves your life in a spill. All operators should have helmets, but only a few will supply them unless you ask and only one or two insist that you wear them; some people now bring their own helmet with them. Quite apart from your own injuries you're likely to be charged a criminally high price for any repairs needed for the bike, so make sure that you are adequately insured, both in the rental agreement and by your own travel insurance – many of these schemes specifically exclude injuries sustained while riding/driving a hired vehicle.

If you drive **your own vehicle** down through Greece you'll need international third party insurance and a carnet in your passport. Bear in mind that Greece has the highest accident rate in Europe after Portugal and that many of the roads, particularly if you're unfamiliar with them, are quite perilous. Crete itself is better, but even here tarmac can turn into a dirt track without warning on the smaller routes and ill-signed roadworks and slow trucks are everywhere.

Should you be involved in any kind of **accident** it's an offence to drive away and you can be held at a police station for up to 24 hours. Often the talk will be out of all proportion to the incident, but if it is serious ring your consul immediately in order to get a lawyer, you have this right. Don't make a statement to anyone who doesn't speak – and write – very good English. In an **emergency** ring the tourist police on ☎104.

TAXIS AND TOURS

Local **taxis** are exceptionally cheap, at least as long as the meter is running or you've fixed a price in advance, and a good proportion of their business is long-distance, taking people to and from the villages around the main towns (in some places, including the airports, there's a printed list of prices to the most common destinations). If you want to visit somewhere where there's only one bus, or hike somewhere and get a ride back, it's well worth arranging for a taxi to pick you up: for four people this generally costs little more than the bus. It's also quite easy to negotiate a day's or half-day's sightseeing trip, by talking a driver.

It does, however, require a certain ability in Greek and faith in the driver, and over long distances can become expensive. A simpler alternative for a one-off is often to take a **coach tour**. Travel agents everywhere offer the obvious ones – the Samarian Gorge; Vái Beach; a local "Cretan night" – and a few offer much more adventurous alternatives. They're worth at least considering as a relatively cheap and easy way to see things you might otherwise be unable to get to – a day trip to the Minoan sites or the Gorge, for example; isolationists can always escape from the rest of the group once there.

HIKING AND CYCLING

The idea of **walking** for pleasure is one that has yet to catch on widely in Crete, but if you have the time and stamina it is probably the single best way to see the island. There are suggestions for hikes – from easy strolls to serious climbing – throughout the guide, and further tips for hikers in the *Contexts* section. The two Cretan books in the *Landscapes* series (*Landscapes of Eastern Crete* and *Landscapes of Western Crete*, each by Jonnie Godfrey and Elizabeth Karslake, Sunflower Books) make excellent further reading. See the "Information and Maps" section for a lament on the lack of adequate walkers' maps of Crete.

Cyclists are even rarer in Crete, not surprisingly, perhaps, in view of the mountainous terrain and fierce summer heat, but again the seat of a bike offers an incomparable view of the island and guarantees contact with locals the average visitor could never meet – provided you are a hardy hill climber. You can bring your own bike in by plane (it's free within your ordinary baggage allowance) or train (in which case it should go free on the ferry). On the island you may have difficulty with bus conductors, always protective of their luggage compartments, but if you stick to older buses you can always throw it on top. In the flatter resorts you'll even find pedal **bikes for hire**: they're very cheap for a few hours exploration, and child seats are sometimes available too.

SLEEPING

There are vast numbers of beds for tourists in Crete, and most of the year you can rely on turning up pretty much anywhere and finding something. In July and August, however, you can run into problems, especially in the bigger resorts and in Iráklion, Haniá and Áyios Nikólaos. The only real solution is to turn up at each new place early in the day, and to take whatever is on offer in the hope that you will be able to exchange it for something better later.

HOTELS AND ROOMS

Hotels are categorised by the tourist police from "Luxury" down to "E" class and all except the top category have to keep within set price limits.

"D" and "E" class hotels are very reasonable (costing around £4–7 for a double room, £3–5 for a single room) but in practice they are rare: only in Iráklion are there many, and these tend to be very dingy. More luxurious establishments, except perhaps in the centres of larger towns, are often fully booked in advance by foreign tour operators.

Far more often, you'll be staying in **"rooms"** (*dhomátia* – but usually spotted by a *Rooms for Rent* or *Zimmer Frei* sign), which once again are officially controlled and divided into three classes ("A" down to "C"). At the bottom end these are cheaper, and generally cleaner and much more congenial, than the hotels. These days the bulk of them are in new purpose-built blocks but some are still, literally, rooms in people's homes – where you'll often be treated with disarming hospitality. At its least, a room implies a bare

concrete space with a bed and a hook on the back of the door, with toilet facilities (cold water only) outside in the courtyard; at its fanciest it could be a purpose-built, fully furnished place with marble bathroom en suite. Between these extremes you may well find that you pay extra for a hot shower (or for a shower at all), that there's a choice of rooms at various prices (they'll always try you on the most expensive first) and that price and quality are not necessarily directly linked: always ask to see the room first. What you pay for a double room could be anything from £4, for a very basic place out of season, to £15 for high-season luxury in a resort.

Areas to look for rooms, and some suggestions for the best, are included in the guide, but as often as not, they find you: owners descend on ferry or bus arrivals to fill any space they have. In smaller places, simply ask in a taverna or kafeneíon – even if there are no official places around there is very often someone prepared to earn extra money from putting you up. (In the larger places there are now signs posted by the tourist police warning against going with people who offer rooms; I have never heard of any trouble, and this may be simply to protect owners of official accommodation. Nonetheless, some caution is sensible – make sure that you at least know where you're being taken.)

It has become standard practice for "rooms" proprietors to ask to keep your passport; ostensibly "for the tourist police", but in reality to prevent you leaving with an unpaid bill. Some owners may be satisfied with just taking down the details, as in hotels, and they'll almost always return the documents once you get to know them, or if you need them for another purpose (to change money, for example).

Prices, for rooms and hotels, should be displayed on the back of the door: if you feel you're being overcharged at a place which is officially registered it should be enough to threaten to go to the tourist police (who really are very helpful in such cases) – small amounts over the odds may be legitimately explained by tax or out-of-date forms. And just occasionally you may find that you have bargained so well, or arrived so far out of season, that you are actually paying *less* than you're supposed to.

CHEAPER OPTIONS: HOSTELS, ROOFS AND CAMPING

If even rooms are beyond your budget, then an alternative can usually be found. There are eight official **youth hostels** (*ksenón neótitas*) on Crete, all of which must be among the least strictly run in the world: they're in Iráklion, Haniá, Mália, Áyios Nikólaos, Réthimnon, Sitía, Mírthios and Plakiás. The last four are particularly good. Facilities are basic – you pay around £1.50 a night for a dormitory bed on which to spread your sleeping bag – but they usually offer cheap meals and/or kitchen facilities, a good social life and an excellent grapevine for picking up work, travelling companions or whatever. I've never known any of them ask to see a YHA card.

A few of the cheaper hotels, especially in Iráklion and Haniá, are run on similar lines as unofficial hostels: here or from a sympathetic rooms or taverna proprietor, you may be able to negotiate **roofspace**. Sleeping on the tiles is better than it sounds – most Cretan buildings have flat concrete roofs where they will provide a mattress for you to lay a sleeping bag on, and there's often an awning for shade. The nights are generally warm and the stars are stunning. It's worth asking about this wherever you go – it can be a cheap and uncramped alternative.

"**Freelance camping**" – outside authorised campsites – has always been the cheapest and in many ways most pleasant means of travel around the Greek islands. In modern Crete, however, it's a dying tradition. For a start, it's officially forbidden – there's been a law since 1977 and once in a while it gets enforced – and, much more significantly, the best sites are gradually being developed, which inevitably means turfing off the "undesirables" (and unfortunately some campers have been undesirable, leaving otherwise scenic sites filthy). Nevertheless, with discretion and sensitivity it can still be done, and just occasionally you may find yourself with nowhere to sleep but the beach. Obviously the police crack down on people camping rough on (and littering) popular mainstream tourist beaches, especially when a large community of campers is developing: elsewhere nobody is really bothered. The ideal is to find a sympathetic taverna near which to sleep out: if you take most of your meals there they'll often be prepared to guard your gear during the day and let you take showers. If you do camp like this, however, take your rubbish away with you.

It's warm enough to sleep out in just a sleeping bag from May until early September, so you don't even need to drag round a tent. A waterproof bag (available from camping shops) or groundsheet is, however, useful to keep out the late summer damp: so too is a foam pad, which lets you sleep in relative comfort almost anywhere. You will always need a sleeping bag, since even in midsummer the nights get cool, but this can be as lightweight as you can find.

Official campsites are surprisingly rare – they're mentioned in the text where they exist – and not, on the whole, very good. They tend to be either very large and elaborate (Iráklion) or else nothing more than a staked-out field. Though prices start at around £1 a night per person at the latter, they begin to mount up once you've added a charge for a tent, a vehicle and everyone in the party. When it's all added up you may feel that a basic room would have been better value.

HOUSES, APARTMENTS AND VILLAS

Another of the great traditions of Greek travel is finding that perfect villa and renting it for virtually nothing for a whole month. In the Cretan summer, forget it. All the best **villas** on the coast are contracted out to one agent or other, and let through foreign operators. Even if you do find one empty for a week or two, you'll discover that renting it in Crete costs far more than it would have done to arrange from home. See the addresses of specialist operators listed under "Packages", on p.4, if you're interested.

Having said that, all hope is not lost if you arrive and decide you want to drop roots for a while. If you don't mind avoiding the coast altogether, then the old cliché might just come true. Pick an untouristy inland village – in the Amári Valley, for example, or up behind Paleóhora – get yourself known and ask about; you might still pick up some fairly wonderful deals. Out of season your chances are again much better – you'd undoubtedly be able to bargain a very good rate even in touristy areas if you wanted to stay anytime between October and March, especially for a month or more on end.

One other alternative is to rent a regular **apartment** in one of the larger towns. Most renters would be expecting longer-term tenants, but you might be able to strike a deal: look for a sign saying *Enoikhiázete*, or check classifieds in the local papers.

EATING AND DRINKING

Greek food has a poor reputation which is not entirely deserved. No one would argue that this was one of the world's great cuisines, but at its best it can be delicious – fresh, simple and flavoured with the herbs which scent the countryside. The most common complaint is that food is often lukewarm and always oily. Both are deliberate, and any local will be happy to lecture you on the dangers of too-hot food and the essential, life-enhancing properties of good olive oil.

You can get a meal at a **tavérna**, an **estiatório** or a **psistariá**. Regular tavernas are by far the most common, *estiatória* are very similar but tend to be cheaper and simpler, perhaps more "Greek". *Psistariés* are restaurants that specialise in fresh prepared plates – predominantly grilled meat but often good vegetables too. They're always worth looking out for. A *psarótaverna* is a taverna which specialises in fish.

Often at traditional *tavérnes* and *estiatória* there are no menus and you're taken into the kitchen to inspect what's on offer: uncooked cuts of meat and fish, simmering pots of stew or vegetables, trays of baked foods. This is a good time to fix prices, since they always seem to turn out higher if you wait until after you've eaten. Even where there is a **menu** in Greek and English it will probably be a standard printed form and bear little relation to what is actually on offer: again, check the kitchen or display case. Where prices are printed you'll be paying the right-hand (higher, inclusive of taxes) set, and often a number of unexpected extras too.

A typical Greek **meal** consists of a starter and main course (only the tourist restaurants serve sweets though there's sometimes fresh yoghurt) and these will often be served at the same time – if you want the main course later don't order it for a while. The main course of meat or fish comes on its own except for maybe a piece of lemon or half a dozen chips; salads and vegetables are served as separate dishes and usually shared. Vegetable dishes (often cooked in a tomato sauce) are often very good in themselves and if you order a few between several people can make a satisfying and exceptionally cheap meal. Some of them, like the tomatoes, peppers or aubergines stuffed with rice and mince (*yemistés*) are basically a main course. And if you're really pushed for money you can always fall back on pasta – macaroni pie and spaghetti are usually available – or soup, which can be filling and delicious.

The **baked dishes** – generally a mixture of meat and vegetables like *moussaká* or *yemistés* – and **stews** – usually some form of lamb with potatoes – are cheaper in general than straight meat or fish dishes. **Meat** usually means lamb, often pretty tough but excellent in its various spit-roasted forms. **Fish** is varied and delicious, but very expensive. If the prices on the menu seem phenomenally high, that's generally because they are per kilo – you select your fish from the slab and they weigh it to determine the actual price (don't leave it to the waiter, or you'll get the biggest).

If you are **vegetarian**, you may be in for a dull time: even the excellent standbys of yoghurt and honey, *tsatsíki* and Greek salad begin to pall after a while, and many of the "vegetable" dishes on the menu are cooked in meat stock or have small pieces of meat added to liven them up. A few restaurants do now cater for vegetarians, especially in areas which see a lot of younger travellers, but they remain rare. At least the **fruit** is wonderful, and seasonal fruits exceptionally cheap – look out for what's on offer in the markets or by the roadside: cherries in spring, melons, watermelons, plums and apricots in summer, pears and apples in autumn, oranges

A FOOD AND DRINK GLOSSARY

Basics and terms

Neró	Water	*Fitofágos/Hortofágos*	Vegetarian
Psomí	Bread	*Avgá*	Eggs
Sitarénio psomí	Wholemeal bread	*Tirí*	Cheese
Sikalénio psomí	Rye bread	*(Horís) ládhi*	(Without) oil
Aláti	Salt	*Katálogo/lísta*	Menu
Yiaoúrti	Yoghurt	*O logariasmós*	The bill
Méli	Honey	*Sto foúrno*	Baked
Kréas	Meat	*Psitó*	Roasted
Psári(a)	Fish	*Sti soúvla*	Spit roasted
Lahaniká	Vegetables	*Tis óras*	Grilled/fried to order

Soups and starters

Soúpa	Soup	*Taramósalata*	Fish roe paté
Avgolémono	Egg and lemon soup	*Tzatzíki*	Yogurt and cucumber
Dolmádhes	Stuffed vine leaves		dip
Fasoládha	Bean soup	*Melitzanosaláta*	Aubergine dip

Vegetables

Patátes	Potatoes	*Kolokithákia*	Courgette
Hórta	Greens (usually wild)	*Spanáki*	Spinach
Radhíkia	Wild chicory	*Fakés*	Lentils
Piperiés	Peppers	*Rízi/Piláfi*	Rice (usually with *sáltsa* –
Domátes	Tomatoes		sauce)
Fasolákia	String beans	*Saláta*	Salad
Angoúri	Cucumber	*Horiátiki (saláta)*	Greek salad (with olives,
Angináres	Artichokes		feta etc)
Yígantes	White haricot beans	*Yemistés*	Stuffed vegetables
Koukiá	Broad beans	*Papoutsákia*	Stuffed aubergine
Melítzána	Aubergine	*Bouréki*	Courgette/potato/cheese pie

Meat and meat-based dishes

Kotópoulo	Chicken	*Kelftiko*	Meat, potatoes and veg cooked
Arní	Lamb		together in a pot or foil; a Cretan
Hirinó	Pork		speciality traditionally carried to
Vodhinó	Beef		bandits in hiding.
Moskhári	Veal	*Pastítsio*	Macaroni baked with meat
Sikóti	Liver	*Païdhákia*	Lamb chops
Patsás	Tripe soup	*Brizóla*	Pork or beef chop
Nefrá	Kidneys	*Keftédhes*	Meatballs
Biftéki	Hamburger	*Loukánika*	Spicy sausages
Moussaká	Aubergine, potato and mince pie	*Kokorétsi*	Liver/offal kebab
Stifádho	Meat stew with tomato and onion	*Tsalingária*	Garden snails

Fish and seafood

Garídhes	Prawns	*Glóssa*	Sole	*Soupiá*	Cuttlefish
Okhtapódhi	Octopus	*Barbóuni*	Red mullet	*Marídhes*	Whitebait
Astakós	Lobster	*Xifías*	Swordfish	*Gávros*	Anchovy
Kalamária	Squid	*Sinagrídha*	Dentex		
Kalamarákia	Baby squid	*Gópes*	Bogue (cheap!)		

Sweets and Fruit

Karidhópita	Walnut cake	*Kasséri*	Hard cheese	*Portokália*	Oranges
Baklavá	Honey/nuts pastry	*Graviéra*	Gruyère type	*Pepóni*	Melon
Rizógalo	Rice pudding		cheese	*Karpoúzi*	Watermelon
Galaktobóuriko	Custard pie	*Fráoules*	Strawberries	*Míla*	Apples
Pagotó	Ice cream	*Kerásia*	Cherries	*Síka*	(Dried) figs
Pastéli	Sesame/honey bar	*Stafília*	Grapes	*Fistíkia*	Pistachio nuts

Drinks

Neró	Mineral water	*Rosé/Kokkinéli*	Rosé	*Gazóza*	Generic fizzy
Enfialoméno		*Tsáï*	Tea		drink
Bíra	Beer	*Kafés*	Coffee	*Boukáli*	Bottle
Krasí	Wine	*Gálakakáo*	Chocolate milk	*Potíri*	Glass
Mávro	Red	*Portokaládha*	Orangeade	*Stiniyássas!*	Cheers!
Áspro	White	*Limonádha*	Lemonade		

and grapes most of the time. They even grow bananas on Crete.

Breakfast is not a meal normally served in Greek restaurants. In the resorts there are now plenty of places offering a choice of English or Continental starts to your day, but mostly these are poor and overpriced. Try to search out instead a *galaktopoleío* (milk bar), which serve puddings and yoghurt (many *kafeneía* also serve yoghurt with honey) or a *zaharoplasteío* (patisserie) for gorgeously sweet and syrupy cakes and pastries. A combination *galaktozaharopoleío* (quite a mouthful in every sense) is not uncommon.

Better still, buy your own yoghurt, bread, eggs or fruit – **shops and markets** open very early, and these things, as well as picnic foods like cheese, salami, olives and tomatoes are always easy to buy. Remember that Greek cheese isn't all *féta* (salty white sheep's cheese) and, if you ask, there are some remarkably tasty local varieties: though all surprisingly expensive. Beach picnics can be further supplemented by tinned foods such as stuffed vine leaves (*dolmadhes*) or baby squid (*kalamarákia*).

Ubiquitous **fast-food snacks** include *souvláki* – small kebabs most commonly in the form of the doner-kebab type *yíros píta* or chunks of *píta-souvláki*, stuffed into a doughy bread (more like Indian Nan than pita bread) along with salad and yoghurt, and quite superb. Or you'll find flaky pies filled with *féta* cheese (*tirópita*), with spinach (*spanakópita*) or even sausage (*louhanikópita*), or better still *boúgatsa*, filled with creamy cheese and sprinkled with sugar. These are all cheap, useful substitutes for a meal, at their best and

most varied in the larger towns: you'll also find places serving varieties of *tost* – bland toasted sandwiches – and pizza; but avoid Cretan hamburgers at all costs.

DRINKING

Wine (*krasí*) is usually *retsína* – though *retsína* is not actually made on Crete – and most commonly comes in half-litre bottles: you may also find it served from the barrel in quarter, half or kilo metal mugs. This resinated wine is an acquired taste, but once you like it you'll start finding some varieties are extremely good. Acquiring the taste is helped by the fact that it is exceptionally cheap: a litre can cost under £1, often less than a litre of beer. Local Cretan wine is generally not resinated (if you want to specify this ask for *aretsínato*): restaurants, especially rural ones, will often have a barrel from which jugs are filled – usually the contents are brown and cloudy, but they're always worth a try. Cretan bottled wine is rather more expensive – brands like *Minos*, which you can get everywhere, are fine if rather boring. The best mainland brands of unresinated wine are by *Boutari* – especially the whites *Lac des Roches* and *Rotonda* and the justifiably famous *Náoussa* red. *Marko* and *Cambas* are also drinkable. **Beer** is standard European lager: *Amstel*, *Henninger* and *Lowenbrau*, all locally brewed, are the most common, in half-litre bottles or smaller cans.

For ordinary drinking you go to a **kafeníon** – simple places filled with old men arguing and playing *távli* (backgammon). They start the day selling coffee (*kafé*) until this is gradually replaced by *óuzo* (an aniseed-flavoured spirit, drunk neat or mixed with water) and, later still, brandy (which is usually *Metaxa* or *Botrys* and graded with 3, 5 or 7 stars) or *rakí*, a burningly strong, flavourless spirit also known in Crete as *tsípouro* or *tsikoudhiá*. The miniature Greek **coffee** is what most Westerners would call "Turkish" and is usually medium sweet or *métrio*. If you want more sugar ask for *glikó* (sickeningly sweet), if none at all *skéto*. Ordinary coffee is also usually available – ask for "Nescafé", which is what it generally is (*Nes me gála* is Nescafé with milk). Iced coffee is known as *frappé*, and is usually excellent. Óuzo and other drinks are traditionally served with small snacks – *mezédhes* –

but nowadays you generally have to order and pay for these. Incidentally, one of the best ways to idle away hours at a *kafeníon* is to join the others playing *távli*, a national obsession. Most places will lend you a set if you ask.

Tea, *tsái*, is often available too, usually served black with a tin of milk to add. It often tastes better with lemon, *me lemóni*, instead.

Real **bars** are rare in traditional Crete, though occasionally you'll find an *ouzerí*, which differs little from a *kafeníon*. Bars for tourists are common in resorts, though, usually either places where you can sit outside sipping exotic, expensive cocktails or combined with discos and serving less exotic but even more expensive concoctions.

COMMUNICATIONS: POST, PHONES AND MEDIA

For a simple letter or card, **stamps** (*grammatósima*) can also be purchased at a *períptero* (corner kiosk). However, the proprietors are entitled to a ten percent commission and never seem to know the current international rates. **Postboxes** are bright yellow: if you are confronted by two slots, *Esoterikó* is for Greek mail, *Exoterikó* for overseas.

If you are sending large purchases home, note that **parcels** should and often can only be handled in sizeable towns, preferably a provincial capital. This way your bundle will be in Athens within a day or two. **Registered** (*sistiméno*) delivery is also available, but it is extremely slow.

Receiving mail, the *poste restante* system is reasonably efficient, especially at the big town post offices. Mail should be clearly addressed and marked *poste restante*, with your surname underlined, to the main post office of whichever town you choose. It will be held for a month and you'll need your passport to collect it. Alternatively you can use the ***American Express*** service in Iráklion: c/o Creta Travel Bureau, Epimenídhou 20–22. You are supposed to carry their cheques or card if you want to use the service.

POST

Local **post offices** are open from about 7.30am to 2.30pm, Mon–Fri; in big towns and important tourist centres, hours may extend into the evening and even weekends. Bigger post offices will change money as well as handle mail. Air mail **letters** take three to six days to reach the rest of Europe, five to eight days to get to North America, and a bit more for Australia and New Zealand. Aerograms are faster and surer; postcards can be inexplicably slow: up to two weeks for Europe, a month to the Americas or the Pacific. A modest express fee (about 50p) cuts letter delivery time to two days for the UK and three days for the Americas.

PHONES

Local calls are relatively straightforward. In many hotel lobbies or cafés you'll find fat red pay-phones which at present take a five-drachma coin and are for local calls only. In the towns you'll also find conventional phone booths. Those with a blue band on top are for local (*topikó*) calls and require five-drachma coins; those with an orange strip are intended for middle and long-distance (*iperastikó*), and are fed five-, ten- and twenty-drachma pieces. A tone in mid-conversation warns you when you need to insert more. Perhaps easier is to phone from a *períptero*. Here the phone is connected to a meter, and you pay after you have made the call: local ones are very cheap, long-distance is subject to a mark-up which only the owner can calculate (since only he/she can see the meter). For this reason, international calls from a *períptero*, though they can be dialled direct quite easily, are slightly risky – first the cost is unpredictable (but definitely higher than from the OTE office) and second the owner may panic at the sight of the spinning meter and cut you off.

For **international long-distance** (*exoterikó*) calls, it's cheaper to visit the nearest **OTE** (*Organismós Tiliepikinoníon tis Elládhos*) office, and you'll have to do this if you want to reverse the charges or do anything else exotic. Operator calls can take well over an hour to connect, but even if you are going to dial direct on their metered phones you should be prepared for a long queue. In Iráklion and Haniá there are branches open 24 hours; in smaller towns OTE can close as early as 3pm. In that case you'll

have no choice but to use a kiosk, or to find a *kafeneíon* with a metered phone: look for a sign saying *Tiléfono me metrití*. If you have access to a private phone you can dial the international operator on ☎161 to get a reversed-charge call put through, or dial direct: ☎00, followed by the country code (44 for UK) and the local number without its initial zero. Calls will cost, very approximately, £2 for three minutes to the UK, $2 a minute to North America.

NEWSPAPERS AND RADIO

British newspapers are fairly widely available in Crete if you are prepared to pay for them. You'll find day-old copies of the tabloids in all the resorts as well as in Haniá and Iráklion, and most of the heavier papers can be found too, though they are in shorter supply and often two days old. Cheaper and more up-to-date, though heavily biased in favour of US press agency reports, the daily *Athens News* is also on sale anywhere there might be a market for it: it has an interesting roundup of selections from the Greek press.

If you have a **radio** you may pick up something more interesting. As well as the BBC World Service, there are also regular news bulletins and bouts of tourist information in English on local Greek stations. American Forces' Radio can be picked up through most of the island, too, often bizarrely incongruous.

OPENING HOURS, HOLIDAYS, SITES AND MUSEUMS

It is virtually impossible to generalise about Cretan **opening hours**, except to say that they

change constantly. The traditional timetable starts early – shops open at 7 or 8am – and runs through till lunchtime, when there is a long break for the hottest part of the day. Things may then reopen in the mid to late afternoon. Tourist areas tend to have adopted a more northern timetable, though, and here shops and offices may stay open right through the day: certainly the most important archaeological sites and museums do so.

Shop hours are theoretically Monday, Wednesday and Saturday from approximately 8am to 2pm, and Tuesday, Thursday, Friday 8am–1pm and 5–8.30pm, but there are so many exceptions to the rule by virtue of holidays and professional idiosyncrasy that you can't count on getting anything done except Mon–Fri from 9.30 to 1 or so. Shut pharmacies are supposed to have a sign on their door referring you to the nearest open one.

All the major **ancient sites** are now fenced off and, like museums, charge admission. This ranges from 50 to 500drs, but with a **student** or FIYTO youth card (p.30) you can get up to fifty percent reductions. Current students of archaeology, classics or history of art can also get a completely free admission permit by writing (well in advance) to the Ministry of Science and Culture (Museums section), Aristídhou 14, Athens.

Opening hours vary from site to site: as far as possible, individual times are quoted in the text, but bear in mind that these change with exasperating frequency and at smaller sites may be subject to the whim of a local keeper. The times quoted are generally summer hours, which operate from around April to the end of September. Reckon on similar days but later opening and earlier closing in winter. If you're a

dedicated archaeology buff you should carry some kind of detailed **guide** with you. On the spot you'll find a glossy tourist picture book at best.

Smaller sites generally close for a long lunch and **siesta** (even where they're not meant to), as do **monasteries**. Most monasteries are fairly strict on dress, too, especially for women: they don't like shorts and often expect women to cover their arms and wear skirts. They are generally open from about 9am to 1pm and from 5 to 7pm.

All of the above will be regularly thrown out of sync by one of a vast range of **public holidays and festivals**. The most important, when almost everything will be closed, are: January 1; January 6; March 25; the first Monday of Lent (February or March); Easter weekend (according to the Orthodox calendar, see below); May 1; August 15; October 28; and several days at Christmas. There may also be a number of local holidays.

ENTERTAINMENT AND FESTIVALS

PANYÍRI: THE ORTHODOX CALENDAR

Most of the big Greek popular festivals have a religious base so they're observed in accordance with the Orthodox calendar: this means that **Easter**, for example, can be one, four or five weeks later than we celebrate it. Easter is by far the most important festival of the Greek year – infinitely more so than Christmas – and taken much more seriously than anywhere in the west.

From Wednesday of Holy Week, the radio and TV networks are given over solely to religious programmes until the following Monday. It is an excellent time to be in Crete, both for the beautiful and moving religious ceremonies and for the days of feasting and celebration which follow. If you make for a smallish village, you may well find yourself an honorary member for the period of the festival.

The first great ceremony takes place on **Good Friday** evening as the Descent from the Cross is lamented in church. At dusk, the *Epitáfios*, Christ's funeral bier, leaves the sanctuary and is paraded solemnly through the streets. Late **Saturday** evening sees the climax in a majestic mass to celebrate Christ's triumphant return. At the stroke of midnight all lights in each crowded church are extinguished and the congregation plunged into the darkness which envelopes Christ as He passes through the underworld. Then there's a faint glimmer of light behind the altar screen before the priest appears, holding aloft a lighted taper and chanting "*Avtó to fos . . .*" (This is the Light of the World). Stepping down to the level of the parishioners he touches his flame to the unlit candle of the nearest worshipper – intoning "*Devthe, levethe fos*" (Come take the

OTHER IMPORTANT FESTIVALS

Epiphany (January 6) The hobgoblins who run riot on earth during the twelve days of Christmas are rebanished to the nether world by various rites of the Church. Most important of these is the blessing of baptismal founts and all outdoor bodies of water. At lake or sea-shore locales the priests cast a crucifix into the deep to be recovered by crowds of young men. Substantial cash prize for the winner, but this custom is now honoured more in the breach owing to recent, serious violence between contenders.

Pre-Lenten carnivals These span three weeks, climaxing over the seventh weekend before Easter.

Clean Monday (*Katharí Dheftéra*) The beginning of Lent, a traditional time to fly kites and to feast on all the things which will be forbidden over the coming weeks.

Independence Day (March 25) Parades and dancing to celebrate the beginning of the revolt against Turkish rule in 1821.

May Day The great urban holiday – most people make for the countryside.

Battle of Crete (May 20–27) The anniversary of the battle is celebrated in Haniá and a different local village each year: sporting events, folk dancing, and ceremonies with veterans of the battle.

Summer solstice/John the Baptist (June 24) Bonfires and widespread celebrations.

Naval Week (late June) Naval celebrations culminate in fireworks – especially big at Soúdha.

Réthimnon Wine Festival (July) A week of wine tasting and traditional dancing.

Iráklion Festival (July and August) A wide variety of cultural events – from drama and film to traditional dance and jazz – at scattered sites through most of the summer.

Metamórfosi/Transfiguration (August 6) Another excuse for feasting.

Sitía Sultana Festival (mid-August) Enjoyable, week-long celebration of the local harvest, with plenty of wine.

Assumption of the Virgin (August 15) Celebrated in many villages, including the town of Neápoli, though the great event is the pilgrimage to the island of Tínos.

Ayios Títos (August 25) Patron saint of the island – big procession in Iráklion.

Cretan Wedding (late August) A "traditional" wedding laid on in Kritsá for the tourists – quite a spectacle nonetheless.

Ayios Ioánnis (August 29) Massive name-day pilgrimage to the church of Saint John Giona on the Rodhopoú peninsula in Haniá.

Chestnut Festival (mid-October) Celebrated in Élos and other villages of the southwest where chestnuts are grown.

Óhi Day (October 28) Lively national holiday – parades, folk dancing – commemorating Metaxas' one word reply ("No") to Mussolini's ultimatum in 1940.

Arkádhi (November 7–9) One of Crete's biggest gatherings celebrates the anniversary of the explosion at the Monastery of Arkádhi.

---

light) to be greeted by the response "*Hristós Anésti*" (Christ is risen). And so it goes round, this affirmation of the miracle, until the entire church is ablaze with burning candles. Later, as the church bells ring, the celebrations begin with fireworks and the burning of effigies of Judas.

Even solidly rational atheists are likely to find this somewhat moving: the traditional greeting, as firecrackers explode all around you in the streets, is *Hristós Anésti* and the reply *Alithos Anésti* (He is risen indeed). In the week leading up to Easter Sunday, you should wish acquaintances "*Kaló Páskha*" (Happy Easter). The Lenten fast is traditionally broken early Sunday morning with a meal of *mayirítsa* (a soup based on lamb offal), and later the rest of the lamb will be roasted.

It's worth bearing in mind that either side of the major festivals many public buildings and banks tend to close, possibly leaving you stranded for days without cash. Keep an eye on the calendar above and plan accordingly.

On top of all these festivals there are literally scores of local festivals, or **paniyíria**, celebrating the patron saint of the village church: and with some 330-odd possible saints' days you're unlikely to travel round for long without stumbling on something. Local tourist offices should be able to fill you in on events in their area.

MUSIC, FILM & OTHER ENTERTAINMENTS

The events of the various festivals aside (and Iráklion's last for much of the summer), Crete can offer little in the way of cultural diversion.

Dancing is of course a tradition here as throughout Greece, but for the real thing you have to go to a *paniyíri*, or else be exceptionally lucky in falling into the right company. Which is not to say that the stuff put on for the tourists isn't enjoyable – it is – simply that it may not be entirely authentic. With regard to **music** it's worth keeping an eye out in the villages for posters advertising *lyra* and *bouzoúki* concerts. These can be highly entertaining and you will often find that you're the only foreigners present, thus ensuring a warm Cretan welcome.

Most of the **discos and bars** are standard European affairs which could be just about anywhere. Cretan **cinema** is probably a more exciting experience. You're unlikely to see any very inspiring films, but most English-language titles are subtitled rather than dubbed, and the open-air screens which can be found in all the major towns in summer are wonderful.

WORK

It's not easy to find work in Crete, and over recent years it has been getting harder, with more people chasing fewer possibilities. Even so, it remains one of the best places in Greece to try your luck at agricultural labour, and there are a few other possibilities. Short-term work will always be on an unofficial basis and for this reason it will generally be badly paid and subject, possibly, to police harassment.

Casual work in **bars or restaurants** around the main tourist resorts is one of the easiest options, though very much more so for women than for men. If you're waiting/serving, most of your wages will probably have to come from tips but you may well be able to get a deal that includes free food and lodging; evening-only hours can leave a lot of freedom, too. The main drawback may be the machismo and/or chauvinist attitudes of your employer. In particular in Haniá, and to a lesser extent elsewhere, many of the bars like to hire young foreign women as decoys, to lure men in and persuade them to drink. This sounds, and to an extent is, easy money – but it can occasionally lead to confrontation with irate clients, and more frequently to harassment by the bar owner, who expects his employees also to be his harem. A common tactic is to threaten to report you to the police, whom the bar is usually paying off.

In this line men ought to aim their sights low and be moderately pleased with washing-up. Trained chefs or cooks will do better. Start looking, if you can, around April–May: you'll get better rates if you're taken on for a whole season.

On a similar level you might be able to get a job touting/selling for **tourist shops**, or if you've got the expertise helping to supervise one of the burgeoning **windsurfing** "schools" or acting as a translator or even a guide for a local travel agent. **Yacht marinas** can also prove good hunting grounds, though less for the romantic business of crewing (still a possibility if you've got the charm and arrogance) than scrubbing down and repainting. Again, the earlier in the year you arrive, the better your chances of getting known and taken on before the competition arrives. One new possibility is **touting for time share**, at the new developments along the north coast.

For a full season's work, relatively slim credentials might also get you a job as a **tour-group courier**. Some firms are willing to take on people (again, women have ·a better chance) waiting to go to university or, more promisingly, having just finished. Nominal pay will be appalling but you'll get a place to live and you can make a lot of money in tips from grateful clients. Scour the brochures as early in the year as possible and turn up at companies' British offices.

Preparations for the tourist season also often require temporary labour, especially if you have a relevant skill: **building**, **painting** or **signwriting**, for example.

Much the most likely source of income, though, is from casual, unskilled **agricultural** labour – invariably low-paid and usually still more so for women whom some Greeks feel they can pay a lower rate. The fields are incidentally quite a rough scene and single women labourers are in a distinct minority. Incidents of violence, non- or underpayment, abuse by employers and police harassment are commonplace. If you're still intent on doing it, hang around hostels in the appropriate geographical areas and ask other travellers for the current situation. Something is being harvested somewhere in Crete through most of the year, and there are various well-known centres where the farmers come if they need labour.

Long-term work is very unlikely, unless you've fixed it up in advance. The main opportunity is **teaching English** at one of the many language schools (*frontistíria*) around the island. If you're already in Crete and want teaching work it looks difficult on paper since you officially need a licence (a complicated procedure). In practice, however, this is very loosely enforced and you

may just strike lucky if you approach schools directly – they're listed in any phone book. The best time of year is from August on, as the start of the school year draws near.

Teaching is essentially a winter exercise – the schools close down from the end of May until mid-September, operating only a few special courses in June and July – so it's general practice to supplement your income by giving private lessons. For this the going rate is around £4–6 an hour. Some teachers finance themselves exclusively on private lessons and, although you still officially need a teaching permit for this, few people experience any problems over it.

The popularity and scale of private English teaching also means that English-speaking women may be able to find work as **au-pairs**. As ever, positions tend to be exploitative and low-paid but if you can use them to your own ends – living reasonably well and learning Greek – there can be mutual benefits. It's unwise to arrange anything until you arrive, so you can at least meet and talk terms with your prospective family. There are a number of specialist agencies in Athens which may be able to help. These include: *International Staff* (Bótasi 12); *Miterna* (Ermóu 28); *Working Holidays* (Níkis 11); *Greek YWCA (XEN)* (Amerikís 11).

DISABLED TRAVELLERS

It is all too easy to wax lyrical over the attractions of Crete: the steep narrow alleys, the ease of travel by bus and ferry, the thrill of clambering round the great archaeological sites. It is almost impossible, on the other hand, for an able-bodied travel writer to see these attractions as potential hazards for anyone who has some difficulty in walking or is wheelchair-bound or suffers from some other disability. The cheering line "facilities for the disabled are not well developed in Greece" is often the only reference to disabled people in the available travel literature.

In all honesty, this guide is barely more practical in this respect than any other. However, don't be discouraged. It is possible to enjoy an inexpensive and trauma-free holiday on the island if some time is devoted to gathering information before arrival. The following guidelines come from a

rheumatoid arthritis sufferer, but the general principles should be applicable to all disabled travellers. For much more advice, plus an account of a visit to Crete by a severely disabled, wheelchair-bound woman, get hold of a copy of *Nothing Ventured – Disabled People Travel the World*, a *Rough Guide* special (Harrap, 1991; £7.99).

There are **organised tours and holidays** specifically for disabled people, but if you want to be more independent, this is perfectly possible too, provided that you do not leave home in the vague hope that things will turn out all right, and that "people will help out" when you need assistance. The best form of assistance, unexpected and unasked for, is likely to be cheerfully given in Crete, but it cannot be relied on. Local attitudes – and comments – may be astonishingly outdated. You must either be completely confident that you can manage alone, or travel with an able-bodied friend (or two). When you have special personal needs, the confidence to travel alone or with one other person, to plan and organise your trip, will come only through preparation.

Become an authority on where you must be self-reliant and where you may expect help, especially regarding transport and accommodation. For example, to get between the terminals at Athens airport, you will have to fight for a taxi: it is not the duty of the airline staff to find you one, and there is no hint of an organised queue.

Be wary, too, since much of what information there is, is **out of date** – you should always try to double check. A number of addresses of contact organisations are published below: the NTOG is a good first step as long as you have specific questions to put to them; they publish a useful questionnaire which you could send to hotels or owners of self-catering accommodation.

It is also vital that you **be honest** – with travel agencies, insurance companies, the organisations you write to for information, companions, the people you meet along the way and, above all, with yourself. Know your limitations and make sure others know them. If you do not use a wheelchair all the time but your walking capabilities are limited, then remember that you are likely to to want to cover greater distances while travelling (often over tougher terrain and in hotter weather than you are used to). So take a wheelchair with you, have it serviced before you go and carry a repair kit: rough roads play havoc with nuts, bolts and tyres.

If you're getting travel **insurance**, read the small print carefully to ensure that people with a pre-existing medical condition are not excluded. And use your travel agent to make your journey simpler: **airlines** or coach companies can cope better if they are expecting you, a wheelchair can be provided at airports and staff primed to help. A medical certficate of your fitness to travel, provided by your GP, is also extremely useful: some airlines or insurance companies may insist on it.

The best place to start is with a **list** of all the facilities that will make your life easier while you are away. You may want a ground-floor room, or access to a large lift; you may have special dietary requirements, or need level ground to enable you to reach shops, beaches, bars and places of interest. Again, be realistic, and accept that you may not be able to expect the level of comfort and convenience you have at home. You should also keep track of all your other special needs, making sure, for example, that you have extra supplies of drugs – carried with you if you fly – and a prescription including the generic name in case of emergency. Any kind of drug, clothing or equipment which might be hard to find in Crete you should carry spares of; if there's an association representing people with your disability, contact them for information on what to take and what to leave behind.

And if all of this sounds like hard work, the rewards should be worth it.

USEFUL CONTACTS

National Tourist Organisation of Greece, addresses on p.13. Their specific information is skimpy and out of date, but they try, and can advise at least on terrain and climate.

Mobility International Hellas, Egnatía 101, 8th Floor, Thessaloníki GR-54635 (☎31/234-489, 206-667). Originated in a specialist travel agency called *Lavinia Tours*, managed by wheelchair user Evyenía Stavropóulo, so have plenty of experience of travel in Greece (limited info on Crete). Involved in disability issues in Greece and internationally. Further details from the British branch, see below.

RADAR (*Royal Association for Disability and Rehabilitation*), 25 Mortimer Street, London W1N 8AB (☎071/637 5400; Minicom ☎071/637 5315). Publishes Holiday Fact Sheets and an annual guide to accommodation and facilities abroad (*Holidays and Travel Abroad – A Guide for Disabled People*;

£4.50 inc. p&p). Issues a list of insurance companies which arrange policies for physically and mentally handicapped people.

Mobility International, 228 Borough High Street, London SE1 1JX (☎071/403 5688). Travel information and advice, plus own programme of leisure and study holidays.

Holiday Care Service, 2 Old Bank Chambers, Station Road, Horley, Surrey RH6 9HW (☎0293/774535). Information on all aspects of travel, plus a specific fact sheet on Crete with accommodation recommendations.

Air Transport Users Committee, 2nd Floor, Kingsway House, 103 Kingsway, London WC2B 6QX (☎071/242 3882). Can supply copies of the British Airports Authority's rather dated leaflet *Care in the Air*, which gives general advice to disabled passengers.

POLICE, TROUBLE AND HARASSMENT

It's now over fifteen years since the Colonels were evicted and Greece ceased to be a police state. As everywhere, there are a few mean characters around, but in general your average Greek policeman is not likely to have too much of a power complex, and you need to do something very insensitive to risk arrest. The most common causes of a brush with authority – all of them technically illegal – are nude bathing or sunbathing, camping outside an authorised site and (a major crime in the Greek book) taking or possessing hash or any other drug.

Nude bathing is, currently, legal on only a very few beaches, and is deeply offensive to many more traditional Cretans: exercise considerable sensitivity to local feeling and the kind of place you're in. As a general rule, stay away from families with children, the main entrance of a beach and any tavernas. If a beach has become fairly established for nudity, or is well secluded, it's highly unlikely that the police are going to come charging in. Where they do get bothered is if they feel a place is turning into a "hippy beach" or nudity getting too overt on mainstream tourist stretches. But there are no hard and fast rules; it all depends on the local cops. Most times the only action would be a warning but you can officially be arrested straight off – facing as much as three days in jail and a stiff fine.

Very similar guidelines exist for **camping rough** – though for this you're still less likely to incur anything more than a warning to move on. The only real risk of arrest is if you are told to move on and fail to do so. In either of the above cases, even if the police do take any action against you, it's more likely to be a brief spell in their cells with perhaps a beating to speed you on your way than any official prosecution.

Drug offences are a far more serious matter. The maximum penalty for "causing the use of drugs by someone under 18", for example, is life imprisonment and a ten million drachma fine. Theory is by no means practice, but foreigners caught in possession of quite small amounts of hash do get jail sentences of up to a year – much more if there's any suggestion they're supplying others.

If you get arrested for any offence you have an automatic right to contact your country's **consul**, who will arrange a lawyer for your defence. Beyond this, there is little they can, or in most cases will, do.

SEXUAL HARASSMENT

Many women travel about Greece on their own without feeling intimidated or constantly harassed – but some undoubtedly are. This has little to do with the way individuals look or behave, and only indirectly relates to the way Greek women themselves are treated. What is important is that different assumptions are made about you as a foreign woman depending on where you are.

In most of the **rural areas**, which are still essentially Greek, you'll be treated first and foremost as a *xénos* – a word which means both stranger and guest – in much the same way as a foreign man. You can sit and drink *oúzo* in the exclusively male *kafenía* (there's often nowhere else) without always suspecting the hospitality and friendliness that's offered.

In the **large resorts and towns**, however, where tourism has for a long time determined the local culture, things can be very different. Here the myths and fantasies of the "liberated" and "available" woman are widespread: not perhaps to the extent of other Mediterranean countries but oppressive nonetheless. Without a good control of the language it can be hard to deal with: words worth remembering for an unambiguous response are *stamáta* (stop it), *afísteme* (leave me alone) and *fíyete* (go away). See also the warnings about work.

It takes no more confidence to **hitch** than in Britain or the States though on long rides the language barrier can add to the strain. In some remote areas there really isn't that much choice, but here the villagers themselves often hitch local farm trucks and the lifts anyway tend to be short.

DIRECTORY

ADDRESSES in Greek are usually written with just the street name followed by the number (Sífaka 11); numbers outside the city centres usually represent a whole block so you may get an individual building number added in brackets. *Odhós* means street; *Leofóros*, avenue; *Platía*, square. In a multistorey building, the ground floor is the *isóyeio*; there may be a mezzanine (*imiórofos*) before the first floor (*prótos órofos*).

AIRPORT TAX There is none on exit – yet.

BAGS If you're visiting Crete as part of a longer trip you may need a rucksack, but unless you're camping or travelling really long-term you're better off with something smaller and lighter – a light nylon holdall bag is large enough to take a sleeping bag and adequate clothes. They are much easier to take on buses (rucksacks often have to be tied on to the roof), far less of a problem when hitching, and create a surprisingly useful aura of respectability – packs often lead to unfortunate assumptions from people and authority ("You have little money and we don't want you . . .") which are good to avoid.

BARGAINING is not a regular feature of life though you'll find it possible with "rooms" and some off-season hotels. A nice line is always to offer to use your sleeping bag, saving the washing of the sheets.

BRING . . . film, an alarm clock for early buses and ferries, and a torch for camping out, visiting caves and churches or finding your way to a midnight swim.

CONSULATES Several countries maintain consulates in Iráklion – British at Papalexándrou 16 (☎224-012), Dutch at 25 Avgóustou 23 (☎246-202), German at Zografóu 7 (☎226-288), Norwegian at Platía Ay. Dimítriou 24 (☎220-536) – for others you'll have to refer to the embassy in Athens.

CONTRACEPTIVES Condoms (*kapótes*) are available from city kiosks or *farmakía*; the pill, too, can be obtained from a *farmakío* – you shouldn't need a prescription.

ELECTRICITY is 220 volt AC (British appliances should work, US ones need a transformer); plugs are usually the standard European pattern of two round pins.

EMERGENCIES ☎100 for police, ☎166 for ambulance, ☎104 for the tourist police.

GAY LIFE There are no overtly gay resorts on Crete, but as throughout Greece attitudes are relaxed. Homosexuality is legal over the age of 17 and (generally, male) bisexuality quite widely accepted.

KIDS/BABIES are worshipped and indulged, perhaps to excess, and present few special problems travelling; for young children, heat and sun are the worst hazards. Baby foods and nappies are widely available and under-8s travel free on the buses (but over-8s pay full fare). A "rooms" establishment is more likely to offer some kind of baby-sitting service than the more impersonal hotels.

LAUNDERETTES are rare, expensive service laundries only slightly more common, but there's almost always somewhere to wash your own clothes. Ask to use the laundry trough rather than risk destroying your room's plumbing.

MOUNTAINEERING Crete offers some exciting possibilities for climbers: contacts for the local mountaineering clubs (*EOS*) in Iráklion, Réthimnon and Haniá are given in their respective listings.

PERÍPTERO A *períptero* is a street-corner kiosk. They sell everything – pens, combs, razors, stationery, postcards, soap, sweets, nuts, condoms, *komboloí* ("worry" beads) – double as phone booths and stay open long after everything else has closed.

SKIING Believe it or not, it is possible to ski in Crete in winter, and there's even a tiny ski lift on the Nídha Plain above Anóyia, while the Kalleryi Lodge in the White Mountains may also open for ski parties. Don't come specially.

STUDENT CARDS give reductions on museum and archaeological site admissions and internal Greek flights. A FIYTO youth card is almost as effective – anyone under 26 can buy one from branches of *STA Travel* in Britain or *Council Travel* in the US.

TAMPONS Sold at *farmakía* and some kiosks.

TIME Greek summertime begins on the last Sunday in March, when the clocks go ahead one hour, and ends on the last Sunday in September when they fall back. Be alert to this, as scores of visitors miss planes, ferries, etc, every year; the change is not well publicised. Greek time is two hours ahead of the UK, three hours when the respective changes to summertime fail to coincide.

TOILETS Public ones, generally foul, are usually in parks or squares, often subterranean. Otherwise try a bus station. Throughout Greece you toss paper in adjacent wastebaskets, *not* in the bowl: learn this habit, or you'll block the pipes. It's worth carrying toilet paper with you – though its provided by the attendants at public facilities, there may be none in tavernas or cafés.

TOURIST POLICE ☎104 for information and help, and see individual towns for local addresses.

WALKING If you're planning on doing some serious walking – such as any of the various gorges – stout shoes or trainers are essential and walking boots with firm ankle support recommended.

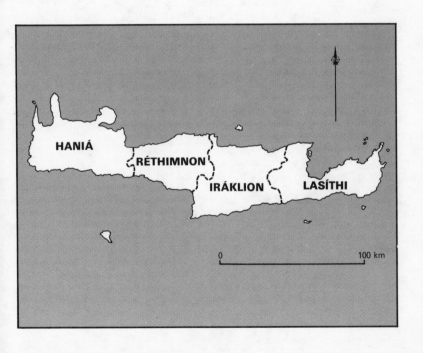

HANIÁ

RÉTHIMNON

IRÁKLION

LASÍTHI

0   100 km

CHAPTER ONE

IRAKLION

T he **province of Iráklion** sees more tourists than any other in Crete. They come for two simple reasons: the string of big **resorts** which lies to the east of the city, only an hour or so from the airport, and the great **Minoan sites**, almost all of which are concentrated in the centre of the island. Knossós, **Mália** and **Festós** are in easy reach of almost anywhere in the province and there are excellent beaches all along the north coast. The price you pay is crowds: **Iráklion** is a big, hustling city, the development to the east is continuous and huge, and in summer the great sites are constantly awash with people.

There seems little here of the old Crete, ramshackle and rural, and yet, by taking the less obvious turn, it is still possible to escape. **West and south** of Iráklion the coastline is less flat, the beaches smaller, the opportunities for hotel builders less obvious. The south coast in particular is far less peopled: the beach accessible only in a handful of places (of which only **Mátala** is at all exploited), the interior traditional farming country.

IRÁKLION AND THE NORTH COAST

Iráklion itself can at first seem a nightmare. Arrive expecting a quaint little island town and you're in for a big disappointment. You find yourself instead in the fifth largest city in Greece; ugly, modern, a maelstrom of traffic, building work, concrete and dust. Stay long enough and you can begin to like the place – but it would take a determined tourist to stay that course. You're better off taking the city for what it has – **Knossós** and the **Archaeological Museum** most famously, but also snatched visions of another city, of magnificent fortifications, a wonderful market, the occasional ancient alley, curious smaller museums – and getting out as fast as practicable. For the most part you'll find the city an exercise in survival.

Knossós apart, the immediate **surrounds of Iráklion** offer little compensation. If you are based in the city with time on your hands then the Minoan remains at **Arhánes** or the views from **Mount Yioúhtas** are worth taking in, and transport to local beaches is excellent. But this is hardly getting the most the island offers.

East of Iráklion, the startling pace of tourist development is all too plain to see. The merest hint of a beach is an excuse to build at least one hotel, and these are outnumbered by the concrete shells of rivals-to-be. It's hard to find a room in this monument to the package tour, and expensive if you do. Some of the resorts – **Mália** and **Hersónisos** most notably – do at least have good beaches and lively nightlife. They wouldn't be at all bad if you were on a package deal from home. But turn up hoping to find somewhere to stay on the off-chance and you won't regard them as the most welcoming of places. As a general rule, the further you go, the better things get: when the road veers inland for an all-too-brief while, the real Crete – olive groves and stark mountains – reveals itself.

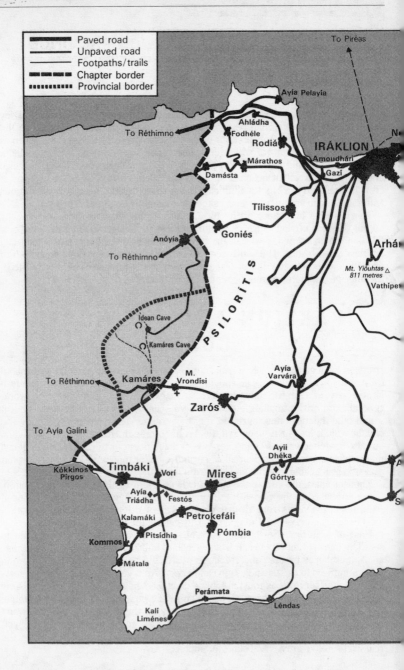

Paved road
Unpaved road
Footpaths/trails
Chapter border
Provincial border

To Piréas

To Réthimno

Ayía Pelayía

Ahládha
Fodhéle

Rodiá

IRÁKLION

Márathos

Amoudhári

Damásta

Gazí

Ne

Tílissos

Anóyia

Goniés

Arháí

To Réthimno

PSILORÍTIS

Mt. Yioúhtas △
811 metres

Vathípe

Ídean Cave

Kamáres Cave

To Réthimno

Kamáres

M.
Vrondísi

Ayía
Varvára

Zarós

To Ayía Galíni

Ayii
Dhéka

Kókkinos
Pírgos

Timbáki

Vorí

Míres

Górtys

Ayía
Triádha

Festós

Kalamáki

Petrokefáli

Pómbia

Kommos

Pitsídhia

Mátala

Perámata

Léndas

Kalí
Liménes

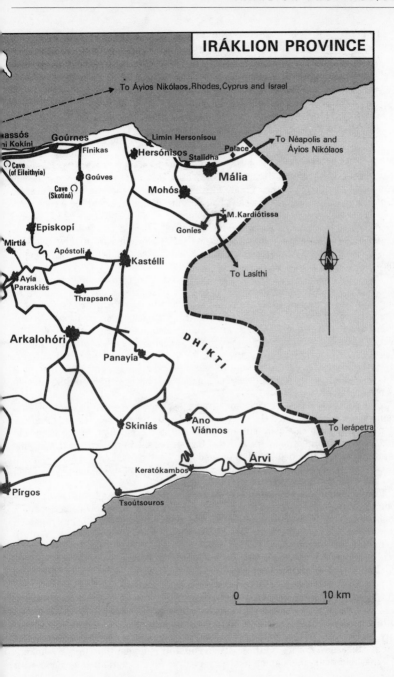

IRÁKLION PROVINCE

To Áyios Nikólaos, Rhodes, Cyprus and Israel

assós
ni Kokíni
Goúrnes
Fínikas
Limin Hersonísou
Hersónisos
Stalídha
Palace
To Néapolis and
Áyios Nikólaos

Cave
(of Eileithyia)
Goúves
Mália

Cave
(Skotinó)
Mohós

Episkopí
M. Kardiótissa

Mirtiá
Gonies

Apóstoli
Kastélli
To Lasíthi

Ayía
Paraskiés
Thrapsanó

DHÍKTI

Arkalohóri

Panayía

Skiniás
Ano
Viánnos
To Ierápetra

Árvi

Keratókambos

Pírgos
Tsoútsouros

0   10 km

To the **west** there's much less, with mountains which drop virtually straight to the sea. There is just one small, classy resort in the bay at **Ayía Pelayía**, a few isolated hotels and, in the hills behind, a number of interesting old villages: at **Fódhele** the birthplace of El Greco, and at **Tílissos** a famous Minoan villa.

Iráklion

The best way to arrive in **IRÁKLION** is from the sea, the traditional approach and still the one which shows the city in its best light, with Yioúhtas rising behind, the heights of the Psilorítis range to the west and, as you get closer, the city walls encircling and dominating the oldest part of town. As you sail in, you run the gauntlet of the great fortress guarding the harbour entrance. Unfortunately the old harbour can't handle ships of this size, and the ferries actually dock at great concrete wharves alongside – a juxtaposition which seems neatly to sum up much about modern Iráklion. The old city has been heavily restored, often from the bottom up, but the slick renovations invariably look fake, pristine and polished alongside the grime which coats even the most recent of new buildings.

Iráklion's name is of Roman origin, taken from a port which stood hereabouts and readopted at the beginning of this century. The present city was founded by the Saracens who held Crete from 827 to 961. In those days it was known, after the great ditch which surrounded it, as El Khandak, later corrupted by the Venetians to Candia, or Candy, a name applied also to the island as a whole. This Venetian capital was in its day one of the strongest and most spectacular cities in Europe: a trading centre, a staging-point for the Crusades and, as time wore on, itself the front line of Christendom. When the Turks finally conquered the city it was only after twenty years of war, culminating in a bitter siege from May 1667 to September 1669.

Under its new rulers the city's importance declined in relation to Haniá's, but it remained a major port and the second city in Crete. It was here, too, that the incident occurred which finally put an end to Turkish occupation of the island. In 1898 fourteen British soldiers and the British consul were murdered, the final straw – where the deaths of thousands of Cretans had not been – which persuaded the great powers to insist on the departure of the remaining Turkish troops and administrators.

Finally united with Greece, Iráklion's prosperity was assured by its central position. Almost all that you see, though, dates only from the last few decades, and a coincidental boom in agriculture, industry and tourism. In 1971 the çity regained the official title of island capital. Its growth continues, as you'll see if you venture to the fringes of town where the concrete spreads inexorably, but it can hardly be said to add to the attraction. Modern Iráklion, indeed, must rank among the least charming of all Mediterranean cities.

Arrival and orientation

Virtually everything you're likely to want to see in Iráklion lies within the walled city, and even here the majority of the interest falls into a relatively small sector, the northeastern corner. **Odhós 25 Avgoústou** is a vital thoroughfare linking the harbour with the commercial city centre. At the bottom it is lined with shipping and travel agencies, car and motorbike hire outlets, but as you climb these give way to banks, restaurants and city-centre shops. **Platía Venizélou** (or Fountain Square), off to the right, is one of two crucial meeting places in the centre: crowded with cafés and restaurants, it is here that Iráklion's youth hang out, while their elders pack the more staid, expensive establishments up in Eleftherías. Behind Venizélou is **El Greco Park**, with the OTE office and more bars, while on the opposite side of 25 Avgoústou are some of the more interesting of Iráklion's older buildings.

Continuing up 25 Avgoústou you reach the traffic lights at Platía Nikíforos Fókas, which is little more than a widening of the street for a major traffic junction. To the right, **Kalokerinoú** leads down to Haniá Gate and out of the city westwards. Straight ahead, Odhós 1821 goes nowhere very much, but adjacent 1866 is given over to the animated **market**. Left, Dhikeosínis heads for **Platía Eleftherías**, paralleled by the touristy pedestrian alley Dedhalou, the direct link between the two squares. Eleftherías is very much the traditional centre of the city, both for traffic, which swirls around it constantly, and for life in general: ringed by expensive cafés and restaurants and in the evening alive with hordes of strolling locals. Most of Iráklion's upmarket shopping is done in the streets leading off the square and it's here that you'll find both the **Archaeological Museum** and the **tourist office** (Mon–Fri 8am–2pm).

Points of arrival

Iráklion **airport**, 4km east of the city, lies right on the coast – you come in to land low over some of the better local beaches. *Olympic* flights are met by a bus which runs direct to their office in Platía Eleftherías, or the #1 bus (also to Eleftherías) leaves every few minutes from a grassy bit of the car park in front of the terminal: buy your ticket (45dr) at the booth before boarding. There are also plenty of taxis outside, and prices to major destinations are posted; it's about 500dr to the centre of town. The airport itself is surprisingly busy (departures can be chaotic, especially when there are delays), but if you arrive in the middle of the night planning to catch an early morning bus it's easy enough to find a corner where you can grab some sleep.

From the wharves where the **ferries** dock, the city rises directly ahead in steep tiers. If you're heading for the centre, for the Archaeological Museum or the tourist office, there's no reason why you shouldn't cut straight up the stepped alleys to Platía Eleftherías. For accommodation, though, and to get a better idea of the layout of Iráklion's main attractions, it's simplest to follow the main roads by a rather more roundabout route. Head west along the coast, past the major eastbound bus station and on by the Venetian harbour before cutting up towards the centre on Odhós 25 Avgoústou.

Arriving **by bus** from anywhere else on Crete you could be at one of four bus stations. Services along the coastal highway to or from **the east** (Mália, Áyios Nikólaos, Sitía etc) use the terminal mentioned above, just off the main road between the ferry dock and the Venetian harbour. Main road services **west**, for Réthimnon and Haniá, run from a smaller terminal just back from the seafront to the west of the Venetian harbour. Head straight up the hill behind this little square and you'll eventually emerge at Platía Venizélou. Buses for the **southwest** – Festós, Mátala or Ayía Galíni – and along the inland roads west (Tílissos, Anóyia) operate out of a terminus just outside Haniá Gate; a very long walk to the centre up Kalokerinoú (or jump on any bus heading up this street). The **southeast**, basically

Ierápetra and points en route, is served by the smallest of the stations, just outside the walls in Platía Kíprou at the end of Odhós Evans. Follow Evans in towards Platía Venizélou, or cut down one of the side streets to the right for Eleftherías.

The Iráklion phone code is ☎081.

Finding a room

Iráklion has a distinct lack of decent, reasonably priced **places to stay**, and at the height of summer a severe shortage of anywhere to stay at all. If possible, arrange to arrive early in the day; rolling up after 8pm or so without a reservation – certainly in the middle of summer – you'd be lucky to find anything at all (though the hostels are always worth a try). One thing worth trying if you're stuck is to ask a taxi driver to take you somewhere, as they often know places out in the suburbs; but make sure they have somewhere in mind before you start driving around. In general, if you do find a room – any room – take it. You can always set out early next day to find something better.

People who can't find anywhere to stay often end up sleeping in one of the parks, particularly the little area down by the east-bound bus station (if you're broke, this has the added advantage that farmers looking for extra hands sometimes come round recruiting in the early mornings), or out around the fortress. But harassment and some robberies have been reported, and this certainly isn't a long-term solution – the police will move you on during the day.

The greatest concentration of **cheaper rooms** is to be found below Platía Venizélou, around Hándhakos and towards the west-bound bus station. Slightly more central, there are a few rather more noisy and marginally more expensive places around El Greco Park and by the bottom of the market; and another small enclave of generally less pleasant places towards the bottom of Kalokerinoú, near the Haniá Gate. None of those in the first list below is likely to offer private bathrooms, but they should all be clean and have (some) hot water. Better **hotels** mostly lie closer to Platía Eleftherías in the more modern business areas. For hotels of C class and above it's usually simplest to approach the tourist office first – they should know where there are available rooms and if they're not too harassed will make the phone calls for you. Just a couple of the more central and convenient medium-price places are included below. At quiet times, if you have the time and patience (or just happen to be passing), it's worth trying some of the B and C class hotels "on spec". During slack periods they'll often make you surprising offers on the quiet – sometimes reducing prices by fifty percent and more.

Hostels and rooms

Youth Hostel, Vironos 5 (☎286-281). In a new location just off 25 Avgoústou: cheap, convenient and likely to have a spare dormitory bed.

Yours Hostel, Hándhakos 24 (☎280-858). Occupies the old youth hostel building, and although they unscrupulously try to pass themselves off as the official youth hostel the place seems well run and is only slightly more expensive. Dorms, single-sex rooms, private rooms and roofspace available.

Rent Rooms Vergina, Hortátson 32 (☎242-739). Basic but pleasant cheap rooms around a courtyard with an enormous banana tree; English spoken.

Rent Rooms Mary, Hándhakos 67 (☎281-135). Decent, cheap rooms place, complete with cold showers and a courtyard to sit and chat.

Hotel Rea, Kalímeráki 1 (☎223-638). Between the two above, a friendly, comfortable D-class place: booking essential.

Pension Karpathos, Gazí 4 (☎241-161). Immediately behind the bus station: handy and not bad value.

Hotel Paladion, Hándhakos 16 (☎282-563). D-class hotel closer to Platía Venizélou with clean but stuffy rooms upstairs, and a pleasant garden at the back with rooms off it.

Rooms Christakos, Evyénikon. One of a number of less enticing rooms places in the backstreets to the west of Hándhakos.

Atlas Guest House, Kandanoleon 6 (☎288-989). Rather run-down old place, slightly more expensive than those preceding, in convenient but noisy alley between Platía Venizélou and El Greco Park.

Georgiades Guest House, Kandanoleon, opposite *Atlas*. Similar prices and conditions to *Atlas*, perhaps slightly cleaner.

Hotel Hellas, Kandanoleon 11 (☎284-400, 225-121). D-class hotel, clean, friendly but again noisy; nice courtyard.

Pension Lion, Andhróyeo 9, alongside San Marco (☎241-194). Across 25 Avgoústou from all the foregoing; pleasant and relatively quiet.

Hotel Idaion Andron, Perdhikári 1 (☎283-624). Behind the Venetian Loggia, tiny E-class hotel around a flowery courtyard. Rooms small and very basic, but good value.

Hotel Creta Sun, Odhós 1866 10 (☎283-217). E-class hotel right above the market stalls at the bottom of 1866, neither quiet nor specially clean, but atmospheric.

Hotel Ionia, Evans 5 (☎281-795). At the corner of Evans and Yiánari, also near the market, offers marginally greater comforts and a good restaurant: may by now have been refurbished and upgraded from E-class.

Hotel Christos, Yiamaláki 17 (☎287-390). One of the better choices (E-class) in the side streets **off Kalokerinoú**, convenient if you arrive at the southwestern bus station – you'll see others, or signs to them, down towards Haniá Gate. Hotels actually on Kalokerinoú – none very good – include the D-class *Venetia* (no. 189, ☎283-239), *Ikaros* (202, ☎283-006) and *Arcadi* (235, ☎282-077).

Moderate hotels

Dedalos, Dedhálou 15 (☎224-391). Very centrally placed on the pedestrianised alley between Venizélou and Eleftherías. Slightly shabby rooms with balconies, but convenient and reasonably priced; C-class.

Olympic, Platía Kornárou (☎288-861). In a more modern part of town at the top of Odhós 1866, another slightly older business-style hotel; again good value for C-class comfort.

Mediterranean, Smirnis 1, Platía Dhaskaloyiánnis (☎289-331–5). B-class hotel, very central and not too noisy or expensive.

Campsites

Camping Iráklion, Amoudara beach about 6km west (☎286-380). The only nearby campsite: enormous but not very attractive with souvenir shop, cafeteria, swimming pool. Strictly run and expensive, it is easily reached by the #6 bus, from outside the *Hotel Astoria* in Platía Eleftherías.

The City

By far the most striking aspect of Iráklion is its walls, which have been marvellously preserved and where necessary restored, though not always with much thought to access. The obvious place to start is the fortress guarding the harbour.

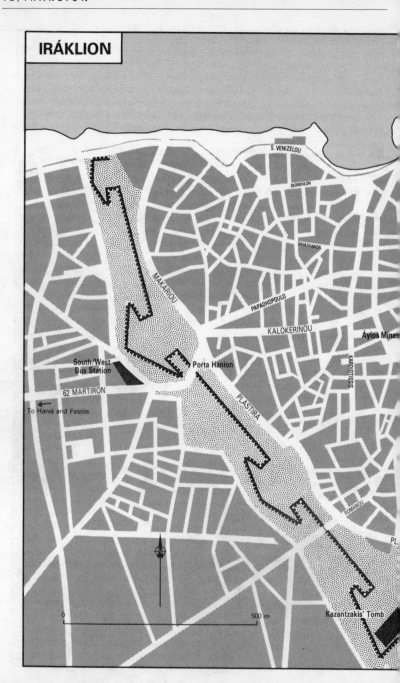

IRÁKLION

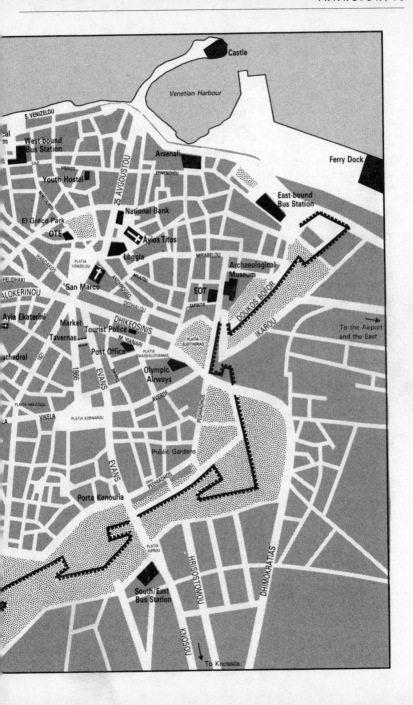

Walls and Fortress

Built between 1523 and 1540, the **Fort** (8.30am–3pm, closed Mon) was known to the Venetians as the *Rocca al Mare*, to the Turks as *Koule*. Painstakingly refurbished, it now often houses temporary exhibitions which may disrupt the standard opening hours. Taken simply as a structure, it is undeniably impressive: massively sturdy walls commanding superb views over harbour and town and protecting a series of chambers (many still piled with cannonballs) in which the defenders must have enjoyed an overwhelming sense of security. It is easy to see here how Venetian Iráklion managed to resist the Turks so long. On the other hand there is something unsatisfying about the way it has been so thoroughly scrubbed, polished and cosseted, losing any hint of atmosphere. While you may know, from the Lions of St Mark adorning the exterior and the simple solidity of the stone, that the fort is the genuine sixteenth-century item, it *feels* as if it had been built yesterday for some swashbuckling Hollywood production.

At night, when the fortress is floodlit, the causeway which leads there is the haunt of courting couples, while the niches in the walls provide temporary accommodation for people awaiting ferries: it's a fine place to watch the ships coming and going.

The only other survivors of the Venetian harbour installations, the vaulted **Arsenali**, are now lost in a sea of concrete and traffic. Here, ships were built or dragged ashore to be overhauled and repaired – close up, you may still find bits of broken boat lying about.

The **walls** themselves are rather harder to penetrate. Perhaps the easiest approach is to follow Odhós Pedhiádhos south from the back of Platía Eleftherías and find your way up one of the dusty tracks which lead to the top of the rampart. With luck and a little scrambling you can walk all the way around from here, clockwise, to St Anthony's Bastion overlooking the sea in the west. There are some curious views as you walk around, often looking down onto the rooftops, but the fabric of the walls themselves is rarely visible – it's simply like walking on a dusty path raised above the level of its surrounds. Few people venture here either; there are tales of petty thievery.

On the Martinengo Bastion, facing south, is the **tomb of Nikos Kazantzakís** (1883–1957, see p.64). Crete's greatest writer, Kazantzakís was denied an Orthodox burial for his unorthodox views, and his simple grave is adorned only with an inscription from his own writings: "I believe in nothing, I hope for nothing, I am free". At the weekend Iraklians gather here to pay their respects and get a free view of the football ground below.

For more impressive views of the defences, from the outside, stroll out through one of the elaborate **gates** – the Pórta Haníon at the bottom of Kalokerinoú or the Pórta Kenoúria at the top of Evans. Both of these date from the second half of the sixteenth century when the bulk of the surviving defences were completed. Originally thrown up in the fifteenth century, the walls were constantly improved thereafter as Crete became increasingly isolated in the path of Turkish westward expansion: their final shape owes much to Michele Sanmicheli who arrived here in 1538 having previously designed the fortifications of Padua and Verona. In its day this was the strongest bastion in the Mediterranean, and at the Kenoúria Gate, where the walls are over 40m thick, you can see why.

If you want to follow the walls in the other direction, from the sea up, simply follow the coastal road west from the harbour – a considerable walk – until you reach them. Not far along the way you pass the **Historical Museum** (Mon–Fri 9am–5pm, Sat 9am–2pm), in a grand old house by the west-bound bus station. The collection is a miscellaneous and often confused one, not helped by English labelling which is eccentric to say the least. Nevertheless it helps fill some of the gap which, for most people, yawns between Knossós and the present day, and since it always seems virtually deserted, wandering around is a pleasure. In the basement you'll find sculptures and architectural fragments from the Byzantine, Venetian and Turkish periods; the ground floor has religious art and documents from the same periods; and the upper floors bring things through to the present. Included here are reconstructions of the studies of Nikos Kazantzakís and of the Cretan statesman (and Greek prime minister) Emanuel Tsouderos; photos and documents relating to the German occupation of Crete; and a substantial selection of folk art – particularly textiles.

Towards the market

Heading inland from the harbour, Odhós 25 Avgoústou offers a less strenuous walk past more obvious attractions. On the left as you approach Platía Venizélou, the much renovated church of **Áyios Títos** commands a lovely little plaza. Originally Byzantine, but wholly rebuilt by the Venetians in the sixteenth century, it was later adapted by the Turks as a mosque and only reconsecrated in 1925. A reliquary inside contains the skull of Saint Titus, which came here originally from his tomb in Górtys (the rest of the body was never found) and was later taken to Venice, where it stayed from the time of the Turkish invasion until 1966: in the Middle Ages the head was regularly and ceremonially exhibited to the people of Iráklion.

On the top side of this square, abutting 25 Avgoústou, stands the Venetian **City Hall** with its famous *loggia*, reconstructed after the work of earthquakes was compounded by the rigours of the last war. Just past here on the left is **San Marco**, a church very much in the Venetian style which, also restored, is used for exhibitions and occasional lectures or meetings. Under the Venetians it was the cathedral and under the Turks a mosque: nowadays the church steps make a handy overflow for the cafés in **Platía Venizélou**. In the square, the Morosini Fountain (hence "Fountain Square") dates from the final years of Venetian rule. On first sight it's a rather disappointing little monument, especially as it's normally clogged with mud and cigarette butts, but the decoration is fine close up and the lions on guard, 200–300 years older than the rest of the structure, wonderful.

Continuing, you reach the crossroads with Kalokerinoú and Dhikeosínis, which is the main through route of the city. Straight ahead, Odhós 1866 is packed throughout the day with the stalls and customers of Iráklion's **market**. This is one of the few living reminders of an older city, with an almost eastern bazaar feel as you push your way up through the crowds. There are luscious fruit and vegetables in particular, but also bloody butchers' stalls, cheese and yoghurt, leather goods, souvenirs, an amazing array of cheap kitchen utensils, pocket knives and just about anything else you might conceivably need. At the far end you emerge in a quiet square, **Platía Kornárou**, the focal point of which is a beautiful Turkish fountain. Heavily restored, as ever, this now houses a café which would be lovely if you could ever find it open. A small Venetian fountain – incorporating a headless Roman torso imported from Ierápetra – stands across the square.

Churches and Icons

Turning right before the market leads you down Kalokerinoú towards the Haniá gate and the main road west. Veer left after about 100 metres, up Áyii Dhéka or one of the streets immediately after, and you'll reach a large open space beside the **Cathedral of Áyios Mínas**. The cathedral – a rather ugly nineteenth-century building – is notable mainly for its size. Just in front, however, stands the tiny original church of Áyios Mínas, which looks very ancient indeed: the interior is worth seeing if you can find someone to open it for you.

Far more worthwhile, and just at the bottom of the same square, is the church of **Ayía Ekateríni** (Mon–Sat 9.30am–1pm; Tues, Thurs & Fri also 5–7pm) which houses a **Museum of Religious Art**. This is the finest collection of Cretan icons anywhere, and some Cretan icons are very fine indeed. Built in the fifteenth century, the church was part of a monastic school which in the following centuries – up to the end of Venetian rule – was one of the centres of the "Cretan renaissance", a last flourish of Eastern Christian art following the fall of Byzantium and mainland Greece. Among the school's students were Vicénzos Kornáros, author of the Cretan classic *Erotókritos*, and many leading Orthodox theologians; most importantly, however, it served as an art school where Byzantine tradition came face to face with the influences of the Venetian renaissance. Among the greatest of the pupils was Mihailis Dhamaskinos, six of whose works form the centre of the collection. It was the much-imitated Dhamaskinos who introduced perspective and depth to Byzantine art, while never straying far from the strict traditions of icon painting; in his later works indeed he reverts to a much purer, earlier style. The most famous Cretan painter of them all, El Greco, took the opposite course – wholeheartedly embracing Italian styles to which he brought the influence of his Byzantine training. Although there is little evidence, it's generally accepted that these two – Dhamaskinos and El Greco – were near contemporaries at the school.

Turning left before the market brings you quickly up to **Platía Eleftherías**, a confused mass of pavement cafés and whorls of traffic. There's a small bust of Nikos Kazantzakís and a larger-than-life statue of Eleftheríos Venizelos, leading figure in the struggle for union with Greece, staring out over the harbour from the ramparts and looking more like Lenin than ever. Beyond the statue you reach the entrance to the **Public Gardens**, as often as not half taken over by a funfair, but generally relatively peaceful; they also shelter some averagely filthy public toilets. Above all, however, Platía Eleftherías offers access to the Archaeological Museum.

The Archaeological Museum

Iráklion's **Archaeological Museum** (Tues–Sat 8am–7pm, Sun 8am–6pm; check hours if possible, as reorganisation work has meant frequent changes) is one of the major reasons to visit the city: far and away the most important collection of Minoan art and artefacts anywhere in the world. There is no doubt that the enjoyment and meaning of a visit to Knossós or the other sites will be greatly heightened if you've been here first (or better still, between two visits). The museum is, however, old-fashioned, poorly displayed and sparsely labelled – always crowded (at least in summer) and at times quite overwhelmed by the stampede of coach parties thundering through. Recent refurbishment has improved matters only slightly. Try to see it early, late, or during everyone else's lunch break. Equally important, the collection is large and to the layman can seem repetitive – unless you're completing a thesis on Minoan pottery you won't want to examine everything in detail. If you've a serious interest, it's a lot more enjoyable in small doses: take in the highlights first time around and go back later for whatever you feel you've missed (tickets are valid for re-entry the same day).

Several detailed, colour brochures are on sale at the museum, but the following should give you some idea of what to expect. Basically, the galleries on the ground floor, which you have little choice but to walk through in order, follow a chronological pattern: they run from the Neolithic era right through to Roman times, with the more important Minoan periods also divided according to where the items on display were discovered. Upstairs, larger rooms show the fabulous Minoan frescoes. Due to the renovation and reorganisation of some rooms in the museum (partly to move the most popular items – which attract the large tour groups – to places where these crowds cause less of an obstruction) some items may not be precisely where stated. However, they should still be in the same room.

Room 1 covers several thousand years, from the earliest signs of human settlement around 6000 BC to the beginnings of Minoan civilisation in the Pre-Palatial period. There's a bit of everything here, of interest mainly because it is *so* old: pottery, among which the blotchy **Vasilikí ware** with elegant elongated spouts points to the great things to come; stone jars from the island of Móhlos displaying an early mastery of the lapidary's craft; also statuettes, including a Neolithic "fertility goddess". Amongst the miniature sculpture don't miss a **clay bull** in Case 12 with tiny acrobats clinging to its horns: an early sign of the popularity of the bull sports so important later. Particularly typical of what is to be seen later, in the central cases is displayed some sophisticated early **jewellery** alongside some intricately engraved **seal stones** – among the latter one from ancient Mesopotamia indicating contacts between the island and its neighbours from very early on.

Room 2 contains objects from the earliest period of occupation of Knossós and Mália (around 2000–1700 BC), along with items found in various peak sanctuaries of the same era. Archaeologically most important is the **Kamáres ware** pottery, with often elaborate white and red decoration on a dark ground. For casual visitors, however, the miniature figures are of far more immediate interest, in particular the famous "**town mosaic**" from Knossós. This consists of a series of glazed plaques depicting multistoreyed Minoan houses, beautiful pieces which look like children's toys but in fact probably fitted together to form a decorative scene. There are also some lovely figurines and tiny animals, mostly offerings found in the peak sanctuaries: look out for the three-columned shrine with a dove perched on the top of each column, thought to represent the epiphany or manifestation of the goddess worshipped there. Note also the **clay statuettes** of the worshippers found at these sanctuaries – their arms crossed or placed on the chest in reverential attitudes – as well as the *taxímata* or sick-symbols representing parts of the human body the deity was requested to heal: a custom that is continued in churches all over Greece today.

Room 3 is devoted to the same period at Festós. Here the **Kamáres ware** is even more elaborate, and it was at Festós that this art reached its peak – exemplified by a magnificent vase with sculptured white flowers in high relief. In Case 30 you'll find the original pieces found in the cave at Kamáres which gave the style its name. There is also the celebrated **Festós Disc**, a large slab of clay with writing on both sides, spiralling in towards the centre. The disc is frequently described as the first known example of printing, since the impressions of hieroglyphs were made with stamps before it was fired. The various signs are divided up into groups, believed to be words. Interestingly, some of these "words" are repeated, leading scholars to suggest that the disc may contain some form of prayer or hymn. An assortment of alternative theories notwithstanding (several books are on sale around the island claiming to "reveal the secret" of the disc), this earliest Minoan script remains undeciphered.

Room 4 represents the "New Palace" period (1700–1450 BC) in which the great sites reached their peak of creativity, rebuilt after the first destruction. Kamáres pottery is now replaced by new styles with patterns painted in dark colours on a light background, and themes drawn from nature (in particular marine life) rather than abstract patterns. The **Jug of Reeds** (or grasses) in Case 49 is a brilliant example of this stylistic development. Again there are other objects far more immediately striking: above all the renowned **Bull's Head rhyton**, a sacred vessel used in religious ceremonial and found in the Little Palace at Knossós. Carved from black stone (steatite) with eyes and nostrils inlaid (the wooden horns are new), the bull is magnificently naturalistic. There are other animal heads here too, including another rhyton in the form of a lioness's head, made from white limestone, and the stunning leopard's-head axe from Mália. In Case 46 are a number of vessels connected with the snake cult; some of them may have been snake containers. These are pertinent to Case 50, where two representations of the **Snake Goddess** – both wearing tight-waisted, bare-breasted dresses and a decorated apron, each with snakes coiling around their hands – may equally be priestesses engaged in sacred rituals. A delicate ivory acrobat, generally accepted to be a bull-leaper, and a faience relief of a *Kri-Kri*, or wild goat, suckling her calf also stand out. The **Gaming Board**, from the "Corridor of the Draughtsboard" at Knossós, is beautiful too – made of ivory, blue paste, crystal and gold- and silver-leaf, with ivory pieces – and a further reminder of the luxurious life which some Minoans at least could enjoy. Room 4 also contains a collection of tools (including two huge saws) and weapons (especially a giant sword from Mália), almost all bronze though with decorations in ivory, gold and semiprecious stones. Finally, in Case 44, two small clay cups could carry important clues to the history of Minoan writing of which so little survives. These vessels bear inscriptions written in Linear A script – developed from the cumbersome hieroglyphic – using cuttlefish ink. This use of ink suggests that other writing materials suitable to this medium probably existed (imported papyrus or even domestically produced palm-leaf paper?) which have since perished in the Cretan climate.

Room 5 is devoted to the last period of the palace culture (1450–1400 BC), mainly at Knossós. Already the objects are considerably less exciting. In pottery, similar decorative themes continue to be used, but with a new formalism and on new types of vessel which are taken to mean that Mycenaean influences were beginning to take hold. Such influences are clear on the giant amphorae standing against the walls. The numerous **Egyptian objects** found at Knossós are interesting too, fine in themselves and important evidence of the extent of trade between the two civilisations (and for archaeologists, vital ammunition in the war over dates). In Case 70a a **clay model house** from Arhánes gives you a fascinating insight into how a modest Minoan dwelling would have looked. With small rooms and tiny windows to keep out the bright Cretan sun (and fierce winds), it also has a small court in one corner which must have served as a light well. The roof terrace above – with typical tapered columns – is similar to those seen on village houses throughout Crete today. Side by side in Case 69, you can also see examples of both Linear A and Linear B scripts.

Room 6 covers finds from cemeteries at Knossós, Festós and Arhánes of approximately the same period. First come some small groups of clay figures from a tomb near Festós, in particular one of a ritual dance inside a circle decorated with horns of consecration – very crude work but wonderfully effective. In the centre of the room is some of the museum's finest **jewellery**: gold signet rings, necklaces of gold and beads, and other gold work demonstrating the fine granulation typical of Minoan style. There is more martial art, too, including some fine gold sword hilts and two fabulous **helmets**, one of boar's tusks (reconstructed), the other of bronze with long cheekpieces. The boar's tusk helmet also makes an appearance on a ceramic amphora in Case 82. Taken with the other weapons displayed here – knives, swords and spear and arrow-heads among them – these items are seen as further proof of the subordination of Minoan culture to the more warlike Mycenaean in this period.

Room 7 backtracks slightly in time to include objects from minor sites – mostly small villas and sacred caves, though including the larger complex of Ayía Triádha – throughout the main palace period and beyond (1700–1300 BC). As you enter you'll see great bronze double axes, erected on wooden poles, stone horns of consecration and bronze cauldrons set about the room. In the cases themselves are some very famous pieces, above all the three **stone vases** from Ayía Triádha and the **gold jewellery** from a grave near Mália. The "Harvesters' Vase" is the finest of the three, depicting in low relief, and vivid realism, a procession returning home from the fields; the harvesters are led by a strangely dressed character with long hair and a big stick, possibly a priest, and accompanied by musicians. The other two show scenes from boxing and wrestling matches and a chieftain receiving a report from an official. All three are carved from black steatite. The jewellery is to be found in a single case in the centre of the room – catch above all the stunningly intricate **pendant of two bees** around a golden disc (supposedly a drop of honey which they are storing in a comb). Beside it are a number of other gold animal pendants, as well as necklaces and rings. Some **bronze figurines** in Case 89 depict worshippers making the ritual "salute" gesture to the deity whilst leaning backwards, and there's also a rare depiction of an older man released from the constriction of the usual tight belt – thus proving that not all Minoans had sylph-like figures as much of their art would lead you to believe. The enormous bronze cauldrons are worth a closer look; superbly crafted from sheets of metal riveted with nails, their discovery at Tílissos led to the excavation of the villas there. More mundane items in Case 99 include large copper ingots, almost certainly used as a form of currency.

Room 8 is given over to finds from the palace at Zákros (1700–1450 BC) and again includes several superlative items. There's a magnificent **rhyton of rock**

crystal with a handle of beads and a collar (hiding a join between two pieces) cased in gold. Its beauty aside, this is always singled out by guides as an example of the painstaking reconstruction undertaken by the museum – when discovered, it was broken into more than 300 fragments. Also striking is the **peak sanctuary rhyton**, a green stone vessel on which a low relief scene depicts a peak sanctuary with horns of consecration decorated with birds and wild goats. Originally covered in gold leaf, this discovery provided valuable information on Minoan religion. In the case parallel to this is a bull's head rhyton, smaller than but otherwise similar to that in Room 4. Room 8 also has a fine display of pottery from both palace and town, mostly from the zenith of the **marine and floral periods**. Finally, there are some outstanding stone and ceramic miniatures – shells and a butterfly in particular – and an assortment of the craftsmen's raw materials: a giant elephant's tusk, burnt in the fire which destroyed the palace, and unused ingots of bronze from the storerooms.

Room 9 contains discoveries of the same period from lesser sites in the east. As usual there is an assortment of pottery and everyday objects, the most important of which are a series of **terracotta figurines** from a peak sanctuary at Piskoképhalo (Case 123). These naturalistic figures are fascinating in that they show what ordinary Minoans must have looked like and how they dressed – albeit for worship. Beside them are some charming miniature animals and models of sanctuaries. In Case 127 you can see a collection of bronze tools and weapons from the workers' village at Gourniá: hammers, picks, cutters and even "razor blades". Also in this room (Case 128) is the museum's largest collection of **seal stones**. Two things stand out about these. Firstly the intricacy of the carving, superbly executed in tiny detail on the hardest of stones, and secondly the abundance of different themes (for obvious reasons, no two seals are the same) which provide pictures of almost every aspect of Minoan life, from portraits of individuals (rare) to religious ceremonies, hunting scenes and, most commonly, scenes from nature. The seals were used to close parcels or clay amphorae and for signing correspondence – a number of impressions of seals in clay have survived from Minoan times, mostly baked hard in accidental fires. Some of the larger seals, especially those in precious stones or with non-natural designs, may also have been charms or amulets.

Room 10 begins the museum's post-Minoan collection, covering a period (1400–1100 BC) when Crete was dominated by Mycenaean influences. The stylisation and repetition of the themes employed in pottery decoration coupled with a near-abandonment of the highly skilled craft of stoneworking are obvious examples of artistic decline. Figurines from the sanctuaries are also far less naturalistically executed; there are many examples of a stereotyped goddess, both hands raised perhaps in blessing. However, an evocative clay sculpture of a **dancing group** with a lyre player from Palékastro (Case 132) does seem to echo past achievements, but even here Mycenaean influences are apparent.

Room 11 continues the theme into the period of the arrival of Dorian Greeks (1100–900 BC). Among the Minoans, the goddess with raised hands remained important. The anguished features of the example from Mount Karfí (Case 148) – a remote mountain above the Lasíthi Plateau whence many Minoans fled from the vulnerable coastal areas – seem to foreshadow the end. Note the horns of consecration on her head. The newcomers introduced stylistic changes: the clay cart drawn by curiously portrayed bodyless oxen is a new form of ritual vessel. The passing of the Bronze Age can be seen in Case 153: the metal of the new age was iron and this metal was now used for the vast majority of weapons and tools. But some Minoan beliefs and traditions survived, such as worship at the cave sanctuary of the Minoan goddess of childbirth, Eileithyia, to the east of Iráklion. Cases 149 and 158 display votive offerings from the cave dating down to Hellenistic and Roman times. Some figurines made of lead portray couples engaged in sexual intercourse or women giving birth – leaving the goddess in little doubt what was required of her.

Room 12 takes the collection up to about 650 BC. The early part of the period shows simply a development of the art of the previous era; the latter half is marked by eastern, notably Egyptian, influences. This is most evident on the pottery, which starts to be decorated with griffins, and with figures who would look at home in Tutankhamun's tomb. An interesting jug in Case 163 is typical of this era: on the vessel's neck two lovers – thought by some to be Theseus and Ariadne – embrace fondly. There are also some fine pottery and bronze figures, and a small treasure of gold jewellery.

Room 13 may well come as a relief, simply because there is nothing small or intricate to look at. Instead it contains a collection of **sarcophagi** from various periods, their painted decoration reflecting the current pottery style. They come in two basic shapes: chests with lids and "bathtubs" (which may well have been used as such during their owners' lifetimes). Minoans were not really as small as their coffins would suggest – they were buried with their knees drawn up to their chests, as a couple of skeletons preserved as they were found attest.

Room 14, the **Hall of the Frescoes**, is perhaps the most exciting in the museum – if by now you're too weary to appreciate it, it deserves another visit. Only tiny fragments of actual frescoes survived, but they have been almost miraculously reconstituted, and mounted on backgrounds which continue the design to show the entire fresco (or at least an entire portion thereof). The frescoes, among the greatest achievements of Minoan art, were originally painted directly onto wet plaster, using mostly plant dyes but also colours from mineral sources and even shellfish, a technique which has ensured their relatively unfaded survival. The job of the restorers was helped to an extent by knowledge of the various conventions, which matched Egyptian practice: men's skin, for example, was red, women's white; gold is shown as yellow, silver as blue and bronze, red.

Most of the frescoes shown in the museum come originally from Knossós, and date from the New Palace period (1600–1400 BC). Along the left-hand wall, after a fragment of a bull fresco, are four large panels from the enormous fresco which led all the way along the Corridor of the Procession at Knossós (an artist's impression shows how the whole might originally have looked). Two groups of youths are shown processing towards a female figure, presumably a priestess or goddess. Between the doors there's the fresco of griffins from the Throne Room at Knossós, and then on the far side a series from the villa at Ayía Triádha, some blackened by fire. Among these, the animation of the wild cat is especially striking; a floor painting of a seascape is also shown here. On the opposite wall it's back to Knossós, with some of the most famous of the works found there. These include the shields which adorn the Grand Staircase; the elegant priest-king, or Lily Prince; the great relief of a bull's head; the beautifully simple fresco of dolphins from the Queen's apartment; and the famous depiction of athletes leaping over a bull. Finally, there are two simple pictures of lilies from the walls of a villa at Amnísos.

As striking as the frescoes themselves is the **Ayía Triádha Sarcophagus**, decorated in the same manner, which stands in the centre of the room. Made of stone – the only such sarcophagus known in Crete – this is covered in painted plaster, and although it was found in an unimportant tomb, it is assumed, from its unique and elaborate nature, that it was made originally for a royal burial and later re-used. On one side is an animal sacrifice, with a bull already dead on the altar and two goats tied up awaiting their fates. On the other are two scenes, perhaps of relatives making offerings for the safe passage of the deceased. The ends feature a scene of goddesses riding in a chariot drawn by griffins, and of two women in a chariot pulled by goats above a procession of men. Also in this room is a wonderful wooden **model of the Palace of Knossós**, reproducing in detail the existing parts and surmising a reconstruction for the rest.

Room 15 has more **frescoes** of the same period. The most famous of them is "La Parisienne", so dubbed for her bright red lips, huge eyes, long hair and fancy dress, but in reality almost certainly a priestess.

Room 16 exhibits yet more **frescoes**, the most interesting being the first, the "Saffron Gatherer": originally reconstructed as a boy, it has since been decided that this in fact represented a blue monkey. The two versions are shown side by side. Here too is "the Captain of the Blacks", a work from the troubled end of the New Palace period. It apparently shows a Minoan officer leading a troop of African soldiers, probably mercenaries – a sign of the period's increasing militarism.

Room 17 breaks the chronological approach to display the accumulations of an Iráklion doctor, the **Yiamalakis Collection**. This covers the entire remit of the museum in a single room, and it has some very fine pieces indeed. Of particular note is a steatopygous ("fat-buttocked" in plain English) Neolithic figurine – perhaps a fertility goddess – from near Ierápetra. There are also stunning gold jewels, especially the bull's head and two other pieces of the "Zákros Treasure"; some fine miniatures, bronze and ceramic; and from later periods, huge Roman figures and a mosaic relaid on the floor.

Room 18, back downstairs, continues the chronological collection right through from the Archaic period to the division of the Roman empire (c.650 BC–400 AD). There's an enormous variety of styles and objects here – among which a sensitively worked bronze of a youth in toga and sandals from Roman Ierápetra stands out – but the period was not one of Crete's artistic high points.

Room 19 goes back a little to display larger pieces from the early years of this final period, the Archaic (650–500 BC), in particular three large bronze figurines of Apollo and Artemis with their mother Leto. These are impressive in their simplicity, and significant as early examples of works made from sheets of hammered bronze, riveted together.

Room 20 is devoted to Classical Greek and Greco-Roman sculpture. Apart from a few good Roman copies of Greek classical works, and some stern portrait busts of members of the imperial families, it's not a terribly inspiring end to the museum.

Food, drink and nightlife

Big city as it is, Iráklion disappoints when it comes to eating – and even more when it comes to going out after you've eaten. The cafés and tavernas of the main squares – **Venizélou** and **Eleftherías** – are essential places to sit and watch the world pass, but their food is on the whole expensive and mediocre. One striking exception is *Bóuyatsa Kirkor*, by the fountain in Venizélou, where you can sample authentic, home-made *Bóuyatsa*, a creamy cheese pie served warm and sprinkled with sugar – absolutely the correct and traditional thing with a strong mid-morning coffee; it's also served at *Ta Leontaria* next door. If you feel you must eat here – and the place certainly buzzes with life at night – then the *Knossos* taverna (across the road from Platía Venizélou at the bottom of Dedhálou) serves the usual fare at reasonable prices. The cafés and restaurants on **Dedhálou** itself, the pedestrian alley linking the two main squares, are popular with tourists too, but again not particularly good value.

For real, sensibly priced **food**, you need to get off this most obvious part of the tourist trail, though not necessarily far. Perhaps the most attractive option is to head for the little alley, Fotíou Theodosáki, which runs through from the **market** to Odhós Evans. It is entirely lined with the tables of rival tavernas, most surprisingly grimy and authentic-looking. During the day, these are frequented by market traders and their customers; in the evening clients are mainly tourists, which means some prices are far higher than you'd expect. As long as you check first, however, and stick mainly to the baked dishes on display, you can still get excellent value. Nearby, at the corner of Evans and Yiánari, the taverna under the *Hotel Ionia* is more straightforward, with a wide selection of baked dishes on display – the sort of place to come if you're in need of a substantial, no-nonsense feed. Again, it can cost more than you expect if you fail to check prices in advance.

Other good tavernas are more scattered. Still near the centre, just off Eleftherías at the entrance to **Platía Dhaskaloyiánnis** (where the post office is), are a couple which are cheap if not wonderful, while Dhaskaloyiánnis itself has a pleasant lunchtime venue, *Omitsos*, where you can eat out beneath shady awnings – a good place to come if you want to take a break during a tour of the nearby Archaeological Museum. This square also has some pleasant cafés – among them *Café Flou*, which has another life at night (see below) – quiet places to sit and read or write your cards. **Nearer Venizélou**, try exploring some of the back-streets to the east, off Dedhálou and behind the Loggia: the *Cyprus Taverna* and the *Curry House* (see below), for example, are easy to spot and there are others nearby. *Taverna Giovanni*, on an alley parallel to Dedhálou (there's a sign near the *Pizzeria Victoria*), is a friendly place with a varied menu and reasonable prices.

Down **around the harbour** you'll find a number of other, slightly more expensive possibilities. *Ta Psaria*, a fish taverna at the bottom of 25 Avgoústou, has been done up recently and prices have risen accordingly, but it remains a fine place to sit and look out over the castle. Right on the water not far west of here is a short line of others, with glass and plastic screens to keep out the worst of the winds (though it can still be cold here in the evenings when the wind gets up). The second along, *Ouzeri to Rembetiko Pareaki*, has live music after about 10pm, often good: excellent varied *mezedhes*, though the main menu is unexciting and expensive. Also in this area, though without the sea view, *Taverna Rizes* at the bottom of Hándhakos is considerably cheaper – a pleasant, quiet courtyard setting, too.

At the more basic end of the range, **takeaways** abound. There's a whole group of *souvláki* stalls, for instance, clustering around 25 Avgoústou at the entrance to El Greco Park – the park itself is handy if you need somewhere to sit and eat. For cheese or spinach pies and a variety of other baked items, there are a couple of bakeries at the top of the park, or try the doughnut place on Platía Nikíforos Fókas at the bottom of Odhós 1821.

Ethnic and other gimmicky restaurants can also be found in the centre. There is, for example, the *Curry House* just off Dedhálou, which advertises both **Indian** and **Mexican** food. If your cravings for something spicy are severe this will assuage them – but don't expect the real thing. There are **Chinese** restaurants on Dedhálou (under the *Hotel Dedalos*) and in Eleftherías behind the *Argo* cafeteria. You can also find decent **pizza** at rival operations on Dedhálou and Platía Eleftherías, or far better at the excellent *Tartuffo* on Dhimokratías (the road towards Knossós) near the *Galaxy Hotel*. Go early, as it's packed with locals.

Bars and nightlife

As for **nightlife**, Iráklion is a bit of a damp squib when compared to many other towns on the island. Much of what does happen takes place in the suburbs or out along the hotel strip to the west. If you're determined, however, there are a couple of city-centre possibilities – and plenty of options if all you want to do is sit and drink.

Bars are mostly to be found in the areas already covered under restaurants. Perhaps the most pleasant place is a quiet square behind Dedhálou (up from the *Taverna Giovanni*), where there are several quietly trendy little bars (including *Flash* and *Avga*) with outdoor tables – popular with students in term-time. The eccentric *Café Flou* on Platía Dhaskaloyiánnis casts off its daytime serenity after ten when locals gather to hear George the chain-smoking DJ play a wide gamut of beat music – 1950s stuff seems to be his speciality. The clientele even start dancing here when it gets really raucous. Around Platía Venizélou are numerous slightly more touristy alternatives: the first-floor Piano Bar/Ladies Café *Loggia*, for example, with a pleasant rooftop bar at the top of the same building, and others in basements along Kandanoléon, off El Greco Park. Iráklion looks a great deal better than you'd expect from above, and there are other, fancier rooftop places above all the restaurants in Platía Eleftherías: the *Café-Bar Doré* for example. This serves food as well, and while it's not exactly the sort of place to wear cut-offs and dirty T-shirt, it's also no more expensive than the restaurants in the square below. Less elevated romance, with recorded jazz background, is to be had at the *Onar* café and tearoom (Hándhakos 36b, north of Venizélou). There's a small terrace and they serve a wide variety of teas as well as great ices, just the thing when you're winding down around midnight. The obliging staff will even play your requests. *Tasos*, on the way down here next to *Yours Hostel*, is a popular hang-out for young hostellers, lively at night and with good breakfasts to help you recover in the morning.

Discos proper include *Trapeza*, behind the *Astoria Hotel* down a street opposite the Archaeological Museum, and *Endasie*, on the street behind the Loggia and Áyios Títos – a white marble place with a Cadillac centrepiece and a relatively laid-back atmosphere. For bigger, brighter places less packed with local lads, the resort strip to the west is better – try, for example, *Stathmos* on the road to Gazi, enormous with a breathtaking light show, or *Apollonia*, out near the *Creta Beach* hotel.

There are also numerous **cinemas** scattered about, for which check the posters by the tourist police office. Most enjoyable is the open-air place by *Camping Iráklion*, on the beach to the west.

Listings

Airlines *Olympic*, on Platía Eleftherías (☎229-191), is the only airline with a permanent office in Iráklion. A bus leaves from this office one hour before each *Olympic* departure. Charter airlines flying in to Iráklion mostly use local travel agents as their representatives. For airport information call ☎282-025.

Airport buses Bus #1 runs from Platía Eleftherías to the airport every few minutes.

Banks The main branches are on 25 Avgoústou.

Beaches For city beaches take a #1 bus east to Amnísos (not one that only goes as far as the airport) or a #6 west to Amoudhári: both leave from Platía Eleftherías. See the following section for details.

Bike and car hire 25 Avgoústou is lined with hire companies, but you'll find cheaper rates on the backstreets. Good places to start – out of dozens – include *Eurocreta* (Sapotie 2; ☎226-700) for cars and *Motor Speed* (Ariadnis; ☎241-938) for bikes, both near the Archaeological Museum and under the same management (15–25% discounts to readers depending on season; free delivery to hotels and airport); *Blue Sea* (Kosma Zotou 7 near the bottom of 25 Avgoústou; ☎241-097; 20–30% discount); *Ritz* in the *Hotel Rea* for cars (Kalimeráki 1; ☎223-638); *Sun Rise* (25 Avgoústou 46; ☎221-609) and *Motorrad* (Vironos 1; ☎281-670) for bikes.

Buses See p.39 for details of where the bus stations are.

Cinema Check details of what's on at the hoardings in front of the tourist police office or by the main entrance to the Public Gardens. There's an open-air cinema next to *Camping Iráklion*.

Consulates See *Basics* p.30.

Festivals The Iráklion Summer Festival runs from mid-June to mid-September. It includes exhibitions, concerts and plays by groups from around the world, some of which are top-notch, others on the level of concerts by American high school choirs. Details from the tourist office. August 25 is St Titus' Day, marked by a major procession from the church of Áyios Títos.

Hospital The main public hospital is reasonably central, on Apollónion southwest of Platía Kornarou, between Alber and Moussoúrou.

Launderette Two can be found in the backstreets below the Archaeological Museum; one on Mirabélou, the other at Sapfous 1. Take plenty of change and follow the signs. Both are open roughly 8am–8pm daily.

Left luggage There's a left luggage office in the east-bound bus station (with limited hours) and a commercial agency at 25 Avgoústou 48 (7am–midnight, 300drs per item per day). If you want to leave your bag while you go off on a bike for a day or two, the hire company should be prepared to store it.

Mountaineering The local *EOS* is at Dhikeosínis 74 (☎287-110).

Newspapers and books English and other foreign newspapers are sold throughout the city centre – best bet is up Dedhálou where you'll find a wide selection of Jackie Collins novels as well as local guides and maps. Towards the bottom of Handhákos there's a more serious bookshop with a decent selection of English-language titles.

Pharmacies Plentiful on the main shopping streets – at least one is open 24 hours on a rota basis, check the list on the door of any. Also traditional herbalists in the market.

Post office Main office in Platía Dhaskaloyiánnis, off Eleftherías: open Mon–Fri 7.30am–8.30pm. In summer there's also a temporary office (a van) in the middle of Platía Eleftherías, handy for changing money.

Shopping The market is best for food as well as for cheap practical goods and for leather-ware and most standard tourist items (herbs make an unusual souvenir from here). More upmarket tourist shops – jewellery and fabrics especially – can be found down Dedhálou: fascinating antiques at *Makis* on the narrow street parallel to Dedhálou near the *Taverna Giovanni* and from two small stores on 25 Avgoústou. Everyday shops down Kalokerinoú and clothes and shoe shops around Averof: good value in late July sales. Opposite the *Xenia Hotel* by the west-bound bus station there's a small supermarket open long hours every day.

Taxis Major taxi ranks in Platía Eleftherías and El Greco Park.

Telephones OTE head office in El Greco Park – often long queues, efficient 24-hour service.

Toilets There are public toilets in El Greco Park and the Public Gardens.

Tourist office The NTOG is opposite the Archaeological Museum (Mon–Fri 8am–2pm; ☎222-487). Friendly but overworked.

Tourist police On Dhikeosínis. Better informed and more helpful than most.

Travel agencies 25 Avgoústou is crammed with shipping and general travel agents. Cheap/student specialists include the extremely helpful *Blavakis Travel* (Platía Kallergon 8, just off 25 Avgoústou by the entrance to El Greco Park; ☎282-541) and *Prince Travel* (25 Avgoústou 30, ☎282-706). Ferry tickets also from *Minoan Lines* (25 Avgoústou 78; ☎224-303), *Arabatzoglou Bros.* (25 Avgoústou 65; ☎282-341) or *Kavi Club* next to the tourist office (☎221-166). For excursions around the island, villa rentals etc, the bigger operators are probably easier: try *Zeus Travel* (25 Avgoústou 48; ☎223-214), *Irman Travel* (Dedhálou 26; ☎242-527) or *Creta Travel Bureau* (20–22 Epiménidhou; ☎243-811). The latter is also the local *American Express* agent.

Work For temporary work your best bet is to sleep out in the dusty park by the east-bound bus station, or else turn up there around dawn when local farmers come recruiting. At the beginning of the season there's a slim chance of poorly paid jobs in travel agents/bike hire places as general gopher and translator.

Amnísos and other local beaches

If all you want to do is escape Iráklion to lie on a beach for a few hours, the simplest course is to head **east**, beyond the airport. These are the beaches where locals go when they have an afternoon off. They are easily reached by public trans-port: the #1 bus runs every twenty minutes or so from the tree-shaded stop oppo-site the *Hotel Astoria* in Platía Eleftherías. Towards the end of the route there's a choice of three sandy patches: a municipal beach, Amnísos and Tobróuk.

Leaving the city through its sprawling eastern suburbs, and through the town of NÉA ALIKARNASSÓS into which they merge, the bus follows the old road as it skirts around the **airport** (make sure that yours isn't going to stop at the airport). Even in spring this manages to be a wasted and dusty-looking landscape – an impression not helped by the ill-camouflaged bunkers of the Greek air force base which shares the runway. Once past the airport, however, the road swings down to the coast and a narrow patch of level ground between the sea and the hills. First stop is at the **municipal beach**: fenced off (you pay to get in) and provided with showers and changing rooms. There seems little point in paying unless you want to study the undercarriages of incoming planes in intimate detail – this beach tends to be crowded and only marginally cleaner than the free sections.

The next halt is **AMNÍSOS**, where there are a couple of tavernas and food stalls immediately behind the beach, and even a huddle of new (surprisingly upmarket) hotels. I wouldn't choose to stay here, but it's not a bad beach to find so close to the city. The main drawback is again the stream of planes coming in to land: on peak weekends there seems to be one every few minutes, during the week quiet periods are enlivened by fighters on low-level runs or coming in to practice their touch-and-go on the runway.

The last of these beaches, **Tobróuk**, is perhaps the best of them, with more tavernas and drink stalls, slightly fewer people, and relative peace to be found if you walk a while along the sand.

Amnísos and Eileíthyia: two minor sites

Amnísos is also a famous name in Minoan archaeology. There was a small settlement here, apparently a port for Knossós, from which the Cretan forces involved in the Trojan War are said to have set sail. In a villa on the site was found the unusual Fresco of the Lilies on display in the Iráklion Museum. It has to be said, though, that the site is not a particularly impressive one – especially as most people's view is restricted to peering through the links in the wire fence. This at least is easy enough, since the remains are right by the road down to Amnísos beach, on the low hill off to the left. This site is also noted for the excavations of Marinatos in the 1930s, when the archaeologist's discovery of pumice fragments amongst the ruins prompted him to develop his theory blaming an eruption of the volcanic island of Thíra for the destruction of the Minoan palaces (see *Contexts*). The scorch marks on many of the remaining stones testify to the intense fire which destroyed the villa during this period.

Behind the main road a sign points inland towards the hills (the turnoff to EPISKOPÍ) indicating another significant ancient site, the **Cave of Eileíthyia**, which gets a mention in *The Odyssey* as one of Odysseus's stopovers on his way home from Troy. Just over 1km up the steep road from the turnoff the cave is signed on the left. Eileíthyia was a goddess, primarily of childbirth, of very ancient origin and this cave was a cult centre from Neolithic times. Inside are two large walled stalactites which were almost certainly regarded as fertility totems. The cave itself is now fenced and locked and if you are intent on making a survey (it's about fifty metres deep) you'll need to get a key from the guardian 7km away at Nirou Hani (see p.71).

To the west

There are also **beaches to the west of the city** – less noisy but also less atmospheric and more touristy. If you take a #6 bus from immediately in front of the *Hotel Astoria* it will run out through the Haniá Gate and into Iráklion's more prosperous western extremities. Eventually you'll end up on the road which runs behind the hotel strip, along by *Camping Iráklion* and on eventually to the luxury *Creta Beach* hotel complex, unappealingly sited immediately before the power station and cement works. You can get off almost anywhere down here to attempt to get to **Amoudhári Beach**. This is not always as easy as it sounds – although the beach itself is public, there are very few access roads to it, and the hotels and campsite try hard to prevent non-residents walking through their grounds. Either ignore the people shouting at you, or get off at one of the roads down and put up with the crowds who tend to congregate at these access points.

Knossós

> ... *a dancing place*
> *All full of turnings, that was like the admirable maze*
> *For fair hair'd Ariadne made, by cunning Daedalus*

Homer, The Odyssey

KNOSSÓS (Mon–Fri 8am–5pm, Sat & Sun 8am–3pm) lies some five kilometres south of Iráklion on a low, largely man-made hill. By far the largest of the Minoan palaces, it thrived over 3000 years ago at the heart of a highly sophisticated island-wide civilisation. Long after Minoan culture had collapsed, a town here remained a power in the land, rivalling Górtys right into the Roman era.

Although only the palace itself is much visited – or regularly open to the public – the hills all around are rich in lesser remains dating from the twentieth century BC through to the second or third AD. Yet less than a hundred years ago this was a place which existed only in mythology. Here it was in legend that King Minos ruled and that his wife Pasiphae bore the Minotaur, half-bull half-man. Here the labyrinth was constructed by Daedalus to contain the beast, and youths were brought from Athens as human sacrifice, until finally Theseus arrived to slay the beast and, with Ariadne's help, escape its lair. Imprisoned in his own maze, Daedalus later constructed the wings which bore him away to safety and Icarus to his death. The excavation of the palace, and the clothing of these legends with fact, is among the most amazing tales of modern archaeology.

Today's Knossós, whose fame can rival any such site in the world, is associated above all with Sir Arthur Evans, who excavated the palace at the turn of the century and whose bust is one of the first things to greet you as you enter the site. The autocratic control Evans exerted over the excavations, his working standards and procedures, and above all the restorations which he claimed were necessary to preserve the building as he worked his way through it, have been the source of furious controversy among archaeologists ever since. It has become clear that much of Evans's upper level – the *Piano Nobile* – is pure conjecture. Even so, his guess as to what the palace might have looked like is certainly as good as anyone else's, and it makes the other sites infinitely more meaningful if you have seen Knossós first. Without the restorations, it would be almost impossible to imagine the grandeur of the multistorey palace or to see the ceremonial stairways, strange top-heavy pillars and brightly frescoed walls which distinguish the site. For an initial idea of the size and complexity of the palace in its original state, take a look at the cutaway drawings on sale outside – somewhat fantastic, but possibly not too far from reality.

The Palace

As soon as you enter the **Palace of Knossós** through its West Court – the ancient ceremonial entrance – it is clear how the legends of the labyrinth grew up around it. Even with a detailed plan, it's almost impossible to find your way around the site with any success. My advice is not to try too hard: wander around for long enough and you'll eventually stumble onto everything. If you're worried about missing the highlights you can always tag onto one of the constant guided tours for a while, catching the patter and then heading back to take in the detail when that particular crowd has moved on. You won't get the place to yourself –

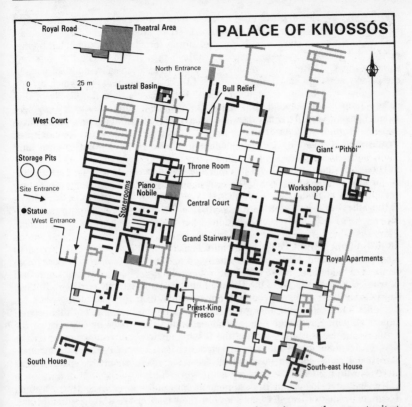

whenever you come – but exploring on your own does give you the opportunity to appreciate individual parts of the palace in the brief lulls between groups. And if you get the opportunity to come back a second time, it will all begin to make a great deal more sense.

The remains you see are mostly those of the second palace, as it was rebuilt after the first destruction around 1700 BC and as occupied (with increasing Mycenaean influence) through to about 1450 BC. At the time it was surrounded by a town of considerable size. The palace itself, though, must have looked almost as much a mess then as it does now – a vast bulk, with more than 1000 rooms on five floors, which had spread across the hill more as an organic growth than a planned building, incorporating or burying earlier structures as it went. In this the palace simply followed the pattern of Minoan architecture generally, extra rooms being added as the need arose. It is the style of building still most common on Crete, where finished buildings are far outnumbered by those waiting to have an extra floor or room added when need and finance dictate.

The West Court and first frescoes

The **West Court**, across which you approach the palace, was perhaps a marketplace or at any rate the scene of public meetings. Across it run slightly raised walkways, leading from the Palace's West Entrance to the Theatral Area, and once presumably on to the Royal Road. There are also three large, circular pits: originally grain silos or perhaps depositories for sacred offerings, but by the end of the Minoan era being used as rubbish tips. If you follow the walkway towards the West Entrance nowadays, you arrive at a typically muddled part of the palace, not at all easy to interpret. First there's a line of stones which marks the original wall of an earlier incarnation of the palace, then the facade of the palace proper and beyond that a series of small rooms of which only the foundations survive. Arriving when the palace was still standing, you would have passed through a guardroom and then followed the **Corridor of the Procession**, flanked by frescoes depicting a procession, around towards the south side of the palace.

Though it's hard to work out which is the corridor, this is still the best way to go. Around on the south side of the central court, you can climb a flight of stairs to admire the reproduction of the **Priest-King Fresco** (also known as the Prince of the Lilies) and look down over the palace. Up here was apparently a whole series of large and airy frescoed chambers, perhaps reception rooms.

Central Court, Throne Room and Piano Nobile

You can climb from this side of the courtyard to the *Piano Nobile*, the upper floor on the west side, but this is best left till later. Proceed instead straight into the **Central Court**, the heart of the Palace. Aligned almost exactly north–south, the courtyard paving covers the oldest remains found on the site, going back to Neolithic times. Some say this was the scene of the bull leaping, but that seems rather unlikely – although the court measures almost 60m by 30m, it would hardly be spacious enough for the sort of intricate acrobatics shown in surviving pictures, let alone for an audience to watch. In Minoan times the courtyard would have had a very different atmosphere from the open, shadeless space which survives, with high walls hemming it in on every side.

The entrance to one of Knossós's most atmospheric survivals, the **Throne Room**, is in the northwestern corner of the courtyard. Here a worn stone throne sits against the wall of a surprisingly small chamber: along the walls around it are ranged stone benches and behind there's a copy of a fresco of two griffins. In all probability this was the seat of a priestess rather than a ruler – there's nothing like it in any other Minoan palace – but it may just have been an innovation wrought by the Mycenaeans, since it appears that this room dates only from the final period of the palace's occupation. Overexposure has meant that the Throne Room itself is now closed off with a wooden gate, but you can lean over this for a good view, and in the antechamber there's a wooden copy of the throne on which everyone perches to have their photo taken. Opposite the real throne, steps lead down to a lustral basin (a sunken "bath", probably for ritual purification rather than actual bathing – it has no drain).

Alongside the Throne Room, a stairway climbs to the first floor and Evans's reconstructed **Piano Nobile**. Perhaps the most interesting feature of this part of the palace is the view it offers of the palace storerooms, with their rows of *pithoi* (storage jars) often still in place. There's an amazing amount of storage space here: in the jars, which would mostly have held oil or wine, and in spaces sunk into the ground for other goods. The rooms of the *Piano Nobile* itself are again rather confusing, though you should be able to pick out the Sanctuary Hall, with stumps of its six large columns. Opposite this is a small concrete room (complete with roof) which Evans "reconstructed" directly above the Throne Room. It feels entirely out of place: inside there's a small display on the reconstruction of the frescoes, and through to the other side you get another good view over the Central Court. Returning through this room, you could climb down the very narrow staircase on your right to arrive at the entrance to the corridor of store-rooms (now fenced off) or head back to the left towards the area where you entered the palace.

The Royal Apartments

Returning to the courtyard allows you to cross to the east side, where the **Grand Staircase** leads into the royal apartments, plainly the finest of the rooms at Knossós. The stairway itself is a masterpiece of design: not only a fitting approach to these sumptuously appointed chambers, but also an integral part of the whole design, its large well bringing light into the lower storeys. Light wells such as these, usually with a courtyard at the bottom, are a constant feature of Knossós and a reminder of just how important creature comforts were to the Minoans, and how skilled they were at providing them.

For more evidence of this luxurious lifestyle you need look no further than the **Queen's Suite**, off the grand **Hall of the Colonnades** at the bottom of the stair-case. The main living room is decorated with the celebrated dolphin fresco and with running friezes of flowers and (earlier) spirals. On two sides it opens to courtyards which let in light and air – the smaller one would probably have been planted with flowers. In use, the room would have been scattered with cushions and hung with rich drapes, while doors and curtains between the pillars allowed for privacy, and for cool shade in the heat of the day. That, at least, is what they'd have you believe, and it's a very plausible scenario. Remember, though, that all this is speculation and some pure con: the dolphin fresco, for example, was found in the courtyard, not the room itself, and would have been viewed from inside as a sort of *trompe l'oeil*, like looking out of a glass-bottomed boat. There are also some who argue, convincingly, that grand as these rooms are, they are not really large or fine enough to have been royal quarters. Those, the argument goes, would have been in the lighter and airier rooms which must have existed in the upper reaches of the palace, and these lower apartments would have been inhab-ited by resident nobles or priests.

The truth hardly matters, for whether or not you accept Evans's names and attributions, the rooms remain an impressive example of the sophistication of Minoan architecture – all the more so when you follow the dark passage round to the **Queen's bathroom**, its clay tub protected behind a low wall (and again prob-ably screened by curtains when in use), and to the famous "flushing" lavatory (a hole in the ground with drains to take the waste away – it was flushed by throw-ing a bucket of water down).

On the floor above the Queen's domain, the Grand Staircase passes through a set of rooms which are generally described as the **King's quarters**. These are chambers in a considerably sterner vein: the staircase opens into a grandiose reception area known as the **Hall of the Royal Guard**, its walls decorated in repeated shield patterns. Opening off it is the ruler's personal chamber, the **Hall of the Double Axes** – a room which could be divided to allow for privacy in one half while audiences were held in the more public section, or opened out for larger functions. Its name comes from the double axe symbol, so common throughout Knossós, which here is carved into every block of masonry.

The Palace Fringes

From the back of the Queen's chambers you can emerge into the fringes of the palace where it spreads down the lower slopes of the hill. This is a good point at which to consider the famous **drainage system** at Knossós, some of whose best surviving sections are visible under grilles. The snugly interconnecting terracotta pipes ran underneath most of the palace (here they have come more or less direct from the Queen's bathroom) and guides to the site never fail to point them out as evidence of the advanced state of Minoan civilisation. They are indeed quite an achievement – in particular the system of baffles and overflows to slow down the run-off and avoid any danger of flooding, which can be most clearly seen down by the external walls. Just how much running water there would have been, however, is another matter – the water supply is at the *bottom* of the hill and even the combined efforts of rainwater catchment and water physically carried up to the palace can hardly have been sufficient to supply the needs of more than a small elite.

From the bottom of the slope you get a fine impression of the scale of the whole palace complex and can circle around towards the north, climbing back inside the palace limits to see the area known as the **Palace Workshops**. Here potters, lapidaries and smiths appear to have plied their trades, and here also are the spectacular **giant pithoi**, where people queue to have their photograph taken with the jars towering over them. There's a good view also of the bull relief fresco set up by the north entrance.

Outside and just beyond the north entrance, if you've walked around from the workshops, the **Theatral Area** is one of the more important enigmas of this and other Minoan palaces. An open space a little like a stepped amphitheatre, it may have been used for ritual performances or dances, but there's no real evidence of this, and again very little room for an audience if that was its function. Beyond it the **Royal Road** sets out. Originally this ran to the Little Palace, and beyond that probably on across the island: nowadays it ends after about a hundred yards in a brick wall beneath the modern road. Alongside are assorted structures variously interpreted as shops, workshops or grandstands for viewing parades, all of them covered in undergrowth.

Back down the Royal Road, you can again re-enter the palace by its **North Entrance**. Beside the entry is a well-preserved **lustral basin**, and beyond that a guardroom. Heading back to the central courtyard, a flight of stairs doubles back to allow you to examine the copy of the **Bull Relief** close to.

Outside the Palace

Of the lesser structures which crowd around the palace, a couple of houses on the south side are particularly worth seeing. The one known simply as the **South House**, reconstructed to its original three floors, seems amazingly modern, and is also wonderfully like the model villas displayed in the museum. Across a little valley from here, outside the fenced site, was the **Caravanserai** where ancient travellers would rest and water their animals. Like the other dependencies and out-buildings of the palace, this is not open for visits. Among the other important outlying buildings are the **Little Palace**, on a site which also contains a mansion and many Roman remains (just up the narrow alley which turns off to the left as you head back towards Iráklion), and the **Royal Villa**, facing the palace from the slope to the northeast. These two are occasionally open for special visits.

Practicalities

Getting to Knossós from Iráklion could hardly be easier. The #2 bus sets out every ten minutes from the city bus stands adjacent to the east-bound bus station, runs up 25 Avgoústou (with a stop just below Platía Venizélou) and out of town on Odhós 1821 and Evans. If you're driving you can take this route, through Evans Gate, or follow the signs from Platía Eleftheriás; from anywhere other than Iráklion turn directly off the bypass onto the badly signed Knossós road.

Arriving, you're confronted first by a string of rather pricey tavernas and tacky souvenir stands. There are several **rooms** places here too, and if you're really into Minoan culture there's a lot to be said for staying out this way to steal an early start. Be warned, though, that the site area is expensive and unashamedly commercial. At the end of all the development, on the other side of the road, is the car park (not nearly big enough at peak times). This is where the bus drops you, and it's through the car park that you enter the site proper, having first run the gauntlet of map salesmen and tour guides and bought your ticket at the turnstiles. To catch the bus again on leaving you have to walk a short way back up the road; a ruse no doubt designed to force you once again past all those souvenir shops.

South to Mount Yioúhtas

The countryside south of Knossós is dominated by the bulk of **Mt Yioúhtas** (811m), which rises alone from a landscape otherwise characterised by gently undulating agricultural country. Seen from the north, and especially the north-west, the mountain has an unmistakeably human profile. Underneath the mountain, the ancient Cretans claimed, Zeus lay buried – an assertion which for other Greeks provided further proof (since the god was immortal) of the saying which claimed "All Cretans are liars", and which may indeed have been the original basis of the reputation.

Beyond Knossós the nature of the journey is transformed almost immediately – the road virtually empty, the country greener. Almost any of these roads south makes a beautiful drive, past vineyards draped across low hills and through flourishing farming communities. Just a couple of kilometres from the site, at the head of the valley, there's an extraordinary **aqueduct** arching along beside the road. This looks medieval, but is in fact barely 150 years old. Just beyond are a couple of tavernas/cafés beside the road – a convenient escape from the Knossós crowds – and just past them is a turning on the left, clearly signposted to Mirtiá.

Mirtiá and the Kazantzakís Museum

The main reason to visit **MIRTIÁ** is for the Kazantzakís Museum in the village, but you don't necessarily need to be a fan of the writer to find the trip worth making. Only enthusiasts are likely to spend long over the exhibits, but it's an enjoyable collection to look over quickly and a lovely drive there on almost deserted roads. Mirtiá itself is larger than you'd expect – as indeed are many of these villages – and bright with flowers planted in old oil cans.

The **museum** (9am–1pm; Mon, Wed, Sat & Sun also 4–8pm; closed Thurs) is on the central platía (well beyond the multicoloured, multilingual signs on the main street at either end of the village), along with three pleasant *kafenía* where you can stop for a drink. It occupies a house where Kazantzakís's parents once lived – a fine bourgeois mansion – and the collection includes a vast quantity of ephemera relating to the great author: diaries, photos, manuscripts, first editions, translations into every conceivable language, playbills, stills from films of his works, costumes and more. There's also a video documentary in Greek.

Briefly, **Níkos Kazantzakís** was born on Crete in 1885, and his early life was shadowed by the struggle against the Turks and for union with Greece. Educated in Athens and Paris, he travelled widely throughout his life working for the Greek government on more than one occasion and for UNESCO, but above all writing: a vast range of works including philosophical essays, epic poetry, travel books, translations of classics (such as Dante's *Divine Comedy*) into Greek, and of course the novels on which his fame in the west mostly rests. *Zorba the Greek* (1946) was the first and most celebrated of them, but his output remained prolific to the end of his life: particularly relevant to Cretan travels are *Freedom or Death* (1950), set amid the struggle against the Turks, and the autobiographical *Report to Greco*, published posthumously in 1961 (he died in West Germany in 1957). He is widely accepted as the leading Greek writer of the century, and Cretans are extremely proud of him, despite the fact that most of his later life was spent abroad, that he was banned from entering Greece for long periods and excommunicated by the Orthodox church for his vigorously expressed doubts about Christianity. There are plenty of people who now regard his writing as overblown and pretentious, but even these admit that the best parts are where the Cretan in Kazantzakís shows through, in the tremendous gusto and vitality of books like *Zorba* and *Freedom or Death*. He himself was always conscious, and proud, of his Cretan heritage.

Arhánes

From the turning to Mirtiá, it's not much further through the vineyards to the junction where you turn right for Arhánes. It was here, a singularly unthreatening spot on a summer afternoon, that General Kreipe was kidnapped on April 26, 1944.

The fork leads, through PATSÍDHES and KÁTO ARHÁNES, to the large agricultural centre of **ARHÁNES** – a town substantial enough to have a one-way traffic system. The centre, with a small square by a restored church and a couple of large, dozy *kafenía*, is on the north-bound side: drive through and double back. The church has an incongruous whitewashed clock tower and a fine collection of icons; elsewhere there are Byzantine frescoes in the church of Ayía Triádha, on the far fringes of town, and much more importantly at the church of **Asómatos**, a couple of kilometres east (follow the road through town, and then the signs east, but ask about the key at one of the cafés first). Its superb fourteenth-century works include a horrific *Crucifixion*, and a depiction of the Fall of Jericho with Joshua in full medieval armour.

Arhánes was a sizeable centre of Minoan civilisation, and there are a number of sites roundabout. All of them are relatively recent discoveries – they have been excavated in the last twenty-five years or so – and not all of the excavations are yet fully published. Consequently they are neither particularly famous nor especially welcoming to visitors, but many of the finds have been important. The largest of the structures is the **"Palace"**, in reality more likely a large villa, which lies right in the heart of the modern town, signed just off the main road. Through the chain-link fence you can see evidence of a substantial walled mansion: this was only part of what once stood here – piecemeal excavation is still going on, and much more remains to be done in areas which currently are built over.

The second of the sites is **Foúrni**, off to the right as you enter the town (immediately before the school) and up a ferociously rocky, steep trail. What has been unearthed here is a burial ground used throughout the Minoan period. Its earliest tombs date from around 2500 BC, before the construction of the great palaces, the latest from the very end of the Minoan era. The structures include a number of early *tholos* tombs – round stone buildings, roofed over and reminiscent of beehives. Each of these contained multiple burials – in sarcophagi and *pithoi* – and since Foúrni also revealed many simpler graves and a circle of seven Mycenaean-style shaft graves, it is by far the most extensive Minoan cemetery known. Its significance was increased by some of the finds made here: most importantly, within *Tholos A*, a side chamber was found which revealed the undisturbed tomb of a woman who, judging by the jewellery and other goods buried with her, was both royal and perhaps a priestess. Her jewellery and rings are now on display at the Iráklion museum, as is the skeleton of a horse apparently sacrificed in her honour.

The size of Foúrni is further evidence of the scale of the Minoan community that once thrived around Arhánes. Yet again, though, its interest is rather diminished by the fact that it is fenced and locked.

Human sacrifice?

If you're going to see a fenced site then **Anemospília** is considerably more worthwhile. This at least has a spectacular setting and a controversial story. The road there heads north from Arhánes: coming from Iráklion you enter the one-way street and turn sharp right, back on yourself, almost straight away, just past a small chapel. Following the best of the roads you begin to climb across the northern face of Mt Yioúhtas, winding around craggy rocks weirdly carved by the wind (*Anemospília* means Caves of the Wind) until you reach the fenced site held in a steep curve of the road.

What stood here was a temple, and its interpretation has been the source of outraged controversy among Minoan scholars since its excavation at the beginning of the 1980s. The building is a simple one – three rooms connected by a northward facing portico – but its contents were not so easily described. The temple was apparently destroyed by an earthquake in the middle of a ceremony, and the ceremony was apparently a human sacrifice: the only evidence of such a ritual found in Minoan Crete and a severe shock to those who liked to portray the Minoans as the perfect peaceable society. The evidence seems hard to deny, though – three skeletons were found in the western room, one with rich jewellery suggesting a priest, another a woman, presumably a priestess or assistant, the third curled up on what was apparently an altar and, according to scientists, already dead at the time of the collapse of the building which killed the others. A large bronze knife was lying on top of this skeleton. Outside, another man was crushed in the corridor, apparently carrying some kind of ritual vase. In the circumstances (and these events have been dated to around 1700 BC, the time of the earthquakes which destroyed the first palaces) it seems easy to believe that the priests might have resorted to desperate measures in a last attempt to calm the god who was destroying their civilisation.

To the summit: Vathípetro

Continuing beyond Arhánes you'll see a sign after a couple of kilometres for the **summit of Mt Yioúhtas**, up a track which is a relatively easy drive. You can also climb to the top in little over an hour from Arhánes, but it seems rather unsatisfying to do this only to discover other people rolling up on their motorbikes or in taxis. The panoramic views are the main lure – back across Iráklion especially, but also west to Psilorítis and east to Dhíkti. South, the view is blocked by another peak crowned with a radio mast. On the summit is a small and not especially interesting chapel, and the trappings of the annual *Paniyíri* to which villagers from all around make their way on August 6. There was once a Minoan peak sanctuary too (of which no significant trace), and on the shoulders of the mountain, not easily accessible, are caves associated with the local Zeus cult.

The main road past the mountain goes on toward **VATHÍPETRO**, which is well signposted along the way. Here, at last, is a site which can actually be examined close to, a large Minoan **villa** which once controlled the rich farmland south of Arhánes. Inside was found a remarkable collection of everyday items – equipment for making wine and oil and other tools and simple requisites of rural life. The house, originally a substantial building of several storeys, has a courtyard with a shrine in it, and fine large rooms especially on the east. The basement workrooms, however, were most interesting: finds included most of the agricultural equipment and (if the custodian is on site with his key) much of it can still be seen *in situ*. When the doors are locked, you can see something of what remains through the barred windows.

West of Iráklion

Heading west from Iráklion the modern highway, cut into the cliffs, is as fast and efficient a road as you could hope to find, and in simple scenic terms it's a spectacular drive; but there's very little in the way of habitation – only a couple of developed beach resorts and the "birthplace of El Greco" at Fódhele until the final few, flat miles into Réthimnon. If you go this way, the point where you join the bypass offers perhaps the best view of Zeus's profile on Mt Yioúhtas – open mouth, prominent nose and chin. If you're in no hurry, forget the highway and try the older roads west, curling up amid stunning mountain scenery. On none of these back roads is there anything very specific to see – the Minoan site at Tílissos is an exception – but they take you through archetypal rural Crete, with half-empty ways travelled by herds of sheep or goats, isolated chapels or farmsteads beside the road, and occasionally a village. City buses will take you west as far as the *Creta Beach* hotel (p.57): to travel any further in this direction you'll need either your own transport or a KTEL bus from one of the west-bound stations.

The new road

Once past the city beaches, the highway heads north, climbing into the foothills of the Psilorítis range as they plunge straight to the sea. Watch out, as you start this climb, for the medieval fortress of **Paleókastro** built into the cliff right beside the road. Even after they've been pointed out, these ruinous fortifications have to be looked for twice, so completely do they blend in against the cliff. Once spotted, though, they're unmistakeable, with immaculately crafted stonework and absolutely smooth joins. Just beyond, the road crosses a bridge over the modern village of Paleókastro in a little gully leading down to the sea: a beautiful setting with wealthy suburban homes and restaurants which are popular for weekend outings.

Ayía Pelayía

As you round the headland, **AYÍA PELAYÍA** is laid out below, a sprinkling of white cubes around a deep blue bay, unbelievably inviting from this distance. Closer to, the attraction is only slightly diminished. By Cretan standards this is a very upmarket resort, with a taverna-lined beach curving round the edge of a sheltered cove. The water is clear and calm, the swimming excellent, and there's water-skiing and other sports to be had if you are prepared to pay. There's a superb view, too, of all the ships which pass the end of the bay as they steam into Iráklion – spectacular at night when the brightly lit ferries pass. Even at weekends, when there are substantial crowds of day-trippers from Iráklion, the place remains faintly exclusive. The atmosphere must be due, in part at least, to the presence of two of the best-looking luxury hotels on the island – the *Capsis Beach* on the promontory overlooking town and the *Peninsula* over on the headland beyond – but it may not last; continuing development is rapidly outpacing what the small beach can cope with.

The chief disadvantage of the place (expense and shortage of accommodation aside) is lack of transport. If you take a long-distance bus you face a steep 3km descent from the main road where you'll be dropped – and if this feels heavy going, wait till you try walking back up. The service direct to Ayía Pelayía is slightly ad hoc: buses run between the *Capsis Beach* hotel and the *Astoria* in Platía Eleftherías five or six times a day. Check at either end for details.

The road down ends in a car park at the end of the beach, Ayía Pelayía's main thoroughfare. **Food** is abundant – if you tire of or can't afford the beachfront restaurants, head into town where there are some more basic takeaways and two or three small supermarkets for the makings of a picnic on the beach – but in season you'd be hard pressed to find anywhere to stay. There are in any event relatively few plain rooms: most **accommodation** here is in studios or apartments with cooking facilities. Out of season these can be excellent value if you're prepared to bargain hard, but through the summer they're mostly block-booked. If you want to stay, it's a question of wandering around asking at every door with a sign – when you come to look closer there are more of these than you might think, and as always the owners will usually know who has a room free (if anyone does). For off-season bargains on apartments, try *Apartments Elena*, for example; *Ayía Pelayía Travel Service*, on the beach just over halfway along, act as agents for many of the other owners as well as offering a general information and money-exchange service.

Fódhele

Turning **inland from the main road** opposite Ayía Pelayía, an old stretch of paved road runs from Ahládha to Fódhele, connecting by rutted, unpaved sections with other old roads inland. If you're simply heading for Fódhele, you can get there more efficiently by taking the later turnoff a few miles west, but if you can afford the time to travel at a more leisurely pace, the old route offers a great deal more to look at. **AHLÁDHA** itself, a couple of kilometres back towards Iráklion, has a spectacular hilltop setting which compensates in large part for the fact that the village itself offers nothing to stop for.

FÓDHELE is firmly established on the tourist circuit as the birthplace of El Greco. Whether or not this claim is true – and there's virtually no hard evidence to substantiate it – the excursion is a pleasant one. The village lies in a richly fertile valley, surrounded by orange and lime groves. On the far side of the river as you drive up are a couple of small Byzantine chapels: there's an ancient church in the village too. Despite the craft and souvenir shops which line the main street to sell local embroidery, and despite the café tables ranged along the river bank, Fódhele most of the time is almost preternaturally sleepy – you can sit at one of these shady tables for half an hour before anyone emerges to take your order, and wait as long again before the order has any effect. Meanwhile, take a few minutes to study the plaque in the village square. Made of stone from Toledo (where Domenico Theotokopoulos settled to produce the bulk of his most famous works and earn the name El Greco), this was presented to Fódhele in 1934 by the University of Valladolid, an authentication of the locale's claim to fame which must be responsible for at least some of its current prosperity.

To get to **El Greco's House** you cross the river, pass the church (which has copies of many of his works) and follow the track which heads northwards out of town. Aside from the fact that it is old enough to have seen him, there's no reason to suppose that this place was in any way associated with the painter, but having got this far you might as well see it – especially if plans to incorporate some kind of display have been completed. Nearby there's an attractive Byzantine chapel.

A couple of **buses** a day run direct to Fódhele from the Haniá Gate terminal in Iráklion, but it's not really practical to use these for a quick visit. On the other hand it's not too far (about 3km) to walk back down to the main road, so you could try catching the afternoon bus up (at 2pm) and then either hitching back or trying to flag down a long-distance bus. There are also occasional tours from Iráklion.

The old roads

Ignoring the benefits of the modern road and taking the slower, mountain route you run at first, behind the beaches, through villages – like GAZÍ – that are mostly industrial and lacklustre. Once under the highway, however, you immediately start to climb into the hills. Almost straight away there's a right turn signed to RODHIÁ, a sizeable village looking back down over the city (with lights which are plainly visible from there at night). This is the short way to Ayía Pelayía and Fódhele, but to get there you face 9km and more of atrocious road to reach Ahládha.

As you apparently start to leave development behind, you promptly come across it again in the form of **Arolithos**, a brand new "traditional village" which is a surprisingly successful attempt to create the atmosphere of traditional Crete in a tourist development. There are craftsmen – potters, weavers, artists, a smith – at work using traditional methods, shops where you can buy their products, a restaurant (with wood-fired ovens), and events such as Greek dancing evenings laid on. There are also some upmarket rooms (A-class hotel standard), though no very good reason to stay. For the moment the place seems half empty except when a coach trip calls by (it's clearly destined to become a popular spot for the "traditional Cretan evenings" beloved of tour operators), but it's worth a look as you pass. Perhaps the most surprising thing about the place is that no one has tried anything like it before.

A little way beyond Arolithos the way divides: the road which used to be the main route from Iráklion to Réthimnon is the one which runs through **MÁRATHOS**. This was itself something of a bypass in its day, and consequently it runs through very few villages of any size. Márathos is attractive, though, famous for the honey which seems to be on sale at every house, and with a couple of *kafenía* if you feel like breaking the journey. Not far beyond the village it's possible to cut down by another pretty terrible track to Fódhele.

These days more people travel by the furthest inland of the roads, the one which climbs up through Tílissos and on via **Anóyia** (p.160). It's a pleasant ride through fertile valleys filled with olive groves and vineyards – a district, the Malevísi, which was renowned from Venetian times for the strong sweet **Malmsey wine** much favoured in western Europe.

Tílissos

The big attraction of the first part of the trip is **TÍLISSOS**, a name famous in the annals of Minoan archaeology as among the first sites to be excavated. Local archaeologist Hatzidakis, working at the beginning of the century, revealed evidence of occupation from the early Pre-Palace period (c.2000 BC), but interest focuses primarily on three large villas from the New Palace era, contemporary with the great periods at Knossós, Festós and elsewhere. They were probably not as isolated in the country house sense as they seem today, but may well have been part of a thriving community, or even a staging post on the route west towards as yet undiscovered centres there. The existence of a rather simpler villa at Sklavókambos, on the road halfway from here to Anóyia, may lend weight to this theory. The site shared in the destruction of the palaces about 1450 BC but new buildings then arose among which was the cistern in the northeast corner. With the arrival of the Dorians Tílissos developed into a Greek city of the classical period, issuing its own coinage. This later construction makes it a bit harder to get a clear picture of what's there.

When you reach the village of the same name, the archaeological **site** (Tues– Sun 8.45am–3pm) is signed to the left at the foot of the main street. While it's not always the easiest of sites to interpret, it is a lovely place to wander round, with few visitors, pine trees for shade, and some evocative remains including staircases and walls still standing six feet tall alongside some unsubtle restoration. Immediately beyond the fence, vineyards and rich agricultural land suggest a (probably illusory) continuity of rural life. Houses A and C are of extremely fine construction and design (C has the more impressive remains) whilst House B has little to look at but its ground plan, but does contain some of the oldest relics here.

A building of finely dressed ashlar stone, **House A** has a **colonnaded court** at its heart with a window lighting the staircase to the west side of this. In **store-rooms** on the north side some of the large reconstructed *pithoi* can be seen with holes near their bases for tapping the contents, probably oil. A number of Linear A tablets also came to light in this area. In the south wing the main rooms open onto a light well with the **central room** having a **lustral basin** – in this case more of a sunken bath – just off it. A stand for a double axe was found in the **pillar crypt** similar to the ones found at Knossós. In this area were also discovered the three

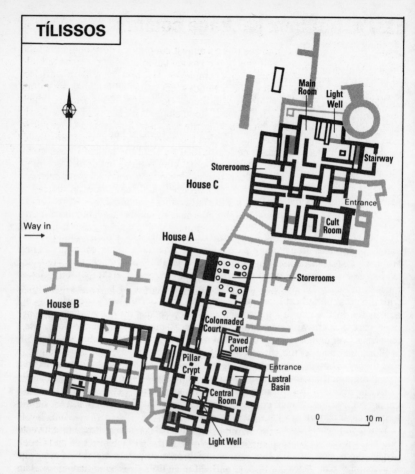

TÍLISSOS

Main Room
Light Well
Stairway
Storerooms
House C
Entrance
Cult Room
Way in
House A
Storerooms
House B
Colonnaded Court
Paved Court
Pillar Crypt
Entrance
Lustral Basin
Central Room
Light Well
0   10 m

enormous bronze cauldrons (now in the Iráklion museum) which originally prompted the site's excavation. Throughout the house fragments of painted stucco had fallen from above, suggesting a luxurious second storey to this dwelling.

House C contains a **cult room** with a central pillar, **storerooms** and, at its northern end, the **living area**. Here a paved **main room** would have been illuminated by a **light well** on its eastern side. At the end of one of many corridors, a Minoan speciality, a staircase would have led to an upper floor. There is also evidence of a drainage system. Outside the house, beside the **cistern** entered by a stairway, is a **stone altar** from the classical period.

Tílissos village, a pleasant enough place, provides food, drink and even a few **rooms** for its visitors. For a delicious Cretan omelette made with local cheese, stop at the *estiatório* fifty metres up the main street after the site turnoff. It's on the left. There's also a regular **bus** service to here from the Haniá Gate, and slightly less regular links on towards Anóyia.

East of Iráklion: package country

Beyond the city beach at Amnísos there's almost continuous development all the way to Mália, as what little remains of the coastal landscape is torn apart to build yet more hotels, apartments and beach complexes. The first recognisably distinct centre is **HÁNI KOKKÍNI**, a grubbily nondescript resort with a long but rather scrabbly beach. There's a **Minoan villa** here – known as *Nirou Hani* – which must have been beautifully sited when it stood alone. With the road immediately outside and concrete apartments blocking the sea view, however, it is harder to appreciate. Excavations of the villa revealed the foundations of a two-storey building dating from the New Palace period (c.1550 BC). All the usual Minoan architectural features – light well, storage rooms, connecting corridors, decorative paving – are present and the site was particularly rich in religious paraphernalia, including tripod altars and some striking bronze double axes now on display in the Iráklion museum. These finds led the excavators to name it the "House of the High Priest". The site is locked but the guardian should be available most mornings and afternoons (except Mondays): enquire at the nearby cafés if he's not immediately apparent. He also holds the key to the **Cave of Eileíthyia** (p.57).

Through **GOÚRNES** and **GOÚVES** things get even worse. At Goúrnes a giant US air force base has been established for years and, despite government pledges of removal, continues to buzz the coast for miles around. The beach stretches unbroken for several kilometres, but for the most part it's a narrow strip of dirty pebbles, windy and exposed. Overlooking it all from the hills are giant radar dishes and if you have a radio you'll also be able to pick up the jingoistic sounds of US forces' broadcasts. At **KÁTO GOÚVES** there's a campsite, *Camping Creta*, with no shade and little to recommend it.

About 5km inland from here, up the turning to Goúves proper, is the **Skotinó Cave**, one of the largest and most spectacular on the island. It's a pleasant walk of some 45 minutes from the coast road, passing through Goúves village, which makes an encouragingly complete contrast with the coastal strip. You can stop here for refreshment and to check directions before continuing to the signed turnoff, on the right, for Skotinó (which means "dark"). Divided into four levels with an awesomely huge main chamber, the cave is 160m deep. It was first investigated by Evans and more scientifically explored in the 1960s by French and Greek archaeologists. A considerable number of bronze and ceramic votive offerings representing periods dating back to early Minoan times indicated that this was an important sacred shrine. The cave remained in use well into the Greek and Roman eras, when the fertility goddess Artemis was worshipped in what is thought to be a substitution for an earlier Minoan female fertility deity, possibly Brytomartis.

Hersónisos

Continuing east along the main coast road, the turning for the direct route up to the Lasíthi Plateau (p.77) is signed 3km beyond the bridge over the Aposolémis winter torrent. Shortly after this you roll into the first of the really big resorts, **HERSÓNISOS** (or, more correctly, Límin Hersonísou; Hersónisos is the village in the hills just behind). If you wanted to stay in a big resort you could do a lot worse than this – Límin Hersonísou has plenty of Eurodisco nightlife, enough restaurants to keep prices down and numerous small patches of sand beach between rocky outcrops. One thing you won't find, though, is a room. Hersónisos village, about a twenty-minute walk uphill, has also been taken over totally by tourism but the developments are more recent and have preserved to a surprising degree the small village feel of the place. There are a couple of pleasantly authentic tavernas and *kafenía* among the narrow streets but, again, no chance of finding a bed. If you were determined to stay, your best bet would be the upmarket **campsite**, *Caravan*, on the coast just east of town.

Along the modern seafront, a solid line of restaurants and bars is broken only by the occasional souvenir shop: in their midst you'll find a small pyramidal fountain with broken mosaics. This is Roman, and the only real relic of the ancient town of **Chersonesos**, a thriving port from Classical Greek through to Byzantine times, handling trade from Lyttos. (Lyttos lay inland near Kastélli – even less survives there.) Around the headland above the harbour and in odd places along the seafront you can see remains of Roman harbour installations, mostly submerged, and on the headland above the more modern church is the fenced and locked site where an early Christian basilica, probably the seat of a bishop, has been excavated. But in the main the new port covers the old.

Stalídha

Hersónisos marks the beginning of the **Gulf of Mália**, around which are ranged some of the island's biggest, best and sandiest beaches. Sadly, just about all of them are heavily developed – where once were isolated coves there are now hotels and apartment complexes, and it's becoming increasingly hard to define where Hersónisos ends and Stalídha begins or where you leave Stalídha and enter Mália. **STALÍDHA** (STALIS) is a rather dull, middle-of-the-road resort. There are palm trees by the beach but little else to interest the casual visitor. If you're planning simply to turn up and find a room, or looking for a bit of life, Mália is a far better bet. There's another side road here that will take you up to the Lasíthi Plateau (see p.78).

Mália

Large enough to be a substantial town in its own right, **MÁLIA** is undeniably commercial, and its beach, long and sandy as it is, becomes grotesquely crowded at times. If you're prepared to enter into the holiday spirit of things, however – party all night and sleep all day – it can be very enjoyable. In terms of both action and accommodation it has a great deal more to offer than any of its rivals along the north coast. And of course there's the Minoan palace just down the road.

The town consists of two distinct halves, fanning out to the north and south of a T-junction where the bus drops you. The more raucous side of town lies along the **Beach Road** which snakes for a good kilometre towards the sea. Here you'll find supermarkets, souvenir shops, tour agents, cafés, restaurants, video bars and nightclubs. To walk the length of this will take you about fifteen minutes – longer if you allow yourself to be enticed by the sales patter along the way. At the end of the road there's a car park, a small harbour and a couple of beaches to the left. The **main beach**, however, stretches away to the right. It will take you another fifteen minutes to walk through the crowds here to get to anywhere with enough room to relax: at this end of the beach there's a small church, and behind are dunes (among which people camp despite the signs forbidding it) and patches of marshy ground alive with frogs. For entertainment you can swim out to a tiny offshore islet. The rocks here are sharp for barefoot exploring, but if you brave them you'll find the white-walled chapel perpetually locked, and the rock pools on the seaward side alive with small crabs, shellfish and sea urchins.

To find a trace of real Cretan life in all of this, turn inland to the north of the main road. Here in the **old town**, with its narrow twisting alleyways and white-washed walls, Mália attempts to maintain a semblance of its self respect – if not lower prices.

Practicalities

For **accommodation**, you're probably best off trying at the numerous **rooms** signed in the old town: the cheaper hotels – mostly located around the T-junction – are invariably full. Tracking back from here along the main Iráklion road there are a number of reasonably priced pensions on the left including *Hotel Argo* (☎31-636) which has rooms with breakfast. Further along this road, on the right after the Mobil station, lies the new **youth hostel** (☎31-555), a worthwhile stop even if you don't intend to stay. Situated in a former banana orchard, the place is being quietly transformed into a leafy garden by its elderly warden, Yiannis Theakakis; Yiannis also keeps a list of rooms in the town for those seeking more private accommodation. There's also help to be had in finding rooms at *Yiassou Travel* – 100m east of the T-junction – who will also change money at reasonable rates and provide general information.

Eating in Mália is unlikely to be a problem: restaurants jostle for your custom at every step, especially along the Beach Road. None of these are particularly good, but that's the price of mass production – the Beach Road also has a reputation for poisonous *souvláki*. One way of avoiding this would be British-style fish and chips, authentically wrapped in newspaper, from the *Electra Café* at the bottom of the Beach Road near the sea; at least as good as the real thing, and much cheaper. But again, the best places to eat are in the old town, inland. Wander up to Platía Áyios Dhímitri, a pleasant square beside the church, where you could try a meal at *Toto-Loto* or, even better, *Taverna Minos Knossos*, after an aperitif at the *Ouzeri Kapillo* where they serve excellent local wine from the wood.

The Beach Road comes into its own when the profusion of **bars**, **discos** and **clubs** erupt into a pulsating cacophony during the hours each side of midnight. The larger joints employ greeters to hand out invitations on the street aiming to tempt you inside, but all are free to enter and part of the fun is drifting in and out of them as the fancy takes you. Among the better bars with dance floors, *Krypton* seems to be the most popular at the moment perhaps because of its imported London DJs. The once all-conquering *Flash* has taken a downturn, whilst the American DJ at *Highway* has built up a crowd. *George's Place* and *Zig-Zag* attract fewer teeny boppers. Alternatively, if all you wanted was a quiet beer, try *Bar Epsilon* on the main road near the bus stop or head up into the old town where you'll find plenty of bars and tavernas maintaining a more Cretan pace.

The practical matters of life are simply attended to – almost everything you need, from bike hire to the *Daily Mirror*, is available on or near the T-junction. There's a **post office** and **OTE** right in the centre; near here, too, are a couple of **banks**, and out of hours you can change money at many of the travel agents or (good rates) in the three-storey tourist emporium called *Malia Maria Market*, a little way down the Beach Road. The best place for **bike hire** is *Moto Euro Tours* (☎31-636), back along the main road going west, where the owner, Pit Frankoulis, will explain all about his lifetime love affair with the motorcycle if you give him the chance. For **car hire** try *Athena* (☎31-705), also on the main road nearby, who do special offers. And if you're shopping for food, look out for cheap bananas: chances are they'll have been grown under plastic sheets in the fields around the town. (Crete, incidentally, has almost the only bananas in Greece: imports are banned to protect the trade, which is strange given the presence of just about every other conceivable import.)

The Palace of Mália

The **Palace of Mália** (Tues–Sat 8.30am–3pm, Sun 9am–2.30pm) lies forty minutes' walk east of the town, just off the main road. Any bus will stop, or hire a bicycle for a couple of hours – it's a pleasant, flat ride. Much less imposing than either Knossós or Festós, Mália in some ways surpasses both. For a start, it's a great deal emptier and you can wander among the remains in relative peace. And while no reconstruction has been attempted, the palace was never reoccupied after its second destruction, so the ground plan is virtually intact. It's a great deal easier to comprehend than Knossós, and if you've seen the reconstructions there it's easy to envisage this seaside palace in its days of glory. Basking on the rich agricultural plain between the Lasíthi Mountains and the sea, it retains a real feeling of an ancient civilisation with a taste for the good life.

From this site, whose Minoan name is unknown, came the famous gold pendant of two bees which can be seen in the Iráklion museum or on any local postcard stand. It was allegedly part of a horde which was plundered and the rest of which now resides (as the Aegina Treasure) in the British Museum. The beautiful leopard's-head axe, also in the museum at Iráklion, was another of the treasures found at Mália. Of the ruins, virtually nothing stands above ground level apart from the giant *pithoi* which have been pieced together and left about the palace like sentinels: the palace itself is worn and brown, blending almost imperceptibly into the landscape. With the mountains behind, it's a thoroughly atmospheric setting.

First discovered by Joseph Hatzidakis early this century, in 1922 the site passed to the French School at Athens who have excavated here since. As at Knossós and Festós, there was an earlier palace dating from around 1900 BC, which was devastated by the earthquake of about 1700 BC. The remains you see today are those of the new palace, built to replace this, which functioned until about 1450 BC, when it was destroyed for the last time in the wave of violence which swept across the island (see *Contexts*).

Entering the Palace: the West Court

You enter the site, as elsewhere, through the **West Court**. As at the other palaces there are raised pathways leading across this, the main one heading south towards the area of the eight circular **storage pits**. These probably held grain – the pillars which survive in the middle of some would have supported a protective roof. In the other direction the raised way takes you to the building's north side, where you can pick up the more substantial paved road which apparently once led to the sea.

Entering the palace itself from this side, through a "door" between two rocks and jinking right then left, you arrive in the **North Court** by the storerooms and their elaborately decorated, much-photographed giant *pithoi*. Off to the right were the so-called royal apartments, on the far side of which is a well preserved **lustral basin**. Nearby lay the **archive room** where a number of Linear A tablets were unearthed. Straight ahead is the **Pillared Hall** – which the excavators, prompted by the discovery of some cooking pots, think may have been a kitchen

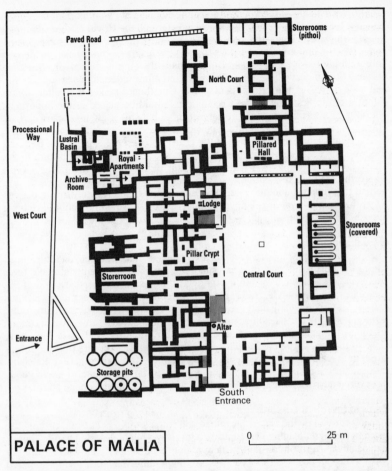

PALACE OF MÁLIA

0   25 m

Paved Road

Storerooms
(pithoi)

North Court

Processional
Way

Lustral
Basin

Pillared
Hall

Royal
Apartments

Archive
Room

West Court

Lodge

Pillar Crypt

Storerooms
(covered)

Storerroom

Central Court

Entrance

Altar

Storage pits

South
Entrance

– with a grand dining room on the floor above looking out over the courtyard. Incidentally, if this view is correct, the location is almost exactly the same as that of the palace kitchen at Zakrós.

The Central Court and Royal Apartments

Mália's **Central Court**, a long, narrow area, about 48m in length by 22m wide, is only slightly smaller than the main courtyards at Knossós and Festós. Look out for the remains of the columns which supported a portico at this northern end and for traces of a similar portico down the eastern side. Post-holes were discovered by the excavators between these columns which seemed to suggest that the court could be fenced in – possibly to protect the spectators during the bull-jumping games? Behind the eastern portico are more storerooms, now under a canopy. In the centre of the court is a shallow pit which may have been used for sacrifices; if this was its purpose it is the only such Minoan sacrificial area known.

On the west side of the courtyard are the remains of two important stairways. The first led to the upper floor beside what is termed the **Royal Lodge** or Throne Room, which overlooks the courtyard. The second, in the southwest corner, comprises the bottom four steps of what was the main ceremonial stair to the first floor, still impressive in its scale. Beside this is the curious *kernos*, or **altar**. The purpose of this heavy limestone disc, with thirty-four indentations around its rim and a single one in the centre, is disputed. One theory makes it an altar, where samples of the first fruit of the Cretan crops would be placed in the hollows as offerings to a fertility goddess at harvest time, but this is by no means certain; other theories make it a point for tax collecting or even an ancient gaming board!

The rooms along the west side of the Court also deserve exploration. Between the two staircases ran a long room which may have gone straight through to the upper floor like a medieval banqueting hall. Behind this is the **Pillar Crypt**, where the double axe symbol was found engraved on the two main pillars. And behind that runs yet another corridor of **storerooms**. Entered only through areas which had some royal or religious significance, these would no doubt have been depositories for things of value – the most secure storage at the palace.

New discoveries

The excavations at Mália are by no means complete. Inside and beyond the fenced site to the north and west digs are still going on as an apparently sizeable town comes slowly to light. Beneath a canopy to the west of the northern end of the palace lies the **Hypostyle Hall**. This building consists of a number of storerooms and two interconnected halls whose function is uncertain. Benches run round three sides of the halls, leading some to suggest that this was some form of council chamber, but again this is pure speculation. Five hundred metres to the north, close to the sea, is the *Chrysolakkos* or **Golden Pit**. This appears to have been a large, multi-chambered mausoleum dating from the Old Palace period. Its elaborate construction suggests a royal burial place as did the wealth of grave goods discovered here – among them the gold honeybee pendant mentioned above.

Back to town – the beach

Leaving the site by the way you came in, a dirt track (50m back) runs around the fence to the right, leading eventually to a lovely stretch of deserted **sand**. There's a makeshift taverna here, and usually a couple of camper vans parked up, but considering its position this beach is amazingly little visited. If you're prepared for the total lack of facilities, it makes a fine place to camp out, picnic or simply take a swim. Moving on, you can easily **walk** along the shore back into town, or back at the road there should be little difficulty flagging down a bus in that direction or on towards Áyios Nikólaos.

Inland: the Pedhiádha

The hinterland east of Iráklion consists mainly of hilly farm country, with large, widely scattered villages. Known as the *Pedhiádha*, this region is quietly prosperous but sees few visitors. Indeed, relying on public transport there's little opportunity to take in a great deal: most of the villages see just their daily market bus. But with wheels of your own it makes for enjoyable aimless touring, and certainly the inland roads are far more attractive than the coastal one.

Frescoed churches

The area's chief village, **KASTÉLLI**, or Kastélli Pedhiádhos, is a pleasant place to pull over for a while, with a number of tavernas and *kafenía* around the cross-roads in the centre of town. There are even some comfortable modern **rooms** (surprisingly expensive) above a bar on the road which leads out to the east. Excitements, however, are few. The chief attraction is the countryside itself, its winding lanes traced by elderly oak and plane trees, and the many smaller villages, often with frescoed medieval **churches**. Look out, as you drive, for signs to such churches – usually worth seeking out simply for the journey off the main ways, even if very often you can find no one to let you in.

One of the more famous is the fifteenth-century **Isódhia Theótokon**, near the village of SKLAVEROHÓRI just a couple of kilometres west of Kastélli. Another is **Áyios Yióryios** at KSIDHÁS about 3km east, which not only has frescoes of its own but also incorporates part of a much earlier basilica. This was probably associated with ancient **Lyttos**, which occupied the height immediately above the village. An important city and rival of Knossós in classical times, Lyttos was eventually destroyed by Knossós in 220 BC but reinhabited on a smaller scale in Byzantine times. What little remains, however, is for specialists only.

A personal favourite among the churches is **Áyios Pandheleímon**, off the road back to Hersónisos just before the village of PIYÍ. To get there, set off north and not far out of Kastélli you'll see a sign directing you onto a dirt track to the right. There are several alternative trails but, providing you don't mind bumpy driving, just about any seems eventually to take you past the church (as long as you stick broadly to the side of the valley, parallel with the paved road). The way is shaded with huge old trees and the church itself – far bigger than you'd imagine – is set in a grove of ancient oaks around a spring. There's a small taverna where you can sit with the local farmworkers while you wait to see if anyone turns up with a key: by no means certain (he's usually either "just left" or, worse, "on his way") and hardly vital. If you do get in, the frescoes are weathered almost beyond recognition but the structure, probably early thirteenth-century, is interesting for the way it incorporates parts of the original tenth-century basilica and uses as columns some much older fragments, possibly scavenged from Lyttos. The aqueduct which once took water to Lyttos passes close by, and you may spot fragments as you drive around looking for the church.

Towards Lasíthi

The one inland route which visitors follow in any number is the drive **up to Lasíthi**. Once again the attractions are simple: scenery which becomes increasingly mountainous as you climb towards the plateau, spreading old trees beside the road, and still older churches in the villages. Starting from Iráklion the normal route is to follow the coast road until just before Hersónisos, where you turn inland towards Kastélli and then east through the Langádha valley to Potamiés and Goníes. Before reaching the turnoff on the right for Kastélli (you continue left), look out for the ruins of the **Roman aqueduct** which carried water from springs in the hills near ancient Lyttos to its port at Hersónisos, visible in a ravine below the road.

Approaching POTAMIÉS you'll see the small Byzantine frescoed chapel of **Sotíros Christos** (locked) to the left, quickly followed by a signed track, also on the left, for the tenth-century monastery of the **Panayía Gouverniótissa** (Assumption of the Virgin), one of the oldest in Crete. The track climbs through olive groves to arrive at a shaded parking space next to the deserted, partly ruined and rather eerie monastery buildings. The enormous ovens that once fed the brethren, now broken, are still in evidence, and precarious staircases (take care) climb to the dormitories above. The tiny **chapel** which attracts visitors and the faithful today stands close by in a peaceful garden with a shady lemon tree. Inside are restored frescoes dating from the fourteenth century with a fine *pantokrator* in the dome. The chapel will probably be locked (key available from the *kafeníon* at the edge of the village), but a restricted view of the frescoes inside can be had through a small glassless window in the apse.

Five kilometres further is AVDHOÚ, where there are more fine (if faded) frescoes from the fourteenth and fifteenth centuries in three churches: Áyios Andónios, Áyios Constantínos and Áyios Yióryios. The churches should be open; if not, enquiries in the village cafés should produce the necessary keys.

Mohós
From Mália, or on a round trip from Áyios Nikólaos, you can take the shorter cut, turning inland at Stalídha and following the road signed for Mohós. This route is probably the most dramatic of the three approaches to the plateau (the third is from the other end, from Neápolis), with **spectacular views** back over the coast as the road climbs dizzily above the Gulf of Mália. After crossing a pass you arrive at the village of **MOHÓS**, its pleasant leafy square edged by tavernas and cafés. There's a major festival here – albeit rather touristy – on August 15 every year.

Krási and Será
Three kilometres beyond the point where the roads join, a loop off the main route will bring you to the curiously named village of **KRÁSI** ("wine" in Greek). Curious because Krási's fame is based on water: a curative spring in fact. The spring is situated in the shade of an enormous plane tree, claimed to be the largest in Europe, and which twelve men cannot girdle. A great crowd of septuagenarians taking the waters certainly seemed revived when I was last there, for they were soon dancing with each other in the pleasant platía. The waters are reputed to be especially good for stomach complaints – worth noting if you have fallen foul of the Mália *soúvlaki* poisoner.

Not much further on, just before the village of KERÁ, the convent of **Panayía Kardhiótissa** (Our Lady of the Heart) lies immediately below the road. The buildings date from the twelfth century, and though from the outside they look like whitewashed modern concrete, the interior is undeniably spectacular, with restored frescoes throughout. These came to light only in the 1960s, when they were discovered beneath successive layers of paint. There is also a copy of a famous twelfth-century icon of the Virgin, the original of which was taken from here to Rome in 1498. In a peaceful garden outside the church one of the three remaining nuns will be on duty at the stone table in the shade of a mulberry tree. If you wanted to try out your Greek, you could ask Sister Theophilate, Sister Dionysia or Sister Theodoti to tell you of how they came to "enter" the order at the age of ten, a story which reflects a darker side to the smiling face of the Orthodox Church in Greece.

The Mountains

After the village of Kerá the road winds on into the Dhiktean mountains, as the views become increasingly magnificent. To the left, **Mount Karfí** looms ominously, its summit over 1100m above sea level. This spire-like peak (Karfí in Greek means "nail") was one of the sites where the Minoan civilisation made its last stand following the collapse of the great centres after the twelfth century BC. To remote refuges such as this the last of the Minoans fled from the Dorian advance, keeping alive shadowy vestiges of their culture. The solitary peak, now identified as a Minoan sanctuary, stands as a silent witness to the end of Europe's first great civilisation.

The road continues to climb until, at Séli Ambélou, you approach a dramatic pass flanked by windmills perched on the ridges above. Once through the crags of rock, the Lasíthi plateau is laid out before you, so sudden and perfect as to be almost a parody of a scenic view. Beyond, almost straight ahead, rise the highest peaks of the range including **Mount Dhíkti** itself – all 2148 metres of it. There's a good taverna here, where you can stop to take in the sights (though it's surprisingly cool once you start sitting around), and don't forget the view seawards as well – on clear days you can see as far as the island of Thíra (Santorini) over sixty miles distant.

On the ridge behind the car parking area, a couple of the stone windmills have been restored and pressed into use as souvenir shops. There's a path from here along the heights leading up to still higher viewpoints and eventually the site of ancient **Karfí**, but this is probably better approached from Tzermiádho on the plateau.

The Lasíthi plateau itself is described in Chapter Two.

ACROSS THE ISLAND

There are a number of roads that run from Iráklion towards the south coast, but almost all the traffic seems to follow the one which heads slightly southwest, **towards Festós and Mátala**. Plenty of buses come this way too, leaving from the Haniá Gate terminal and heading for Festós, Mátala, Léndas or Ayía Galíni via Timbáki. Míres, in the heart of the Messará plain, is the southern junction for switching between these various routes. The only other regular bus service across the island from Iráklion runs southeast **towards Ierápetra**, via Áno Viánnos and Mírtos.

The southern half of the province is very different from the north. There's just one resort of any size – at **Mátala** – and a day-trip route which takes in the sites of **Górtys**, **Festós** and **Ayía Triádha**. The rest is countryside and very little developed for tourism. Which is not to say it's an undeveloped area, for this is the island's single most important agricultural centre, and the **Messará plain** above all has always been a vital resource; its villages are widely distributed and wealthy.

The coast, Mátala excepted, is relatively little visited, and indeed a good part of it is quite inaccessible: east of **Léndas** (where there's excellent sand and a growing young travellers' scene) stretches well over 30km of shore which simply can't be reached overland, and even beyond this **Tsoútsouros** and **Keratókambos** are accessible only by steep, rough tracks.

Towards Festós

Crossing the island from Iráklion is not, on the whole, the most exciting of drives: you leave the city westwards (through the Haniá Gate) and on the outskirts turn south, under the highway, following the signs to Festós. From the beginning the road climbs, heading up to the island's spine, through thoroughly businesslike countryside. This is more of what traditionally was the Malevísi, or Malmsey, wine producing region: though some wine is still made, most of the grapes you'll see now are grown for eating.

Ayía Varvára and a minor road west
AYÍA VARVÁRA is the chief village of this area, a place known as the *Omphalos* (the navel) of Crete. The great chapel-topped rock which you see as you arrive is by this account the very point around which the island balances, its centre of being. Not that this makes for any great tourist attraction. There are plenty of cafés and shops, but they cater mostly for local farmers in search of a bag of fertiliser or a tractor part.

On the southern fringe of the village a turning takes off to the west, following the flank of the Psilorítis range **towards Kamáres** (p.162) and eventually on to Réthimnon or down to Ayía Galíni. This is a beautiful drive and a relatively good, empty road: ZARÓS is a particularly attractive village (with a lovely C-class hotel, the *Idhi*, should you want to stay) and along the way there are a number of ancient churches. The only one of these you have much real hope of finding open is the **Moni Vrondísi**, above the road about 3km beyond Zarós. Here there are fourteenth-century frescoes in the church and a collection of icons taken from the nearby church of Áyios Fanoúrios – Vrondísi itself has given up the finest of its artworks, the six great panels by Dhamaskinos, to the museum in Iráklion. Even without them, though, this is a wonderful setting, with trees for shade, cool water, a gushing fifteenth-century fountain in elaborate Italian taste, and views towards Festós and the Gulf of Messará. Áyios Fanoúrios, all that survives of the **Moni Valsamónero**, is reached by a track from the next village – VORÍZIA. The frescoes in this church are said to be among the best in Crete: but if you get in to see them you'll have achieved more than I ever have.

There's also a great short **gorge walk** to be had just outside Zarós. One kilometre west of the village, turn right up a track signposted to Áyios Nikólaos (another frescoed church that is usually locked), which ends after about 2km in a car park by the church. You can continue to climb, on foot, for a further 2km to the entrance to the Gorge of Zarós. This is some 3km long and a path, including steps and bridges for the difficult bits, has been constructed to take much of the strain. It's rarely visited, and the rewards are spectacular views of the Psilorítis range and – depending on the time of year – plenty of bird, plant and even animal life.

The Messará Plain
Continuing by the main road south from Ayía Varvára the way becomes genuinely mountainous, and very soon you cross the Pass of Vourvoulítis (650m) and enter the watershed of the Messará. The **Messará plain**, a long strip running west from the Gulf of Messará, is the largest and most important of Crete's fertile flatlands. Bounded in the north by the Psilorítis range and the lower hills which run right across the centre of the island, in the east by the Dhiktean mountains, and in the south by the narrow strip of the Kófinas Hills, it is watered, somewhat

erratically, by the Yeropótamos. Heavy with olives, and increasingly with the fruit and vegetable cash crops that dominate the modern agricultural economy, the plain has always been a major centre of population and a vital link in the island's economy. Evidence of this importance abounds, not only at Górtys, Festós and Ayía Triádha but at a wealth of lesser, barely explored sites: today's villages are obviously prosperous, too, surrounded by neat and intensive cultivation.

As you descend to the plain by a series of long, looping curves, the main road heads west through Áyii Dhéka. A left turn, eastwards, takes you across far less travelled country and potentially (see p.95) all the way to Ierápetra.

Áyii Dhéka

ÁYII DHÉKA is the first village you reach on the Messará, and the most interesting. The place takes its name from ten early Christians martyred here around 250 AD under the emperor Decius. The **Holy Ten** are still among the most revered of Cretan saints: regarded as martyrs for Crete as much as Christianity – the first in a heroic line of Cretans who laid down their lives opposing tyrannous occupation. On the southwestern edge of the village are two churches associated with them. The older, originally Byzantine, has an icon portraying the martyrs and the stone block on which they are supposed to have been decapitated. Steps beneath the more modern chapel nearby lead to a crypt where you can see six of their tombs. Perhaps more authentic reminders of the village's ancient past are the scavenged pieces of Górtys – Roman statues, pillars and odd blocks of masonry – which can be seen everywhere: re-used in modern houses, propping up walls or simply lying about in yards. In the centre where the main road passes through there are a number of roadside cafés and restaurants and a few signs offering **rooms** – a pleasant place to break your journey.

Górtys

GÓRTYS (known traditionally as Gortyn or Gortyna) is a large, fragmented site, taking in a great deal more than the fenced area by the road which most people see. The best way to get some idea of its scale is to follow the path through the fields from the village. This heads off, more or less parallel to the road, opposite the chapel of Áyii Dhéka: it's an easy walk to the main site, and along the way you'll skirt most of the major remnants of the Roman city.

Settled from Minoan times at least, when it was a minor subject of Festós, Górtys began its rise to prominence under the Dorians, becoming by the eighth century BC a significant commercial power and in the third century BC finally conquering its former rulers at Festós. The society was a strictly regulated one, with a citizen class (presumably Dorian) ruling over a population of serfs (presumably "Minoan" Cretans) and slaves. Even for the citizens life was as hard and orderly as it was in classical Sparta.

Evidence of early Górtys has survived thanks largely to the remarkable law code found here (see below) and to a lesser extent through treaties known to have existed between the Górtys of this era and its rivals, notably Knossós. Hannibal fled to Górtys briefly after his defeat at Rome. It was under the Romans, however, from 67 BC on, that the city reached its apogee: as the seat of a Roman Praetor it was capital of the province of Crete and Cyrenaica, ruling not only the rest of the island but much of Egypt and North Africa as well. It was here that

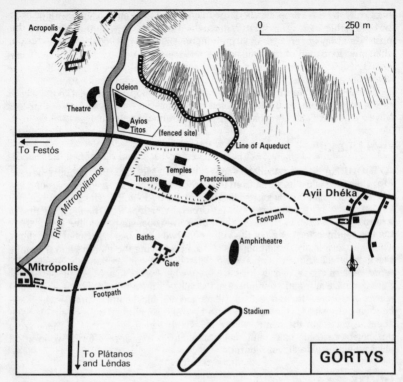

Christianity first reached Crete, when Saint Titus was despatched by Saint Paul to convert the islanders. After the Saracen invasion in the ninth century Górtys was abruptly abandoned.

South of the road

In the fields en route to the site it is the **Roman city** which is in evidence, and if you wanted further proof of its extent you could walk south to the remains of the city gate, or beyond that to the Stadium. The city once stretched from the edges of Ayii Dhéka to the far banks of the Mitropolitanos (then known as the Lethe) and from the hills in the north as far south as the modern hamlet of Mitrópolis (where a small Roman basilica with good mosaics has been excavated). For most people, though, the ruins along the main path, and others seen standing in the distance or suspected unexcavated beneath hummocks along the way, are quite enough. In another setting, or individually, these might seem unimpressive, but with so many of them, abandoned as they are and all but ignored (fenced to keep souvenir hunters out, but not guarded nor advertised) they are amazing – you feel almost as if you have discovered them for yourself.

The **Praetorium** (the governor's palace) is the most extensive remain, a vast pile built originally in the second century AD, rebuilt in the fourth, and occupied as a monastery right up to the time of the Venetian conquest; within the same fenced area is a courtyard with fountains and the **Nymphaeum**. Somewhere in this area, too, was the terminus of the main aqueduct, which brought water from the region of modern Zarós. Further on, the **Temple of Pythian Apollo** was the most important of the Roman city's temples, again later converted to a church, while the **Theatre**, though small, is very well preserved.

Áyios Títos and the Law Code

From the theatre you can cut up to the road and cross to the parking area which marks the entrance to the main, fenced **site** (Mon–Sat 8am–7pm, Sun 8am–6pm). As you enter, it is the church of **Áyios Títos** which immediately grabs the eye, the back of its apse rising high in front of you. This is the only part of the church which survives intact, but the shape of the rest is easy enough to make out. When it was built (around the end of the sixth century) it would have been the island's chief church: you can see the extent to which it is still revered in the little shrine which operates at the end of one of the surviving aisles.

Beyond the church lies an area which was probably the ancient Forum, and beyond this the most important remain of ancient Górtys, the **Odeion** (or covered theatre) and its **Law Code**. The law code, a series of engraved stones some 9m long and 3m high, dates from around 500 BC, though presumably codifying laws which had been established by long practice before then. It is a fascinating insight into a period of which relatively little is otherwise known; the laws are written in a very rough Doric Cretan dialect and inscribed alternately left to right and right to left, so that the eyes can follow the writing continuously (a style known as *boustrophedon* after the furrows of an ox plough). What they set out (and the code is not a complete system of law, more a series of rulings on special cases) reflects a strictly hierarchical society in which there were at least three distinct classes – citizens, serfs and slaves – each with quite separate rights and obligations. Five witnesses were needed to convict a free man of a crime, only one for a slave; raping a free man or woman carried a fine of a hundred *staters*, a serf only five. The laws also cover subjects such as property and inheritance rights, the status of children of mixed marriages (ie between free people and serfs) and the control of trade.

As you see them, the panels on which the law is inscribed are incorporated into the round Odeion, which was erected under Trajan around 100 AD and rebuilt in the third or fourth century (the brick terrace which protects the inscriptions from the elements is modern). This was just the latest incarnation of a series of buildings on the site, in which the code had apparently always been preserved – obviously this was a city which valued its own history. When they were discovered in the late nineteenth century, these ruins were entirely buried under eroded soil washed down from the hills behind.

Across the river

Beside the fenced site the river runs by an abandoned medieval mill and on the far bank you can see a larger **Theatre**, in rather poor repair, set against the hillside. In Roman times the river ran through a culvert here and you would have walked straight across – nowadays you have to go back to the road and over its bridge to explore this area. The guard at the site – who, though he speaks no English, is very keen to encourage people to explore the outlying areas – will give you directions to the easiest path up to the **Acropolis** on the hilltop above the river. Hardly anyone makes it up there (it's a stiff climb in the heat) but the ruins are surprisingly impressive, with Roman defensive walls and a building known as the *Kastro* (though apparently not a castle) still standing in places to a height of six metres. The lesser remains are among the earliest on the site, and include scant relics of a Greek temple which was later converted to a church. From the hill you also get a fine overview of the layout of Górtys and can trace the line of the aqueducts coming in from the north.

Míres

From Górtys it's about 6km to **MÍRES**, a town of some size and the transport centre for the area. It could hardly be described as attractive, but as a centre for local commerce as well as passing tourists, Míres at least has plenty of life, with scores of places to eat and drink, the only bank for miles around, and cheap **rooms** easy to find if you happen to be stranded between buses. On Saturday mornings there's a busy market. If you are changing **buses** – and you can get to Léndas or Mátala on the coast from here, to Zarós and Kamáres in the mountains (very occasionally), through Timbáki to Ayía Galíni or Réthimnon and even (once a day) to Réthimnon via the Amári Valley – watch out for the fact that there are two termini some distance from each other along the main road. One serves the Iráklion-based routes, the other those into Réthimnon province: check well in advance which you need. Heading direct for Festós there's usually no need to stop.

Festós and Ayía Triádha

The palace of **FESTÓS** (Mon–Sat 8am–7pm, Sun 8am–6pm) was excavated by Federico Halbherr (also responsible for the early work on Górtys), at almost exactly the same time as Evans was working at Knossós. The style of the excavations, however, could hardly have been more different. Here, to the approval of most traditional archaeologists, reconstruction was kept to an absolute minimum – it's all bare foundations, and walls which rise at most a couple of feet above ground level. As at Knossós, most of what survives is the Second Palace, rebuilt after the destruction of c.1700 BC and occupied to c.1450 BC. But at Festós the first palace was used as a foundation for the second, and much of its well-preserved floor plan has been uncovered by the excavations. Fascinating as these superimposed buildings are for the experts, they help make Festós extremely confusing to find your way about, and difficult to understand. Taken with an apparent lack of elaboration, at least in the decoration of the palace, this adds up to considerable disappointment for many visitors. Since much of the site is also fenced off, it becomes almost impossible to get any sense of the place as it once was.

Although there are major differences between Festós and the other palaces, these are in the end however, outweighed by the multitude of similarities. The rooms are set about a great central courtyard, with an external court on the west side and a theatral area north of this; the domestic apartments are as usual slightly apart from the public and formal ones; there are the same lines of storage magazines and pits for grain; and on the east side are workshops for the palace craftsmen. While no traces of frescoes were found, it does not follow that the palace wasn't luxurious: the materials – marble, alabaster, gypsum – were of the highest quality; there was sophisticated drainage and bathrooms; and remains suggest a large and airy dining hall on the upper floors overlooking the court. Bear in mind, as you explore, that part of the palace is missing – there must have been more outbuildings on the south side of the site where erosion has worn away the edge of the ridge and a corner of the central court itself has collapsed.

Entry: the West Court and Grand Stairway

You enter the palace from above, down steps leading past a **Tourist Pavilion** and approaching the northwest corner of the complex through the Upper Court. Step down first into the **West Court** and integral **Theatral Area**: as at Knossós there are raised walkways leading across the courtyard, and here one of them runs right up the steps which form the seats of the theatral area. On the west side of the court are circular walled pits, probably for storing grain. The West Court itself is a survivor of the original palace – the main walkway leads not up the stairs into the new palace but past them and into the entrance to the old. From there, much of the facade of the old palace can be seen as a low wall in front of the Grand Staircase which leads into the new. When the palace stood, of course, this would not have been apparent; then the court was filled with rubble and levelled (though not paved) at the height of the bottom step of the stairway.

The **Grand Staircase** was a fitting approach to Festós, a superbly engineered flight of twelve shallow stone steps, 14m wide. Some of the steps are actually carved from the solid rock of the hill, and each is slightly convex, higher in the

PALACE OF FESTÓS

middle than at the ends, in order to improve the visual impact. The entrance facade was no doubt equally impressive – you can still see the base of the pillar which supported the centre of the doorway – but it's hard to imagine from what actually survives. Once inside, the first few rooms were perhaps deliberately cramped, either for security purposes, to prevent a sudden rush, or as contrast to the larger, lighter spaces beyond. At the end would have been a blank wall, open to the sky, and a small door to the right which led out onto stairs down towards the central court. Standing in the entrance area now, you can look down over the **storerooms**, and going down the stairs you can approach them more closely through a larger room which was apparently an office. Exposed here is a store-room from the old palace with a giant jar still in place. At the far end more *pithoi* stand in a room apparently used to store olive oil or other liquids; there's a stool to stand on while reaching in and a basin to catch spillage, while the whole floor slopes towards a hole in which any slops would collect.

The Central Court and Royal Apartments

From the stores "office", quite an elaborate room, you can pass into the **Central Court**, which is by far the most atmospheric area of the Palace. In this great paved court, with its scintillating views, there is a rare sense of Festós as it must have been. Look for the black smudge on the face of Psilorítis which marks the entrance of the Kamáres cave. The views aside (and of course they would have been pretty much blocked by the two storeys, at least, on either side), the court-yard remains impressive. In particular its north end was positively, and unusually, grand. The doorway, flanked by half-columns and niches (possibly for sentries) covered in painted plaster, can be plainly made out. To the left as you face this are a couple of *pithoi* (put there by the excavators) and a stepped stone which some claim was a block from which athletes would jump onto bulls: the equally unlikely and unprovable counter-theory is that it was a base for a flowerpot.

Along each of the long sides of the courtyard ran a covered **portico** or veran-dah, the bases of whose supports are still visible: in the southwest corner are vari-ous rooms which probably had religious functions, and beyond these, hard to distinguish from them, parts of the old palace which are mostly fenced off. Also here, right at the edge of the site, are the remains of a **Greek temple** of the clas-sical era, evidence that the site was occupied long after the Minoans and the destruction of the palace.

Heading up through the grand north door – notice the holes for door pivots and the guardroom just inside – a corridor leads through the **North Court** toward the **Royal Apartments**. These have been covered and shut off to avoid damage from people walking through, and it's hard to see a great deal of the Queen's rooms or the King's behind them. Above the King's rooms, however, is a large **Peristyle Hall**, a colonnaded courtyard much like a cloister, open in the centre. On the north side this courtyard was open to take in the view of Psilorítis. It must have been a beautiful place – perhaps also one of religious significance. Staircases linked the hall directly with the royal apartments (and the **lustral basin** on the north edge of the King's rooms); nowadays it is easier approached from the palace entrance, turning left up the stairs from the Propylon.

Palace dependencies

Continuing past the royal quarters on the other side, you come to the dependent buildings on the northeast side of the palace, buildings which almost certainly predate much of the palace itself. Among the first of these is the so-called **Archive** where the famous Festós disc (see p.48) was discovered in one of a row of mud-brick boxes. A little further on is the **Peristyle House**, probably a private home, with an enclosed yard similar in style to the Hall. From here, stairs lead back down to the level of the Central Court, into the area of the palace **workshops**. In the centre of another large courtyard are the remains of a furnace, apparently used for metalworking – though it may also have been a kiln. The small rooms roundabout were the workshops, perhaps even the homes, of the craftsmen. Walking back to the Central Court, another suite of rooms, with its own small peristyle hall, lies on your left. These are usually described as the **Prince's rooms**.

Ayía Triádha

AYÍA TRIÁDHA (8.45am–3pm, Sun 9.30am–2.30pm; closed Fri) lies about 3km from Festós on the far side of the hill, an easy drive or a walk of about 45 minutes by a well signed road around the south slope. (There is also an old footpath around the north side, but check with the guards at Festós about the current feasibility of the walk – it seems to have fallen into disuse). The site remains something of an enigma; nothing to compare with it exists in what is known of Minoan Crete, nor does it appear in any records. Even the name has had to be borrowed from a nearby chapel.

In sharp contrast with unadorned Festós, however, Ayía Triádha has provided some of the most delicate Minoan **artworks** found. From this site came the three vases of carved black steatite – the Harvester Vase, the Boxer Vase and the Chieftain Cup – on display in the Iráklion museum, as well as some of the finest works in the Fresco Hall there, including the unique painted sarcophagus. And the ruins yet again enjoy a magnificent hillside site, looking out over the Gulf of Messará. The modern view takes in the coastal plain with Timbáki airstrip in the foreground (built by the Germans during the war, its runways are now more often used for motor races), but in Minoan times the sea would have come right to the base of the hill. Despite this beauty and wealth, Ayía Triádha is plainly not a construction on the same scale as the great palaces: the most commonly accepted explanation is that it was some kind of royal villa or summer retreat, but it may equally have been the home of an important prince or noble, or a building of special ceremonial significance.

You approach the site from the car park, above. As ever the remains, in which buildings of several eras are jumbled, are confused and confusing. This matters much less than usual, however, for it is the atmosphere of Ayía Triádha which really makes the place – the absence of crowds, the beauty of the surroundings and the human scale of the villa with its multitude of little stairways and paved corridors between rooms.

The Site

To your left as you climb down are the bare ruins of a Minoan house older than most of the other remains (the villa was broadly contemporary with the new palace at Festós) and beyond them a **shrine** which contained a frescoed floor and walls now on show in the Iráklion museum. If you keep to the higher ground here you come into the courtyard of the villa, perhaps the best place to get an impression of its overall layout. L-shaped, the building closed the courtyard only on its north and west sides, and the north side is further confused by a much

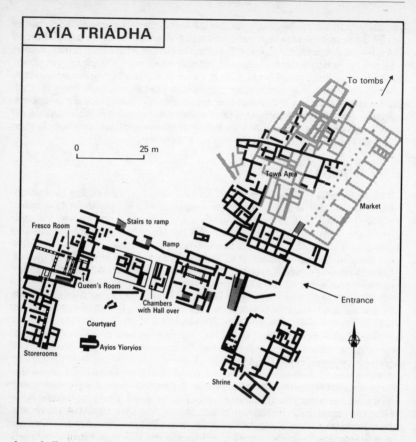

AYÍA TRIÁDHA

0   25 m

To tombs

Town Area

Market

Fresco Room

Stairs to ramp

Ramp

Queen's Room

Chambers with Hall over

Courtyard

Ayios Yioryios

Storerooms

Entrance

Shrine

later hall, apparently a Mycenaean *megaron*, built over it. To the south of the courtyard is the early fourteenth-century chapel of **Áyios Yióryios**, in which there are fragments of frescoes.

The **royal villa** now lies mostly below the level of the courtyard, but in Minoan times it would not have appeared this way: the builders made use of the natural slope to create a split-level construction, and entrances from the court would have led directly into upper levels above those you see today. The finest of the rooms were those in the corner of the L looking out over the sea; here were found the best of the frescoes, including the famous stalking cat. The quality of workmanship can still be appreciated in these chambers with their alabaster-lined walls and gypsum floors and benches. Beside them to the south is a small group of storerooms, while from the hall and terrace out front you can walk around the ramp which runs beneath the north side of the villa. The Italian excavators named this the *Rampa del Mare* and claimed that it once ran down to the sea, though there seems little evidence for this.

Follow it the other way instead and you can head down to the lower part of the site, the **town area**. By far the most striking aspect of this is the **market**, a row of shops which are once again unique in Minoan architecture. The shops, identically sized, fronted by a covered portico, run in a line down the hill: in front of them is an open space and across that the houses of the town. Only one problem spoils the easily conjured image of the Minoan populace milling around the market while their rulers looked benignly on from above – this area apparently dates only from the declining years of the Minoan culture and is contemporary, not with the villa, but with the megaron erected over it. Beyond the shops (and outside the fence) lies the **cemetery**, where remains of two *tholos* tombs and many other graves were found, including the one containing the Ayía Triádha sarcophagus.

Festós practicalities

Bus services to the Festós site are excellent, with some nine a day to and from Iráklion (the last leaves just before the site closes – fewer run on Sunday), five of which continue to or come from Mátala. There are also services direct to Ayía Galíni. All of them stop right by the Festós parking area. Prospects for hitching shouldn't be bad either with so many tourists about. If you're arriving in the afternoon, plan to visit Ayía Triádha first, as it closes early.

The **Tourist Pavilion** at Festós serves drinks and poor food and also has a few beds, though these are very rarely available (thanks to advance bookings) and pricey when they are. There are a few more **rooms** to be found in the nearby village of ÁYIOS IOÁNNIS, along the road towards Mátala, or alternatively you should find something in the first larger place you strike in almost any direction: Míres, Timbáki or Pitsídhia.

West towards Timbáki

Continuing west from Festós, towards Ayía Galíni or Réthimnon, the final stretch of the Messará plain, with its acres of polythene greenhouses and burgeoning concrete sprawl, must be among the ugliest places in Crete. **TIMBÁKI** may also be the drabbest town. It's a place of some size, which means there are cafés and restaurants along the main street, shops and banks, and even a couple of hotels. But there's no reason to stay here longer than you have to.

Just beyond, a turning leads to **KÓKKINOS PÍRGOS** on the coast. If this can seem reasonably attractive, it is only by way of contrast, for here too plastic and concrete are the overwhelming images (if you've come from anywhere else, it simply seems ugly). The sole advantages of the place are cheap **rooms**, of which there are plenty, and the lack of crowds on the none-too-beautiful beach. These do not amount to enough of a reason to come here.

Inland: Vóri to Kamáres

Having written this part of the island off, it's worth remembering that yet again all you have to do is turn off the main road to escape altogether. **VÓRI** lies only a very short distance north, and it's quite a big place, yet already it's far more pleasant, a working village almost entirely off the beaten track. That some tourists do come here is thanks to the excellent new **Museum of Cretan Ethnology** (daily 10am–6pm), advertised by large signs along the main road. Once in Vóri, finding the museum becomes less easy, but it's worth seeking out (behind the church) for a comprehensive view of traditional country life in Crete

– better than the equivalent museum in Réthimnon. The collection is a miscellany of agricultural implements, building tools and materials, domestic utensils, furniture, basketware, pottery, musical instruments, weaving and embroidery, some familiar, some entirely new; well labelled and fascinating. There are a couple of *kafenía* in the village square if you need refreshment before continuing on your way.

If you're heading for Ayía Galíni you have little choice but to return to the main road, but for the Amári Valley and Réthimnon it's also possible to take the new road up to Kamáres, another lovely, climbing drive. If this road turns out not to have been completed yet, don't despair: you can get through on old tracks, albeit on a dire, bumpy surface made worse by construction vehicles.

Mátala

MÁTALA is much the best-known of the beaches in the south of Iráklion province. You may still meet people who will assure you that, with its cave-dwelling hippy community, this is *the* travellers' beach on Crete. But that's history. It's about as far from modern reality as the fact that Mátala was the place where Zeus swam ashore in the guise of a bull with Europa on his back, or that it was once one of the chief ports of Górtys. The entry to the village should prepare you for what to expect, as you drive in past a couple of kilometres of new hotels and "Welcome to Mátala" signs and pull up at the huge car park on the edge of town. It does get better, and development is still relatively small-scale, but the town never feels anything other than wholly touristy: coach tour arrivals in the afternoon take up every inch on the sand and prices, for rooms especially, are high.

On the plus side, Mátala beach really is quite spectacular, a broad, curving swathe of sand tucked under the cliff in which the famous caves are carved. And the town crowds – there are always crowds – are relatively young, the atmosphere boisterous. If you are prepared to walk, there are other beaches with far fewer people on them. And you will never be short of somewhere to enjoy a cocktail at sunset. If you enjoy that, Mátala remains one of Crete's better resorts. If you're after isolation, or a cheap room, try somewhere else.

Caves and beaches

The **caves** started it all. Nobody knows quite who started the caves, which are entirely man-made, but it seems likely that the first were Roman or early Christian tombs: they have been so re-used and added to ever since that it is virtually impossible to tell. The cliff in which they are carved, an outcrop of compacted sand, is soft enough to allow surprisingly elaborate decor: some caves have windows and doorways cut out as well as built-in benches or beds (which may originally have been grave slabs); others are mere scooped out hollows. Locals inhabited the caves, on and off, for centuries, and during the war they made a handy munitions dump, but it was in the Sixties that they really became famous, attracting a large and semi-permanent foreign community. Name a famous hippy and there'll be someone to claim that he or she lived here too – Cat Stevens and Bob Dylan are only the most frequently mentioned. It has, however, been a very long time since the caves were cleared out; nowadays they're fenced off, open by day but searched by the police at closing time every night.

The **beach** below the caves is the focus for most of the town's activity, and during the day everyone hangs out either on the sand or in the tavernas overlooking it. The swimming is great – if surprisingly rough when the wind blows – with gently shelving sand in the centre, underwater remains of the Roman port around the base of the rocks on both sides (but watch out for sea urchins), and multicoloured fish everywhere. If the crowds on this town beach get too much, you can head south, climbing over the rocks behind town in about twenty minutes, to another excellent stretch of sand known locally as **Red Beach**. This can be quite a tough walk, scrambling over loose scree on the way down, but the beach is excellent. Usually half empty, it has curious dark reddish-brown sand and wonderfully clear water over a sandy bottom. On the way you pass more caves, many of which *are* inhabited through the summer: indeed when you know where to look it turns out that there are a number of cave dwellings around, all some way from the village and the exact whereabouts of the better ones a closely guarded secret.

Practicalities

For all practical purposes, Mátala consists virtually of a single street, the continuation of the main road into town as it curves round behind the beach. The "market" and many of the places to eat lie to the right, between the road and the beach, the "old town", such as it is, is crammed against the rocks to the left.

Finding a **room** can take some time, but with so many alternatives there usually seems to be something available. The most attractive place to stay would undoubtedly be in the old town on one of the little backstreets – but there are very few places here. More realistic, and still right at the centre of things, is to take the little street to the left at the entrance to town, behind the huge new *Zwei Brüder* hotel, which is almost entirely lined with purpose-built rooms places. Among the first and best of these is the *Hotel Sofia* (☎0892/42-134), although rooms facing towards the town square here can be very noisy. Quieter and mostly slightly cheaper alternatives further up the street include *Matala View*, *Red Beach*, *Fantastik* and *Silvia*. If you have no luck here then you'll have to start trudging out along the road by which you entered town, asking at every place along the way; potentially a long walk. Out of season, of course, you may well be in a position to bargain; but Mátala does have a very long season – it's a popular Easter destination for Greek families. There's a large, well-equipped **campsite** right beside the beach by the bottom of the cliffs.

Finding something to **eat**, at least, is not going to cause problems. There's a solid line of tavernas facing out into the bay, with sufficient competition to keep prices within reason. Among the best of these is the last, *Neosicos*, but menus and prices are generally very similar. For an alternative, quieter view of town try *Olympia*, pretty much at the highest point, where there's a candlelit, rooftop restaurant/bar looking down over all the action. Takeaway food and ingredients for picnics can be found in the stalls of the "market".

The chief **entertainment** in the evening is watching the invariably spectacular sunset. Almost every bar and restaurant has a west facing terrace, from the *Sunset* taverna on the beach to the bars on the rocks above the harbour. Although there are a couple of **discos** (*Zorba's* on the road out of town, for example), nightlife is generally low-key, cocktail bar stuff. There are one or two rowdier bars on the main street: follow the noise to find out where the action is. The *Zwei Brüder* bar/taverna, in the square as you arrive in town, is the longest established meeting place, with music and reasonably cheap food.

Almost every other practical need is easily taken care of: newspapers and books, **car and bike hire** and **currency exchange** are all around the main square or up the single main street; there are also a couple of **travel agents** who have phones for long-distance calls. There's a **post office** van parked throughout the summer near the entrance to the market, with competitive exchange rates as well as stamps for your postcards. The **OTE** also occupies a temporary building, this time in the middle of the car park behind the beach – it generally seems uncrowded and helpful. The covered **"market"** still has a couple of authentic market stalls selling fruit and veg, but these are rapidly being displaced by souvenir shops, general stores and travel agents. Finally, if you want to escape, there are **boat trips** from the harbour (in addition to all the usual coach excursions on offer at the travel agents): a taxi service to Red Beach and Kómmos, and twice-weekly trips to Ayía Galíni and Préveli.

Alternative bases: Pitsídhia and Kalamáki

An alternative base to Mátala, and a good way of saving some money and also enjoying rather more peace, is to stay at **PITSÍDHIA**, sprawling around the main road about 5km inland. This is already a well-used option, so Pitsídhia is no unspoilt village, and nor is it quite as cheap as you might expect, but there are plenty of rooms, lively places to eat, and an affable young international crowd.

KALAMÁKI, which is right on the beach a similar distance from Pitsídhia as Mátala, is another possibility. At the moment it seems unfinished, a dusty, ugly place caught halfway between being a beach with a taverna on it and a full-blown resort, but there's plenty of accommodation in half-built rooms places, several bike rental companies with hardly any customers, a number of places to eat, and a long, empty, windswept beach. The road down there seems to run out halfway (unless they've completed the new paved one), but any of the dusty tracks seems to find its way to the coast eventually.

Kómmos

At the southern end of the long beach that starts in Kalamáki, almost halfway to Mátala, lies the archaeological site of ancient **KÓMMOS**, a Minoan harbour town which was probably the main port for Festós and Ayía Triádha. The site can also be approached from Pitsídhia by a track signed on the right, 1km west of the village.

Sir Arthur Evans was the first to report signs of Minoan occupation here, but real excavation started only a decade ago when Joseph Shaw began work, funded by the American School of Classical Studies. The work carried out in the seasons since then has made it clear that Kómmos is destined to become a major site of the future. Meanwhile, the excavations are fenced off and not strictly open to visitors – but this does not prevent you taking a look at what's been uncovered.

There are three main **excavation areas** to the north, centre and south; none of them more than a stone's throw behind the beach. It is thought that the whole area will eventually yield evidence of occupation. The **northern area**, on a low hill close to the sea, contains domestic dwellings among which is a large house (on the south side) with a paved court and a limestone winepress. The **central group** – behind a retaining wall to prevent subsidence – has houses from the

New Palace era, with well preserved walls and evidence, in the fallen limestone slabs, of the earthquake around 1600 BC which caused much destruction here. A rich haul of intact pottery was found in this area, much of it in the brightly painted Kamáres style.

The most remarkable finds to date, however, came in the **southern sector** where what you see is partly confused by being overlaid by a classical Greek sanctuary. Minoan remains here include a fine stretch of limestone **roadway**, three metres wide and more than sixty metres long, heading away inland, no doubt towards Ayía Triádha and Festós. The road is rutted from the passage of ox-drawn carts and would also have been pounded by the feet of countless Minoan mariners. Note the drainage channel on its northern side. To the south of the road one building contains the longest stretch of Minoan wall on the island: over fifty metres of dressed stone. The function of this enormous building isn't known but it may well have had a storage purpose connected with the port. Just south of this was another large building (now partly overlaid by a later Greek structure – probably a warehouse), 30m long and 35m wide, divided into five sections with its seaward end open to the sea. This was a shipshed or **dry dock** where vessels were stored out of the water during the winter (or non-sailing) season.

An interesting **temple** lies to the western side of this area, nearest the sea. Here an early tenth-century BC Dorian temple – one of the earliest in the whole of Greece – was replaced by a later one, apparently devoted to a pillar cult similar to that of the Phoenicians who had founded a trading empire based upon modern Lebanon. The excavators think that the Phoenicians may have erected the temple here for use by their sailors who would have made frequent trading missions to Kómmos. The other remains and altars in this area date from the Hellenistic period when the site became a revered sanctuary. When fully excavated and opened to the public, Kómmos may well emerge as among the most important Minoan sites yet explored.

Léndas and Kalí Liménes

South of the Messará, two more beach resorts – Léndas and Kalí Liménes – beckon on the map. Léndas has a couple of buses a day from Iráklion and in an undeveloped way is quite a busy place. Kalí Liménes, for reasons which will become apparent, is hardly visited at all. If you have your own transport, the roads around here are all passable but mostly very slow: the Kófinas Hills, which divide the plain from the coast, are surprisingly precipitous and even on the paved roads you have to keep a sharp eye out for sudden patches of mud, potholes and roadworks (the only halfway decent road to the coast here is the one from Górtys to Léndas via Mitrópolis; follow the signs carefully). Other than the direct Léndas–Iráklion service, public transport is very limited indeed – you'll almost always have to travel via Míres.

Léndas

Many travellers who arrive in **LÉNDAS** think they've come to the wrong place. The village at first looks filthy; the beach is small and rocky; and the rooms are frequently all booked. Quite a few leave without ever correcting that first impression. For the real attraction of Léndas is not here at all but beyond the point to the west, 3km or so along the coast road. Here you come upon an enormous sandy beach, where three good taverna/bars, each with a few basic rooms, overlook the sand from the roadside and tents and makeshift shelters provide accommodation for many more down on the sand. This beach is almost entirely nudist, and largely German-speaking (all the menus are written in German).

Once you've discovered why Lendás is so popular, the village itself begins to look slightly more welcoming. If it remains a rather scrappy and primitive place, that's the way it is. The bus drops you in a sandy yard which also serves as a car park for those who drive – from here you pick your way down to the beach as best you can. There is no proper street, and the few paths which look promising mostly end up in someone's back garden to the outrage of a barking dog or rooting piglet. But at least the village has most of the facilities you'll need, including a shop which will change money and sells newspapers and souvenirs, a couple of food shops, numerous places to eat (including *Taverna Iris*, with a long-distance phone available 8am–noon & 2–10pm), and several bars (the *Pink Panther* serves pizzas and cocktails).

If you want to **stay** you'll see all the options pretty much straight away – some of the newer ones, like *Lendas Bungalows* on the village "square", are relatively luxurious. Perhaps the nicest of the **tavernas** is the light blue place around to the far right of the beach. Out at the good beach (if you're walking, you can save time by cutting across the headland), the third and newest of the places, *Taverna Sifis*, has the best rooms, though it's also the most expensive.

East of Léndas, you can also explore some smaller, near deserted beaches, and the hilltop remains of ancient **Levín** (or Leben) overlooking them from immediately outside the village. This was an important healing sanctuary, with at its centre an *Asklipion* by a spring of therapeutic waters; people were still coming here for cures as recently as the 1960s when the spring was diverted and the site became neglected. At its height, from the third century BC on, the sanctuary maintained an enormous temple and was a major centre of pilgrimage. You can still see ruins spread over an extensive area, but sadly, little of their nature can be discerned. There's an arch through which the water once flowed, otherwise only the odd segment of broken wall survives, along with a few severed columns or statue bases, and isolated fragments of mosaic. Much closer in, just above the main part of the village, are the more substantial remains of an early Christian basilica, with a much smaller eleventh-century chapel still standing in their midst.

Kalí Liménes

Leaving Lendás **to the west**, past the beach, you can follow a mostly unpaved road along the coast all the way to Kalí Liménes. It's a very bumpy drive, but far from impossible, and on the way you'll pass a number of smaller beaches. The only one of these with any sort of permanent habitation is PLATIÁ PERÁMATA, a sandy little village with a couple of stores, a few basic rooms and usually the odd camper. It's really not the best of beaches, though. In each of the last two bays before Kalí Liménes small rooms places have recently opened above little beaches; the first a very basic affair of bungalow/shacks, the second slightly bigger.

KALÍ LIMÉNES itself was an important port in Roman times, the main harbour of Górtys and the place where Saint Paul put in, as a prisoner aboard a ship bound for Rome, in an incident described in *Acts 27*. He wanted to stay the winter here, but was overruled by the captain of the ship and the centurion acting as his guard: setting sail they were promptly overtaken by a storm, driving them past Clauda (the island of Gavdhós) and on eventually to shipwreck on Malta.

Today Kalí Liménes is once again a major port – for oil tankers. Which has rather spoilt its chances of becoming a resort. Personally, I like the place: the constant procession of tankers gives you something to look at (they discharge their loads into tanks on an islet just offshore); there are a number of places offering **rooms** (including the excellent *Kanavourissia Beach*, a kilometre or so east of the main village where the road from Pómbia arrives); the coastline is broken up by spectacular cliffs; and as long as there hasn't been a recent oil spill the beaches – lined by shacks, a couple of which serve simple food and drinks – are reasonably clean and almost totally empty. But it has to be said that it's a long way from the postcard image of Crete.

Back towards Míres

Heading **back to the Messará** you're in for a bit of mountain driving, and total contrast once you hit the plain on the far side. Leaving Kalí Liménes, don't attempt to drive out of the west end of the village or you'll soon grind to a halt on precipitous rocks: the road inland heads off a short way east, back towards Léndas. At PIGAIDÁKIA you rejoin tarmac for the very steep hairpin descent to PÓMBIA, a large agricultural centre. Beyond here you can either head straight on to Míres or take a left turn for PETROKEFÁLI (where there's a simple pension should you want to stay) and the short route towards Mátala. Touring around here, through quiet and prosperous villages surrounded by their crops of oranges, pomegranates or olives, is a wonderfully peaceful contrast to the traffic of the main road.

Across the south: to Áno Viánnos and Árvi

The road **east across the Messará**, from Áyii Dhéka through Asími to Áno Viánnos in the shadow of the Dhíkti mountains, may finally be paved all the way by the time you read this; a process which has taken years and at the time of writing was still not complete. Assuming it has been finished it should be an enjoyably empty drive – there are no buses across, very little traffic of any kind in fact – although there's not a great deal to stop for along the way.

From **Iráklion** the road cuts across the centre of the island, through ARKALOHÓRI, to join this route at MÁRTHA and continue through Áno Viánnos towards Ierápetra. In this direction there are a couple of daily buses, but you'll still have to change or hitch the final stretch if you hope to hit the coast before Mírtos.

The coast: Tsoútsouros and Keratókambos

Coming across the island, the first point at which you can head down to the coast comes shortly before SKINIÁS: thirteen kilometres of trail which wind alarmingly down to **TSOÚTSOUROS**. This is not an effort I would particularly recommend, for Tsoútsouros, despite its apparent isolation, is amazingly developed. Who it is that occupies the place and how they get here is a mystery – nevertheless the small grey beach can barely cope.

Far better to hold out for **KERATÓKAMBOS**, a tranquil fishing village 10km along a terrible coastal trail from here or a similar distance by a much better route from the main road. The road down, via the highly picturesque village of HONDRÓS, is now paved, which no doubt bodes development. For the moment, though, Keratókambos remains tiny and quiet, very much a locals' resort. A single street of houses interspersed with cafés and tavernas faces a tree-lined sand and shingle beach with a shower on it. Two of the tavernas rent out a few **rooms** which must be among the most basic in Crete: stone cells with a couple of cots and no washing facilities at all. For more luxury you could retrace your steps two kilometres or so to the point where the road emerges at the coast – this is Kastrí Keratókambos and here you'll find *VE Rooms*. If you do stay, or you want to **camp** in isolation, you could explore better patches of deserted sand along the coast road in either direction.

Áno Viánnos

Moving on, the **coast road** gets better as you head towards Árvi, passing beneath a great crag of rock with a ruined castle perched upon it. Again, however, the direct approach is the turning off the main road, heading first through the large village of **ÁNO VIÁNNOS**, clinging to the southern slopes of the Dhíkti range. The air is much sharper up here, even in high summer, and the eating fare more substantial than on the sweltering beaches far below. On my last visit in early August, I pulled into the square and an old lady led me by the arm to her daughter's taverna where I was sat down in front of a plate of steaming lamb stew. It tasted fine. The traditional centre of this part of southeastern Iráklion province, Áno (or upper) Viánnos' importance has waned as the coastal settlements have grown. But it's still a substantial village with a couple of interesting churches containing well-preserved fourteenth-century frescoes. These, Ayía Pelayía and Áyios Yióryios, are located up a narrow, stepped side street close to the enormous plane tree on the village's eastern extremity.

The Ierápetra road leads east out of the village, skirting an alarming precipice, and continues on through AMIRÁS, where you turn off for Árvi by a giant memorial to Cretans killed in the last war. A paved road winds gradually down to sea level and emerges on the coast through the gorge of a stream which waters the exotic fruits grown around Árvi.

Árvi

Standing on the site of the ancient Roman town of Arvis, and hemmed in by rock cliffs which trap the heat – creating a microclimate among the hottest in Crete – **ÁRVI** has surprisingly not been overwhelmed by development. This may have something to do with a long but pebbly beach and the villagers' greater interest in the wealth to be made from growing bananas, oranges and pineapples in this near-tropical environment. There are **rooms**, but not always enough in high season: try the *Hotel Ariadne* (☎71-300), near the entrance to the village with balcony sea views, or the slightly cheaper *Gorgona* or *Rooms Galaxy* (☎71-373), towards the centre. Failing these, follow the usual street-corner signs. Once you've settled in there's not much else to do apart from baking in the sun, which is something you can often do comfortably here even when the rest of the island is too cold to contemplate it. When you need shade, there are numerous shops, bars, cafés and tavernas behind the beach; there's even a **bank**. On the hillside that overlooks the village lies the monastery of Áyios Andónios which now has only a couple of monks in residence.

Along a bumpy track **to the east** lie more isolated beaches leading eventually to the coastal hamlets of FAFLÁNGOS and, after 6km, AKROTÍRI SIDONÍA, which has a superb beach although no rooms or other facilities. It should be possible to **camp** here, but be aware of local sensitivities: these are not resorts but ordinary villages on the sea. Some maps don't mark it, but the dirt track continues to TÉRTSA and MÍRTOS (p.142), some 12km in all which makes a pleasant walk.

travel details

Buses

Iráklion–Réthimnon/Haniá (1hr 30min/3hr; old road 2hr/5hr) 25 daily from 5.30am to 7.30pm, a couple of them via the old road.

Iráklion–Ay. Nikólaos (1hr 30min) 24 daily, 6.30am to 9pm.

Iráklion–Sitía (3hr 30min) 5 daily, 8am to 5.30pm.

Iráklion–Ierápetra (via Ay. Nikólaos; 2hr 30min) 8 daily, 7.30am to 6.30pm.

Iráklion–Áno Viános/Ierápetra (2hr 30min/ 3hr) twice daily, 6.30am and midnight.

Iráklion–Hersónisos/Mália (45min/1hr) every half-hour, 6.30am–9pm.

Iráklion–Milátos (1hr 30min) 2 daily, 8.30am and 3pm.

Iráklion–Ay. Pelayía (30min) 4 daily, 8.45am–5pm.

Iráklion–Arhánes (30min) 12 daily, 7am–8.30pm.

Iráklion–Plateau Lasíthi (2hr) 2 daily, 8.30am and 2.30pm.

Iráklion–Festós (2hr) 10 daily, 6.30am–5.30pm.

Iráklion–Mátala (2hr) 7 daily, 7.30am–4.30pm.

Iráklion–Ay. Galíni (2hr 30min) 9 daily, 6.30am–5.30pm.

Iráklion–Léndas (3hr) 2 daily, 10am and 1.30pm.

Iráklion–Anóyia (1hr) 6 daily, 6.30am to 4.30pm.

Iráklion–Fódhele (1hr) 2 daily, 6.30am and 2pm.

Iráklion–Omalós (4hr 30min) daily at 5.30am.

Mália/Hersónisos–Plateau Lasíthi (1hr 30min) daily at 8.30am.

Some of these services are restricted on Sundays

Ferries

To Pireás (12hr) 2 daily, at 6.30pm and 7pm.

To Thíra (2hr 30min fast boat/4hr) at least once daily, early morning.

To the Cyclades daily to Thíra, Íos and Páros; most days to Míkonos and Náxos; at least twice weekly to Tínos, Skíros, Skíathos and Anáfi.

To Kárpathos/Rhodes (10hr/12hr) Wed 2am, Fri 7am.

To Rhodes (11hr) Thurs 2am, Sun 3am.

To Thessaloníki Tues, Thurs & Sat 7pm.

To Limassol (Cyprus) and Haifa (Israel) (28hr/ 36hr) Tues & Fri 9am.

To Alexandria (27hr) Every 8 days.

To Venice (63hr) Every 8 days.

To Ancona (56hr) Tuesday midnight.

To Marmaris (39hr) Sunday midnight.

These are summer timetables – schedules severely restricted in winter

Planes

To Athens (50min) 7 daily.

To Thessaloníki (1hr 30min) 2 a week.

To Rhodes (40min) daily.

To Thíra/Míkonos (40min/30min) 3 a week.

To Páros (45min) 3 a week.

Summer timetables – no island flights and others restricted in winter

ΑΓ ΠΕΛΑΓΙΑ	Αγ Πελαγία	Ay. Pelayía
ΑΜΝΗΣΟΣ	Αμνήσος	Amnísos
ΑΝΩ ΒΙΑΝΝΟΣ	Ανω Βιάννος	Ano Viánnos
ΑΡΒΗ	Αρβή	Arví
ΑΡΧΑΝΕΣ	Αρχάνες	Arhánes
ΒΑΘΥΠΕΤΡΟ	Βαθύπετρο	Vathípetro
ΓΙΟΥΧΤΑΣ	Γιούχτας	Yioúhtas
ΓΟΥΡΝΕΣ	Γούρνες	Goúrnes
ΓΟΡΤΥΣ	Γόρτυς	Górtys
ΗΡΑΚΛΕΙΟ	Ηράκλειο	Iráklion
ΚΑΛΟΙ ΛΙΜΕΝΕΣ	Καλοί Λιμένες	Kalí Liménes
ΚΕΡΑΤΟΚΑΜΠΟΣ	Κερατοκάμπος	Keratokámbos
ΚΝΩΣΟΣ	Κνωσός	Knossós
ΛΕΝΤΑΣ	Λέντας	Léndas
ΜΑΛΙΑ	Μάλια	Mália
ΜΑΤΑΛΑ	Μάταλα	Mátala
ΜΟΙΡΕΣ	Μοίρες	Míres
ΤΣΟΥΤΣΟΥΡΟΣ	Τσούτσουρος	Tsoútsouros
ΤΥΛΙΣΟΣ	Τύλισος	Tílissos
ΤΥΜΠΑΚΙ	Τυμπάκι	Timbáki
ΦΑΙΣΤΟΣ	Φαιστός	Festós
ΦΟΔΕΛΕ	Φόδελε	Fódhele
ΧΕΡΣΟΝΗΣΟΣ	Χερσόνησος	Hersónisos

CHAPTER TWO

LASITHI

Eastern Crete, at least in the minds of most visitors, is dominated by **Áyios Nikólaos** and the mass tourism it attracts. Travellers who come here to see a more traditional face of the island tend not to look on the area with much favour. But while Áyios Nikólaos itself is undeniably overcrowded, it can also be a lively and exciting base, whilst the countryside roundabout – the **Lasíthi Plateau** and **Krítsa** in particular – are worth a good few days of anyone's time.

Things improve, too, as you move towards the **far east** of the island, which is under the sway not of Áyios Nikólaos but of **Sitía**, a large and traditional town where tourism has had little outward effect. At the eastern tip the Minoan palace at **Zákros** and the laid-back beaches around **Vái** offer wildly contrasting escapes.

Along the **south coast**, there is generally far less development, though **Ierápetra** and its environs would win few beauty prizes. Not far away, however, at **Mírtos** and **Ayía Fotiá** for example, there are beaches as good as any in the province.

THE LASÍTHI PLATEAU AND ÁYIOS NIKÓLAOS

The **northwestern corner of Lasíthi** may be the gathering ground for almost all the province's visitors, but it's not just about resorts. Stay for a few days in the **Lasíthi plateau** and you experience a very different world; make your way east along the coast to **Goúrnia** and you can enjoy one of the best minor Minoan sites in near isolation. And at **Áyios Nikólaos**, of course, there is genuine fun to be had, in what is perhaps Crete's most cosmopolitan enclave.

Transport, at least along the main roads, is excellent. There's a constant stream of buses between Iráklion and Áyios Nikólaos, stopping at major points en route, and good local services from both Áyios Nikólaos and the inland centre of Neápoli.

Mália to Áyios Nikólaos

Driving into Lasíthi from Mália you've a choice of route. The **new road** is fast and wide. Leaving the palace at Mália behind, it embarks almost immediately on the long climb inland – rising at first through the **Gorge of Selinári** where travellers would traditionally stop at the chapel and pray to Saint George for safe passage. There's still something of a truckstop here, but most traffic roars straight past and on through the tunnel blasted beneath the old pass. It's a tremendous engineering achievement, though beyond – having bypassed Neápoli – there's little else to see until you emerge high above Áyios Nikólaos to spectacular views of the Gulf of Mirabéllo.

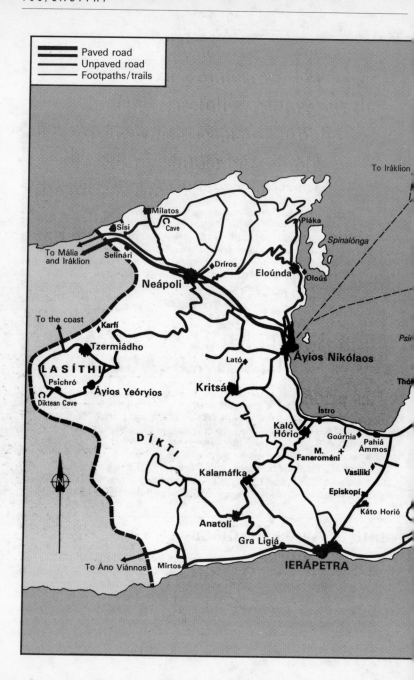

Paved road
Unpaved road
Footpaths/trails

To Iráklion

Mílatos
Sísi
Cave
Pláka
To Mália
and Iráklion
Selinári
Spinalónga
Oloús
Dríros
Eloúnda
Neápoli
Psír
To the coast
Karfí
Tzermiádho
Lató
Áyios Nikólaos
LASÍTHI
Psichró
Áyios Yeóryios
Kritsá
Thó
Diktean Cave
Ístro
Kaló
Hório
DÍKTI
Goúrnia
Pahiá
Ámmos
M.
Faneroméni
Kalamáfka
Vasilikí
Episkopí
Káto Horió
N
Anatolí
Gra Ligiá
To Áno Viánnos
Mírtos
IERÁPETRA

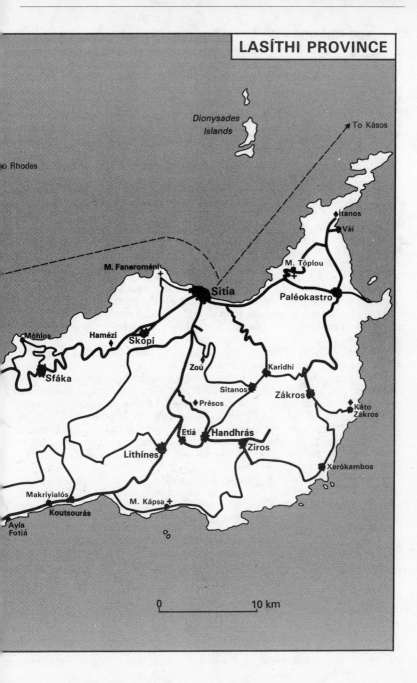

LASÍTHI PROVINCE

Dionysades Islands

To Rhodes

To Kásos

Sítanos

Vái

M. Faneroméni

M. Tóplou

Sitía

Paléokastro

Móhlos

Hamézi

Skopí

Zoú

Karídhi

Sfáka

Sítanos

Zákros

Présos

Káto Zákros

Etiá

Handhrás

Lithínes

Zíros

Xerókambos

Makriyialós

M. Kápsa

Koutsourás

Ayía Fotiá

0   10 km

Sísi and Mílatos

The **old road** follows the coast for a while longer, rolling on through Sísi with a branch off to Mílatos. **SÍSI** is becoming developed, but for the moment this amounts only to scattered apartments, and the local beaches remain quiet and small-scale. EPÁNO SÍSI, the village on the road, has one or two possibilities for rooms but a more tempting stop is SÍSI PARALÍA, 2km away on the coast. Here a tiny harbour is overlooked by some slow-moving tavernas. However, new construction work on the western side of the lovely cove means that the tranquillity may not last. Scattered around the village are numerous **rooms**, or there's *Camping Sísi*, just over a kilometre to the west, with its own swimming pool and plenty of shade.

MÍLATOS remains almost untouched, possibly because of its uncomfortable pebble beach (sun beds for hire). Once again **rooms** are available both in the village and at the beach settlement 2km away. Here, two tavernas, a shop and little else hug the seafront – the *Mary-Eleni* taverna specialises in reasonably priced fresh fish. Though you'd never guess from what remains today, **ancient Mílatos** has a distinguished story and the glory of a mention by Homer in the *Iliad* as one of the seven Cretan cities that sent forces to fight at Troy. In mythology (backed up by recent archaeological finds) it was also from Mílatos that Sarpedon, King Minos's brother whom the king had defeated to take the throne, sailed to found Miletus – destined to become one of the greatest of all the cities in Asia Minor. Unlike its namesake in modern Turkey, however, little has survived on the site to the east of the beach. The city faded into obscurity in antiquity and by Roman times no longer existed (see Dríros below).

There's more recent history to be seen at the **Mílatos Cave**, 3km east of the village and signed up a good dirt road. More a series of caverns than a single cave, this appears to go back for miles: with adequate lighting you might be able to discover just how far. Less adventurously, there's a small chapel right at the entrance, a memorial to the events which earned the cave its notoriety. Here in 1823, during one of the early rebellions against the Turks, some 2700 Cretans (that at least is the number claimed) took refuge, were discovered and besieged in the cave. Eventually, having failed to break their way out, they were offered safe conduct by the Turkish commander – only to be killed or taken away into slavery as soon as they surrendered.

Beyond the cave, you could continue around the Áyios Ioánnis peninsula, or across to Neápoli, by a variety of dirt roads. Back through Mílatos village, however, the scarcely used paved road to Neápoli is an equally beautiful, and certainly an easier, way to zigzag through the mountains.

Neápoli and Dríros

NEÁPOLI, despite its size, history (Pope Alexander V was born here) and location, sees virtually no tourists other than those who stop for a coffee in the square between buses or as they drive through. A charming provincial town, it was formerly the capital of Lasíthi (a role now usurped by Áyios Nikólaos) and remains the seat of the local government and of the provincial courts. There's a small museum (rarely open, but ask and someone will be found to let you in) as well as a cheap D-class **hotel** (the *Neapolis*), various other **rooms**, and, around the square, tavernas, *kafenía* (try *soumadha*, a local almond drink), post office and banks. It's a peaceful place to stay, and it is from here that one of the roads up to the Lasíthi Plateau (see following section) sets out.

Continuing instead towards Áyios Nikólaos you very soon pass a turning signed towards **Dríros**, a route that curls steeply up above the old and new roads (which here run almost exactly parallel). Following the signs you eventually come to a dead end beneath a rocky hillside, and scrambling up you'll find ruins of the ancient city – its earliest remains dating back to the eighth century BC. A canopy covers the **Temple of Apollo Delphinios**, one of the earliest temples known in all of Greece. It was dedicated to a cult that celebrated Apollo transformed into a dolphin, a guise the god used when guiding Greek sailors. That the chief sanctuary of Miletus in Asia Minor was devoted to the same cult is further evidence of a link between this area and the founding of the colony there. In the centre of the temple can be seen the remains of a sunken hearth. Here were found three hammered bronze statuettes (among the earliest known) as well as two Eteocretan inscriptions (Greek letters used to write a Cretan, possibly Minoan tongue). Finding anything else of note among the thorny bushes and ruined dry-stone walls roundabout is virtually impossible – and deciphering it once you do is even harder. Nevertheless, if you make it to the top of the hill the views make the climb worthwhile, whilst the drab desolation all round is a startling contrast to the green country around Neápoli.

If you've come this far and want to continue east by the most scenic possible route, take the road through KASTÉLLI, FOURNÍ – with its dramatic entry road lined with eucalyptus trees – and PÍNES, which winds down to Eloúnda with yet more wonderful views of the Gulf of Mirabéllo.

The Lasíthi Plateau

Scores of coach tours toil daily up to the **LASÍTHI PLATEAU** to view its famous sea of white cloth-sailed windmills. Most must leave disappointed, for few of the mills remain in operation, and even these operate only for limited periods. Even if you see none unfurled at all, however, the trip is still worth making for the drive alone, and if you're into mountains this is a great place to stay.

From Neápoli a long and winding road, twenty slow kilometres of it, climbs into the mountains which ring the plain. When you finally come upon the plateau laid out below you, it seems almost too perfect – a patchwork circle of tiny fields enclosed by the bare flanks of the mountains. Closer to it's a fine example of rural Crete at work, with every inch given over to the cultivation of potatoes, apples, pears, cereals and almost anything else that could conceivably be grown in the cooler climate up here.

The area has always been fertile, its rich alluvial soil washed down from the mountains and watered by the rains which collect in the bowl. In spring there can be floods, which is why the villages all cluster on the higher ground around the edge of the plain, but in summer the windmills traditionally come into use pumping the water back up to the drying surface. Although the plateau was irrigated in Roman times – and inhabited long before that – this system was designed by the Venetians in the fifteenth century, bringing the plain back into use after nearly a century of enforced neglect (during which time cultivation and pasture had been banned after a local rebellion). Where they survive, the windmills have barely changed since then. In the past twenty years or so, however, most have been replaced by more dependable petrol driven pumps. The other windmills – the stone ones standing guard on the ridges above the plain, also mostly ruined – were traditional grain mills.

Come on a day trip and you will see all this. Stay overnight and you'll see a good deal more, as the tourists leave and a great peace settles over the plateau. The excesses of Mália or Áyios Nikólaos seem a world away as you climb into your cot to the sound of braying donkeys and a tolling church bell outside, and wake to the cock's crow the next morning. If you feel inclined to rise with the lark you'll see a diaphanous white mist floating over the plain and its windmills in the sparkling early morning sun. Ideally you'd arrive at either end of the season: in late spring the pastures and orchards are almost alpine in their covering of **wild flowers**, an impression reinforced by the snow lingering on the higher peaks; in autumn the fruit trees can barely support the weight of their crop, and the villagers seem not to know what to do with the mountains of produce they have cultivated. Whatever time of year, though, bring some warm clothing. The nights get extremely cold.

The villages

A paved circular road links the villages on the plateau's edge. **TZERMIÁDHO**, the largest and most important of them, comes complete with post office, OTE, a number of cafés and tavernas, and even a couple of hotels (the *KriKri* is cheap and comfortable). Whichever point you arrive at on the circuit you'll be assailed by villagers encouraging you to buy their handmade rugs and embroidered work. If you're tempted to buy, don't jump at the first opportunity; the other villages further on usually offer better quality for lower prices. And don't be afraid to bargain.

From the road on the edge of Tzermiádho there's a sign up to the **Trápeza Cave**, in which Evans and Pendlebury discovered assorted remains and tombs going back to Neolithic times. If you don't take up the offer from one of the many elderly "guides" who may accost you en route, you'll need to look out for a slope on the left where the track narrows. Follow this to the top and be alert for the narrow, unmarked cave entrance. As you wander in the murky darkness (a torch is essential) it's easy to imagine that this is where Crete began: Stone Age peoples huddled around fires no doubt telling stories in the manner of primitive tribal groups today. From these modest beginnings sprang the Minoans and then, under their tutelage, the Greeks.

From Tzermiádho there's also an ascent to the ancient site of **Karfí**, perched on the southeast slope of Mount Karfí. Ask in the village for directions to the start of the track which is located near the health centre. The climb will take a good hour and you'll need sturdy footwear. When you reach it you'll find a site, founded around the eleventh century BC, spread across a saddle between two peaks. In this enclave the Minoans attempted to preserve vestiges of their culture, now threatened by the Dorian advance. Amongst the ruins (excavated by Pendlebury in the 1930s) it's not easy to make out a shrine where the clay goddesses now in the Iráklion museum were found – nor to make much sense of the dwellings intersected by a number of paved alleyways. But this desolate settlement is certainly atmospheric and the descent offers fine views over the plateau.

Clockwise from Tzermiádho, the next village of any size is **ÁYIOS KONSTANTÍNOS**, which is where the Neápoli road emerges on the plain. Here, too, you could find a **room** if you wanted one, and because it is the first (and last) village most people meet, it is packed with souvenir shops. Watch out particularly for a priest and his wife selling embroidered fabrics: these two could sell ice to Eskimos.

ÁYIOS YIÓRYIOS, next in line, is larger and less commercial. Given the choice, I'd stay here for the most authentic of welcomes. There's a small and entertaining **Folk Museum** (daily, summer only, 10am–4pm), which also contains a fascinating photo-biography of Crete's great writer, Níkos Kazantzakís. Excellent value rooms and food (and home-made wine) are to be had at the *Hotel Dias* (☎31-207), or try the *Hotel Rea* (☎31-209), along the street, if this is full.

Whichever village you stay in you can catch the **bus** as it circles the plain (or hitch quite easily between villages), or more enjoyably walk through the fields from one to another. The path is rarely direct, but it's easy enough to pick your way by the trails – even right across the plain, from Psihró to Tzermiádho, is a bare hour and a half's walk.

Most people's destination is **PSIHRÓ**, base for visiting Lasíthi's other chief attraction, the Dhiktean cave. Here there are a couple of more expensive pensions and restaurants but also some traditional (if rather dingy) village rooms – try the *Dikteon Andron*. If you find everything full – as is likely during the big local festival over the last three days in August – there's an unofficial campsite by the *Taverna Panorama* (you're expected to eat there) at the western end of the village.

The birthplace of Zeus

The **Dhiktean Cave** (Tues–Sat 8am–6pm, Sun 10am–4pm) lies just past the village, up a trail for which mules are on offer but which is in reality neither particularly long nor dauntingly steep. According to legend it was in the Dhiktean Cave that Zeus was born to Rhea. His father, Kronos, had been warned that he would be overthrown by a son and accordingly ate all his offspring. On this occasion, however, Rhea gave Kronos a stone to eat instead and left the baby concealed within the cave, protected by the Kouretes who beat their shields outside to disguise his cries. From here Zeus moved to the Idean Cave, on Psilorítis, where he spent his youth (p.161). That at least is the version generally told here, and though there are scores of variations on the myth, it is undeniable that the cave was a cult centre from the Minoan period on, and that explorations around the turn of the century retrieved offerings, to the Mother Goddess and to Zeus, dating through to Classical Greek times.

If you resisted the guides at the bottom of the path you'll find them more persistent still at the entrance to the cave. Whatever they say, a guide is not compulsory, and in the middle of the day there are so many tours going through that there is plenty of light and commentary to be had without one. However, if you have neither torch nor an extremely lurid imagination, a guide is not a bad investment. It takes long experience and a Cretan eye to pick out such intimate details as the nipples the baby Zeus sucked on from the rest of the stalactites and stalagmites. Hokum aside, though, when you look back from the depths of the cave towards the peephole of light from the world you have left behind, framed in a blue haze caused by the damp atmosphere, it's not hard to believe that this may well have been the infant Zeus's first sight of the world destined to become his kingdom.

Two general points. To avoid the crowds and savour the cave's mystical qualities to the full, try to arrive before noon. Also watch out for damp and extremely slippery stones underfoot on the way down: non-slip shoes are essential.

Áyios Nikólaos

Sited on the picturesque Gulf of Mirabéllo, "Ag Nik", as **ÁYIOS NIKÓLAOS** is known to the majority of its English-speaking visitors, was originally the ancient port for Lató, one of the dominant cities of this area in Hellenistic times. This settlement faded in the Roman period and seems to have been abandoned in Byzantine times. The Venetians built a fortress here – of which nothing remains – and gave the surrounding gulf its name Mirabéllo ("lovely view"). The town came slowly back to life and by the nineteenth century the port was again busy. After union with Greece in 1913, Áyios Nikólaos was confirmed as the capital of Lasíthi Province. A quiet harbour town for most of this century, it was discovered in the Sixties by international tourism and later by the BBC, who used the resort as a backdrop for its series *Who Pays the Ferryman?*

The attractions were – and are – obvious: a setting on a small, hilly peninsula around a supposedly bottomless lake, now connected to the sea to form an inner harbour. It is wonderfully picturesque, and it knows it. Exploitation of the beauty is the order of the day: the lake, the harbour and the coast all around are jostled over by restaurants, bars and hotels, all of them charging well above the odds and packed solid with tourists from May to September. If you're after clubs, crowds and expensive souvenirs, then this is the place for you. But if you're looking for a beach, forget it – the few small patches of sand are either closely guarded by expensive hotels or standing room only by the time you've finished breakfast.

The phone code for Áyios Nikólaos is ☎0841

Practicalities

Arriving, you'll get a far better impression of Áyios Nikólaos if you come by ferry and can walk straight into the centre of town where it's at its prettiest. The **bus station** is very much on the low-rent side of town, where the concrete modernity is at its most apparent and the traffic noise never stops. Arriving here – or driving in on the one-way system – head up the hill to Platía Venizélou, and then down into the picturesque areas past the souvenir shops which line both Koundoúrou and 28 Oktovríou. The lake marks the centre of town in every way, and the narrow bridge over its channel is a notorious bottleneck for traffic and strolling visitors. From here Aktí Koundoúrou curves around the sides of the harbour, and M. Sfakianáki strikes over a small hill to the cove of Kitroplatía. Almost all the action in Áyios Nikólaos takes place around these streets.

Rooms

Wherever you arrive, you should take a **room** straight away if you are offered one. They are almost impossible to come by in mid-season – in any price range – and the later it gets, the worse your chances. Once established, you can set out on the long trek to find something better for the next day or the day after that. One factor in your favour is that there are literally thousands of rooms, scattered all about the town.

The possibilities **around the bus station** are fairly obvious. You cannot, for example, miss the *Atlantis* (☎28-964) right in front of you, or the various "Rooms"

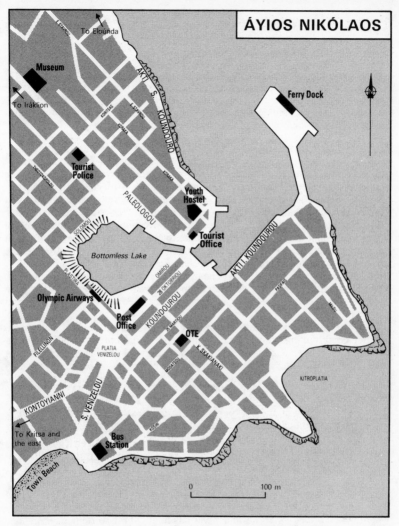

ÁYIOS NIKÓLAOS

To Eloúnda

Museum

To Iráklion

AKTI S. KOUNDOUROU

Ferry Dock

Tourist
Police

PALEOLÓGOU

Youth
Hostel

Tourist
Office

Bottomless Lake

AKTI I. KOUNDOUROU

Olympic Airways

Post
Office

KOUNDOUROU

28. OKTOVRIOU

OMIROU

OTE

PSAROS

MAOU

PLATIA
VENIZELOU

K. SFAKIANAKI

FILELLINON

KITROPLATIA

KONTOYIÁNNI

S. VENIZELOU

To Kritsa and
the east

Bus
Station

Town Beach

0   100 m

signs up the alleyways behind the ticket office. If you don't mind the noise of the
early buses and the general scruffiness of this area there are many others: retrace
the path your bus took and you'll emerge on Kontoyiánni where the large *Hotel
New York* (☎28-577) often has places, albeit not particularly good value.

Across town you may have to search longer, but rooms up in the (relatively)
older parts of the town to the north and west are generally a great deal better.
Right in the centre of town – and perhaps the best chance of a bed if everything
appears booked up – lies the **youth hostel**, at Stratigoú Kóraka 3 (☎22-823).
Despite its excellent position this is extremely grim, very much a last resort.
Further up Kóraka, and in the other streets parallel to Paleológou as it runs up the

hill out of town, are many of the **best of the room options**. The higher you climb, the cheaper these will be. Best of the bunch is the excellent *Pension Marilena* at Erithoú Stavroú 14 (☎22-681). Others worth a try are *Pension Katerina* (☎22-766), at Stratigoú Koráka 30, and *Pension Perla* (☎23-379), nearby at Salaminos 4.

Should all these fail, try the **tourist office** (☎22-357), back down by the bridge: they're open from 8.30am to 10pm and claim to list every room in town. They will also **change** cash and travellers' cheques at fair rates. In high season Áyios Nikólaos is a place where **ringing ahead** will save a lot of toil and sweat.

Food

At least when it comes to **eating** there's no chance of missing out altogether, even if the prices are often fancier than the restaurants. There are tourist oriented restaurants all around the lake and harbour: two facing each other across the bridge, the *Pizzeria* and the *Café Bar Stelios* (with cheap omelettes and "English" breakfasts) have kept their prices surprisingly reasonable, while if you want to pay for a good meal the places around the Kiroplatía are generally fair value. But mostly what you're paying for is the location. Slightly back from the harbourside here is *Trata*, at the end of Sfakianáki, still moderately priced with a tempting roof garden for sultry nights. Further back along the same street, at the junction with Pasifais, lies a real gem: *O Vios Einai Oneirou* ("Life is Beautiful"). This new *ouzerí*/taverna is the creation of a woman architect, carpenter and chef, Maro Dayiantis. She not only decorated the restaurant but made all the furniture for it as well. There's an elegant plant-filled terrace beside the main room and superb music.

The streets **around Platía Venizélou** back towards the bus station are another good hunting ground for economy food. The *Itanos*, up a side street on the east side of the square, serves Cretan food and wine and has a terrace across the road outside. Going down the hill along El Venizélou towards the bus station you'll find the equally good value *Posidon* on the right, and over the road the *Taverna Roumeli*, specialising in grilled fare.

Action

After you've eaten, you can start to get into the one thing which Áyios Nikólaos undeniably does well: **bars and nightlife**. Not that you really need a guide to this – the bars are hard to avoid, and if you want to carry on you can just follow the crowds. Among the places for a **quieter drink** is the *Hotel Alexandros* on Paleológou, with a rooftop bar overlooking the lake. Great views, reasonably priced cocktails and frequent live music here. The *Café Kastro*, among the disco bars on Koundoúrou harbourside, is a surprisingly civilised haven of sanity where Greek professionals unwind at various hours of the working day. Another place for a pleasant drink around midnight when the crowds have gone are the cafés along the lakeside. *Café Takis* seems to stay open the latest, around 3.30am if you can survive that long.

Quiet drinking, however, is really not what it's all about in the more popular places, all of which are packed and deafening. Among the **disco bars** to try are *Lipstick* and *Bora Bora*, on Koundoúrou harbourside, for standard Eurodisco sounds; *Skyline*, nearby, specialising in theme nights, and *Jimmy's*, in the second left off Sfakianáki, with English DJs and fanatical teenyboppers, provide the main opposition. There are more bars to try at the bottom of 25 Martíou (known as "Soho Street") where it heads up the hill, among which are *Tequila* and *Aquarius*.

Each year Áyios Nikólaos also mounts a summer-long **cultural festival**, "the Lato", which includes music, dance and theatre from Crete, Greece and elsewhere. Keep an eye out for posters advertising the various events or ask at the tourist office.

Necessities

One of the advantages of being in such a major resort is that the practical things of life are easily taken care of: you can change money until late at night, buy books and newspapers, send letters home, and generally sort yourself out. The **OTE** office, open till midnight, is on N. Sfakianáki just above 25 Martíou; the **post office** is on 28 Oktovríou above the lake, and **Olympic Airways** are not far away, looking down over the lake from the west (Plastíra 20; ☎22-033). For information about **ferries** out, the main agent is *Massaros Travel*, on Koundoúrou not far from the post office (☎22-267); other **travel agents**, for local tours, are all around. **Bike hire** – from dozens of outlets mainly in the harbour area – tends to be very expensive in season when demand is huge: away from the summer months shopping around might bring you a real bargain. Try *Adonis* on Akti Koundoúrou or *Mike Manolis*, who has a pitch at the junction of 25 Martíou and Sfakianáki near the OTE, for cheaper alternatives. **Boat trips** to points around the gulf mostly leave from the west side of the harbour just below the youth hostel, and if you walk around here and along Akti Koundoúrou northwards you'll be assaulted by their operators.

The Town

Things to do in town by day are pretty limited – you're not supposed to have recovered from the night before so soon. There's the museum (see below), but for most visitors the days are taken up strolling the area around **Lake Voulisméni** – allegedly over 60m deep – nosing around in the shops, and heading for the strips of **beach**. In the little cove at Kitroplatía there's a rocky foreshore from which you can swim; north of town by the *Dolphin* taverna you'll find a narrow length of gritty sand; or there's a municipal beach (with entry fee) beyond the bus station on the south side of town. This at least is clean and sandy, but again it's terribly crowded. Most people simply end up diving off the rocks which line the foreshore north of town, or else they get out altogether: the sandy beach of ALMIRÓS is 2km south and there's a constant stream of people walking there; further in this direction by bus or bike there are good beaches around Kaló Hório, or in the other direction around Eloúnda (see following sections). The boat trips to beaches around the bay are also popular, and usually enjoyable.

The Archaeological Museum

The **Museum** (Tues–Sat 8.30am–3pm, Sun 9.30am–2pm) is modern and well laid-out, and as ever it will mean a lot more after you've visited a few sites in the area. Following some interesting Neolithic finds in Room 1, you come to Room 2 and the museum's star exhibit, the extraordinary **Goddess of Mírtos**. This goose-necked early Minoan (c.2500 BC) clay figurine – actually a jug – was found in the excavation of the superbly sited Bronze Age settlement at Fournoú Korifí, near Mírtos. Note the pubic triangle, breasts and the square panels thought to portray a woven garment. The beak-spouted jug she's holding (which is also the vessel's mouth) is similar to vases in the museum from the same period. In Rooms 1 and 2 are also displayed some fine examples of **Vasilikí ware**, named after the early Bronze Age site on the isthmus of Ierápetra where it was first discovered. The lustrous mottled finish of this pottery was achieved by uneven firing, an effect which obviously pleased its creators. Even more remarkably, these flawless artefacts – including a "teapot" and a beak-spouted ewer dating from around 2500 BC – were made not with the wheel, but on the clay "turntables" exhibited in Room 1. The potter's wheel only reached Crete some six hundred years later and you can see an early example in Room 2 from a tomb at Kritsá.

Room 3 displays some fine Marine-style pottery which, although found in a villa near Makriyialós, is thought to have come from the Knossós workshop. Also here is some interesting **jewellery**, including a beautiful gold pin bearing an intricately crafted bramble motif and a long inscription in Linear A on the reverse. The message, could we but understand it, would no doubt be as fascinating as the jewel. In the same room is a wonderful collection of Late Minoan clay sarcophagi or *larnakes* decorated with birds, fish and the long-tentacled octopus which seems to have delighted the Minoan artists. The archaeologists assumed, when they turned up these items, that they were all burial chests. But when they turned up more of these painted tubs with clearly identifiable plug-holes in the bottom the Minoans had the last laugh – they were obviously avid bathers.

Room 4 contains a rare Minoan infant burial displayed exactly as found at its site at Kryá, near Sitía. Dating from the Late Minoan period, the transferring of the whole thing from site to museum by Kostis Davaras "without displacing a single stone" must have been some headache. Finally, in Room 7, there's an eerie grinning skull from the Roman cemetery at Potamós, on the edge of Áyios Nikólaos, to send you on your way. A wreath of gold olive leaves is still in place about its crown as was the silver coin – originally in the mouth of the deceased – now displayed separately in the case. This was the traditional fare paid to the boatman Charon, who ferried the dead across the River Styx to the underworld.

The Gulf of Mirabéllo

North of Áyios Nikólaos the swankier hotels are strung out along the coast road – flashest of them the *Minos Beach* with its bungalows, private pools and jealously guarded beach – with upmarket restaurants, discos and cocktail bars scattered between them. Among them, and by way of contrast to this hedonistic beach life, a signed road leads off to the right towards the sea and the Byzantine church of **Áyios Nikólaos**, from which the modern resort takes its name. To get in you'll need to enquire at the tourist office back in town for the key, but should you make the effort you'll be rewarded with some of the earliest fresco fragments found in Greece, dating back to the eighth or ninth century. The geometric patterns and motifs that survive are the legacy of the Iconoclastic movement, which banned the representation of divine images in religious art.

Soon after this the road begins to climb above the **Gulf of Mirabéllo**: looking across, Psíra and Móhlos can be made out against the stark wall of the Sitía mountains, while nearer at hand mothballed supertankers are moored among the small islands sheltering in the lee of the peninsula. One of the largest of these islets, ÁYIOS PÁNDES, is a refuge for the island's wild goat, the *kri-kri*. The animals have an elusive reputation, carefully avoiding the cruise parties from Áyios Nikólaos which put in to see them.

Oloús and Eloúnda

The road drops back down to sea level as it approaches Eloúnda. Before you reach the centre of the village, however, there's a track signed off to the right to the "sunken city" of OLOÚS. This leads down to a natural causeway which is the only link between the peninsula of Spinalónga (often known as "big Spinalónga" to distinguish it from the more famous island of the same name) and the mainland. All around the causeway on both sides you'll find people swimming from small patches of beach or basking on flat rocks. Protected by it are the remains of Venetian salt pans, now fallen into disrepair. Oloús itself lay around the far end of the causeway and along the coast to the right. Though it is known chiefly for having been the port of Dríros, what little remains is Roman: there's a fenced enclosure behind a small taverna in which you can see the floor of a Roman basilica with an odd, almost patchwork-style black and white mosaic; and among the rocks a little further round (watch out for sea urchins) are the sunken traces of harbour installations. The site has never been excavated, however, and this is about the extent of what survives. If it weren't for the beaches, the excursion would hardly be worth it. On the far side of the peninsula there are better beaches still – tough to get to except by boat.

ELOÚNDA, though it's a fair-sized resort these days, with one very exclusive hotel (the *Elounda Beach*) and scores of new apartment developments, is a very different proposition from Ag Nik – low-key and slow moving. At its heart is an enormous square with cafés, shops and hotels on three sides, the seafront promenade on the fourth. This is where you park if you've driven, it's where the bus stops, and it's also where the boats to Spinalónga leave from. Just about everything else in Eloúnda is in the immediate vicinity. Post office, OTE, bank and car rental can all be seen as you stand in the square, and there are even a few **rooms** advertised, though finding a vacancy is another thing. However, Chronis Daskalakis, the manager of *Olous Travel* (☎41-324), next to the post office, promises that he will find a room for any travellers who come to him at the price they want to pay, whatever the season. You can quote the *Rough Guide* on this! The agency also serves as a local information office

Spinalónga

The great majority of people visiting the fortress rock of **SPINALÓNGA** leave from Eloúnda (though there are also boats direct from Áyios Nikólaos and from Pláka) and it is certainly the most convenient way of getting there, with reasonably priced caiques making the trip every half-hour or so.

The islet was fortified by the Venetians in 1579 to defend the approach to the Gulf and more particularly the sheltered anchorages behind the peninsula of Spinalónga. Like their other island fortresses it proved virtually impregnable and was handed over to the Turks only in 1715, by treaty – some fifty years after the rest of Crete had surrendered. The infamous part of the island's history is much more recent, however. For the first fifty years of this century, Spinalónga was a leper colony, the last in Europe. Lepers were sent as outcasts – long after drugs to control their condition had rendered such measures entirely unnecessary – to a colony primitive in the extreme and administered almost as if it were a detention camp. Its jail was frequently used for lepers who dared complain about their living conditions.

Even today there's an unnerving sense of isolation when the boat leaves you here, at a jetty from which a long tunnel leads up into the fortified centre. There are still just two easily sealed entrances: this tunnel, and a jetty on the seaward side (which you see if you approach from Áyios Nikólaos) which leads up to the old castle gate with its Lion of Saint Mark. Around the base of the castle a real town grew up – Turkish buildings mostly, adapted by the lepers using whatever materials they could find. Although everything is in decay, you can still pick out a row of shops and some houses which must once have been quite grand.

Pláka

The colony's mainland supply centre was at **PLÁKA**, about 5km north of Eloúnda, and if you ask at *Manoli's Taverna* there you can still get someone to run you across to the island, whose settlement is clearly visible across the narrow strait. Pláka itself remains a very quiet spot. There are three or four tavernas, of which *Manoli's* serves fresh fish at reasonable prices and a couple of the others rent out cheap **rooms**. There's beautifully clear water and a beach on which the pebbles are rather too large for comfort. Only at weekends, when locals come to escape the crowds elsewhere, does the place lose its tranquillity – and even then it's quieter than anywhere else around. Walking, you could continue to the point of the cape in around an hour and a half, following the road almost as far as the next village, VROUHÁS, before taking off along a track above the sea.

Kritsá and Lató

The other excursion everyone from Áyios Nikólaos takes is inland to Kritsá, a "traditional" village about 10km away. Despite the commercialisation, this is a trip well worth making for a break from the frenetic pace of Ag Nik; buses run at least every hour from the main station. Along the way two sites delay you, each worthy of a visit.

Panayía Kirá

About 1km before Kritsá the road runs straight past the lovely Byzantine church of **Panayía Kirá** (Mon–Sat 9am–3.15pm, Sun 9am–2pm; closed Fri), inside which is preserved perhaps the most complete and certainly the most famous set of Byzantine frescoes in Crete. Of the three naves (the buttresses and lantern are later additions), the larger, central one is the oldest, though the frescoes have all been retouched and restored to such an extent that it is impossible to say with certainty which is the most ancient. All of them originate from the fourteenth and perhaps early fifteenth centuries. Those in the south aisle, through which you enter, depict the life of Ann, mother of Mary – her marriage to Joachim, the birth of Mary – and the early life of the Virgin herself up to the Journey to Bethlehem. In the centre of the church Mary's story is continued and there are scenes from the life of Christ including the Nativity, Herod's banquet and a superb Last Supper. And in the final aisle there are vivid scenes of the Second Coming and Judgement, along with the delights of Paradise and assorted interludes from the Lives of the Saints (especially Saint Anthony). Throughout, the major scenes are interspersed with small portraits of saints and apostles. Alongside the church is a small taverna and a shop selling excellent, but expensive, reproduction icons.

Lató

Just beyond the church you can turn off towards the second of the detours, the archaeological site of **LATÓ** (daily 8.30am–3pm), about 3km up a well-signed dirt road. Although there's as much to be seen here as in many of the more cele-brated sites it's very little visited: presumably because most visitors' interests are directed to the Minoans, and this was a much later settlement, Doric in origin but flourishing through to Classical times. Even the archaeologists shared this lack of curiosity, for systematic excavation of the site started only in 1967 under the French School.

The city's name derives from a Cretan Doric corruption of Leto, the mythical mother of Artemis and Apollo. Homer relates in the *Odyssey* how Eileithyia (the Minoan goddess of childbirth) attended Leto when she gave birth to the god Apollo on the island of Delos: it is thus fitting that Eileithyia became the patron goddess of Lató, as coins turned up in the excavations here proved. That it was an important city is clear from the sheer extent of the ruins, which the more you wander around, the more you realise spread in every direction. It is a magnificent setting – this city of sombre grey stone sprawled across the saddle between the twin peaks of a, dauntingly craggy hill – and standing on the peak you can look down onto the white cluster of Áyios Nikólaos (Lató's ancient port), with the bay and Oloús, a major rival of Lató in its heyday, beyond, or inland to the valleys and climbing peaks of the Dhiktean mountains. Ruins aside, these views would be

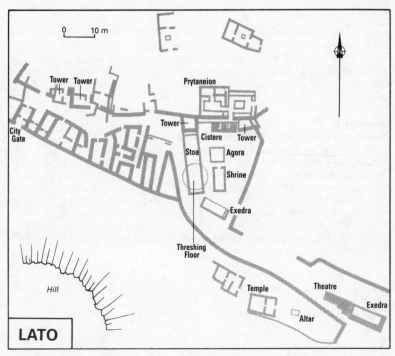

0   10 m

Tower Tower

Prytaneion

City Gate

Tower

Cistern   Tower

Stoa   Agora

Shrine

Exedra

Threshing Floor

Hill

Temple

Theatre

Exedra

Altar

LATO

worth the sweat getting up. The exposed position can't have been all that practical, however, and wearing a toga must have been a hazardous business in the fierce summer winds which gust from all directions.

You enter the city, artificially, by stepping straight over the broken defensive wall into its very heart. The open area of the **agora** is an interesting fusion of early Greek and older Minoan influences. This pentagonal space was a meeting place for citizens but also incorporates a tier of steps on its northern side, reminiscent of the theatral areas at Minoan sites such as Knossós and Festós. The steps ascend between the remains of two towers to the **prytaneion**, or town hall, with small rooms at the rear which held the city's archives. In the centre of the agora is a deep square cistern and a shrine, flanked on the western side by a colonnaded **stoa**, a shady place to converse or shelter from the elements. The southern end of this has been cut through by a relatively modern circular threshing floor. The **exedra** nearby was a sort of public seating area. In the southeast corner of the site is another exedra with what is termed a "theatral area" beside it – a broad flight of steps again similar to the Minoan style – which leads to a raised terrace containing a well preserved fourth-century BC temple with a stepped altar just before it.

To the east, a stepped path leads downhill to a rectangular area with a gateway which would have been the original entrance to Lató. Climbing back up the street you can see the shops and workshops abutting the city wall on the right, with defensive towers and gateways into the residential areas on the left.

Kritsá

If you wanted, you could retrace your steps from Lató to where the track divides, and then turn right to head down to FLAMOURIANÁ on the Lakonía plain, from where there's a paved road (and buses) back to Áyios Nikólaos. Most people head for **KRITSÁ**, however. Always a sizeable place (known as "the largest village in Crete"), Kritsá has in many ways suffered from its own popularity and its fame as a handicrafts centre. Nowadays it feels more like a small town, with every street lined with tourist shops selling (mostly) leather goods or embroidery. Despite the commercialism prices are a great deal better than in Áyios Nikólaos – though you can still pay as much as £400 for some of the wonderful, elaborately woven rugs – and if you manage to avoid the tour bus crowds (early morning and mid-afternoon are the best times) the place reverts to a friendly semi-somnambulance in which you're free to wander and browse under no pressure at all. Kritsá's other chief claim to fame lies in its situation, with views back over the green valley up which you arrived and the mountains rising steeply behind. You get little impression of this at street level, other than an awareness that you are climbing quite steeply, so try to get out onto one of the balconies at the back of the cafés along the main street, where you can look back over the town and towards Áyios Nikólaos.

Staying in Kritsá is a surprisingly easy and attractive option. There are usually beds to be found – certainly more chance than on the coast – and it's an ideal place to stay close to the action but also get something approaching a genuinely Cretan atmosphere. A number of places offer **rooms**. A start can be made at *Pansion Kera*, up the hill on the right from the bus stop on the main street. The proprietor here will provide information about other rooms if she is full, or simply ask around in the street outside. There are plenty of decent places to eat too, many of them regular targets of "Greek Nights Out" from Ag Nik. If you want to explore further, you'll find more frescoed churches here and in the immediate surrounds. **Áyios Yíoryios**, for example, is on the edge of the village, signed uphill to the left as you walk through: the frescoes here are contemporary with those at the Panayía Kirá, though in a very much worse state of preservation. Further in this same direction, **Áyios Ioánnis** lies a kilometre or so down the road to KROÚSTAS. These churches will probably be locked – enquire as to accessibility from the guardian at the Panayiá Kirá.

South to the Isthmus

The main road south and then east from Áyios Nikólaos is not a wildly exciting one – a drive through barren hills sprinkled with villas and above the occasional sandy cove. Beyond the beaches at ALMIRÓS and AMOUDHÁRA there's little temptation to stop until you reach the cluster of development around **KALÓ HÓRIO**. Here there are two good tavernas just above the road, and a little further on a *Mini-Market* and a few houses. Below them paths wind down, quite steeply, to a couple of excellent small beaches. On the first of them there's a taverna by the outflow from a small river. Immediately beyond is ÍSTRO, where the *Istron Bay Hotel* hangs from the cliff above a spectacular cove with a fine sandy beach. If you walk confidently through the hotel grounds you can get down to enjoy this and the hotel's beach bar: there's no such thing as a private beach on Crete, but apparently nothing to prevent all the approaches being privately controlled.

Five kilometres further on, a track is signed on the right for the **Moní Faneroméni**. The track is a rough one and climbs dizzily skywards for 6km, giving spectacular views over the Gulf of Mirabéllo along the way. The view from the monastery itself, when you finally arrive there, must be among the finest on Crete. To get in to the rather bleak-looking monastery buildings, knock loudly (and repeatedly if necessary). When you gain entry you will be shown up to the chapel, built into a cave sanctuary where a sacred icon of the Virgin was miraculously discovered, the reason for the foundation of the monastery in the fifteenth century. The frescoes, although late, are quite brilliant – especially that of the Panayía Theotókou, the Mother of God. The monk who unlocks the chapel has been known to be a little mean with the time (and electric light) you need to view the artworks – more time can usually be "purchased" with a discreet contribution to monastic funds.

Gourniá

Back on the coast road, another 2km brings you to the site of **GOURNIÁ** (daily 8.30am–3pm), slumped in the saddle between two low peaks. A look at the map tells you much about ancient Gourniá's strategic importance, controlling the narrow isthmus with its relatively easy communication with the southern seaboard at modern Ierápetra. The overland route avoids a hazardous sea voyage around the eastern cape – a crucial factor in ancient times, especially in winter when sailing usually stopped because of rough seas.

This is the most completely preserved of the Minoan towns, and in its small scale contains important clues about the lives of ordinary people and perhaps about the nature of the communities from which the palaces evolved. The desolation of the site today – you are likely to be alone save for the sleeping guard –

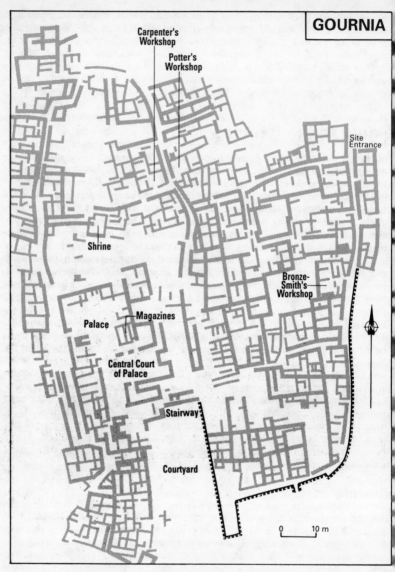

GOURNIA

Carpenter's Workshop

Potter's Workshop

Site Entrance

Shrine

Bronze-Smith's Workshop

Magazines

Palace

Central Court of Palace

Stairway

Courtyard

0   10 m

only serves to heighten the contrast with what must have been a cramped and raucous community three and a half thousand years ago.

There is evidence of occupation at Gourniá as early as the third millennium BC, but the remains you see today are those of a town of the New Palace period (c. 1500 BC). Around 1450 BC, as happened elsewhere, the town was destroyed by fire. A limited rebuilding occurred during the era of Mycenaean rule at

Knossós and the shrine may date from this late period. But the site was soon abandoned again and disappeared beneath the soil where it lay unsuspected until the awakening of archaeological interest in the nineteenth century. Evans, as usual, was the first to scent Minoan occupation of this area and then a young American, Harriet Boyd-Hawes, started digging in 1901. The site, a budding archaeologist's dream, made her reputation.

The narrow, cobbled alleys and stairways – built for pack animals rather than carts – intersect a throng of one-roomed houses centred on a main square and the house of a local ruler or, more likely, governor. The settlement is not a large place, nor impressive by comparison with the palaces at Knossós and elsewhere, but it must have been at least as luxurious as the average Cretan mountain village of even twenty years ago. Among the dwellings to the north and east of the site are some which have been clearly identified, by tools or materials discovered, as the **homes of craftsmen**: a carpenter, a smith and a potter. It's worth remembering that the rooms may not have been as small as they appear – many of these are in fact basements or semi-basements reached by stairs from the main rooms above, and the floor plans of those did not necessarily correspond with what you see today. The houses themselves were mainly built of stone on the lower courses and mud brick above, with plaster-daubed reeds for roofing.

The **palace** (or governor's quarters) occupied the highest ground, to the north of a courtyard containing a familiar L-shaped stairway. With a smaller court at its heart, the whole is a copy in miniature of the palaces at Knossós or Festós. About twenty metres to the north of the palace a **shrine** was discovered. It is easily identified by the sloping approach path paved with an intricate pattern of evenly matched cobbles. The shrine itself, up three steps, is a small room with a ledge for cult objects. Here were unearthed a number of terracotta goddesses with arms raised, as well as snake totems and other cult objects, now on display in the Iráklion museum.

Across the island: Pahiá Ámmos and Vasilikí

It is tempting to cross the road from the Gourniá site and take one of the paths through the wild thyme to the sea and a swim. Don't bother – this seemingly innocent little bay acts as a magnet for every piece of floating detritus dumped off Crete's north coast. If you backtrack a little you could head instead to the rather bizarre **campsite** of *Gournia Moon*, with its own small cove and beach. There's almost as much junk washed up here, but at least the people who run the site make an effort to clear it up, and there's a campsite café/shop.

There is a much larger beach, as well as rooms to rent and tavernas, at **PAHIÁ ÁMMOS** in the next valley. As you climb the road above Gourniá, be sure not to miss looking back over the site, its street plan laid out like a map. Even its best friends wouldn't describe Pahiá Ámmos as an attractive town, but this windswept mess of concrete does possess an eccentric Greek charm. However, the **pollution** problems mentioned above are, sad to say, even worse here. Apparently local political battles have stymied a grand clean-up plan (with huge moles to keep out the junk) and much of the time it is positively dangerous to swim here. A close look at the sea should convince doubters. That said, should you still wish to stop over, Pahiá Ámmos at least has every basic facility you're likely to need (including a large supermarket) and your stay may be enlivened by a coastal freighter loading up in the small port.

This is the narrowest part of the island, and from here a fast new road follows the ancient route through the Monastiráki gorge **towards Ierápetra** in the south. To the left the awesome slopes of the Thriptí range bear down on the road until some 3km along it you reach a turnoff for **VASILIKÍ** on the right. The archaeological site (permanently open) is visible from the main road, with an entrance from the lane a short distance down on the left.

This Pre-Palatial settlement, dating from about 2650–2200 BC, may not be much to look at, but it's important for the light it throws upon the hazy millennium preceding the Minoan great period. Remains from this period occur at Knossós and other palaces but cannot be properly excavated because of the important buildings constructed on top of them. Vasilikí was the first of these early sites to be found in a pristine condition, due to its being abandoned after a fire about 2200 BC.

The site contains two main buildings, originally surrounded by numerous smaller (and simpler) dwellings. The remains of the edifice nearest to the entrance, on the lower slope of the hill, are slightly earlier than that on the crown. The **Red House**, as the former is named, has a number of interesting features. It is orientated with its corners towards the cardinal points of the compass, a practice normal in Mesopotamia and the Near East but alien to Egypt and the Aegean (a clue to Minoan origins?). In the southern corner deep basement rooms allow you to gain an idea of early Minoan building techniques: holes to support the absent wooden beams are visible as well as large patches of hard, red lime plaster, the forerunner of what later artists were to use as the ideal ground for the wonderful palace frescoes. This material gives the dwelling its modern name. The pottery known as Vasilikí ware, orange or red with dark, blotchy decoration, takes its name from this site where the fine examples on display in the museums at Iráklion and Áyios Nikólaos were discovered.

Unless you wish to continue on up the lane into the village of Vasilikí, for another glimpse of rural Crete, the main road continues towards Ierápetra via EPISKOPÍ, almost exactly halfway across the isthmus. Here, below the road beside a pleasant raised *platía* where old men play backgammon in the shade of eucalyptus trees, lies a charming blue-domed Byzantine church. The arched drum dome with elaborate blue tile decoration, together with an unusual ground plan, make this church unique on the island. Entry is difficult due to the continued absence of the *papás* who apparently possesses the only key, but anyway it's the church's exterior which gives it its standing in Byzantine architecture.

The road's next stop is Ierápetra, 7km further (p.138).

THE FAR EAST

The far east of Crete marks yet another dramatic change in scenery and tempo. Although much of it is rocky, barren and desolate, it is an area of great natural beauty. With the exception of **Ierápetra**, a scruffy and oddly crowded resort, the towns and villages are slower and quieter, life conducted at an easier pace. **Sitía**, in particular, seems a contented city unperturbed by its visitors. The north coast has few beaches, and in the main the mountains drop straight to the sea (the drive towards Sitía is as dramatic as any in Crete), but there are a couple of coves which are just about accessible, and beyond Sitía, as the heights tail away, there's more opportunity for swimming. The far east is much visited only in two spots –

the overrated palm beach at **Vaí** and the superb Minoan palace at **Zákros**. Away from these it's a great area for escapists. On the south coast there are a number of excellent sandy beaches: at **Makriyialós**, at **Ayía Fotiá** and the coast east of Ierápetra, and at **Mírtos**.

Bus connections and main roads continue to be good: there are very frequent rapid services from Áyios Nikólaos to Ierápetra, and equally good connections along the north coast to Sitía. Onwards from Sitía it's easy enough to continue to Vái or Zákros or to cut back south to Ierápetra, and from Ierápetra – rather less readily if you're relying on public transport – you can carry on west, across the centre of the island, to Iráklion.

The road to Sitía

Beyond the isthmus, the tawny bulk of the Sitía mountains makes a formidable barrier to further progress and the road at first is carved into the cliff face, teetering perilously above the gulf. The views back become more expansive all the time, until at PLÁTANOS you reach a famous viewpoint, with a couple of tavernas where you can sit and stare down on the island of Psíra, the site of a Minoan settlement, or west across the gulf to Áyios Nikólaos. Past here the road runs further inland, emerging only occasionally to glimpses of the sea far below.

Of the tempting beaches you see many are inaccessible, although THÓLOS, where there's a quiet beach but not much else, can be reached 4km down an asphalted road.

Móhlos and Psíra

A more inviting alternative is **MÓHLOS** – and this involves tackling five or more kilometres of dusty hairpin bends. There is no bus connection down to the coast, which leaves you with the options of a taxi or walking. Shortest of the routes down is a dirt track signed soon after Plátanos, but you may have difficulty persuading the bus to stop here, and it is also the least attractive route, past a large quarrying operation. There are equally obvious ways to follow down (in one and a half hours or less) from the villages of SFÁKA, TOURLOTÍ (a trail not marked on the maps) and MIRSÍNI, all of which are standard halts for the bus. The Sfáka road is now mostly asphalted (if potholed) and the way to go if you have transport. You could also get to Móhlos by boat from Áyios Nikólaos – a regular trip in summer which includes a stop at Psíra.

Tiny and out of the way as it is, Móhlos has plenty of tavernas (serving excellent fish) as well as two small hotels, *Sofia* (☎94-179) and *Mochlos* (☎94-205) and numerous houses which rent out **rooms**. There are some new hotel developments, too, but fortunately these are far enough out not to affect the village much. Not that the place is wholly unspoilt: rooms are surprisingly expensive and often booked up in high season, and some of the bars and tavernas much fancier than you'd expect. This appears to be mainly because American teams are still excavating on the islet offshore, and they and their followers often spend whole summers here, occupying most of the available space. No matter, the atmosphere remains sleepy and there's plenty of space if you need to camp out, plenty of rather rocky foreshore to swim off during the day.

The **islet** looks within swimming distance – and it is when the weather is calm – but it's easier to arrange a ride with a local fisherman if you want to go over. Inhabited from the Pre-Palatial period, in Minoan times this barren rock was almost certainly a much less barren peninsula, and the sandy spit linking it to the mainland would have been used as a harbour (anchorages which could be approached from either side were a great advantage for boats that could sail only before the wind). You can see remains of late Minoan houses on the south side of the island, and there are more below the current sea level where recent excavations have also identified remnants of the ancient harbour. But the important discoveries at Móhlos were in the much more ancient tombs built up against the cliff. Here were found very early seal stones (including one from Mesopotamia), some spectacular gold jewellery (now in the Iráklion museum), and a fine collection of marble, steatite and rock crystal vases (Áyios Nikólaos and Sitía museums).

The larger island of **PSÍRA**, this time genuinely offshore, was also a Minoan port, and here the remains are of a town a little like Goúrnia but built amphitheatrically around a good natural harbour. It was first excavated in 1907 by an American, Richard Seager, who revealed a settlement which again was occupied from the early Minoan era. During the Neo-Palatial period, this community of merchants, sailors and fishermen shared in the general prosperity of the time. A long, stepped street climbs away from the harbour and most of the dwellings here have a hearth in one of their rooms. No palaces or obvious public buildings were discovered but the site has produced rich finds of painted pottery. One jar, now on display in the Iráklion museum, is noted for its decoration of bulls' heads interspersed with the double axe symbol. Trading with overseas areas such as Egypt and the Levant must have been necessary to import the essential requirements of life to such a parched, infertile place. The remains of what is thought to be an ancient well have been found – although the island is completely dry these days. The site was another of those destroyed about 1450 BC: later the Romans used the island for strategic and navigational purposes, and you can still make out the remains of their lighthouse and military settlement on the island's crown. As with the islet, you should be able to arrange a ride over to Psíra with a fisherman, or you could take a more organised visit from Áyios Nikólaos.

Heading back from Móhlos to the main road involves a more serious walk, of two hours or more, which you might want to bypass by taking – or with luck sharing – a taxi.

The final stretch

From here to Sitía the road, lined with a riot of pink oleander flowers in summer, continues to toil through villages clinging to the mountainside, now high above a deserted bay, now enfolded by mountains, until the final approach to the city, and a descent in great loops through softer hills. As you progress, the familiar olive groves are increasingly interspersed with vineyards and there are some fine local wines to be had in the village cafés (especially in ÉXO MOULIANÁ). Most of the grapes, however, go to make sultanas: in late summer, when they are laid out to dry in the fields and on rooftops all around, the various stages of their slow change from green to gold to brown make a bizarre spectacle.

Of the villages en route, **MIRSÍNI** has an attractive church built around, and entirely enclosing, a frescoed fourteenth-century chapel. This is well worth visiting if you can find the priest to let you in.

Near to the ruined stone windmills on the final crest before the Bay of Sitía, a track is signed on the right for the ancient site of **HAMÉZI** (the village of the same name is further on). The track will eventually lead you to a Minoan site with a spectacular hilltop setting after about a fifteen-minute walk. Once on the track, take the second turning right, the one just beyond the windmills – this should bring you to a beekeeper's hut with hives stacked beside it. The fence circling the site on its conical hilltop is visible from here. Should you get lost on the way – which isn't difficult – head for the nearby village of PARASPÓRI, where the boys at *Yiordanis' Bar* will be only too pleased to direct you. *"Archaeológiki anaskafí"* are the words you need, but make sure you are heading for the hilltop site or they may think you want Ahládia (see below).

Dating from the Pre-Palatial period (c.2000 BC), this grey stone ruin has a unique importance in Minoan archaeology, for it is the only known structure to have had an oval ground plan, possibly dictated by the conical shape of the hill. It was thought at first to be a peak sanctuary, but the discovery of a cistern made a dwelling, or even a fortress, seem more likely. The ground plan sketched out by the walls – more than a metre high in places – consists of a number of rooms grouped around a central courtyard where the cistern is located. A paved entrance is visible on the south side. Whatever the building's function, it certainly had a commanding view over the surrounding terrain. While you're taking this in, keep an eye out for the rare Eleanora's falcon which breeds on the offshore island of Paximádha – the valley to the east is one of its favourite hunting grounds.

If you still have the appetite for more ruins, nearby at AHLÁDIA are the remains of an impressive *tholos* tomb dating from the Mycenaean period, as well as a Neo-Palatial Minoan villa. The **tomb** lies just to the east of the village of Paraspóri up a track to the right, whilst the **villa** lies up another track one kilometre further on. Both should be signed.

Moní Faneroméni

Further along the main Sitía road, just beyond SKOPÍ, you'll come to a track signed on the left for the **Moní Faneroméni**. Ignore this as the road is unfinished and leads only to a dead end in a ravine. The monastery is best approached by another track 5km closer to Sitía. What you'll find when you reach it is a charming monastic church overlooking a gorge near to the sea.

In many ways a metaphor for more recent Cretan history, the church has been battered but still stands unbowed. In 1829 the monastery and tiny church were looted and burned by the Turks, and most of the frescoes destroyed. The beauty of what was lost is visible from one scarred remaining fragment depicting a saint reading. The three indentations across his face are bullet holes, again Turkish. By the iconostasis hangs a curtain embroidered with a gold Greek cross which you may be tempted to peer behind. The remains of the founder here are not for the squeamish. The shoals of silver *taxímata*, or sick symbols, hung on the icon of the Virgin to implore her miraculous intervention attest to the importance of the shrine locally today – a tradition stretching back to Minoan times and probably beyond. There's a path from here, which would take you on foot to Sitía in less than two hours.

Sitía

After the excesses of Mália or Áyios Nikólaos, arriving in **SITÍA** can seem something of an anticlimax, even dull. But don't be fooled; Sitía's charms are subtle. Allow yourself to adjust to the more leisurely pace of life here and you may, like many other visitors before you, end up staying much longer than intended. The town certainly makes an ideal base from which to visit the other attractions in the region. Not even Sitía, of course, can entirely escape the tourist boom, and the increasing number of tourists attracted to the port has led to a great deal of new development at the fringes; the old atmosphere may not survive much longer. Hopefully, though, the planners will heed the lessons of mistakes made elsewhere. Many of the new visitors are French or Italian, a legacy perhaps of the French troops who garrisoned the place under the Great Power protection at the end of the nineteenth century, and the Italians who occupied during World War II.

This area was settled, as *Eteia*, in Classical times, and later there was a Roman town of some size; but very little is known of either. It was under the Venetians that the port really took off (they called it *La Sitia* – hence Lasíthi), as part of a conscious attempt to exploit the east of the island. For all their efforts, the area remained cut off by land from the rest of Crete and although what was in effect a separate fiefdom developed here, it never amounted to a great deal. Perhaps the most significant event of this era was the birth of Vicenzo Kornaros, author of the epic Cretan poem, the *Erotókritos*. More physical remains are few, prey to earthquakes and the raids of Barbarossa. Where once there was a walled city, now you'll find only the barest remains of a castle.

The town is set on a hill tumbling down towards the western end of the picturesque Bay of Sitía. Its oldest sections, hanging steeply above the harbour, look east over the bay and the long ribbon of new development along the coast. Life concentrates on the waterfront, around Platía Venizélou in the corner of the bay. North towards the port and ferry dock is a seafront promenade crowded with the outdoor tables of rival tavernas. South, the main road runs behind the beach, flanked for miles by a rambling jumble of development.

> The phone code for Sitía is ☎0843

Arrival – somewhere to stay

The **bus station** in Sitía is chaotic and you should get away from it as soon as possible. Rooms are rather scattered, but except at the busiest times you should be able to find something. There's a **youth hostel** (☎22-693), one of the better ones, at the top of Odós Therísou – you pass it on the right as you drive into town. Quiet and good value **rooms** can be found in the older streets leading up the hill from the waterfront, especially behind the OTE and in the nearby streets off Kapetan Sifi. **Odhós Kondhiláki**, which runs down the side of the OTE, has numerous possibilities. At the near end the homely *Pension Venus* (Kondhiláki 60; ☎24-307) and the unnamed *Rooms* next door are worth a try, as is Maria Hamilaki at no. 35 (☎22-768). At the far end is the pleasant *Hotel Arhontiko* (Kondhiláki 16; ☎28-172), with a mature orange tree in its front garden. Two streets up from the OTE along Sifi will bring you to *Rooms Iris* at Riga Fereou 15

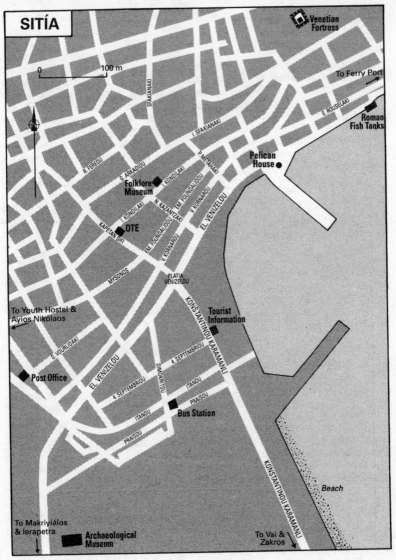

SITÍA

0   100 m

To Ferry Port

Venetian Fortress

Roman Fish Tanks

E. ROUSELÁKI

SFAKIANAKI

I. SFAKIANAKI

P. METAHAKI

Pelican House

R. FEREOU

G. ARKADIOU

K. KONDILAKI

Folklore Museum

I. KONDILAKI

N. KAZANTZAKI

EM. FOUNDALIDOU

V. KORNAROU

EL. VENIZELOU

KAPETAN SIFI

OTE

EM. FOUNDALIDOU

V. KORNAROU

MYSONDS

PLATÍA VENIZELOU

To Youth Hostel & Ayios Nikólaos

Tourist Information

G. VOURLIOAKI

KONSTANTINOU KARAMANLI

Post Office

EL. VENIZELOU

4. SEPTEMBRIOU

DIMOKRITOU

4. SEPTEMBRIOU

ITÁNOU

PRASOU

ITÁNOU

Bus Station

PRASOU

KONSTANTINOU KARAMANLI

Beach

To Makriyiálos & Ierápetra

Archaeological Museum

To Vai & Zakros

(☎22-494). To the south of the OTE there are a number of places along the more commercial **Odhós Missónos**. Paying rather more, you could stay out along the beach road where **hotels** of all types are scattered: at the beginning, around the bottom of Itánou, are a number of characterless C- and D-class places, the *Elisvos*, *Asteria* and *Elena* among them. A short walk along the Ierápetra road there's also *Pension Victoria* (☎28-080), which has a garden and communal kitchen. Finally, near to the ferry port, the *Hotel Nora* (Rouseláki 31; ☎23-017) is a friendly establishment run by women. Should you still need help, the **tourist office** (☎24-955) is at the start of the beach road.

Other practicalities

The basics in Sitía are easily attended to. There's a branch of the National **Bank** at the bottom of Odhós Sífi facing Platía Venizélou; the **OTE** is further up the same street; the **post office** over by the road into town in the triangle of streets at the end of Kornárou. **Bike rental** places are located on Itánou below the bus station. Best of the bunch is *Petras Moto* (☎24-849), who provide helmets, or try *Kazamias* (☎24-074), around the corner at Présou 2. The **ferry agent** (for boats to Kásos and the Dodecanese) is *Tzortzakis*, on the harbour front down towards the dock; **Olympic** have an office at Venizélou 56, just off the platía, for their expensive local flights to Kásos, Kárpathos and Rhodes.

The Town

Sitía is an absorbing place to wander around, doing no more than enjoying the atmosphere. The narrow streets behind the seafront are packed with the everyday happenings of a Cretan provincial town: villagers in to stock up on news and necessities and shops which cater to their every conceivable need, from steel drums to wooden saddles, seed to pick-up trucks. While you're people-watching, one thing not to be missed, especially on Sundays, is the *vólta*, when it seems that the whole town puts on its finery to parade in front of their neighbours. Get a seat around six in the evening at a table adjacent to the road behind the waterfront for this remarkable show.

You'll not be in town long, especially around the harbour area, before you bump into **Níkos**, a resident pelican who is also the town's pampered mascot. When he was first trapped in fishermen's nets some years ago, Níkos's wings were clipped to force him to stay. Now that his wings have grown again he shows no signs of wanting to leave. This may have something to do with the town council providing him with his own purpose-built house on the harbourside together with a daily supply of fresh fish. When not waddling proprietorially along the seafront greeting visitors, Níkos indulges a delinquent streak by dive-bombing bathers from a great height (he rarely hits them!), and flopping onto the sails of capsized windsurfers, making them impossible to right.

In spite of the potential hazards posed by Níkos, the heat will eventually propel you towards the beach: the **town beach** is swimmable and windsurfers are on hire from the *Black Hole* disco along the beach road. However, the better beaches are a few kilometres further east towards Ayía Fotiá – the bus to Vái will drop you off.

Aside from wandering the streets, sitting in the cafés or lying on the beach, things to do are limited. The **Folklore Museum** on Kondhiláki (Mon–Sat 9.30am–3pm) offers an entertaining look at traditional life: Adam Hopkins's book *Crete* includes a wonderful section on his stay with a family in Sitía, revealing the extent to which the old lifestyle survives to this day. If you continue north to the end of the same street you'll arrive at the restored **Venetian fort**, now used as an open-air theatre. Climbing down towards the port from here, you can see the ruined remains of some **Roman fish tanks**, just along the harbour front from the pelican's house. In these semicircular constructions, freshly caught fish were kept until they were needed.

The Archaeological Museum

To gain a clearer picture of the past, however, the **Archaeological Museum** (Tues–Sun 8.30am–3pm), on the Ierápetra road, contains an interesting collection of finds from the surrounding area and the palace at Zákros. You enter by the main room, where finds from the early Minoan cemetery at nearby Ayía Fotiá are displayed, as well as some fine stone vases from Móhlos and its island neighbour, Psíra. The **Zákros section** comes next: interesting exhibits here include a bronze saw, a winepress from a Minoan villa near the palace and a collection of sea shells. Archaeologists claim these had a sacred function, but it would be nice to think that the Minoans used them for decorative purposes as we do today – perhaps they even put them to their ears to listen to the sea.

Further on lies one of the museum's great treasures, a case full of **Linear A tablets** – so rare that many of the world's leading museums don't even have one. They were discovered by archaeologist Nikólaos Pláton in the archives room at the palace – note how the Minoan characters have been delicately scratched into the soft clay. Some show evidence of being burned by the fire which destroyed the palace, and in fact it was the fire that preserved them, for as unbaked clay tablets they would have crumbled to dust. A nearby case illustrates the **domestic life** of the kitchen, the only one so far positively identified at any palace. Among the cooking pots and other utensils there's a superbly preserved terracotta grill, probably used for cooking some form of *souvláki* – a method used in the Greek world since pre-Mycenaean times and mentioned by Homer.

After the Hellenistic and Roman sections, don't miss the barnacle-encrusted tangle of Roman pots (probably from a wreck) which has been preserved by placing it inside a fish tank of salinated water. This artistically stunning idea was the brainwave of the museum's founder, the eminent Cretan archaeologist Níkos Papadákis: his guide to the monuments of Sitía and Eastern Crete is on sale at the museum and is recommended.

Food, bars and nightlife

A line of enticing outdoor **tavernas** – the biggest of which is *Zorba's* – crowds the harbour front, many with a display of dishes and fresh fish out front to lure you in. Tempting as they are, eating at these seafront places can work out very expensive if you're not careful: though *Remegio*, just along from *Zorba's*, serves excellent food at average prices. Cheaper (and more interesting) eats are available away from the water: *Erganos*, at Dhimókratou 4 (between Venizélou and Itánou, one block inland), is a new place cooking Greek dishes with flair. If you want to mix in with the locals there's *Kali Kardia* ("Good Heart"), on Foundalídhou two blocks in from the waterfront, an *ouzerí* where you can wash down a fish *mezé* with house retsina. *Mixos*, one block nearer the sea at Kornárou 117, does traditional charcoal cooking on a spit in the street and serves it up with a very strong local wine. Further afield, another restaurant to be recommended is *Neromilos* (☎25-205), off the road to Ayía Fotiá. Housed in a converted mill high above the bay, it offers magnificent views as well as good Greco-French dishes created by the chef-owner, Panyotis. It might be worth considering a taxi to this one, as the road down can be pretty tortuous in the dark.

If you're just looking for a snack, the *Picadilly* pastry shop, on the corner behind *Zorba's*, sells excellent *tirópita* and delicious-looking chocolate cakes;

bakeries and cake shops are something of a local attraction, in fact, and there are a couple more good ones along Kornárou.

Nightlife, mostly conducted at an easy Sitían pace, centres around drinking and disco-bars. These are concentrated in two areas: up at the north end of Kornárou, and out along the beach road (officially named Karamanli). In the first group there's the low-key *Glyfada* – on the seafront after the pelican's house – whose terrace has a great view over the bay. One block in from here the louder *Kazarma* caters for a younger crowd. Closer in along the harbour, if you fancy being deafened in near-darkness, try the *Time In* cocktail bar. At the other end of town lie Sitía's two discos: the *Black Hole* (along the beach road) can be a bit lifeless if you arrive on the wrong night, and *Revans*, a new place on Vourdilaki, near the post office. Young Sitían professionals gather at their own open-air hideaway, *Status*, on the Ierápetra road, 100m past the Archaeological Museum. Here, beneath a giant palm tree – which is spotlit at night – you can sip cocktails and dance to a disco on a crazy-paving floor. Recommended for those who like their nightlife laid back, but don't arrive before ten.

During the middle of August (16–20) Sitía goes into fête, when the annual *Sultanina* or **sultana festival** marks the start of the grape harvest. The local export is celebrated with traditional music and dancing, and all the locally produced wine you can consume is included in the entrance fee to the fairground beyond the ferry port. Tickets for this are sold at a booth on the corner of the harbour, which also has tickets and information for the summer-long **cultural festival** – concerts, dance, theatre – the *Kornaria*.

Towards the east: Vái And Palékastro

Vái beach, with its famous grove of palm trees and silvery sands, features alongside Knossós, the Lasíthi Plateau and the Samarian Gorge on almost every Cretan travel agent's list of excursions. For years it was a popular hang-out for backpackers, but repeated fires followed by a clean-up campaign to attract a more well-heeled crowd have resulted in a ring fence around the beach with a guard to enforce the new regulations which prohibit overnight stays. People still claim to be able to sleep there, but it hardly seems worth the hassle. In spite of its popularity it is a really superb beach, and the trip to Vái is certainly an enjoyable one.

From Sitía the road runs along the beach, tracking a rocky, unexceptional coastline past **AYÍA FOTIÁ**, a small cove that now supports a cluster of new development. Here, in 1971, the largest Minoan graveyard yet found in Crete was excavated, revealing over 250 chamber tombs from the early Pre-Palatial period. Among the outstanding finds of vases, fish hooks, daggers and stone axes (now in the Sitía and Áyios Nikólaos museums) were a number of lead amulets which suggest that these early Minoans regarded lead as well as silver as a precious metal. The cemetery lies near to the sea to the west of the *Mare Sol* hotel.

After some 7km the road turns inland, climbing into quite deserted, gently hilly country, the slopes covered in thyme, heather and sage with the occasional cluster of strategically sited beehives. In summer the deep violet thyme flowers prove an irresistible attraction for the bees which feed on them almost exclusively, creating the much sought after *thimárisio* (thyme honey). It's worth picking a sprig for your buttonhole.

Tóplou Monastery

Not long after you leave the coast, there's a road signed up to the **Monastery of Tóplou**, which is also the short way to Vái. As you approach, the monastery looks more like a fortress, standing defiant in an otherwise empty landscape. And indeed it has a warlike history. The name Tóplou is Turkish for "with a cannon" – a reference to a giant device with which the monks used to defend themselves and uphold the Cretan monastic traditions of resistance to invaders. And they needed it. The monastery was sacked by pirates and destroyed in 1498, and in the 1821 rebellion it was captured by the Turks, who hung twelve monks from the gate as an example. In World War II it again served as a place of shelter for the resistance. The opening above the main gate harks back to these troubled times: through it the monks hurled missiles and boiling oil on those attempting to gain entry.

A forbidding exterior and grim history notwithstanding, Tóplou is startlingly beautiful within: a flower-decked, cloister-like courtyard with stairways leading up to arcaded walkways off which are the cells. The blue-robed monks keep out of the way of visitors as far as possible, but their cells and refectory are left discreetly on view. And in the church is one of the masterpieces of Cretan art, the eighteenth-century **icon** *Lord Thou Art Great* by Ioannis Kornaros. This is a marvellously intricate work, incorporating 61 small scenes full of amazing detail, each illustrating, and labelled with, a phrase from the Orthodox prayer which begins "Lord, thou art great . . .". Outside you can buy enormously expensive reproductions of the icon.

As you leave the church, take a look at the stone **inscription** set into the exterior wall. It records an arbitration by Magnesia, a city in Asia Minor, dating from the second century BC, concerning a territorial dispute between nearby Ítanos and Ierápytna (modern Ierápetra). At this time, when the Romans held sway over Crete, these deadly rivals clashed constantly and finally Rome, unable to placate the two, called in the Magnesians to act as honest brokers. The inscription records part of their judgement (in favour of Ítanos) and was placed in the monastery wall at the suggestion of the English traveller and antiquarian Pashley, when he found it being used as a gravestone in 1834.

The monastery is reputed to be incredibly wealthy – it owns most of the northeastern corner of the island – and this is no doubt how they can afford the extensive restorations which seem set to destroy the romance of the place. The sheer weight of numbers visiting doesn't help either. These days there's a monk assigned to sit outside the church judging the dress of those going in and refusing entry to anyone deemed wanting in propriety – though only women ever seem to offend him.

Beyond Tóplou the road descends towards Vái through the same arid, rock-strewn landscape as before. This area is another where you might catch a sighting of the rare **Eleonora's falcon**, which breeds on the Dionysádes islands to the north – Tóplou and Cape Síderos (a closed military zone) are regular hunting grounds.

Vái and Ítanos

VÁI BEACH makes for a thoroughly secular contrast to the spiritual tranquillity of Tóplou. Famous above all for its palm trees, the sudden appearance of what is claimed to be Europe's only indigenous wild date-palm grove is indeed an exotic shock. Lying on the fine sand in the early morning, the dream of Caribbean islands is hard to dismiss. During the day, however, the sand fills to overflowing as buses – public ones from Sitía and tours from all over the island – pour in to the car park in numbers which really can't be justified by a few palm trees. The boardwalks laid out across the sand are not there only to protect feet from the burning sand, but also to guarantee a route through the mass of baking bodies. Even the adjoining beaches, where those in the know used to hide out to escape the swarm, get pretty crowded nowadays.

The buses are packed, the beach is worse, the café and taverna charge over the odds once you've endured the long queue, you pay to have a shower or use the toilet, and still people come here to camp rough. As everywhere, notices warn that "Camping is forbidden by law", and for once they really do seem to mean it – at least within the confines of the park which protects the palm trees. However, you can climb the steps cut into the rock behind the taverna to the cove to the south, or with rather more difficulty clamber over the rocks to that to the north, and join thriving little communities at either. If you do sleep here, watch your belongings: rip-offs abound. Having endured all this you may just, for a couple of hours at each end of the day, be able to enjoy Vái the way it ought to be. Alternatively, avoid the high season if you can.

The sand may be less good, but for my money the emptiness of the three small beaches at ÍTANOS, 1.5km north of the turning to Vái, makes them far more enjoyable. There's still the odd palm tree scattered around, and if you're at a loss for something to do you can explore the remains of the ancient city here. Inhabited from Minoan times, Ítanos became important later, flourishing through the Classical Greek and Roman eras when she vied with Ierápytna (modern Ierápetra) for control of eastern Crete. One twenty-year squabble between these two led to the Arbitration of Magnesia in 132 BC, part of the stone record of which is preserved at Tóplou monastery. The settlement here remained prosperous until the medieval Byzantine era when it was destroyed, most likely by Saracen pirates. All sorts of messy ruins strewn with potsherds survive beneath the twin acropolis, but little which retains any shape. There are two early basilicas you might be able to make out, as well as the beautifully cut lower courses of a Hellenistic wall on the western hill.

Palékastro

The main road to Vái, and all the public buses, run via **PALÉKASTRO**, some 9km south. It's a pleasant little farming village and a good place to stay close to the beaches – with a couple of excellent tavernas on the main square which are worth breaking your journey for if you're simply passing through. However, the place is now starting to realise the potential of its position and tourism is expanding – there's even a rather incongruous nightclub. For accommodation, try *Hotel Itanos* (☎61-205) on the main square (not connected with the restaurant below it – enquire instead at the supermarket next door), or the *Palekastro* (☎61-235), 100m along the road to Sitía on the left. Don't be misled by a drab exterior here; the pleasant new rooms lie beyond a courtyard behind. There are also plenty of signs indicating **rooms**.

The **Minoan site of Palékastro** lies towards the beach, about twenty minutes' walk from the village. Follow the signs to the *Marina Village Hotel* and then to the beach. For archaeologists this was a very significant place, the largest

Minoan town yet discovered and the source of much information about everyday Minoan life. It is an obvious site to settle, a broad and fertile agricultural plain set on an excellent bay beneath the protection of a high, flat-topped bluff: and indeed the area was extensively inhabited both before and after the Minoan era. Much of the site is disappointing for the casual visitor, with only a few odd walls lost among the fields: many of the excavations were later infilled to protect them. Still, some of the latest excavations are open to view and offer fascinating glimpses of dwellings, stairways and streets. Try to resist entering the excavation areas through the broken fences as the delicate walls are still being made safe for posterity by the archaeologists. When you've had your fill of wandering among the olive groves seeking out some of the further-flung remnants, there are some excellent beaches not far beyond where you could easily camp out. The better sands are around the bay further to the south, but the only facilities are on the first stretch of beach you reach: a taverna by the makeshift car park where the track arrives at the coast, and another around to the left, in the shadow of the bluff.

Zákros and the far southeast

Palékastro is also the crossroads for the road south to Zákros, a beautiful drive through country where the soil is a strange pinkish-purple colour, as if indelibly stained with grape juice (although actually it's olives which grow around here). The few hamlets you pass on the way are so small that they make **ZÁKROS** (or more properly Áno Zákros) seem positively urban when finally you get there. A slow-moving little town, it boasts three or four restaurants around the square and a small hotel, the *Zakros* (☎61-284). What little trade they see, however, is almost exclusively passing through, since Káto (or lower) Zákros, and the palace, are on the coast 8km further on. Locally, Zákros enjoys a certain fame for its numerous springs which feed the lush vegetation hereabouts and which were also an attraction for the Minoans. If you follow the sign up to the right as you come into the town, or simply climb the hill from the centre, you'll reach a little chapel from where in five minutes a path leads beside the stream to its source and some pleasant, shady picnic spots.

Leaving the village by the Káto Zákros road, you'll soon pass the remains of a Minoan villa dating from the late Neo-Palatial period (c.1500 BC); here was turned up a winepress which is now in the Sitía museum. Pressing on towards the coast, a good new road winds spectacularly down to approach the small bay from the south. There are even better views if you turn left down the purple track which runs straight into the back of the village, past the palace.

KÁTO ZÁKROS is a delight. There's a pebbly sand beach, three good tavernas and a few places offering **rooms**, of which *Poseidon* (☎93-388) – on a rocky outcrop with spectacular sea view – is the best. Along with a tiny harbour with a couple of fishing boats in it, this is about all the village amounts to. Everything you really need you can find – they'll change money in the tavernas and let you use their showers and toilets, you can even make long-distance phone calls – but there is absolutely nothing else, not even a shop. Not for Club 18-30, perhaps, but ideal if it's tranquillity you're after.

Although in summer a couple of daily buses do run all the way to Káto Zákros, most transport still stops in the upper village. From here you could hitch the rest of the way quite easily, but it's also worth considering the **walk**, less than two hours to the palace via a beautiful ravine known as the **Valley of the Dead**. The easiest route traces the road for almost half an hour, before turning left onto a track which brings you out above the ravine. Getting to the bottom is something of a scramble, which may need hands as well as feet, but once you're down the trail is easy to follow along the left-hand side of the stream bed, marked by the usual red waymarks in case of confusion. It's a solitary but magnificent walk, brightened especially in spring by plenty of plant life. High in the cliff walls you'll see the mouths of caves: it is these, used as tombs in Minoan times and earlier, which give the ravine its name. At the bottom you rejoin the dirt road, which runs through groves of bananas and olives and into Káto Zákros past the palace. As an alternative you can follow the waymarked path all the way from Áno Zákros, avoiding the road altogether. This is more easily attempted on the way back, when getting lost is difficult; to find the way down, you'd have to get someone to guide you through the fields behind the village and onto the start of the trail.

The Palace of Zákros

The valley behind Káto Zákros was explored by a British archaeologist, David Hogarth, at much the same time as the other great Cretan palaces were being discovered, around the turn of the century. But Hogarth gave up the search, having unearthed only a couple of Minoan houses, and it was not until the 1960s that new explorations were begun by a Greek, Nikólaos Pláton. Pláton found the palace almost immediately, just yards from where Hogarth's trenches ended. The **palace of Zákros** (daily 9am–4pm) thus benefited from the most modern of techniques in its excavation and, having been forgotten even locally, it was also unlooted. The site yielded an enormous quantity of treasures and everyday items, including storerooms with all their giant *pithoi* still in place and a religious treasury full of stone vases and ritual vessels.

For the amateur, Zákros is also full of interest, and a great deal easier to understand than many of the other Minoan sites. Here the remains are of one palace only, dating from the period between 1600 and 1450 BC. Although there is an earlier settlement at a lower level, it is unlikely ever to be excavated – mainly because this end of the island is very gradually sinking. The water table is already almost at the palace level, and anything deeper would be thoroughly submerged. Even the exposed parts of the palace are marshy and often waterlogged – there are terrapins living in the green water in the cistern. When it is really wet you can keep your feet dry, and get an excellent view of the overall plan of the palace, by climbing the streets of the town which occupied the hill above it.

Though the palace is a small one, it can match any of the more important Minoan centres for quality of construction and materials. And it is unique in the way that so much of the town – a place very like Goúrnia – can still be made out all around. The original destruction of the palace appears to have been a very violent one, with only enough time for the inhabitants to abandon it, taking almost nothing with them. This again contributed to the enormous number of artefacts found here, but more importantly the nature of the destruction, in which the palace was flattened and burnt, is an important prop in the theory that it was the explosion of Thíra which ended the Minoan civilisation. Large lumps of pumice found among the ruins are supposed to have been swept there by the tidal wave which followed the eruption. However, many archaeologists take issue

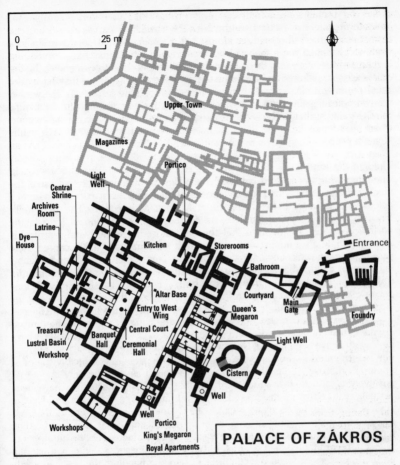

PALACE OF ZÁKROS

0   25 m

Upper Town

Magazines

Portico

Light Well

Central Shrine

Archives Room

Latrine

Dye House

Kitchen

Storerooms

Bathroom

Entrance

Altar Base

Courtyard

Entry to West Wing

Queen's Megaron

Main Gate

Treasury

Lustral Basin

Workshop

Banquet Hall

Central Court

Ceremonial Hall

Light Well

Foundry

Cistern

Well

Workshops

Well

Portico

King's Megaron

Royal Apartments

with this hypothesis and question both its chronological accuracy and the type of destruction (eg fire), seeing the palace's demise as being more consistent with human rather than natural causes.

Entrance

A paved **road** led from the site to its **harbour**, the chief reason why a palace existed here at all. The harbour installations have disappeared beneath the sea, but two large houses excavated along the road are enough to show that this must have been a significant port: the first landfall on Crete for trade from Egypt, the Nile Delta and the Middle East. Among the ruins were found ingots of copper imported from Cyprus, elephant tusks from Syria, and gold and precious materials from Egypt.

The road nowadays forms the **entrance** to the site, leading directly towards the main gateway of the palace in its eastern corner. Before entering the palace proper the remains of a foundry dating from the Old Palace period can be seen beneath a protective canopy on the left. The road then curves round into the town, passing the palace entrance to the left. Entering the palace, the **main gate** leads to a stepped ramp followed by a **courtyard** which may have served as a meeting place between the palace hierarchy and the townspeople. In the northeast corner here is a **bathroom** where visitors to the palace may have been required to wash or purify themselves before proceeding further. To the west of the courtyard lies the main or **central court**, a little over 30m by 12m, or about a third the size of that at Knossós. Crossing the north edge of the court you come to an **altar base**, with the lower courses of the west wing wall in grey ashlar stone beyond.

The West Wing

The **west wing*** is entered between two pillars and this is where, as usual, the chief ceremonial and ritual rooms were located. A **reception room** leads into a colonnaded **light-well**, the hallmark of Minoan architecture. The light-well's black stone crazy paving survives, as do the pillar bases and a drain in the northwest corner. It was here that the excavators unearthed what is arguably Zákros's single most important find: the **peak sanctuary rhyton**, a carved stone vase depicting a peak sanctuary with wild goats from which was gleaned valuable information about Minoan religion. The light-well illuminated the **ceremonial hall** beyond which lay the **banqueting hall**, originally a lavish room with frescoed walls and an elaborate floor. Pláton gave the room this name because of the large number of cups and drinking vessels discovered scattered about the floor.

At the heart of a complex of rooms behind the banqueting hall is the **central shrine** which contains a ledge and niche, similar to the shrine at Goúrnia, where idols would have been placed. Nearby is the **lustral basin**, necessary for purification before entering the shrine. Here, too, was the **treasury**, probably the most important discovery from the excavators' viewpoint as it is the only one so far positively identified. In a number of box-like compartments (which have been partially restored) were discovered almost a hundred fine stone jars and libation vessels including the exquisite rock crystal rhyton – crushed into more than 300 fragments – with its delicate crystal bead handle and collar that the Iráklion museum is so proud of. Next to the treasury in the **palace archive**, hundreds of Linear A record tablets had been stored in wooden chests. Sadly, only a handful on the top layers survived the centuries of rain and flooding; the rest had solidified into a mass of grey clay, depriving the archaeologists of potentially priceless clues in their attempts at deciphering the script. On the opposite side of the treasury is a **workshop** where pieces of raw marble and steatite were found. The remaining stone slabs most likely supported a craftsman's workbench. More workshops and storerooms lay to the west of the shrine, and one of these has been identified as a **dye-house**. And if you were wondering where the occupants of this end of the palace answered the call of nature, a lavatory with a cesspit outside the wall was found nearby. Further west, beyond the palace confines, new excavations are still going on.

---

*Actually the northwest wing, as Zákros is not truly aligned north–south. None of the major palaces, in fact, were exactly laid out on compass bearings – though others were closer than this – but for convenience the excavators always refer to the rooms on each side of the central court as the north, south, east and west wings.

North, South and East Wings

On the **north** side of the central court was the palace **kitchen**, the first to be posi-tively identified at any of the palaces. Bones, cooking pots and utensils were found strewn around the floor both here and in the storeroom or pantry next door. The **south** wing was devoted to **workshops**: for smiths, lapidaries, potters and even, according to Pláton, perfume makers – possibly a borrowing from Egypt. The **well** that serviced this area still flows with drinkable water.

Two large rooms regarded as **royal apartments** flank the **eastern** side of the central court behind a portico. The larger of the two, to the south, is called the king's room and the smaller is claimed to be that of the queen. However, one of these may have been the throne room and there would have been elaborate rooms on the first floor, possibly with verandahs overlooking the courtyard below, which might more realistically have been where the rulers lived. Next to a light-well in the eastern wall of the king's room lay the colonnaded **cistern hall** which, with its eight steps leading down to the water contained in a plaster-lined basin, may have served as a royal aquarium or even a swimming pool (if so, the only one known). It is ingeniously designed to maintain the water at a constant level with the excess draining into the **well** to the south, which lay outside the palace wall and was probably used by the townsfolk. The water from the spring was, as at Knossós, piped throughout the palace and traces of the pipework are still to be seen around the site.

Beyond these royal apartments lay other **residential areas**, but much has been destroyed by centuries of ploughing combined with frequent waterlogging of the land here. At nearby Pelikata was recently discovered the quarry from where the tufa limestone used to build the palace was taken.

Onwards: the coast

Hardly any tourist ever ventures **south of Zákros**, and indeed there's little in the way of habitation in the whole of the southeastern corner of the island, nor any public transport whatsoever. Even the boulder-strewn dirt roads seem to be left in this condition to discourage the adventurous. A little effort, however, is rewarded with excellent beaches – mostly deserted – and a challenging route by which you can circle back to Sitía, taking in an archaeological site at Présos along the way.

Leave Áno Zákros on the new road and you'll shortly reach a track to the right, with a hand-painted sign for "Ambelos and Liviko View". It's not a bad surface, descending through olive groves and giant greenhouses to run along a deep ravine. After 10km, and just when you're convinced you're lost, a brilliant turquoise sea and white sandy beaches divided by rocky outcrops appear below. The tiny village of **KSERÓKAMBOS**, a short way inland, is the place to make enquiries if you want a **room**. The village consists of one street, two tavernas and no shops of any kind, so bring essentials with you: both tavernas will provide information and keys for rooms (if available, which they may not be in August). Try ringing ahead to *Liviko View* (☎91-473), run by a couple of Greek-Australians, John and Katerina Hatzidakis. The cooking here is recommended and at week-ends they even put on the occasional *lyra* concert. Archaeologists argue as to whether this is the site of ancient Ambelos (in spite of a location of this name nearby): artefacts discovered in the area and a looted peak sanctuary certainly suggest there was a settlement of some kind here in ancient times.

Completing the circle: Zíros and Handhrás

If you are unfazed by Cretan dirt roads you can complete a circle back to Sitía via Zíros, although as the road climbs inland the going does get a good deal rougher. Make certain your vehicle is up to it – it's not the sort of area to be stranded in. As the hills enfold you all views are dominated by a giant radar dome on the mountain top, and the road itself is surrounded by "No Photography" signs. At the top of the climb the road, now tarmac, levels to a plateau surrounded by rock cliffs in the midst of which lies the fair-sized farming village of **ZÍROS**. Tumbling down a hillside towards a busy centre, it's a welcoming place with a neat platía circled by willow and acacia trees with whitewashed trunks. There's even an occasional bus to Sitía. If you come in late July, you may be lucky enough to catch the annual festival – something not to be missed. Then the women of the village produce huge trays of delicacies, which are laid out on tables in the square and washed down with gallons of *rakí* to the accompaniment of *bouzouki* and *lyra*. For quieter times there are sixteenth-century frescoes to be seen in the church of Ayía Paraskeví, but you may prefer to lazily soak up the atmosphere of this stone-country with a drink at a table in the square. In the early evening, when the rocky heights crowd in on all sides, it seems that places like Zíros are the real heart of Crete.

Gluttons for punishment could turn back onto the dirt and head down to the south coast at Goúdhouras (see below), but the easy way is via HANDHRÁS. The reasons for Zíros's size and prosperity are evident along the road out, as it cuts through olive groves and vineyards said to be among the best on the island.

A turning at Handhrás leads after 4km to **ETIÁ**, a hamlet where a ruined **Venetian mansion** stands in memorial to the glory days of the Italian city's power in Crete. Built by the Di Mezzo family in the late fifteenth century, this once elegant edifice was badly damaged in 1828 when the local populace vented their rage on the Turks who had been using it as an administrative base; nowadays the ground floor, with its impressive entrance hall and vaulted ceiling, is all that remains of the three-storey building. Because few country houses of the Venetian period survive on Crete, however, the mansion has been declared a national monument under the care of the Greek Archaeological Service.

Continuing along the Handhrás–Présos road, a lane just outside Handhrás is signed on the right for VOILÁ, a **ruined medieval village** that you can just see at the foot of the hill. With its gothic arches and silent paved streets this is a distinctly eerie place to wander round; two ornamental fountains which were a Turkish contribution to this Venetian stronghold are still functioning. The twin-naved Áyios Yióryios church, usually locked, but with an interesting sixteenth-century gravestone fresco in an interior recess, and a tower of the Turkish period, dominate the site. If you still have the energy, there's a ruined Venetian fort on top of the hill above the village.

Ancient Présos

The archaeological site of **PRÉSOS** lies close to the modern village of the same name. This is another of those sites where what you see – in this case very little – cannot begin to match the interest and importance of the history. But even without ruins it would be worth taking the walk around the site for the scenery alone. From the centre of the village, opposite a *kafeníon* with a raised terrace, a dirt road is signposted downhill. Keep your eyes peeled as this sign has been known to take holidays: if in doubt, ask. After about 1.5km you'll come to a signed gate for the "First Acropolis". This is where to leave your vehicle if you have one.

Présos first came to light in 1884, when the Italian archaeologist Federico Halbherr turned up a large number of clay idols and some unusual inscriptions written in an unknown tongue – very likely the same as that of the Linear A tablets – using Greek characters. Set out with lines reading alternatively right to left and left to right, these Eteocretan ("true Cretan") inscriptions are now believed to be evidence of the post-Bronze Age Minoans who fled the Dorian invasions to these remote fastnesses in the east of the island in an attempt to preserve their civilisation. Présos seems to have been one of their principal towns, controlling the sanctuary of Dhiktean Zeus at Palékastro, probably an earlier Minoan shrine. With harbours on the north and south coasts of the island her power eventually led to conflict with the leading Dorian city of the region, Ierápytna (modern Ierápetra). Following final victory about 155 BC, Ierápytna razed Présos to the ground and the city was never rebuilt. With this defeat the long twilight of Minoan civilisation, lasting more than a thousand years after the palaces had fallen, came to an end.

From the entrance follow the path west to a saddle between the two hills where the ancient city lay. On the summit of the **First Acropolis** you can make out the foundations of a temple. On the western slope of this hill are the remains of a substantial **Hellenistic house** excavated by the British archaeologist Bosanquet at the turn of the century. Dating from the third century BC, the outer walls of superbly cut stone define the main living rooms at the front of the house with workrooms at the rear. In the largest workroom was found an olive press together with a stone tank for storing the oil. A stairway to the left of the main door led down to a cellar.

A hundred-metre walk across the saddle to the **Second Acropolis** will reveal cuttings in the rock on the south side which formed the foundations of dwellings. The defensive wall which encircled these two hills can still be made out in places.

Sitía to Ierápetra

The main road across the island **from Sitía to the south coast** cuts between the east and west ranges of the Sitía mountains, giving some fine views in the hill country of the central section before descending towards the sea plain.

Just before PISKOKÉFALO, less than 2km out of Sitía, Minoan enthusiasts may want to pause at the remains of a **Minoan villa** (signed) cut through by the road. Dating from the late Neo-Palatial period (1550–1450 BC), it had two floors and is terraced into the hillside with the well-preserved staircase giving access to an upper floor. The villa's view would have encompassed the river valley below the road, where its farm lands were probably located.

At the entrance to Piskokéfalo itself a dirt road is signed to the left for ZOÚ, 6km further on, where there's **another Minoan villa** of the same period. Follow the road, which crosses a dry riverbed and then turns right (signed), eventually becoming asphalt as it winds up into the hills towards Zoú. The villa – not easily spotted and with no sign – lies on a high bank to the right of the road just before the village. Excavated by Nikólaos Pláton, the excavator of the palace at Zákros, this is more a farmhouse – cultivating the land in the valley to the east – than simply a country dwelling. The rooms seem to be divided between those for domestic life and others for work and storage of farm equipment. A pottery kiln (for making olive oil containers?) was discovered in one room, whilst two deep pits near the entrance probably stored grain.

Back on the main Sitía–Ierápetra road, it's a long climb to the island's spine, past EPÁNO EPISKOPÍ and the turning to Présos (see above), before the road dips towards LITHÍNES. Just after this the islands of Koufonísi, to the east, and Gaidhouronísi, to the west, become visible beyond the coastal plain out in the Libyan Sea. You emerge, eventually, on the south coast at PILALÍMATA. For empty beaches you should get off just past here, where a track on the left is signed for the Moní Kápsa and Goúdhouras. There's a fair stretch of rather pebbly grey beach – known as KALÁ NERÁ – no more than 1km from the road. If you have transport, however, there are better strips of sand to be found scattered all along this rocky foreshore.

East: Moní Kápsa and Goúdhouras

The **Moní Kápsa** enjoys a spectacular setting on a ledge in the cliffs just above the road, and an abiding reputation for miracles. The original monastery, probably founded in the early Venetian period, was destroyed by Turkish pirates in 1471. It was rebuilt, but most of the present buildings were constructed in the nineteenth century, thanks to the energies of "Yerontoyiannis", a monk who earned himself a name as a Robin Hood-style hero as well as a healer. Locally he is revered as a saint, and although he never conducted a single service due to his illiteracy, and is denied canonisation by the church, Cretans flock in to leave their offerings beside his silver encased cadaver in the monastery chapel. You may also visit the cave behind the church to where he often retreated. As you enter the monastery, pairs of baggy trousers and other battered old items of clothing are hung on pegs by the door, for use by anyone who turns up in shorts or otherwise "unsuitably" attired. But most times of the year you will have the place to yourself, and the people around the monastery, lay workers mostly, always seem to have time to sit you down for a chat and a cold drink.

Further along the same road, now asphalt, you come to the best beach of all, just before **GOÚDHOURAS**. There should be little problem camping around here, taking advantage of three or four tavernas in the village. It has to be said, though, that Goúdhouras itself is an exceptionally unattractive, plastic-wrapped little place.

West: Makriyialós and beyond

Westwards, the route to Ierápetra passes ANÁLIPSI and **MAKRIYIALÓS**, villages which have merged into each other along the road. Makriyialós has one of the best beaches at this end of Crete, with tavernas and sand which shelves so gently you begin to think you are going to walk the 200 miles to Africa. But while it is by no means overrun, heavy building has ensured that it's no longer exactly pretty either – and in any case it's not somewhere you're likely to find a cheap room. Still a very pleasant place to stop for a swim or a quick meal – and dead easy to get to on the bus – it's no longer the attraction it once was as a day trip from the bigger resorts.

As you leave Makriyialós, you pass yet another **Minoan villa** (signed only from the western approach), 200m inland from the road. Leave any transport and follow the level track starting to the west of the sign; this eventually climbs up to the site beside a farmhouse. It was long suspected that such a tempting area would not have escaped the attentions of the ancient peoples and in 1971 Kostas

Davaras began excavations which eventually unearthed an important villa of the late Neo-Palatial period (1550–1450 BC). As can be seen from the remains, it had strong outer walls and some fine stone-flagged floors. The ground plan is not unlike that of the palaces, with rooms situated around a central court, where an altar was also identified. The excavation also revealed that the house was destroyed by fire – yet more evidence for the endless debate over what caused the downfall of the Minoans.

There's a second bay immediately beyond Makriyialós, with a smaller, emptier beach, and the road then runs along what is for the most part an exposed and rocky coast, with only the occasional scrubby beach. KOUTSOURÁS, the main village hereabouts, has little to commend it.

Butterfly Gorge

Things look up 2km further on, where a hand-painted sign on the right announces **Red Butterfly Gorge**. Officially named *Dásakis* ("small forest"), this is an embryonic national park administered by the forestry department of Áyios Nikólaos: embryonic because it has not yet reached the minimum size to be granted full national park status. Surprisingly, this is the only pine forest in Crete which starts from the beach and continues uninterrupted to the mountains – and if it looks a bit threadbare today, that's because it was burnt down by the German army in the last war in order to root out resistance forces. Leave your vehicle by the café at the entrance and walk the 500m through the woods to the gorge entrance. In summer, it shouldn't be long before you're surrounded by dozens of the fluttering **red butterflies** which give the gorge its name. The gorge is also a haven for some interesting bird life. The café manager, Yiorgos Yeorgamlis, is a committed Green and a fount of information on the park. He is also fighting a battle with the local villagers who apparently wish to destroy the park to erect more plastic hothouses. They've even been cutting down the saplings he's planted. The more energetic may wish to **walk** the gorge into the mountains of the Thriptí range, ending up at the picturesque village of ORINÓ (sturdy footwear required). Alternatively, there's a **scenic road** there also, signed 2km further along the main road.

Ayía Fotiá

For a while after this there's a genuinely mountainous stretch, until the road dips down to a beach with a taverna on it, and in the following bay a poorly signed track leads down to **AYÍA FOTIÁ**. Hidden from the road in a wooded valley, Ayía Fotiá usually has quite a travellers' scene going on, and whether you like it or not depends on just how many other people determined to get away from it all you want to share your solitude with. The place certainly has its attractions: cheap **rooms** in the village; an excellent beach just a couple of minutes' walk away down the stream bed; cafés and tavernas with good music; and places to camp out if that's what you're looking for.

Ayía Fotiá is, sadly, the last place from here to well beyond Ierápetra which could be described as inviting. The final 10km of road runs fast across a flat plain, unimaginatively developed for tourism along the coast and for hothouse agriculture inland. Neither FÉRMA nor KOUTSONÁRI has much to offer, despite the latter's much vaunted "tourist village", a group of abandoned houses which have been restored to rent as holiday villas. Just past here, however, are two **campsites** – *Koutsounari* and *Ierapetra* – which are the nearest to town if you want to be based at Ierápetra. This is also the beginning of the aptly named **Long Beach**, a windswept line of sand (and the wind can really blow here) which stretches virtually unbroken along the final 5km of shore to Ierápetra.

Ierápetra

IERÁPETRA has various claims to fame – the largest town on the south coast of Crete, the southernmost in Europe – but charm is not one of them. It's a sprawling, messy, concrete place; a supply centre for the region's farmers which until recently attracted an amazing number of package tourists and not a few backpackers looking for work. But the boom years appear to be on the wane: many of the package companies are pulling out, the tourist office has closed down and the town seems to have given up trying. Even the excellent beach – which used to be Ierápetra's saving grace – seems no longer to be the great attraction it once was.

Though you'd never know it to look at the town today, Ierápetra has quite a history. Early knowledge is sketchy, but it's almost certain that there was a settlement, or at least a port, here in Minoan times. A look at the map suggests a link across the isthmus with Goúrnia and it was probably from Ierápetra and other south coast harbours that the *Keftiu*, as the Egyptians called the Cretans, sailed for the coast of Africa. However, it was as a Doric settlement that **Ierápytna**, as the place was then known, grew to real prominence. By the second century BC she occupied more territory than any other Cretan city.

Ierápytna became a bastion of the Greek Dorians against their bitter enemies the Eteocretans: the final victory over Eteocretan Présos in 155 BC ended the last Minoan presence in eastern Crete. Those Eteocretans not killed in battle or put to flight were sold into slavery, a sombre end to the last vestiges of a great civilisation. Only Ítanos, near Vái, now stood between Ierápytna and the complete domination of the eastern end of the island. Prolonged wars and disputes rumbled on for almost a century, and were finally brought to an end only by Rome's ruthless conquest of the entire island. Even then Ierápytna stubbornly resisted to the last, becoming the final city to fall to the invading legions. When Rome then joined Crete to Cyrene in northern Libya, forming the province of Cyrenaica, Ierápytna embarked on a new career as an important commercial centre in the eastern Mediterranean – trading with Greece and Italy as well as Africa and the Near East. During this period much impressive building took place – theatres, amphitheatres, temples – of which virtually nothing survives today. From the Romans to the tourists is a chronicle of steady decline. The Venetians (who favoured Sitía as their administrative centre in the east) left behind a small **fortress**, now restored, defending the harbour entrance. The Turks, under whom Ierápetra languished as a backwater, are represented by a nineteenth-century **mosque** and nearby Ottoman fountain.

Arrival

Arriving, you get Ierápetra at its worst. The **bus station** is in a state of permanent confusion and the one-way traffic system invariably jammed, not helped by many streets being shut off by static roadworks. Nor is it easy to orientate yourself – without any real focus the town takes a day or two to find your way around with any confidence. For a better impression, head down towards the water, past the

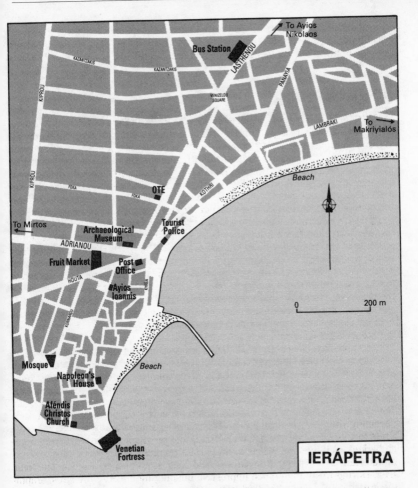

IERÁPETRA

souvenir shops and stalls selling German newspapers, to the seafront and promenade. Here, with a string of restaurants and bars stretching out in either direction – to the left behind the beach, right towards the fortress and the harbour – Ierápetra can be genuinely picturesque.

Accommodation

There are **rooms** to be had in Ierápetra, but sometimes they take a bit of finding – especially if you turn up late in the day during high season. In the centre try the spacious and good value *Hotel Ligia* (☎28-881), right on the square by the post office, or if you don't want to stray far from the bus station there's the homely *Four Seasons* (☎24-390), a couple of hundred metres up Odhós Kazantzakís. Failing these, you could try the slightly more expensive *Hotel Creta* (☎22-550), on Platía Venizélou, or the nearby *Ersi Hotel* (☎23-208). Another decent possibility is

Cretan Villa (☎28-522) at Lakerda 16, to the northeast of Platía Venizélou. If you get really stuck you could try the tourist police on the seafront – but don't count on much help. Alternatively, you could stay at the **campsites** 7km out along the Sitía road (see above) and come in to town in the evenings for the food and the nightlife.

Food and entertainment

When it comes to eating and drinking Ierápetra's scorecard starts to improve. On the **food** front, simply because there is so much competition, prices at the places on the waterfront are reasonable and quality fair. At night, with the lights reflected in the harbour and most of the town blotted out, it's a pleasant setting too. You could try the *Argo* or the *Acropolis*, but to be honest it doesn't make much difference which you choose. Two blocks in from the sea on Platía Venizélou there's the extraordinary *Rex* – surely Crete's only cinema-into-restaurant conversion! It still looks like a cinema with its name up in neon, and the food isn't bad. The only problem is a lack of atmosphere due to the place's inability to tempt the crowds away from the seafront pizazz.

The **bars and discos** are concentrated in the streets immediately behind the seafront, mainly along Kyrba. This too is the area to find more basic food and takeaways. If you fancy taking in some **bouzouki** you have a choice of live action: the pub atmosphere at *Bora Sita* at the start of Kyrba, or the well-heeled variety at *V.I.P.'s* nightclub, 4km out of town on the Sitía road.

The Town

Things to do in Ierápetra by day – apart from lie on the beach – are severely limited. The morning **fruit market** near the archaeological museum can provide a colourful and entertaining half-hour; the **Museum** itself is rather less colourful. Its dusty rooms (officially open Tues–Sat 9am–3pm) are known to close at a moment's notice, but it's probably worth the effort if only to see a fine Minoan terracotta **larnax**, excavated at nearby Episkopí. Dating from the very end of the Neo-Palatial period (c.1300 BC) the *larnax*, or clay coffin, has fascinating painted panels, one of which depicts a mare giving suck to her foal. Other scenes revel in the stalking of the *kri-kri* or wild goat by hunting dogs. The Greek and Roman section contains a selection of statuary, mostly headless because iconoclastic Christians tended to regard the stone craniums as places where the spirit of the devil was lurking. One recent discovery, however, managed to hang on to hers: a wonderful second-century statue of the fertility goddess, **Demeter**, holding an ear of corn in her left hand. On top of her head is a small altar encoiled by two serpents, symbols of her divinity.

Elsewhere in town, two churches which stand out from a miscellaneous collection are the twin-domed **Aféndis Christos** (near the fort), a fourteenth-century building with a fine carved wooden iconostasis; and **Áyios Ioánnis**, an equally ancient, but now restored, former mosque. There's also an old house in which locals claim that **Napoleon** spent the night of June 6, 1798, on his way to Egypt.

If you're staying in Ierápetra and it finally becomes too much, there are a number of ways out. Simplest is the day trip by caique to **GAIDHOURONÍSI** (Donkey Island), some 10km offshore. A real desert island, Gaidhouronísi has some excellent sandy beaches and plenty of room to escape – although you wouldn't want to miss the boat back.

Alternatively, there are more beaches along the coast in either direction, with good bus services along the main road behind them. If you want to **hire a bike** the best deal is at *Moto Cross* (☎23-432) at Kothri 36, just behind the waterfront. They provide helmets and also goggles, which you'll appreciate when the sand starts to fly in the summer winds. Alternatives are *Galaxie* at Metaháki 1, or *Omega Motors* at Lampraki 1.

West to Mírtos

Heading west from Ierápetra, the first stretch of coast is grey and dusty, the road jammed with trucks and lined with drab ribbon development. Where the concrete runs out, the plastic greenhouses start. If you're travelling under your own steam, there's a **scenic detour** worth taking at GRA LIGIÁ. The road, on the right, is signed for Anatolí and climbs to MÁLES, a village clinging to the lower slopes of the Dhíkti range. Here would be a good starting point if you wanted to take a **walk** through some stunning mountain terrain. Otherwise, the dirt road down (signed for Míthi) has spectacular views over the Libyan Sea and eventually follows the Mírtos river valley down to Mírtos itself.

Two Minoan sites: Néa Mírtos and Pírgos

Continuing along the coast road at Gra Ligiá, it's eight kilometres further to **NÉA MÍRTOS**, where a Minoan site excavated in the Sixties by a British team yielded important evidence concerning early Minoan settlements. Known locally as **Fournoú Korifí** ("Kiln Hill"), the site is located beyond the village on the peak to your right, just after a chapel on the coastal side of the road. Immediately after the hill you'll see a sign for "Minoan Villa". Follow a level track 50m inland and leave your vehicle. A path to the right will eventually lead you up to the site; there are thorns for the last fifty metres.

The excavations – which are not always easy to make sense of – revealed not a villa but a much earlier stone-built village of nearly one hundred rooms spread over the hilltop. Probably typical of numerous other settlements sited on the coast of eastern Crete during the early Pre-Palatial period (c.2500 BC), these rooms contained stone and copper tools, carved seals and over 700 pottery vessels. Some of these were Vasilikí-type jugs with their intriguing mottled finish, and many were no doubt used to store the produce of the surrounding lands, then less arid than today – olives, vines and cereals. In a room in the southwest corner of the site was located the oldest known Minoan domestic shrine which produced the most important of the finds: the goddess of Mírtos, a clay idol with a stalked neck and carrying a ewer. (It's now in the Áyios Nikólaos museum, along with the rest of the finds from this site and Pírgos.) Around the goddess broken offering vessels were strewn about the floor, many of them charred by the fire which destroyed the site about 2200 BC. The riddle of the fire, which seems to have left no casualties and provoked no rebuilding, is yet another of the unresolved Minoan questions. However, the site of Pírgos may offer a few clues.

Pírgos
PÍRGOS, just 2km further on, is considerably easier to get to and has a superb view over the coast. The sign to this Minoan villa comes immediately before a

large bridge across the Mírtos river and leads into what appears to be a quarry, which makes it hard to work out the way up. Once you spot it, though, the trail to the top is obvious and it's a bare ten-minute walk to the site.

The settlement here was inhabited at much the same time as Fournoú Korifí and was also destroyed by fire around 2200 BC. Unlike Fournoú Korifí, however, Pírgos was reoccupied and rebuilt following its destruction, when it appears to have incorporated the former's lands. By the time of the Neo-Palatial period (c.1600 BC), the community occupying the lower slopes was dominated by a two- or three-storey country villa spread over the crown of the hill. A **stepped street** flanked by some well-cut lower courses of the villa's outer wall leads into a **court-yard** partly paved in the purple limestone of the region. At the rear of the villa (furthest away from the sea) on the west side, it's possible to make out a **light-well** floored with the same purple limestone. Many of the walls carry marks of the ferocious blaze which destroyed the villa around 1450 BC, lending credibility to the Thíra explosion theory, especially when volcanic material was discovered amidst the rubble. But it now seems that whilst the villa was burned, the surrounding settlement was untouched. Another puzzle to contemplate as you savour the magnificent sea view from the courtyard.

On your way down, take a left turn at the bottom of the stepped street and follow the hill around to see the remains of an enormous plastered **cistern** dating from the Pre-Palatial era (c.1900–1700 BC), the largest found in Minoan Crete. When it burst over the northern side of the hill in ancient times it was not repaired. Beyond this a fine stretch of **paved road** survives from the early period: this led to a burial pit, now excavated.

Mírtos

Across the bridge, the main road turns sharply inland, while a turnoff cuts back down to the coast and **MÍRTOS**. Razed to the ground by the German army in 1943 as a punishment for resistance activities, Mírtos today is an unexpected pleasure after the drabness of what has gone before. This charming white-walled village is kept clean as a whistle by its house-proud inhabitants, and most of the summer you'll find space to breathe on the long shingle beach. Behind the beach lies a short promenade lined with bars and tavernas: *Votsalo* is recommended.

In August the place can get pretty full, often with young travellers who sleep on the beach to the irritation of the authorities. But Mírtos takes all this in its easy stride and refuses to be overwhelmed to the point where it is taken over – and so long as there are no big hotels it doesn't seem likely to be. Most of the time there are plenty of **rooms** signed throughout the village, on every street it seems. Try *Rooms Angelos* or *Rooms Mertini* (☎51-386 for both). There's also a small hotel, the *Mirtos* (☎51-215). There are more good **beaches** and a pleasant **walk** to be had out along the dirt track which follows the coast west to TÉRTSA, 6km away, and then on to Árvi (p.96). Head out here also to find places to **camp**, where you should be undisturbed.

Inland, the character of the main road, now heading towards Áno Viánnos (p.96) and Iráklion, changes immediately as it begins to climb around the south side of the Dhíkti range. Here you're back into the traditional Crete of small mountain villages and alarming precipices.

travel details

Buses
From Áyios Nikólaos
To Mália/Iráklion (30min/1hr 30min) 32 daily, 6.30am–9.30pm.
Sitía (2hr) 8 daily, 6.30am–7pm.
Plateau Lasíthi (2hr) 2 daily, 8.30am and 2pm.
Ierápetra (1hr) 12 daily, 6.30am–8pm.
Eloúnda (30min) 14 daily, 7.15am–8.30.
Kritsá (30 min) 15 daily, 6am–8pm.

From Sitía
To Ay. Nikólaos/Iráklion (2hr/3hr 30min) 7 daily, 6.15am–7.15pm.
Makriyialós/Ierápetra (1hr/2hr) 6 daily, 6.15am–8pm.
Vái (1hr) 7 daily, 9am–6.15pm.
Zákros (1hr 30min) 3 daily, 6.15am, 11.30am and 2.30pm.

From Ierápetra
To Ay. Nikólaos/Iráklion (1hr/2hr 30min) 11 daily, 6.30am–8.30pm.

Áno Viános/Iráklion (30min/3hr) 2 daily, 10.30am and 4.30pm.
Some of these services are restricted on Sundays

Ferries
To the Dodecanese *Sifnos Express* leaves Ay. Nikólaos Wed am for Sitía, Kásos, Kárpathos, Hálki, Rhodes, Sími, Tílos, Nísiros, Kós, Kálimnos, Astipalía, Amorgós, Páros and Pireás; Sat am to Sitía, Kásos, Kárpathos, Hálki and Rhodes. *Lasithi* sails Saturday pm from Ay. Nikólaos to Rhodes.

To the Cyclades *Sifnos Express* sails Sat pm from Ay. Nikólaos to Anáfi, Thíra, Folégandros, Mílos, Sífnos and Pireás.

These ferries operate very infrequently in winter

Planes
From Sitía Twice weekly to Kásos, four times a week to Kárpathos and Rhodes, twice to Athens. *These flights summer only*

ΑΓΙΟΣ ΝΙΚΟΛΑΟΣ	Αγιος Νικόλαος	Áyios Nikólaos
ΑΓΙΑ ΦΩΤΙΑ	Αγία Φωτιά	Ayía Fotiá
ΒΑΙ	Βάι	Vái
ΓΟΥΡΝΙΑ	Γούρνια	Goúrnia
ΕΛΟΥΝΤΑ	Ελούντα	Eloúnda
ΖΑΚΡΟΣ	Ζάκρος	Zákros
ΙΕΡΑΠΕΤΡΑ	Ιεράπετρα	Ierápetra
ΚΡΙΤΣΑ	Κριτσά	Kritsá
ΛΑΣΙΘΙΟΥ	Λασίθιου	Lasíthi
ΜΑΚΡΥΓΙΑΛΟΣ	Μακρύγιαλος	Makríyialos
ΜΙΡΤΟΣ	Μίρτος	Mírtos
ΜΟΧΛΟΣ	Μόχλος	Móhlos
ΝΕΑΠΟΛΗ	Νεάπολη	Neápoli
ΠΑΛΑΙΚΑΣΤΡΟ	Παλαίκαστρο	Palékastro
ΣΗΤΕΙΑ	Σητεία	Sitía
ΣΠΗΝΑΛΟΓΚΑ	Σπηναλόγκα	Spinalónga
ΤΖΕΡΜΙΑΔΟ	Τζερμιάδο	Tsermiádho
ΨΥΧΡΟ	Ψυχρό	Psihró

CHAPTER THREE

RETHIMNON

Réthimnon province is dominated by mountains: its borders defined to the east by the island's highest peaks, including the looming mass of Psilorítis, to the west by the outflung reaches of the Lefká Óri. The towns, even the provincial capital Réthimnon, feel compact and hemmed in, and so do many of the beaches – especially along the often wild and inaccessible southern coast.

Not surprising, then, that it is **the interior** which offers the greatest attractions – in the villages ranged around the **Psilorítis massif** and in a series of wilderness hikes originating from them. A few days here are strongly recommended, for casual ramblers and committed hikers alike. The actual peaks are approached most easily from **Anóyia**, a high mountain town with a reputation for homespun weaving and embroidery that makes a good first base. From here you can hike across to the south side of the mountains or down, via the **summit of Psilorítis**, to the villages of the **Amári Valley** – some of the least visited and most traditional places in Crete.

On the north coast, Réthimnon is at the centre of some of Crete's most drastic resort development, hotels and apartments spreading ever eastwards along a narrow strip of plain. The town, though, has just about managed to keep its priorities straight, and a core of life continues relatively unaffected. To the west a sandy coastline, still not greatly exploited, runs all the way to the borders of Haniá. But for time by the sea, it's across the island, on the **south coast**, that the province has most to offer. Here there are just two resorts of any size, overblown **Ayía Galíni** and its fast-emerging rival, **Plakiás**. Away from these enclaves is the Crete of old: little-known pockets of sand, hard of access but well worth it.

Réthimnon

Although the third largest town in Crete, **RÉTHIMNON** never feels like a city, as Haniá or Iráklion do. Instead, it has an air of the provincial: a place that moves slowly and, for all the myriad bars springing up along the seafront, preserves much of its Venetian and Turkish appearance. Arriving, especially if you approach from the east, in the evening, it looks exactly as it does in old engravings or in Edward Lear's watercolours – dominated by the bulk of a Venetian fortress, the skyline picked out with the delicate spires of minarets.

All of this is increasingly under commercial threat, but for the time being it's an enjoyable place to spend some time, with a wide, sandy beach and palm-fringed promenade right in front of the tangled streets of the old town. There are hundreds of tavernas, bars, cafés and discos, but the big hotels are all out of town, stretching for miles along the shore to the east. Staying in town, away from the front, you'll find things relatively quiet at night, noisily animated during the day.

Arrival – somewhere to stay

Most people arrive in Réthimnon by road. There is no bypass here and apparently no plans for one – so all the traffic on the coastal highway is funnelled straight through the centre, currently via a series of complicated and occasionally dangerous roadworks. If you're driving, you should head straight for the waterfront, the easiest place to find and to park. The two **bus stations** are at the corner of Dhimokratías and Moátsou, diagonally opposite each other, one for the long-distance and north coast services, the other for trans-island and village buses. If you come in on the **ferry** you'll be more central still, over at the western edge of the harbour.

To get your bearings from the bus station, walk straight down towards the front, following Dhimokratías and then Kalérgi or one of the narrower alleys of the old town. You'll emerge on the beach virtually opposite the **tourist office** (Mon–Fri 8am–3.30pm; ☎29-148), where you can pick up maps, timetables and accommodation lists. Alternatively, turn left on Arkadhíou to head straight for the centre and most of the accommodation. From the ferry, simply walk into the old town directly ahead of you.

The phone code for Réthimnon is ☎0831

Accommodation

There's a great number of places to stay in Réthimnon, and only at the height of the season are you likely to have difficulty finding somewhere; though you may get weary looking. The greatest concentration of **rooms** is in the tangled streets west of the inner harbour, between the Rimondi Fountain and the museums: there are also quite a few places on and around Arkadhíou.

HOSTELS AND CHEAP ROOMS

Youth Hostel, Tombázi 41 (☎22-848). Cheapest beds in town are in the youth hostel dormitories (or on the roof). It's large, clean, very friendly and popular, and there's food, showers, clothes-washing facilities and even a library of books in an assortment of languages.

Pension Vrisinas, Heréti 10 (☎26-092). In a narrow street parallel to Kalérgi, worth checking as you walk in from the bus station, but often full. Lovely rooms, though some are noisy.

Pension Zania, 3 Pavlou Vlastou (☎28-169). Right on the corner of Arkadhíou by the old youth hostel building, a well-adapted old house, but only a few rooms.

Pension Corina, Dambergi 9 (☎26-911). Very friendly place with a couple of good balcony rooms at front, several darker ones behind.

Barbara Dokimaki, Plastíra 14 (☎22-319). Strange warren of a rooms place, with one entrance at the above address, just off the seafront behind the *Hotel Ideon*, and another on Damberg, opposite *Corina*; some excellent rooms.

Pension Anna, Katehaki (☎25-586). Comfortable place in a quiet position on the street which runs straight down from the entrance to the fortress to Melissinou. A couple more new rooms places are very close by.

Rooms George, Himáras (☎27-540). Just below the Archaeological Museum as you head up from town, a new place with a taverna below.

Atelier, Himáras (☎24-440). Practically next door to *George*, and very similar.

Stelios Soumbasakis, 98 Nikiforou Foka, corner Koronaíou. Good taverna with some rooms to rent above, and contacts with many small rooms places in the surrounding streets.

Mary Lee Rooms, Melissinou. Good standard rooms place.

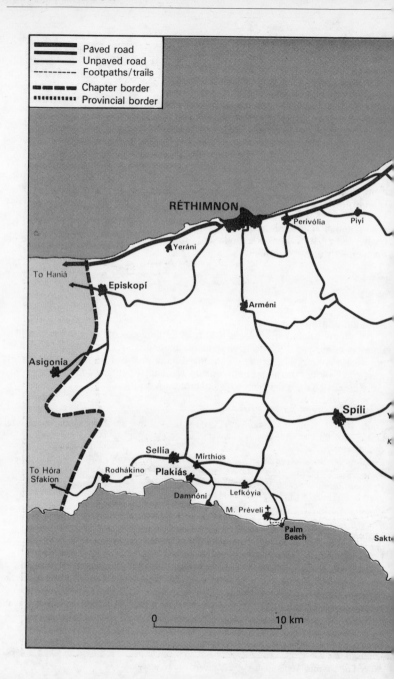

Paved road
Unpaved road
Footpaths/trails
Chapter border
Provincial border

RÉTHIMNON

Perivólia   Piyi

Yeráni

To Haniá

Episkopí

Arméni

Asigonía

Spíli

Sellía   Mirthios

To Hóra   Rodhákino   Plakiás
Sfakíon
                    Lefkóyia
            Damnóni
                M. Préveli
                        Palm
                        Beach   Sakt

0   10 km

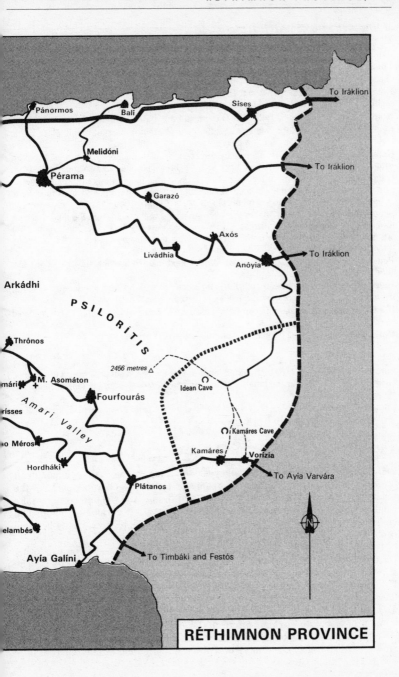

RÉTHIMNON PROVINCE

MODERATE ROOMS AND HOTELS

The cheap **hotels** are on the whole less good value than rooms, but on the other hand more likely to have space; there are several along or just off Arkadhíou. There are also a few more comfortable than usual rooms places. The higher-category hotels are all modern and businesslike.

Hotel Ahillion, Arkadhíou 151 (☎22-581). E-class, rambling and very run-down (worn lino, sagging furniture), but clean and a good position.

Hotel Minoa, Arkadhíou 60 (☎22-508). D-class, still very basic, but better than the above.

Rethimnon Haus, V Kornarou 1 (☎23-923). Very pleasant, upmarket rooms place in old building just off Arkadhíou. Bar downstairs.

Hotel Leo, Vafe 2 (☎29-851). Slightly more expensive than the above, and slightly better, with lots of wood and traditional feel. Price includes breakfast, and there's a good bar.

Olga's Rooms, Souliou 57 (☎29-851, 23-493). Nice old building on this touristy street with some very good rooms, some cheaper – including roofspace. Pleasantly Sixties atmosphere. Several other relatively upmarket rooms places can be found on Souliou.

Seeblick, Plastíra 17 (☎22-478). On the seafront as you walk round from the inner harbour towards the outer wall of the fortress. Rooms with sea view cost more than most rooms, but are good value for the position; some cheaper rooms without views. They prefer to rent by the week and won't even consider a single-night stay in season.

Pension Lefteris, Plastíra 26 (☎23-803). Almost next door to *Seeblick*, they also don't like short stays but will at least consider it.

Hotel Ideon, Platía Plastíra 10 (☎28-667). B-class place with brilliant position just north of the ferry dock; little chance of space in season, though.

Hotel Brascos, Dhaskalaki 1, corner Moatsou (☎23-721). B-class comfort, international blandness.

Hotel Olympic, Moatsou, corner Dhimokratias (☎24-761). Ditto.

CAMPSITES

Camping Elizabeth (☎28-694). Pleasant, large site on the beach about 4km east of town; all facilities. Take the bus for the hotels (marked *Scaleta/El Greco*) from the long-distance bus station to get there.

Camping Arkadia (☎28-825). Only a few hundred metres from *Elizabeth*, further east along the beach. Bigger and slightly less friendly, similar prices.

The City

Réthimnon is a thoroughly enjoyable place to wander round. Although much of it has succumbed to the commercial reality of fast food and supermarkets, the buildings themselves have changed little, and there's still the odd corner where English or German are not automatically spoken, a few curious old shops and craftsmen working away in their traditional get-up of high boots, baggy trousers (*vrákes*) and black headscarves (*tsalvária*).

The monuments described below don't amount to a great deal on paper, but walking between them is often every bit as interesting as getting to them. The streets themselves are a fascinating mix of generations of architecture, the Venetian buildings indistinguishable most of the time from the Turkish and all of them adapted and added to by later generations. Ornate wooden doors and balconies are easily spotted, ancient stonework crops up everywhere, and there are a number of elaborate **Turkish fountains** hidden in obscure corners: one by the Kara Pasha mosque, another below the south side of the fortress at the corner of Smírnis and Koronaíou, two more on Patriárhou Grigoríou leading up from here towards the Public Gardens.

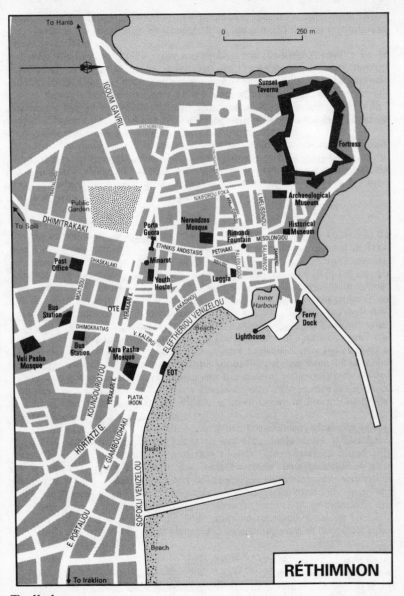

RÉTHIMNON

The Harbour

Most people's time in Réthimnon is split between the beach and the tavernas immediately behind it, with an occasional excursion as far as the inner harbour or up to the Rimondi Fountain and another cluster of tavernas. So the **waterfront** seems a logical place to start.

The impressive breakwaters, which are constantly being added to, reveal some of the problems with the **harbour**. Originally created by the Venetians, it has spent the centuries since constantly silting up, and until very recently had given up on trying to handle really big ships or ferries: when the locals decided to set up their own ferry service to Pireás (the *Arkadhi* was bought by public subscription) the whole thing had to be completely cleared out, and only a constant dredging operation keeps it open. Even now, the ferry is virtually the only large ship to call here: the inner harbour is for small fishing caiques and pleasure craft only; the outer part is given over almost entirely to tourists.

The Fortezza

If you follow the shoreline round to the west you'll emerge beneath the walls of the massive **Venetian Fortress** (Tues–Fri 8am–8pm, Sat–Mon 9.30am–6pm). Said to be the largest Venetian castle ever built, this was a response, in the last quarter of the sixteenth century, to a series of pirate raids (by Barbarossa in 1538, Uluch Ali in 1562 and 1571) which had devastated the town. Whether it was effective is another matter – the Venetian city fell to the Turks in less than 24 hours (they simply bypassed the fort); and when the English writer Pashley visited in 1834 he found the guns, some of them still the Venetian originals, entirely useless. Walk around the outside, preferably at sunset, to get an impression of its vast bulk and fearsome defences, plus great views along the coast and a pleasant resting point round the far side at the *Sunset Taverna*.

The **entrance**, however, is not on the seaward side but in the southeastern corner, opposite the new Archaeological Museum. As you walk in through the walls there's a small café/bar in what must have been some sort of guardhouse within the bastion, and then you emerge into the vast open space within, dotted with the remains of all sorts of barracks, arsenals, officers' houses, earthworks and deep shafts, and at the centre a large domed building which was once a church and later a mosque. It was designed to be large enough for the entire population to take shelter within the walls, and you can see that it probably was. Although much is ruined now, it remains thoroughly atmospheric, and you can look out from the walls over the town and harbour, or in the other direction along the coast to the west.

Among the most impressive remains are the **cisterns** where rainwater would have been collected: deep and cool, and dimly lit by slits through which shafts of sunlight penetrate. The **church/mosque**, currently in the midst of renovation, has a really fabulous dome and a pretty carved *mihrab* (a niche indicating the direction of prayer), both of which are Turkish additions. Just to the north of this are some fine arched foundations and a stairway leading down to a gate in the seaward defences. This was in theory for resupplying the defenders, but in practice it was through here that the Venetians fled from the Turkish attack.

Archaeological and Historical museums

Réthimnon's **Archaeological Museum** (Tues–Sun 8.30am–3pm) has recently been moved to a building almost directly opposite the entrance to the fortress. This was built by the Turks as an extra defence for the entry, and later served as a prison, but it's now entirely modern inside: cool, spacious and airy. Unfortunately the collection has not been improved to go with the new surroundings. Nevertheless, it's worth a look, especially if you're going to miss the bigger museums elsewhere: there's Minoan pottery and sarcophagi, and lots of Roman coins, jewellery, pots and statues, all of them from Réthimnon province.

The **Historical and Folk Art Museum** (Mon–Sat 9am–1pm & 7–9pm), not far away on Mesolongíou, is even smaller but a good deal more enjoyable. It's also different – the only other museum like it is the little visited (and even better) one in Vorí (p.89). Inside, in just two not particularly large rooms, are gathered musical instruments, old photos, basketry, farm implements, an explanation of traditional bread-making techniques, smiths' tools, traditional costumes and jewellery, lace, weaving and embroidery, pottery, knives and old wooden chests. Much of this looks as if it has just come out of someone's attic – as it sometimes has – and the displays include explanations (most of them translated) of how they've gathered the items, often as a result of a traditional craft workshop, farm or bakery closing down. It's a fascinating insight into a fast disappearing rural (and urban) lifestyle, which had often survived virtually unchanged from Venetian times to the 1960s, and well worth a look.

The Rimondi fountain and town centre: some mosques

The centre of town, at least as far as tourists are concerned, is probably the area from the Loggia to the Rimondi fountain; with streets of shops, restaurants and bars radiating in every direction. The seventeenth-century Venetian **Loggia**, which used to house the museum, is currently being converted into a library. The **Rimondi fountain**, at the other end of Paleológou, is also seventeenth-century Venetian. Half-hidden under a blocked-off arcade, the fountain's lion-head spouts still splash water down to a marble bowl, and nowadays they look out over one of the liveliest areas in Réthimnon – Platía Petiháki. Straight up from the fountain, a line of cafés and tavernas leads into Ethníkis Andistásis, the **market** street. Turn right just before this and the backstreets will lead you to the **Nerandzes Mosque**, whose minaret (daily 11am–7pm), ascended by a steep spiral stair, has the best views in town. The body of the mosque is now a meeting hall, often used for concerts.

Up through the market area, the old city ends at the only surviving remnant of the city walls, the **Porta Guora**. To the left here, more tangled backstreets lead towards the youth hostel, and another minaret: through the gate you emerge into the Platía Tessáron Martíron with its ugly, unfinished modern church. Almost directly opposite are the quiet and shady **Public Gardens**, a former Turkish cemetery now laid out with a fine variety of palms and other trees. In July, the gardens play host to the festivities of the **Réthimnon Wine Festival**.

Wandering further afield into the newer parts of town, two more **mosques** almost complete the roll of Réthimnon's acknowledged "sights". **Veli Pasha**, up behind the bus station, has a fine minaret and may by now be open to the public after restoration; **Kara Pasha** by Platía Iróon is older, but only part of the facade survives, with a small garden planted in front.

The beach

To find the **beach** you hardly need a guidebook: the broad swathe of tawny sand in the centre of town advertises itself. There are showers and cafés here, and the waters protected by the breakwaters are dead calm (and ideal for kids). Sadly they are also crowded and none too clean. Outside the harbour, less sheltered sands stretch for miles to the east, only marginally less crowded but with much cleaner water. Interspersed among the hotels along here is every facility you could need – travel agents, bike hire, bars and restaurants.

Food and nightlife

Immediately behind the town beach are arrayed the most obvious of Réthimnon's **restaurants**, all with large and colourful illustrated menus out front and most with waiters trained as salesmen who will run off their patter in English, German, French, Swedish or whatever else seems likely to appeal. These are not always bad value – especially if you hanker after an "English breakfast" – but they are all thoroughly touristy. Look out, here and throughout town, for the wonderful fresh fruit juices and shakes which have become a local speciality: melon is particularly good. Around the **inner harbour** there's a second, rather more expensive group of tavernas, specialising in fish and in intimate atmosphere – though as often as not this is spoilt by the stench from the harbour itself.

Although they lack the sea views, the cluster of *kafenía* and tavernas **by the Rimondi fountain** and the newer places spreading into the streets all around generally offer considerably better value. There are a couple of good pizza places here, too, and a number of old-fashioned *kafenía*, a couple of which serve magnificent yoghurt and honey.

Takeaway food means either **souvláki** – numerous stalls including a couple on Arkadhíou and Paleológou (this one also has spit-roast chicken) and *O Platanos* at Petiháki 44 – or buying your own. **Market** stalls are set up daily on Andistásis below the Porta Guora and there are small general stores scattered everywhere, particularly on Paleológou and Arkadhíou; east along the beach road you'll even find a couple of mini supermarkets. The **bakery** *I Gaspari*, on Mesolongíou just behind the Rimondi Fountain, sells the usual cheese pies, cakes and the like, and it also bakes excellent brown, black and rye bread, a godsend for anyone who's been travelling long-term. There's a good *zaharoplasteío* on Petiháki.

Music and drink

Nightlife is concentrated in the same general areas. At the west end of Venizélou, approaching the inner harbour, a small cluster of noisy **music bars** rock the beach. Up around the corner of Arkadhíou and Paleológou are some slightly quieter places, candle-light and acoustic guitar style. Larger **discos** are mostly out to the east, among the big hotels, but there are one or two in town.

The best entertainment on offer, however, comes at the annual **Wine Festival**, staged in the Public Gardens in the second half of July. The entrance fee includes all the wine you can drink from barrels set up around the gardens, and there are also food stalls and entertainment laid on. You'll need to take your own cup or else buy one of the souvenir glasses and carafes on offer outside. Though it's touristy, the locals go too, and as the evening progresses and the barrels empty the organised entertainments give way to spectacular displays of the local dance steps.

Tavernas and restaurants

Vangela, Platía Petiháki. Right by the fountain, consequently very well known and patronised, and slightly more expensive than its neighbours. Good food, which you can choose in the kitchen; chaotic service, conducted volubly in a mixture of shouted French and broken Greek, can be great, can be incredibly rude.

Agrimi, Platía Petiháki. Just one of the places queueing for your custom as you walk up from the fountain; usually reliable.

Stelios Soumbasakis, Nikiforou Foka 98, corner of Koronaíou. Very friendly, simple taverna.

Taverna Kargaki Haroulas, Melissinou by Mesolongíou. Big, cheap breakfasts plus standard taverna fare at reasonable prices.

La Crêperie, Arabatzoglou 10. Not far from the fountain – a welcome change of diet if you've been here a while.

Sunset Taverna, on the coast road round at the far side of the fortress. Mostly visited for views not food, but the meals are good and tables right by the edge of the sea – the waiters have to cross the road to the kitchen.

Linda & Joe's Snack Bar, Tombázi opposite the youth hostel. Cheap grub, popular with hostellers.

O Zefyros, inner harbour. One of the less outrageously priced places here.

Seven Brothers, inner harbour. Another of the least expensive on the harbour.

Palazzo, inner harbour. One of the nicest on the harbour, with rooftop tables as well, but very pricey.

Alana, Salaminos 11. One of the new breed, a romantic, tree-filled courtyard setting for candlelit tables and mildly international menu. Average food and high prices, however.

Cafés and bars

Zanfoti, Platía Petiháki. Long-established *kafenío* overlooking Rimondi fountain (the one with dark brown tables). Prices higher than your average *kafenío*, but a great place to people-watch over a coffee; good yoghurt and honey, too.

Galera, Platía Petiháki. Next to *Vangela*, the modern equivalent of *Zanfoti*. Large beers and toasted sandwich-type snacks.

Hotel Leo, Vafe 2, just off Arkadhíou. Pleasant, quiet bar inside.

To Diporto, Vafe 7. Another good place for a quiet drink or coffee, off the main streets.

Rouli's, El. Venizelou behind the end of the beach. One of the cheapest and liveliest of several noisy bars here.

Fortezza, inner harbour. Big, glitzy disco-bar; not much action till midnight.

Loggia, Nearchou. Just round the corner from *Fortezza*, on alley which connects with Arkadhíou and is fast becoming the nightlife centre. This is a bar with loud music and a small dance space – other bar-discos next door.

Odysseas, El. Venizelou right by inner harbour. Touristy Cretan music and dancing place, with live performances every evening from 9.30.

To Melo, Arkadhíou, behind the inner harbour. "The Apple" started life as the *Swan Pub*, and still has the fake beams and Olde Englishe look. Now a fairly loud bar, busy late.

Luvaffair Bar, Arabatzoglou. The name says it all.

Listings

Airlines *Olympic* office at Dhimitrakáki 6 (☎22-257), facing the Public Gardens. There's a bus from here to connect with flights at Haniá, 2hr 15min before departure.

Banks The *National Bank* is at Tsoúdheron 18, between Arkadhíou and the youth hostel. Others on Koundouriótou.

Bike and car hire Best place to hire a bike is on Paleológou, where there are several competing outlets – *Stavros* (☎22-858) and *Katrizidaki* (☎29-263), for example – or else down around Platía Iróon and out along the beach road: *Direct* (for cars; on the square, ☎25110; also at Arkadhíou 230); *Arkadi* (bikes; S. Venizelou and Papandreou, ☎29-134); *Pioneer* (cars; S. Venizelou 64, ☎20-312).

Boat trips Two boats, the *Scorpios* and the *Alexandros*, offer day trips to Pánormos and Balí or to Yeoryioúpoli, plus various evening cruises and fishing expeditions. Both tout for custom around the inner harbour.

Cinema Several, including the open-air *Asteria* on Melissinou beneath the south side of the fortress – a lovely place, but usually poor films.

Ferries The agent for the Réthimnon–Pireás ferry, *Rethymniaki*, is at Arkadhíou 250 (☎29-221, 21-518)

Launderette At Tombázi 45, by the youth hostel: open 9am–2pm and 5–9pm.

Left luggage The Haniá–Iráklion bus station has a small and chaotic office.

Mountain climbing, The local EOS is at Arkadhíou 143 (☎22-710, 22-411).

Newspapers and books English and other foreign newspapers are sold at several places along the front. Best for these and for new books in English is the bookshop on Petiháki, between the Loggia and the harbour. There's also an excellent second-hand bookshop (lots of old English paperbacks) on Souliou.

Pharmacies Scattered about the main shopping streets, especially Koundouriótou and Arkadhíou. Check the rota on the door for late/weekend opening. The NTOG has a list of English-speaking doctors.

Post office The main post office (Mon–Sat 7.30am–2pm, Sun 9am–1.30pm) has a smart new building on Moátsou, opposite the *Hotel Brascos*. There's also a temporary office, in season, just behind the beach at the bottom of the eastern breakwater (on S. Venizélou; Mon–Sat 8am–8pm, Sun 9am–6pm).

Shopping Most of the tourist and souvenir shops are along Arkadhíou, Paleológou and Souliou. For food try the market on Andistásis: more general stores are along Arkadhíou and Koundouriótou. Souliou has perhaps the most upmarket tourist shops and some really nice goods (including one shop that sells nothing but herbs and herbal remedies), but prices throughout town – for leather, for example – are markedly higher than in Haniá. For beach games and fishing or diving gear, try *Spiros Spor* on Petiháki. Official shop hours are Mon, Wed & Sat 8am–2pm, Tues, Thurs & Fri 8am–1pm & 5–8pm.

Taxis Ranks in Platía Tessáron Martíron and Platía Iróon. Call ☎22-316 for a radio taxi.

Telephones The OTE office at Koundourióti 28, open 7am–midnight.

Toilets Public toilets on the beach by the tourist office (clean!), opposite the Loggia and in the Public Gardens.

Tourist office The very helpful NTOG is in the concrete building on the beach. Open Mon–Fri 8am–3.30pm (☎29-148).

Tourist police On Arkadhíou just down from the Loggia (☎22-231). The town police and visa section is on Platía Iróon Politehníou below the southwestern corner of the castle, harbour police on the inner harbour.

Travel agents Several along Paleológou, Arkadhíou and Koundouriótou, and also around Platía Iróon and along S. Venizélou. *Aloha Travel* (Paleológou 25; ☎21-537), *Rethymno Tours* (upstairs on Platía Petiháki; open daily 8am–midnight), *Caroline Tours* (Platía Iróon; ☎24-351) and *Creta Travel* (S. Venizelou; ☎22-915) can all arrange excursions and ferry tickets; though for flights home you'd be better off in Haniá or Iráklion.

Work This is not somewhere many people come looking for work – the usual early season possibilities exist of course, but little in the way of farm jobs. Best centre for contacts is the youth hostel.

Out from Réthimnon: Arkádhi Monastery

Of all the short trips which could be taken out of Réthimnon, the best known is still the most worthwhile. This is to the **MONASTERY OF ARKÁDHI** (daily 6am–8pm), some 25km southeast of the city. Immaculately sited in the foothills of the Psilorítis range, Arkádhi is something of a national Cretan shrine. During the 1866 rebellion the monastery served as a Cretan strongpoint in which, as the

Turks took the upper hand, hundreds of Cretan guerrillas and their families took refuge. Here they were surrounded by a Turkish army until, after a siege of two days, the defences were finally breached on November 9, 1866.

As the attackers poured in, the ammunition stored in the monastery exploded: deliberately fired, according to the accepted version of events, on the orders of the abbot. Hundreds (some sources claim thousands) were killed in the initial blast, Cretan and Turk alike, and most of the surviving defenders were put to death by the enraged assailants. The following year the British philhellene J. Hilary Skinner, fighting with the insurgents, could still describe "scores of bodies unburied, half-buried, sun-dried, and mangled, to be seen within the monastery". That he was here at all is proof of the international sympathy for the cause of Cretan independence which this ultimate expression of the cry of "*Freedom or Death*" did much to promote. Figures as disparate as Victor Hugo, Garibaldi and the poet Swinburne were moved to public declarations of support, and in Britain money was raised for a ship (the *Arkadhi*) to run the Turkish blockade. Though Crete's liberty was still some way off, the monastery remains the most potent symbol of the struggle. There are celebrations of the anniversary of the blast every November, from the 7th to the 9th.

The buildings

Nowadays you can peer into the roofless vault beside the cloister where the explosion took place, and wander about the rest of the well-restored grounds. Despite the carnage, the bulk of the monastery buildings, including the others around the central cloister, were relatively unscathed and Arkádhi is still a working monastery. Before its notoriety, indeed, it was one of the richest in Crete and already a well-known stopover for travellers (Edward Lear spent one of his better-tempered nights here) and a centre of resistance. Pashley, for example, relates a story of events over forty years prior to the famous blast, when eighty Muslims, who had occupied the monastery to pacify local rebels, were captured and put to death: in retaliation, many of the buildings were burnt. More recently the monastery lent assistance to guerrilla fighters during World War II: George Psychoundakis, for example, describes handing over to the monks supplies from a parachute drop.

Of the surviving buildings the **church** is much the most impressive, with a rich mix of styles which places it among the finest Venetian structures left in Crete. Its highly decorative facade, dating from 1587, features on the 100-drachma note – isolated here in the Cretan countryside, it seems startlingly out of place. The rest of the monastery is mainly seventeenth-century (though it was originally founded as early as the eleventh) and more familiar in layout and style. Across the courtyard from the scene of the explosion a small **museum** devoted to the exploits of the defenders of the faith contains a variety of mementoes and tributes, blood-stained clothing and commemorative medals.

Getting there

Getting to Arkádhi is straightforward. In addition to all the tours, there are **buses** from Réthimnon at 6am, 10.30am, noon and 2.30pm, returning at 7am, 11.30am, 1pm and 4pm. Going up at 10.30 and back at 1 gives you about the right amount of time, but these are the most popular buses, and consequently can be crowded; alternatively hitching a lift down should be no problem – the road ends here and the only place any traffic can go is back down to the coast. You could also try walking on to Thrónos in the Amari valley (p.165) – get someone at the monastery to set you on the right track.

The **road up** is attractive in itself: if you're driving take the old route out of Réthimnon via PERIVÓLIA and then follow the signs which lead under the highway towards the monastery via ÁDHELE and PIYÍ. As you climb into the lower reaches of the mountains the road, and the valley through which it runs, gradually narrow until at the end it's a real ravine. This opens out quite suddenly into the small plain at whose centre stands the monastery: you'll pass a modern monument to the martyrs of independence and arrive at a huge spreading tree where the bus stops and cars park. There is **food** available, but this is also a quiet place to picnic, either on benches around the outside of the monastery or walking out into the meadows which surround it.

West towards Haniá

Heading west from Réthimnon the roads are easy and efficient, but they offer little in the way of diversion. As you leave the city, you immediately start to climb; within a couple of kilometres the old road peels off to head inland, while the **highway** carries on above the coast.

Following the highway, you drop back to sea level at **YERÁNI**, 6km from Réthimnon, with a rocky cove good for a swimming break. There's a sign here to the Yeráni cave, site of a Neolithic cult rediscovered when the road was built, but despite plans the cave is not actually open to the public. Beyond, after another brief flirtation with the hills, the road finally levels out beside the **Gulf of Almirós**, from where it traces the shore, flat and straight, the rest of the way to Yeoryióupoli (p.201). A long and windswept sandy beach follows it all the way, separated from the road by straggling bushes of oleander: there are frequent spaces to pull over and park if you want a swim, and just a few new developments beginning to spring up. The beach itself is virtually deserted much of the way, but there can be dangerous currents so don't venture too far out: it gets further from the road and considerably more sheltered as you approach the development at Yeoryióupoli.

The old road

The **old road**, much more scenic, is by comparison quite populous. You'll pass through five or six prosperous little villages before arriving at EPISKOPÍ, something of a local market centre. Here you're approaching the fringe of the White Mountains, which rise with increasing majesty ahead. To the left a road runs up to some of the smaller villages, a rarely travelled route where the old life continues little affected. **ASIGONÍA**, at the end of a perpetually cloudy cul-de-sac, has been a particular favourite of students of traditional Cretan culture (like Michael Llewellyn Smith in *The Great Island*), partly, perhaps, because it was the home village of George Psychoundakis (see "Books" in *Contexts*). There's an interesting local festival, on April 23, when at dawn flocks of sheep are brought to the church to be milked, sheared, and dedicated to Áyios Yioryios, their patron saint and protector. Continuing west, the road soon divides, the main way descending steadily towards Yeoryióupoli, a secondary route climbing through the village of Kournás (p.203) and then dropping steeply to the lake.

East by the coast road

Leaving Réthimnon to the east, you can strike almost immediately onto the new road, which runs fast, flat and dull along the coastal plain, or follow the old, squeezed into the narrow gap between this and the sea. This way you'll pass through a string of village suburbs, connected now by an almost continuous string of hotel development for some 10km. At STAVROMÉNOS the old road cuts under the highway and heads inland; the new continues to hug a featureless coastline, now with barely any development at all, past the odd rocky beach.

PÁNORMOS marks a distinct break (still more marked if you are coming the other way, suddenly to emerge on the flat): the end of the level ground and the start of a spectacular, swooping mountain drive which continues virtually all the way to Iráklion. Here, too, is the last of the large hotels for some time, curving round a headland above a small bay and beach. The village of Pánormos is just a short detour off the road, a pretty little place with a couple of bars and tavernas by the harbour and a small, sandy beach. Unfortunately, there are also lots of new **rooms** places as well as the large hotel, and combined with the boat tours from Réthimnon this can mean that the place (which is really tiny) is swamped in midsummer. Out of season, it wouldn't be a bad place to stay for a few days. Surprisingly, this is an ancient settlement (a tiny river runs through to the sea) with the ruins of what was once a large sixth-century basilica, probably destroyed in the ninth-century Saracen invasion, and of a later Genoese castle.

Balí

The next stop you might consider making is at **BALÍ**, a small resort set around a series of small coves. Here the road drops down briefly from the heights to a desolate patch of low ground behind a bay. There's a large petrol station (where the bus will drop you), opposite which a road runs around the bay towards the village. On foot, this last stretch is further than it looks – a couple of kilometres to the village, more to the best beach. What you see first, though, is a fair-sized scrabbly beach at the end of the bay: grey and stony, this often shelters a considerable collection of camper vans and tents. Sadly, it's no longer really worth the effort of walking any further: although the beaches are still spectacular, they're very much overrun, and Balí has become a package resort too popular for its own good. Only well out of season, when there are bound to be bargains given the number of rooms here, is it worth staying; though it still makes a handy spot for lunch and a swim if you're driving this way.

Balí proper consists of three coves. The first has a pebbly beach and a couple of tavernas and rooms places: here too is the *Bali Beach Hotel*, the first and still much the most luxurious hotel. In the second cove is the original village, with most of the local shops as well as more hotels, rooms and tavernas. One side of this cove has been concreted to form a harbour (there are day trips by boat from Réthimnon), on the other you can swim, though rarely with much space. The third cove is known as Paradise Beach, and though it's still much the best for swimming – with a patch of sand and, on either side, crags of rock with level places to sunbathe – it's too crowded and overlooked to really deserve the name any more. Just outside the cove, but still well sheltered within the larger bay, are a couple of rocks to dive from. It's a beautiful place to splash about, surrounded by mountains which seem to rise direct from the sea to impressive heights.

After Balí, the next access to the coast is at Ayía Pelayía, 25km further on (p.67). Nor is there much else to stop for: **SÍSES** has wonderful views from its perch beside the highway, and a few rooms, but little else. From the village a track with an appalling surface cuts up to the old road. Don't be deceived by maps which show some kind of way through above Balí – there is no other practicable route inland between Pánormos (from where there's a good road to Pérama) and Fódhele.

East on the mountain roads

Taking the old roads east, inland through the fringes of the Psilorítis range, there are a variety of alternate routes and a number of interesting detours off them. The old main road, through DHAMÁSTA, has least to offer, though it's a pretty enough drive. Striking higher into the mountains is more rewarding. For a combination of relatively easy driving and interest, perhaps the best option is the road up through Garázo and Axós to **Anóyia**, though you can also reach Axós on an even higher road from Pérama.

Margarités and Eleutherna

Whichever route you follow, you'll leave the coast at STAVROMÉNOS and head up through VIRANEPISKOPÍ. The first potential detour comes some 5km further on, a right turn to **MARGARÍTES** and PRINÉS. Margarítes has a long tradition of pottery manufacture; you can normally see work in progress at the workshops, and you can buy the results at shops strung out along the steep main street. There are cafés at the top of the village, pleasant places to sit outside and rest a while.

Continuing on a deteriorating road, the site of ancient **ELEUTHERNA** is a brief climb beyond Prinés. Imposingly situated on a ridge between two streams, the city was originally approached on a road cut from the rock, at the town end of which stood (and in large part still stands) a hefty tower. There are few other significant remains but the setting is tremendous and if you find the cisterns cut from the rock you may be able to spot remains of the aqueduct which fed them. Eleutherna was a city of some power from as early as the seventh or eighth century BC through to medieval times: most of what you see is Roman or Byzantine, though the cisterns may be earlier.

Recently, archaeologists made a potentially very significant discovery here: traces of a human sacrifice made in front of the funeral pyre of some local magnate. It apparently dates from the late eighth century BC, about the same time that Homer was describing very similar sacrifices of Trojan prisoners in front of the funeral pyre of Achilles. The victim, who was bound hand and foot and had died in a ritual during which his throat was cut, may well have been expected to serve the dead man in the next world – also found in front of the pyre were sacrificed animals and offerings of perfume and food. Other cremations on the site (some twenty have been found, though only one human sacrifice) had offerings including gold, jewellery and fine pottery, as well as four tiny, superbly crafted ivory heads: among the best work of their time (c.600 BC) yet discovered anywhere. There's said to be a practicable walk from Eleutherna to the monastery at Arkádhi, less than 5km away as the crow flies, but you'll have to check out the route locally. Otherwise you've little choice but to retrace your steps to the main road.

Pérama to Axós

PÉRAMA is a substantial place, an agricultural centre which also has a little light industry, and its businesslike main street is lined with banks, shops and cafés. The chief interest in this is the rarity value of seeing a town of such size in Crete that owes nothing whatever to tourism. Even if you do no more than drive through it's a refreshing sight, and you may well find yourself passing this way more than once if you take one of the local detours available.

The Melidhóni Cave

The most obvious of these is to **MELIDHÓNI**, a bare 5km from Pérama. The village itself is unremarkable, but a half-hour's walk (or a short drive, signed from the village) leads to a great **cave**, whose series of chambers are thick with stalactites and stalagmites. This was the legendary home of Talos, a bronze giant who protected the coasts of Crete by striding around the island thrice daily (or perhaps only three times a year) hurling rocks at unfriendly ships: the Argonauts were greeted thus when they approached the island. Far more infamously, however, the Melidhóni cave was also the setting for one of the most horrific atrocities in the struggle for Cretan independence. Here, in 1824, around 300 local villagers took refuge, as they had often done before at time of war, in the face of an advancing army. This time, however, the Muslim commander demanded that they come out: when the Cretans refused, and shot two messengers sent to offer safe conduct, he attempted to force them out by blocking the mouth of the cave with stones, and cutting off the air supply. After several days of this, with the defenders opening new air passages every night, the troops changed their tactics, piling combustible materials in front of the cave and setting light to them. Everyone inside was asphyxiated*.

The bodies were left where they lay for the cave to become their tomb. Ten years later Robert Pashley became one of the first to enter since the tragedy, to find in places "the bones and skulls of the poor Christians so thickly scattered, that it is almost impossible to avoid crushing them as we pick our steps along". A shrine near the entrance to the cave today commemorates the dead.

Axós

Back through Pérama, the main road wends along the valley of the Yeropótamos all the way to the turning for **GARÁZO**, a small village where hardly anyone seems to stop. If you do, you'll find that the simple roadside cafés are friendly and exceptionally good value. **AXÓS**, especially if you arrive at lunchtime, makes a surprising contrast. Where the main road passes through, it is lined with weaving and embroidery for sale (mostly rather poor) and with tavernas crowded with tourists. This is largely because the village serves as a lunch stop for "Photo-Safari" day trips from Iráklion and Réthimnon. If you catch it without the crowds, Axós is undeniably attractive; there's a small (and locked) frescoed church and the site of a post-Minoan settlement, also called Axós, barely accessible on a ridge above the village. The upper road from Pérama, via LIVÁDHIA and ZONIANÁ, emerges in Axós by the church.

---

*This grisly event was far from unique – numerous other caves around the island have similar histories, although none claimed so many victims.

Anóyia

The focus of this trip is **ANÓYIA**, a small town perched beneath the highest peaks of the Psilorítis range. It is the obvious place from which to approach the Idean Cave and, for the committed, the summit of Psilorítis itself. The weather, refreshingly cool when the summer heat lower down is becoming oppressive, is one good reason to come, but most people are drawn by the proximity of the mountains or by a reputation for some of the best woven and embroidered work in Crete. The last is greatly exaggerated (most of what is on display is tacky in the extreme) but the town still makes a very pleasant break from the coast.

As you drive through, it seems that Anóyia has two quite distinct halves: from what appears to be the older, lower part, the road takes a broad loop around, to re-emerge in the modern looking platía of the upper town. In many ways this appearance is deceptive. A series of steep, sometimes stepped alleys connect the two directly, and however traditional the buildings may look, closer inspection shows that most are actually concrete. This reflects a tragic recent history – the village was one of those destroyed as reprisal for the abduction of General Kreipe (see p.166) and at the same time all the men who could be rounded up here were killed. The local handicrafts tradition is in part a reflection of this history, both a conscious attempt to revive the town and the result of bitter necessity with so large a proportion of the local men killed. At any rate it worked, for the place is thriving today, though there do still seem to be large numbers of elderly widows anxious to subject any visitor to their terrifyingly aggressive sales techniques.

The impression of an old and a new town persists even when you know it to be false. The upper half of the village has almost all the **accommodation** as well as the **bank** (no foreign exchange), **post office** (reluctant foreign exchange), police, most of the non-tourist shops and a large platía where the younger residents hang out. The more antique feel of the lower half is reinforced by the elderly men, baggy trousers tucked into their black boots, moustaches bristling, who sit at the *kafenía*, and by the black-clad women sitting outside their shops, ferociously hawking their handmade wares. In the square in the lower half of town stands a statue and next to it a wooden carving of Venizélos, arm in a sling – the carver's workshop is nearby, full of similar bizarre works. Walk the lanes between the two halves of town and there's a real country feel: empty houses and garages closed up with wire and used to stable livestock; goats grazing in vacant lots; and more workshop/homes where the craftswomen have set up showrooms in their front parlours.

Anóyia sees a lot of day-trippers, but most stay only an hour or so. Linger a while, or stay overnight, and it's surprisingly uncommercial. It shouldn't normally be hard to find a **room** in the upper half of town, where you'll see signs leading off all along the main street. The one drawback to staying is that there's hardly anywhere to **eat**: one taverna on the main road where it loops out of the lower village (*Prásini Foliá*, with a large open-air space for dancing which occasionally hosts "Cretan Evening" tours) and a *souvláki* place near the top of the town. Neither of these seems to serve anything other than the excellent barbecued lamb which is a local speciality: vegetarians are advised to buy their own bread and cheese (local cheese is also excellent).

Psilorítis and its caves

Heading for the mountains, a rough track leads the 13km from Anóyia to the **Nídha Plateau** at the base of Mount Psilorítis. It's a steady climb most of the way, and a road travelled little except by the shepherds who seasonally pasture their sheep up here (and who nowadays travel back and forth by pick-up). Along the way you'll pass some of the stone huts – many of them ruinous – in which traditionally the sheep's milk yoghurt and cheese would be made. Somewhere near the highest point a track leads off to the **ski area**: an unlikely thought in summer, although it does see plenty of snow in season. Soon after, the small plateau and its bare summer pastures fan out below you, and the road drops to skirt around its western edge.

Zeus and the Idean Cave

At what is effectively the end of the road (shortly beyond, it peters out in a net of trails across the plateau), a modern taverna stands looking over the plain. Since this was the only place for miles which offered rooms or sustenance it seems both unfortunate and surprising that it should have been forced to close. But it has. The rooms and kitchen are now used only by private climbing groups. Opposite the taverna, a short path leads up to the celebrated **Idean Cave** (*Idhéon Ándhron*), a rival of that on Mount Dhíkti (p.105) for the title of Zeus's birthplace. Though scholarly arguments rage over the exact identity of the caves in the legends of Zeus, and over the interpretation of the various versions of the legend, locals are in no doubt that the Idean Cave is the place where the god was brought up, suckled by wild animals.

Certainly this hole in the mountainside, which as Cretan caves go is not especially large or impressive, was associated from the earliest of times with the cult of Zeus, and at times ranked among the most important centres of pilgrimage in the Greek world. Pythagoras visited the cave, Plato set *The Laws* as a dialogue along the pilgrimage route here, and the finds made within indicate offerings brought from all over the eastern Mediterranean. Current excavations have revealed that the cave cult had a much longer history than this, too. First signs of occupation go back as far as 3000 BC, and though it may then have been a mere place of shelter, by the Minoan era it was already established as a shrine, maintaining this role until about 500 AD. Sadly for visitors, a major new dig is still going on inside, which means the whole cave is fenced off: there has even been a little railway constructed to carry all the rubble out. Unless you befriend an archaeologist, you can do no more than stand outside and stare at the blank mouth.

To the summit

The taverna also marks the start of the way to the **summit of Psilorítis** (Mount Ida), at 2456 metres the highest mountain in Crete. Though it's not for the unwary or unfit, the climb should present few problems to experienced, equipped climbers. The route, which diverts from the path to the cave just beyond the small spring and chapel, is marked with red dots: a guide who knows the mountain would be useful, since it's not always obvious which is the main trail, but is by no means essential. Don't attempt it alone, however, as you could face a very long wait for help if you ran into trouble. If you do make the climb, it should be a seven-to-eight-hour round trip to the chapel at the summit, though watch out in spring for thick snow which will slow you down. It's wise to carry enough food, water and warm gear to be able to overnight in one of the shelters should the weather turn on you – in any event a night at the top, with the whole island laid out in the sunset and sunrise, is a wonderful experience.

For the first half-hour or so **the climb** trails south across the mountainside, a gradual ascent until you reach a gully where it starts in earnest. Head west here, away from the plain, on a rocky path up the left-hand side of the gully. After about an hour and a quarter of this you reach an open height with a stone shelter and good views back the way you came: do not follow the most obvious trail at this point, which leads only to one of the lesser peaks (Koussákas, 2209m), but follow the ridge *downhill* and south instead, unlikely as this may look. After barely fifteen minutes you reach a basin where several trails meet, and where there is spring water and stone huts for shelter. Turn right, northwest, and an obvious uphill trail will take you all the way to the summit, though it is only in the last twenty minutes that the peak itself becomes visible and the ground starts to fall away to reveal just how high you are. The summit itself is marked by another shelter and the chapel of **Tímios Stavrós** (a name by which the peak is sometimes known locally); nearby there's water in a cistern, which you are advised to boil or purify before drinking. When it's clear, the panoramas from the top make the climb well worthwhile. Usually, though, conditions are very cold and windy and the views are spoilt by cloud or heat haze.

Other routes: the Kamáres Cave

While the route outlined above is probably the easiest to follow without a guide, there are any number of **alternate routes** up and down. **From the west** you can climb from virtually any of the Amári villages below the peak (especially Fourfourás, p.166), but although this is relatively straightforward in the sense that you can see the peak almost all the way, there are no real trails and you may run into difficulty with patches of thorny undergrowth or loose scree. **South**, Vorízia and Kamáres also make possible starting/finishing points. If you want to **descend towards KAMÁRES**, the trail divides in the basin mentioned above, about halfway from Nídha to the summit. It's not hard to follow, heading south from the basin, but is a good deal steeper and longer than anything outlined above: perhaps six hours down to Kamáres, seven to eight hours for the ascent. About halfway, there's a junction with a trail to the huge **Kamáres Cave**, in which the first great cache of the elaborate pottery known as Kamáres ware was found (it's now in the Iráklion museum). From the cave you either backtrack to this trail to continue to the village or carry on east to another trail, equally steep.

If you're prepared to camp on the plateau (plenty of water but plenty cold too) or can prevail on the taverna to let you in, an even more attractive option is to tackle the peak in one day, and continue south next day **from the Nídha plateau**. This is a beautiful hike – at least, as long as the road they're attempting to blast through here is out of sight – and it's also a relatively easy one, four hours or so down to **VORÍZIA**, five or six to Kamáres. For either, track around to the southern edge of the plateau, where a gully (soon to become a considerable ravine) leads off. Large red arrows direct you towards Kamáres on the trail which passes east of the cave. For Vorízia, you follow the ravine for about an hour until a faint trail climbs out on the left (soon after this, the stream bed becomes impassable). Above the ravine there are fine views and a heady drop for another hour, when you must turn left (east) again. This is not obvious, but you should begin to see signs of life – goat trails and shepherds' huts. You cut past the top of a second, smaller ravine to a stone hut and then descend, zigzagging steeply, to a dirt road and Vorízia.

Vorízia and Kamáres both have **rooms and food** and at least one **bus** a day to Míres. Hitching to Míres should also be simple enough.

Across the island

Heading south across the island, towards Plakiás or Ayía Galíni, the road takes off from the very centre of Réthimnon, running along the side of the Public Gardens and then climbing rapidly above the town. Look back from the final bend and you have the city, its castle and harbour laid out like a map below you, but once the view has been blocked out, and you've passed the large petrol station which marks the end of the populated north coast, there's very little to stop for before the Libyan Sea. It's a scenic drive, though, on a good road.

A little under 10km from Réthimnon, just before the village of **ARMÉNI**, a sign to the right points the way to the **Minoan cemetery** of the same name. Important discoveries were made here and a couple of the chamber tombs, reached by long passages cut into the soft rock of the hillside, can be seen. However, no excavation has yet been done on the large settlement which must have existed to provide the cemetery with its customers. The site is a relatively late one, occupied only in the Late Minoan period after the fall of the great palaces (from around 1400 BC).

Another 10km takes you to the first of the turnoffs **towards Plakiás**: this one on a new road through ÁYIOS IOÁNNIS and down the Kotsifoú Gorge. Just by this turning there's a café/truck stop which is the best place to change buses if you are travelling between Ayía Galíni and Plakiás or vice versa (there's a timetable posted outside). There's also a good chance here of a lift with passing tourists or a local truck. Only a little further the alternative route to Plakiás takes off – through KOXARÉ and the Kourtaliótiko Gorge. Either way, the drive is a pretty spectacular one.

Spíli

Sticking to the main route south, **SPÍLI** is 30km from Réthimnon: the one place on this road where you might spend some time for its own sake. The town doesn't look much as you drive through – although the mountainside which hovers over the houses is impressive – but if you get off the main road, into the alleys which stagger up towards the cliff, it is wonderfully attractive. A sharp curve in the road marks the centre of town, by a small platía with a broken statue. Just above there's a fountain, with a long row of lions' heads splashing cold water into a trough, and above this begins a steep mosaic of flowered balconies, cobbled lanes, shady archways and giant urns and chimneypots. On occasion, Spíli can become quite crowded – many of the coach tours passing along the road make a brief stop here, usually for lunch – but between times and in the evenings it is quiet and rural. Stay overnight and you'll be woken early by the sounds of the farmyard and an agricultural community starting work.

There are numerous places offering **rooms** spread out along the main road –
the flower-decked *Green Hotel* at the north end of town is good, as is the large,
nameless place similarly positioned in the south, or there are plenty of smaller,
private houses with rooms advertised. Right on the corner by the fountain, a new
establishment offers comfortable but (during the day anyway) rather noisy
accommodation. The few places to **eat** (local yoghurt and honey are excellent)
and most of the local shops and businesses cluster close around the central
square: there's a post office and bank on the main road, and a metered phone in
the souvenir/newspaper shop on the corner by the fountain. If you can stay
longer there are some challenging hikes which start in Spíli – across to Yerakári
in the Amári valley for example – though the new road linking the two places
makes this seem less of an achievement than it once was.

Beyond Spíli, the road towards Ayía Galíni follows a long valley between Mount
Kédhros and the lesser summit of Sidhérotas. Apart from the odd patch of
extremely bad road surface it holds few excitements.

The Amári Valley

An alternative route south from Réthimnon, and a far less travelled one, is the
road which turns off south on the eastern fringe of town to run via the **Amári valley**.
Amári is one of those areas, like Sfakiá, which features large in almost everything
written about Crete – and especially in tales of wartime resistance – yet which is
hardly explored at all by modern visitors. Shadowed by the vast profile of
Psilorítis, its way of life survives barely altered by the changes of the last twenty,
or even fifty years. Throughout the valley, isolated hamlets subsist on the ubiquitous olive, with the occasional luxury of an orchard of cherries (especially around
Yerakári), pears or figs, and throughout there are a startling number of richly
frescoed churches. It's an environment conducive to slow exploration, with a
climate noticeably cooler than the coast: in midsummer the trees, flowers and
general greenery here make a stunning contrast to the rest of the island.

Three **buses** a day run from Réthimnon to the crossroads at AYÍA FOTINÍ:
onwards from there the service is sporadic to non-existent. It's best to explore on
foot – in which case a water bottle and the best map you can find are essential
equipment – but the main roads are fine if you have your own transport, and hitching is at least a possibility. As for staying in the valley, there are officially **rooms**
only in Thrónos and Yerakári, but don't let this deter you from asking in other
villages: villagers are often only too happy to have a paying guest for a night or
two, and traditional hospitality here has not yet been killed by abuse.

Whenever you come, but in July or August especially, you may be lucky
enough to stumble on a village **festival** in honour of the local saint, the harvest or
some obscure historical event. They're worth going out of your way for, so keep
an eye out for notices pasted to *kafenion* windows with details of when and whereabouts. Beginning in a distorted cacophony of overamplified Cretan music, the
celebrations continue until the participants are sufficiently gorged on roast lamb
and enlivened by wine to get down to the real business: the dancing. Cretan dancing at an event such as this is an extraordinary display of athleticism and, as often
as as not, endurance. If the party really gets off the ground locals will dig out
their old guns and rattle off a few rounds into the sky to celebrate. It should prove
an experience not swiftly forgotten.

The eastern slope: Thrónos

There are two roads through the Amári valley, one following the eastern side and clinging to the flanks of the Psilorítis range, the other tracing the edge of the lesser Kédhros range on the western side. Both are scenically spectacular, but the eastern route probably has the edge in terms of beauty and places of interest.

Going this way, the first of the real Amári villages is **THRÓNOS**, situated just off the main road at the head of the valley beneath the site of ancient Sybritos. Like so many others here, Thrónos seems lost in the past, with its beautifully frescoed **church** – Panayía – and majestic views across the valley and up to the mountains. There are more ancient remains, too. In the Byzantine era this was the seat of a bishop (hence *Thrónos*, throne) and these early Christian days are marked by the remains of a mosaic which spreads under the village church and oozes beyond its walls, with traces both inside and out. The new building, in fact, is only about a quarter the size of the original church, whose floorplan, guarded by a low rail, can be clearly seen. The elderly keeper will usually appear with the key as soon as you start to take an interest in the church; if not, ask the local kids, who will no doubt be watching your every move, or in the café/shop alongside. On the hill above the village are still earlier remains of the acropolis.

If you want to stay, simply follow the crude "Rent Rooms" signs through the ramshackle streets to a modern concrete structure with pink cinderblock balconies. The building is an aberration, but once inside it's out of sight and the balconies have the best view in the village; staying is somewhat bizarre, though. When it was built, this place clearly had aspirations, but the customers never came – the rooms are large and quite fancy, but their cooking facilities no longer seem to work, and lack of guests has left the place damp and musty. If you arrive in the afternoon you'll probably have to wake the owner from his siesta in one of the rooms, and in the evening the taverna downstairs (with stuffed eagles and a weasel) is where everyone gathers to play video games and watch TV – but not to eat. If you want some food (and this is the only place to get it, though during the day there's a *kafepantopolíon* open in the village), you eat whatever they have. The one exception is when the yard outside is pressed into use for periodic big *bouzouki* get-togethers, with dozens of tables put out and fires lit for barbecueing; keep an eye out for the posters, as these are well worth attending.

From Thrónos a relatively easy path leads north through the foothills in a couple of hours to the Moní Arkádhi (p.154) where you can pick up buses again; but get directions, as the way divides more than once. South, a paved road runs back into the main valley via KALÓYEROS, also an extremely easy stroll from Thrónos. Fifteen minutes' walk beyond this village, a narrow path leads uphill to the small stone church of **Áyios Ioánnis Theológos**, whose fine frescoes date from 1347 – ask about the key in the village on the way.

Amári

From here, back on the main road, the **Moní Asomáton** is only a little further. The buildings are Venetian, though the monastery itself is older; having survived centuries of resistance and revolution it finally became an agricultural school in 1931. It's not open to the public, but no one seems to mind if you wander in and look over the lovely old buildings, with their palm trees and huge spreading maples.

Outside, a line of fir and eucalyptus marks the beginning of the 5km paved road to the village of **AMÁRI**, the chief village of the valley. This is another beautiful drive or manageable walk, although the second half climbs quite steeply up the hill of Samítos which rises right in the middle of the valley. On the way you pass through two gorgeous villages, MONASTIRÁKI and OPSIGIÁS, but Amári itself outdoes them: it looks like nothing so much as a perfect Tuscan hill village. There's really nothing to do here – even the couple of *kafenía* seem to close for a siesta in the afternoon – but there are scintillating views across to Psilorítis, which seems really close here. For a bird's-eye view, climb the Venetian clock tower which dominates the narrow alleyways (the door is always open). It's not immediately obvious how to get here, but keep climbing and circling the hill and you'll make it eventually. Just outside town, the church of **Ayía Ánna**, reached down a track opposite the police station, has some extremely faded frescoes – and well they might be: dated 1225, they have a fair claim to being the oldest on Crete. As well as a police station, Amári also boasts an OTE and post office, and there's a daily bus at about 4pm for Réthimnon.

Continuing south to FOURFOURÁS and beyond, there are more lovely villages, with the peak of Psilorítis now almost directly above and the softer lines of Mount Kédhros behind the Samítos hill on the other side. Fourfourás is a traditional place to begin the climb of Psilorítis, although no one seems to tackle the peak from here any more (Anóyia and Kamáres are more convenient); it is also the trailhead of some arduous hikes to the lesser peaks. At NÍTHAVRIS the road divides. South, with the coast coming into view, you can head down to Ayía Galíni (see below) or follow the flank of the mountains around through Kamáres (p.162). Turn off west and you can curve round to complete a circle of the valley through the villages on the lower slopes of **Kédhros** (1777m).

The western side

The villages on this side of the valley look little different, but in fact they are almost entirely modern – rebuilt after their deliberate destruction during the war. George Psychoundakis watched the outrage from a cave on the slopes of Psilorítis:

> *"I stayed there two or three days before leaving, watching the Kedros villages burning ceaselessly on the other side of the deep valley. Every now and then we heard the sound of explosions. The Germans went there in the small hours of the twenty-second of August and the burning went on for an entire week. The villages we could see from there and which were given over to the flames were: Yerakari, Kardaki, Gourgouthoi, Vrysses, Smiles, Dryes and Ano-Meros. First they emptied every single house, transporting all the loot to Retimo, then they set fire to them, and finally, to complete the ruin, they piled dynamite into every remaining corner, and blew them sky high. The village schools met the same fate, also the churches and the wells, and at Ano-Meros they even blew up the cemetery. They shot all the men they could find."*

Officially these atrocities – other villages around Psilorítis, from Anóyia to Kamáres, were also burned – were in reprisal for the kidnap of General Kreipe, four months earlier. But Psychoundakis, for one, believed that it was a more general revenge, intended to destroy any effective resistance in the closing months of the German occupation. Today the villages of MÉRONAS, ELÉNES, YERAKÁRI, KARDHÁKI and VRÍSSES mark the southward progress of the German troops with etched stone **memorials** dated one day apart. ÁNO MÉROS has a striking war memorial of a woman wielding a hammer.

Even here, a number of frescoed **churches** survived the terror. Between Vrísses and Kardháki one such lies off to the right of the road, lying low in a field of grain and apparently forgotten. Push the sticky door aside, however, and the gloom gradually reveals beautiful Byzantine paintings around the altar. **YERAKÁRI** is a bigger, more modern and prosperous-looking village than most, with several places to stop for a drink or some food, and a couple of simple rooms establishments, one above a taverna (☎51-013), the other above the supermarket (☎22-313). Just to the south you'll pass the unusual **Monastery of Áyios Ioánnis Theológos**, with a spreading oak tree in front providing shade for a tapped spring. There are thirteenth-century frescoes in an exposed side chapel, and slightly later ones as you enter the church, all very battered. Finally, at **MÉRONAS**, to the right of the road, a soft pink Venetian-style church shelters frescoes from the fourteenth century: you'll need to ask for the key across the road. Again, it takes time to adjust your eyes to take in the painstaking detail of the artwork, darkened with age as it is; a torch would allow you to see a great deal more than the candles or nightlights which usually provide illumination.

Ayía Galíni

Twenty years ago **AYÍA GALÍNI** must have been an idyllic spot: an isolated fishing community of some five hundred souls nestling in a convenient fold of the mountains which dominate this part of the south coast. The village itself is barely a hundred years old, its inhabitants having moved down from the mountain villages of MÉLAMBES and SAKTOÚRIA as the traditional threat of piracy along the coast receded. Catch it out of season and Ayía Galíni, its streets of white houses crowded in on three sides by mountains and opening below to a small, busy harbour, can still appeal. But this is a face which is increasingly hard to find. Packed throughout the season with package tourists, and confined by the limits of its narrow situation, the village's old houses are rapidly being squeezed out by ever larger blocks of rent rooms and concrete hotels. As you drive in down the steeply looping spur off the main road, you'll find the fringes of this development crawling out of the gulch like some mummy leaving its coffin in a bad horror flick. Since the beach was never up to much anyway, there's little reason to stay here long in summer. The lack of a decent beach is a shame, for otherwise there's something appealing about Ayía Galíni's relatively staid and respectable brand of tourism. It's a nicer place than it looks, or than you'd expect from first impressions; largely because despite the development the people have stayed friendly and the atmosphere Cretan.

Practicalities

Buses to Ayía Galíni terminate at the bus station by the church, near the top of the village proper. It's a handy spot to get your bearings since few of the streets are named and such names as there are seem rarely used. The nucleus of the place is built around three streets which run down to the harbour. The first of these (technically Venizélou) is a continuation of the main road into town: along it you'll find post office, bakery, doctor and a couple of car hire places. In the narrow street parallel to this to the east is the petrol station and shops; the next street along is packed with tavernas (and known locally as "Taverna Street"). All of this falls within an extremely small area where nothing is more than a couple of minutes' walk away.

Accommodation

Rooms are equally tightly packed, and there are so many that you can usually find something – though for much of July and August all but a handful are pre-booked by tour operators. Prices are very closely linked to demand: for most of the summer both are high, but away from peak seasons you may get an exceptional bargain. Probably the best place to start looking is at the top of the town, either walking down to the left from the main road as it arrives, or up Taverna Street and round to the right. The latter is the best way to *Rent Rooms Acropol*, a very basic place with an unbeatable location right on the edge of the cliff. The daughter of the people here runs the *Hotel Acropolis*, not far away on the main road, which is much more likely to have room but also much less well positioned. Between the two you'll pass dozens of other possibilities – the hotels *Candia* and *Dedalos* are promising – and you'll need to ask at each one. Check the room before taking it, too, as some of these places have seen better days. A number of newer places which might be worth trying are in the streets on the other side of the main road, west of where the bus drops you, near the OTE: this is an area only just being developed.

There's also a **campsite**, *Camping Agia Galini*, to the east near the mouth of the river, reached either by a dirt track which takes off from the main road about 1km outside the village, or by walking out along the beach. The campsite itself may be full in midsummer, in which case, despite official discouragement, there's rarely any shortage of people sleeping on the beach.

Food and nightlife

One major and undeniable benefit which the crowds have brought to Ayía Galíni is a vast range of **food and drink**: much of it excellent and thanks to the competition not overpriced. The bulk of the tavernas are located, surprisingly enough, along Taverna Street, which in the evening is choked with pedestrian traffic. There are plenty of good places here with tables spilling out into the street. Good value for a great setting is the *Restaurant Onar*, overlooking the harbour from a rooftop at the bottom of the street. Places which are not on Taverna street, and hence less easy to find, include *Horiatis Taverna*, near *Biggis Bikes* opposite the bus stop, quiet and out of the way; *Babi's Pizza/Snackbar*, right by the bus stop and hence handy for a quick snack while you wait (they have a sign claiming to employ the fourth best chef in the world, which must breach all rules of advertising honesty); and *Stelios Café*, on the square below this on the main road, where they have good drinks and breakfasts and occasionally serve freshly made *loukoumadhes*.

There are plenty of **bars and discos** where you can carry on after you've eaten, mostly around the bottom of Taverna Street and around the harbour. *Zorba's* is a long-established favourite and right next door is *Prison*, where you can go to dance. *Whispers* is one of the best of those actually overlooking the harbour.

The basics

As far as more **practical matters** go, you'll again find everything you need in a very small space. The lone exchange office run by the *National Bank* (by the

Stelios Café) can have long queues, but the post office or just about any shop or travel agent will be happy to change your money: just make sure you know the rates. *Candia Tours*, for example, will exchange cash, travellers' cheques and Eurocheques. Other shops, including several mini supermarkets, are well scattered about, as are travel agents, offering a variety of local and island tours, and **bike hire** places. *Biggis Bikes*, more or less opposite the bus stop, is good, as is *Soulia car rental* (☎91347). There's a new OTE office (9am–1pm only) up the hill to the west of the bus stop: it's signed from there. **Telephones** that operate longer hours can be found in *Minos* shop on Taverna Street (near the top) and at the nearby kiosk.

Beaches and day trips

The **beach** at Ayía Galíni is astonishingly small when you consider the number of people who expect to use it. It's not even very sandy or attractive – once the few patches of soft sand have been claimed you have to hire a chair if you hope to lounge in any comfort. It lies to the east of the village, reached by a narrow path that tracks around the cliff from the harbour front, or by one that descends from the top of the town (or you can drive round and park by *Camping Agia Galini*). Walking round by the cliffs, you'll pass caves which in the war served as gun emplacements. You can get food and drink at a number of places immediately behind the beach.

Further afield **to the west** are some much better patches of sand, although thanks to regular boat trips (details from any travel agent, or get your ticket at the harbour) these are rarely deserted either. **Áyios Yióryios** is also fairly easily reached on foot: take the main road up past the bus station and at the crown of the first bend follow a left turn towards a group of apartments. Just beyond these you cross a dry river bed and head up the hillside on a fairly well-worn path marked with splashes of red paint. The beach is getting on for two hours away, a shingly cove with two tavernas, one of which has rooms; there are a couple of other, less attractive coves along the way. **Áyios Pávlos** is much further, but also much more attractive, with some striking rock formations around a sheltered bay, and excellent snorkelling. The boat is much the easiest way to get here, but you can also drive via SAKTOURIA, with the final 6km on a very rough, unsurfaced road. The quicker route is to take the main road towards Spíli out of town and then turn left (signed) after about 12km, but the old road via MÉLAMBES has been newly sealed and is an excitingly winding route with great views. Driving has the advantage that (if you choose a day with no boat trip) you can have the place almost to yourself – and it's small enough to be easily ruined by too many people. There are two taverna/rooms places, *Ayios Pavlos* immediately above the beach and the *Hotel Livikon* a little way up the road, plus a couple of modest apartment developments.

Plakiás and around

Thirty kilometres west, Plakiás is beginning to rival Ayía Galíni as a south coast resort. Commercialised as it is, though, it still has a very different feel: accommodation is simpler, less of it is booked in advance, and the nearby beaches are infinitely better. The people who stay here are on the whole much younger too.

There are two main approaches to the area, both off the Réthimnon to Ayía Galíni road. The first is on a newly surfaced road down through the **Kotsifóu Gorge**; the second, just a few kilometres further on, via the even more impressive **Kourtaliótiko Gorge**. Either way, it's worth pulling over in the gorge to take time to appreciate the scenery and the wildlife (from snakes by the water to birds of prey soaring above). On the first route the gorge eventually opens out to leave you on the main coast road west of Plakiás: turn right for Sellía, left for Mírthios and Plakiás. On the second there are parking places about halfway through the gorge and steps leading down to the chapel of Áyios Nikólaos near the bottom. Further on you have a choice of turning right for Lefkóyia and Plakiás or continuing to follow the course of the stream all the way down to Préveli.

Mírthios

MÍRTHIOS hangs high above the Bay of Plakiás, with wonderful views down over it. It's a small village but, thanks to a large and friendly **youth hostel** (☎31-202), one which sees a fair number of young travellers and is extremely lively. The youth hostel is hard to miss, a garishly painted building just above the road in the very centre of the village. Facilities are pretty basic (though you can cook), but it's a popular meeting place and a good source of local information; if you want more luxury, several other places offer **rooms**. Along the road opposite the hostel are a few tavernas with terraces hanging over the hillside, and a general store. *Giorgio's Taverna*, right under the youth hostel, is particularly friendly and recommended.

For other facilities you have to go down to Plakiás, about twenty minutes' steep downhill walk on a path which sets off from the platía/car parking space opposite the hostel. The long walks to the beach (and much longer climbs back) are the chief disadvantage of staying here, but you are rewarded with considerably lower prices and friendlier atmosphere – locals still just about outnumber visitors. And, of course, if you're a keen walker it's heaven: ask at the youth hostel about some of the more substantial hikes, to almost entirely deserted coves to the west, or up into some of the gorges. The Plakiás bus usually comes up to Mírthios after it has dropped most of the passengers, but check with the driver. You may get left by the junction, about ten minutes' walk away, on the way in.

Plakiás

PLAKIÁS itself is growing all the time, and it's no longer the unspoilt village all too many people arrive here expecting – *SunMed* took over some years ago. Even so, it's still some way from the really big league, and if it's not that attractive in itself it does make a good base for the beautiful countryside and excellent beaches all around. The road comes in from the east, behind the beach, and runs straight into the heart of things along the harbour front. There's basically just a single street that runs inland, rapidly deteriorating into paths which wind up towards Sellía and Mírthios, otherwise everything is strung out in a line facing the sea or in tiny new streets, no more than three or four houses long, built off the main road. The coast road very rapidly deteriorates into an extremely rough track west of the last houses, eventually ending altogether at Souda Beach after some 3km.

Accommodation

There are loads of new hotels and **rooms** in Plakiás, indeed there's little else, but even so you may have difficulty finding a vacancy. As ever, it's a question of wandering around and asking everywhere: those up the backstreet, which of course lack the sea views (but are also quieter), are usually the last to fill. Among the better possibilities are *Pension Asteria* and *Garzonieres*, both up the main inland street near the *Secret Nest* restaurant, and the slightly more expensive *Hotel Livikon* (☎31-216), right by where the buses stop. Thanks to its position this can be noisy, also the problem at rooms above *Christos Taverna*, a little further round the front. The more luxurious B-class *Hotel Lamon* (☎31-279), back a way on the main road, is less pricey than it looks and also has regular-priced rooms in another building. Various more peaceful places can be found off the road before you really arrive in town: look for the signs to, for example, *Panorama* and *Finikas*, each a five-minute walk or so from the centre. In the other direction, new places are starting to open along the coastal track west of town, and if you have a vehicle it's worth driving through to check these out: *Geronimos* taverna/rooms, for example, is set some way above the road, very isolated.

Out here too is the small but noisy **youth hostel** (☎31-306), almost the first building you pass as you come into town; this seems to attract a more party crowd than the Mírthios one, and the music rarely stops. There's also a small and rather scruffy **campsite**, *Camping Plakias*, just behind the town. Wherever you stay, be warned that Plakiás is periodically plagued with **mosquitoes**: the pyrethrin coils or electric devices sold locally are the most effective deterrent.

Eating, entertainment and the basics

Once you're settled there's little else to discover in town. Right on the front at the centre of town is a little row of **tavernas** and bars with tables right out by the water, none of them terribly cheap (in fact food is generally costly here by Cretan standards). *Sofia's* here is just about the longest established place in town, serving huge portions of reasonably good food, but expensive. *Gorgona* next door is very similar; *Christos*, a few doors down, slightly cheaper, with a pleasant tree-shaded terrace and usually at least one vegetarian dish. Back towards the bridge at the entrance to town, *Zorbas* serves pizzas and pasta as well as the usual staples (and a huge chef's salad); on the other side of the bridge, set down a bit, *Lysseos* strives for a romantic, candlelit atmosphere. The ambience and food seem rather more authentically Cretan at another small cluster of places round the corner from *Christos*, facing west along the shore: *Apanemo*, next to the *On The Rocks* bar, *Café Skinos* and *Kedros*. On the way here you pass *Julia's Place*, English-run and not in the most attractive setting, but the plain vegetarian food, with only the slightest Greek influence, can make a welcome change. They also serve home-made cakes. Finally *Secret Nest*, at the back of town, is a pretty regular, basic taverna.

The **bars** don't take much finding, since the music will lead you there. Most are lined up on the waterfront, keeping people who stay here awake. Real late-nighters can move on to the fancy *Hexagon Club*, among the new development on the road in, or to the far less pretentious *Meltemi* disco, in a wooden hut out near the youth hostel. Things don't start to liven up here till midnight or so.

There are relatively few other facilities in Plakiás, but there's at least one of everything you could really need. A bright yellow **post office** van is parked by the harbour, and although there's no bank you can **change money** here or at many of the travel agents or new supermarkets. Also right in the centre are a couple of **bike hire** places (try *Motoplakias*; ☎31-400) and numerous **travel agencies** (*Plakias Tours* also rents cars) – speciality boat trips to Souda Beach, Préveli and even Loutró. There's a **launderette** (Mon–Sat 10am–1.30pm & 5.30–9pm) round at the western edge of town near *Julia's Place*. Some of the tackiest souvenirs in all Crete can be bought at the *Forum* **supermarket**, in the new development on the road in; they also have books, suntan oil and some food.

Beaches

Getting to the **beach** need involve no more than a two-minute walk. The town is set at the western end of the bay, and east of the paved harbour grey sand curves around in an unbroken line to the headland a mile or more away. Unfortunately this beach is not as good close up as it appears from a distance. The long open sweep of the bay means it can be exposed and windy, and there tends to be a fair amount of rubbish lying about. There's plenty of space – especially towards the far end where there's a large hotel and a beach bar – but you'll find much better sands beyond the headland at Damnóni (below), or to the west at Souda Beach.

Souda Beach is just over half an hour's walk west of town, past signs of encroaching development, and there are places to stop for a swim along the way. The sand is grey and coarse, but there's plenty of room and the water at the far end is reasonably sheltered. Above the very end of the beach, the *Galini* taverna enjoys a lovely position in a miniature palm grove.

Damnóni and Lefkóyia

Just to the east of Plakiás Bay, beyond a headland riddled with caves and wartime bunkers and gun emplacements, lie some of the most tempting beaches in central Crete, albeit ones which are already a very poorly kept secret. Three splashes of yellow sand, divided by rocky promontories, go by the general name of **DAMNÓNI**. To get there on foot, follow the main road east and turn right just after the "Welcome to Plakiás" sign, where a track leads through the olive groves. After a while you'll see the beach below you and a path which runs down to it – about thirty minutes in all. Alternately, but slightly longer, you can walk right to the end of the beach, past the big hotel, and on over the headland. Driving, you have to go much further round: follow the road towards Lefkóyia and turn down at the sign for Damnóni or, much further on, for Amoúdhi.

Damnóni beach itself is the first you reach, and the only one that has so far really seen the beginning of the development: a big new hotel, the *Minoan Prince*, is going up on the hillside behind, and there are numerous new rooms places (*Pension Socrates*, on the road in, is not a bad place to stay, set in a little oasis of greenery). When the hotel is finished it may change things forever, but for now Damnóni still consists of two tavernas, a wonderfully long strip of yellow sand and super-clear water. The taverna right on the beach always seems very unfriendly, and they have some particularly dank rooms, but they'll generally let you camp, which is more pleasant; there's better food at the place immediately behind.

At the far end of Damnóni beach you'll usually find a few people who've dispensed with their clothes, and the little cove which shelters the middle of the three beaches (a scramble over the rocks, or there's a just passable track) is entirely nudist. This little enclave can get very crowded, and at times looks like an illustration from *Health and Efficiency* magazine – blow-up Nivea beach balls and all – but it's a good-humoured crowd and, exceptionally, there are usually quite a few Greek naturists too. Again, the water is beautiful and there are caves at the back of the beach (around which people camp) and rocks to dive from. There's some great snorkelling to be had around these rocks with their caves and passages. Continuing over the rocks you pass another tiny pocket of sand (also nudist) before **Amoúdhi Beach**, where there's a rather more sedate atmosphere and another taverna (very friendly, with much better rooms for rent and a huge, unfinished extension).

If lying on beaches was your only plan, you'd have less far to walk, and probably spend less, staying in the village of **LEFKÓYIA** rather than Plakiás. Lefkóyia is barely twenty minutes' walk from Amoúdhi and has a couple of supermarkets, four or five pleasant rooms places, and a couple of tavernas (try *Stelios*) by the main road: its chief disadvantage is that it is not itself on the coast, and that it has no other facilities at all. For the people who stay here, these are also its chief advantages. Don't, incidentally, try to walk to the *Beach Hotel* signposted from the village – it is an extremely long way.

Moní Préveli and "Palm Beach"

Some 6km southeast of Lefkóyia the celebrated **Monastery of Préveli** (8am–1pm & 3–7pm) perches high above the sea. Its fame was capped in the last war when the monks provided shelter for allied troops stranded on the island after the Battle of Crete, feeding the soldiers and organising them into groups to be taken off nearby beaches by submarine. There's a monument commemorating the evacuations and alongside the icons in the church a number of offerings from grateful individuals and governments. The church also houses a cross said to contain a fragment of the True Cross; there's a small museum with other relics and religious vestments; and a fountain in the courtyard with the Greek inscription "Wash your sins, not only your face". There are also fine views out to sea.

The road to Préveli turns off the main road between Lefkóyia and ASÓMATOS, a badly signed dusty track at first, but paved later as it climbs towards the monastery. Not far before the Préveli Monastery you pass the ruinous **Monastery of Áyios Ioánnis** (Kato Préveli), long abandoned and with only the church standing whole amid the broken walls and roofless cells.

Palm Beach: Paradise Lost
Earlier still you'll have passed an ancient-looking bridge (actually a nineteenth-century copy of a Venetian original), where a sign indicates a left turn to a Taverna and Palm Beach. Almost immediately you turn right, shortly crossing another cobbled Venetian bridge, beyond which the track leads eventually (after perhaps twenty minutes' tortuous, rough driving) to *Amudi* rooms/taverna, one of two on a not terribly attractive beach alongside Palm Beach. From here it's a ten-minute scramble around the cliff, a narrow, slippery path for which you need decent shoes and at least one hand free to hold on with – though once you've managed the first bit it gets a lot easier. Alternatively, you can head down the cliffs from Préveli, which is even tougher: a track (barely driveable, or fifteen minutes' walk) takes off about 1km before the monastery, and at the end a marked path clambers steeply down over the rocks, for about half an hour. If you don't feel confident of climbing, the boat will get you here with a great deal less fuss.

Sadly, **Palm Beach** is no longer worth all this effort – at least not if you're here in the middle of the season. It still looks beautiful – a sand-filled cove right at the end of the Kourtaliótiko Gorge, where a freshwater estuary feeds a little oasis complete with palm grove and cluster of oleanders – but too many visitors have ruined it. On any given day you may have three or more day-trip boats, plus people who've walked in and a sizeable community of campers. The worst problem is that there's no toilet for any of them, so almost every sheltered corner stinks, and there are also vast piles of accumulated rubbish, mostly plastic water bottles. If you do come (and at the beginning of the season it's still lovely), take all your rubbish away with you. Behind the beach, you can walk up the palm-lined riverbanks or paddle through the icy water upstream. Lots of people camp along the banks, a lovely setting, but again they have no way of disposing of their rubbish and sewage – in fact here these back to nature types (unusually) seem the worst offenders. Further upstream, before the gorge becomes too steep to follow, are a couple of deep pools nice to swim in. On the west edge of the beach, a small bar sells drinks and a few basic provisions, mostly tinned. A strange thought as you lie on the crowded sands here is that it was from here, forty years ago, that many of the soldiers who sought refuge at the monastery were eventually evacuated by submarine.

West of Plakiás: Sellía and Rodhákino

Heading west from Plakiás, towards Frangokástello, it's a stiff climb up towards Mírthios and then round, hugging the mountainside, to **SELLÍA**. Looking up from Plakiás or across from Mírthios you would imagine that Sellía had the best views of all over this area, but if you do no more than drive through you see nothing – it is the backs of the houses which face out towards Africa. If you want to stop and take a look it's easy enough to find a path through or, better still, head for the church and cemetery at the western edge of town. There's a track from the centre of the village down to Plakiás, about half an hour's walk steeply below, and there's a pleasant long circular hike from Plakiás up here and then back down via Mírthios.

Beyond Sellía the nature of the country changes and there's a real feeling of the approach of western Crete. The road runs high above a series of capes and small coves, quite a good surface all the way apart from a brief unpaved section just outside ARGOULÉS. The only village of any size is **RODHÁKINO**, set on steep streets above a ravine which leads down to a small beach (where General Kreipe was finally taken off the island after his kidnap). There are a few rooms and a taverna here, but it's a very quiet, unvisited place.

Beyond Rodhákino a number of beaches look incredibly tempting far below, but only one seems at all easy to get to; heading down a vertiginous dirt track just before the tarmac on the main road runs out.

travel details

Buses

Réthimnon–Iráklion (1hr 30min) 28 daily, 6.30am–9.45pm, a couple via the old road (2hr).
Réthimnon–Haniá (1hr 30min) 28 daily, 6.15am–10pm, a couple via the old road (3hr).
Réthimnon–Omalós (2hr 30min) daily at 6.15am and 7am.

Réthimnon–Plakiás (45min) 5 daily, 6.15am–5.30pm.
Réthimnon–Spíli/Ay. Galíni (40min/1hr 30min) daily at 6.45am, 9am, 10.30am and 2.15pm.
Réthimnon–Arkádhi (50min) daily at 6am, 10.30am, noon and 2.30pm.

Réthimnon–Anóyia (1hr 30min) daily at 5.30am and 2.30pm
Réthimnon–Amári (1hr) twice daily.
Ay. Galíni–Plakiás/Hóra Sfakíon (1hr 30min/ 2hr 30min) daily at 8.30am.
Ay. Galíni–Plakiás (1hr 30min) daily at 8.45am and 4pm.
Ay. Galíni–Festós/Iráklion (30min/2hr) 9 daily, 8am–8pm.

Ay. Galíni–Réthimnon (1hr 30min) daily at 7am, 10.30am, noon, 2.30pm and 4pm.
Plakiás–Ay. Galíni (1hr 30min) daily at 10am and 6.30pm.
Some of these services are restricted on Sundays

Ferries
To Pireás Tues, Thurs and Sat 7.30pm
To Thíra Sun 7am, plus seasonal day trips.

ΑΓ ΓΑΛΗΝΗ	Αγ Γαλήνη	Ay. Galíni
ΑΝΩΓΕΙΑ	Ανώγεια	Anóyia
ΑΣΙΓΩΝΙΑ	Ασιγωνία	Asigonía
ΑΞΟΣ	Αξός	Axós
ΕΠΙΣΚΟΠΗ	Επισκοπή	Episkopí
ΘΡΟΝΟΣ	Θρόνος	Thrónos
ΚΑΜΑΡΕΣ	Καμάρες	Kamáres
ΛΕΥΚΟΓΕΙΑ	Λευκόγεια	Lefkóyia
Μ. ΑΡΚΑΔΙΟΥ	Μ. Αρκαδίου	Arkadhi Monastery
ΜΠΑΛΙ	Μπαλί	Balí
ΜΥΡΘΙΟΣ	Μύρθιος	Mírthios
ΠΕΡΑΜΑ	Πέραμα	Pérama
ΠΛΑΚΙΑΣ	Πλακιάς	Plakiás
ΠΡΕΒΕΛΙ	Πρέβελι	Préveli
ΡΕΘΥΜΝΟ	Ρέθυμνο	Réthimnon
ΣΠΗΛΙ	Σπήλι	Spíli
ΦΟΥΡΦΟΥΡΑΣ	Φουρφουράς	Fourfourás
ΨΗΛΟΡΕΙΤΗΣ	Ψηλορείτης	Psilorítis

CHAPTER FOUR

HANIA

Haniá, Crete's westernmost province, is still its least visited. This alone is a significant part of its attraction. And although tourist development is spreading fast, and has already covered much of the coast around Haniá, the west is likely to remain one of the emptier parts of the island, partly because there are no big sand beaches to accommodate resort hotels, partly because the great archaeological sites are a long way from here. In their place are some of the most classic elements of the island: scattered coves, rural, unexploited villages and, spectacularly, a great vista of mountains.

The city of **Haniá**, island capital until 1971, is reason in itself to come – unequivocally the most enjoyable of Crete's larger towns, full of harbour life, and littered with oddments from its Venetian and Turkish past. To either side, almost along the whole **north coast** of the province, spreads a line of sandy beach – at times exposed, and increasingly developed, but still with numerous reaches where you can escape the crowds. It is broken by three great peninsulas: **Akrotíri**, enclosing the magnificent natural harbour of the **Bay of Sóudha**; **Rodhópou**, a bare and roadless tract of mountain; and at the western tip of the island **Gramvoúsa**, uninhabited and entirely barren. Akrotíri is overshadowed by NATO, with air bases on land and naval installations in the bay (Haniá itself is often crowded with servicemen and buzzed by low-flying aircraft), but it's still worth a day trip, with a couple of excellent beaches, **Stavrós** above all, and two beautiful monasteries. Most of the region's tourists stay to the west, on the coast between Haniá and Rodhópou, in one of a number of villages now joined together by a string of low-key development through **Ayía Marína** and **Plataniás**, with the villas and apartments thinning out as you head further from the city.

The south is dominated by the peaks of the **Lefká Óri** – the **White Mountains** – whose grey bulk, snowcapped through to June, indeed fills every view in western Crete. Although marginally less high and considerably less famous than the Psilorítis range, they're far more rewarding for walking or climbing. Along the south coast the mountains drop straight to the Libyan Sea and the few towns which exist here do so in their shadow, clinging to what flat land can be found around the bays. Through the heart of the massif there's no road at all, and nor is there any driveable route along the south coast: unless you want to travel back and forth across the island you'll rely on boats here, or on foot. As far as **walking** goes there is, above all, the great hike through the National Park in the **Gorge of Samariá**, Europe's longest gorge. Despite the hordes who thunder through all summer long, it's still a stunning experience. With a little more adventure and preparation there are scores of other, deserted, hiking routes to take.

The south coast communities beneath the mountains see plenty of visitors, mostly gorge trippers passing through, but none could really be described as a resort. **Ayía Rouméli** and **Loutró** can be reached only on foot or by boat. The former, where the walk through the gorge ends, nevertheless manages to be a crowded, overdeveloped little place. If you want somewhere to stay over after your exertions, the serenity of Loutró is a much better bet. **Hóra Sfakíon** is similarly given over to processing day-trippers, and though this capital·of the wild region known as Sfakiá is a pleasant and interesting enough place to stay, you'll find far more peace down the coast a little, at the superb beaches by the Venetian castle of **Frangokástello**.

The west end of the island, beyond Rodhópou, is very sparsely settled. The port of **Kastélli** is the only town of any size, while at **Paleohóra** in the south there's one growing resort. **Sóuyia**, thanks to a new road, may be the next to fall; for the moment it seems curiously in limbo, awaiting developments. The whole of the mountainous southwestern corner, an area known as **Sélinos**, is worth exploring in fact: with rough roads leading to untouched mountain villages and little-known ruins and churches. On the west facing coast – hard to get to but well worth the effort – are two of Crete's finest beaches, **Falásarna** and **Elafonísi**.

THE NORTH COAST

With **Haniá as a base**, getting around the **north coast** is easy enough: it's a heavily populated region with excellent roads and a stream of buses along the main routes. The problem comes in relying on public transport to get off the beaten track, or into the interior. On Rodhópou, for example, there are no services at all, and whilst most inland villages are served by at least a couple of daily buses, they're frustrating if you want to get to several in a single day.

Hiring wheels, then, is a good investment, and there are plenty of outlets in Haniá. Just remember that this is mountainous country – the smaller mopeds are more or less all right for one but with two people on board they simply won't make it up many of the hills.

Haniá

HANIÁ, as any of its residents will tell you, is the spiritual capital of Crete, even if the nominal title rests in Iráklion's urban sprawl. And with its shimmering waterfront, crumbling masonry and web of alleys, it *is* an extraordinarily attractive city, especially if you can catch it in spring when the Lefká Óri's snowcapped peaks seem to hover above the roofs. It leaves you in no doubt, too, that you are in a city as well as a resort. The permanent population of the town – fast expanding into hill and coastal suburbs – always outnumbers the tourists and visitors (many of whom are sailors or airmen from the NATO bases at Soúdha or Akrotíri). For travellers, it adds up to a city worth getting to know, and where you'll almost certainly stay longer than intended, making use of plentiful accommodation, excellent markets, shops and nightlife, and most other facilities you could hope for.

One of the longest continuously inhabited city sites anywhere in the world, Haniá's more recent history (it was a hotbed of nationalist sentiment under the Turks and most of the heavy fighting in the Battle of Crete took place nearby) has left it with little in the way of monuments. It remains an enticing place to wander round, though, with odd reminders of the past at every pace, and antique material used and re-used in the most unlikely settings.

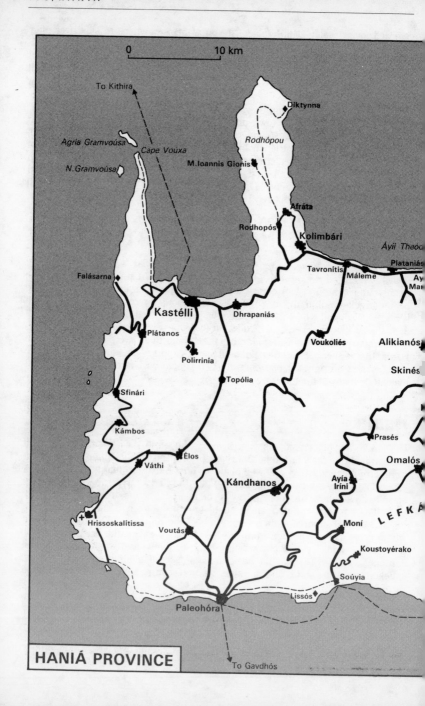

HANIÁ PROVINCE

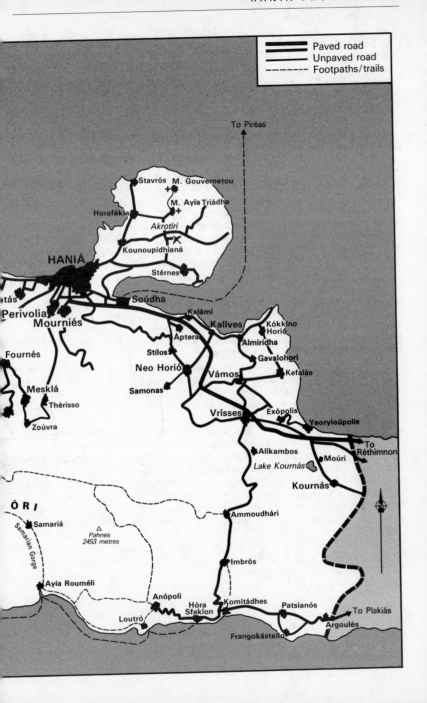

Paved road
Unpaved road
Footpaths/trails

To Piréas

Stavrós M. Gouvernetou

M. Ayía Triádha

Horafákia

Akrotíri

Kounoupidhianá

HANIÁ

Stérnes

tás

Perivolia

Mourniés

Soúdha

Kalámi

Kalives

Kókkino Horió

Áptera

Almirídha

Fournés

Stílos

Gavalohori

Neo Horió

Vámos

Kefalás

Mesklá

Thérisso

Samonas

Zoúvra

Vrisses

Exópolis

Yeoryioúpolis

To Réthimnon

Alíkambos

Moúri

Lake Kournás

Kournás

ÓRI

Ammoudhári

Samariá

Pahnes
2453 metres

Imbrós

Ayía Rouméli

Anópoli

Komitádhes

Hóra Sfakíon

Patsianós

To Plakiás

Loutró

Argoulés

Frangokástello

As **Kydonia**, it was a Minoan community of obscure status: only scattered remnants have so far been brought to light, but many believe that there's a major palace still to be discovered somewhere in the vicinity. After the collapse of the Minoan palace culture, it grew into one of the island's most important cities – well enough known for its citizens to earn a mention in Homer's *Odyssey* – and remained so through the classical Greek and **Roman** eras. The hillside area known as Kastélli served as the city's acropolis (as it remained until this century) but dwellings spread at least as far as the extent of the walled city which can be seen today. Roman mosaics have been discovered beneath the Cathedral Square and up around the area of the present market.

In the early Christian era, Kydonia was the seat of a bishop, and under the protection of Byzantium the city flourished along with the island. As the Byzantine empire became increasingly embattled, however, so its further outposts, Kydonia (and Crete) included, suffered neglect. Not until the thirteenth century is much heard of the place again, when the Genoese (with local support) seized the city from the Venetians and held it for some twenty years from 1263 to 1285.

When the Venetians finally won it back they acted quickly to strengthen the defences, turning the city – renamed **La Canea** – into a formidable bulwark in the west. The city walls were built in two stages. In the fourteenth century Kastélli alone was fortified: within these walls stood the original Cathedral and the city administration. Later, in the sixteenth century, new walls were constructed as a defence against constant raids by pirate corsairs – in particular against the systematic ravages of Barbarossa. It is these defences, along with the Venetian harbour installations, which define the shape of Haniá's old town today. Within the walls, meanwhile, a flourish of public and private construction left La Canea perhaps the island's most beautiful city.

In 1645, after a two-month siege of terrible losses (mostly on the Turkish side – their commander was executed on his return home for losing as many as 40,000 men), Haniá fell to the **Turks**. It was the first major Cretan stronghold to succumb, becoming the Turkish island capital and seat of the Pasha. Its churches were converted to mosques, the defences more or less maintained, and there must have been some building at least: today it is barely possible to distinguish Venetian buildings maintained by the Turks from originals or Turkish workmanship.

For the rest, it is a history of struggle: for independence during the **nineteenth century**, then in **resistance** against the Germans in the last war. In the independence struggle, the city's most dramatic moment came in 1897, following the outbreak of war between Greece and Turkey, when the Great Powers (Britain, France, Russia and Italy) imposed a peace and stationed a joint force in the waters off Haniá. From here, in one famous incident, they bombarded Cretan insurgents attempting prematurely to raise the flag of Greece on the hill of Profítis Elías (see p.196). When the Turkish administrators were finally forced to leave, Prince George, the High Commissioner chosen by the powers, established his capital here for the brief period of regency before Crete finally became part of the Greek state. More **recent history** has been disturbed only by World War II. With most of the German landings and the bulk of the fighting on the coast immediately west of the city, Haniá suffered severe bombardment in the opening stages of the battle, destruction eventually compounded by a fire which wiped out almost everything apart from the area around the harbour. In the final six months of their occupation of the island, the Germans withdrew to a heavily defended perimeter centred on the city.

Arrival

Sizeable city though it is, you should have little problem working out Haniá's geography once you've reached the centre. The old city clusters around the harbour and most tourists rightly confine themselves to this area or the fringes of the new town up towards the bus station. You may get lost wandering among the narrow alleys, but it's never far to the sea, to one of the recognisable main thoroughfares or to some other obvious landmark.

Points of arrival

Arriving **by boat**, you'll anchor at the port and naval base of Soúdha, at the head of the magnificent Bay of Soúdha. Given the choice, this is the right way to come, with unparalleled views of the Lefká Óri – the pale heights visible from miles out even when they're not topped with snow – as you approach the island. SOÚDHA itself is about 10km from Haniá and there are city buses approximately every fifteen minutes which will run you in to the marketplace. You wouldn't choose to stay in Soúdha – the hotels are right above the constant traffic of the main road and it's a grubby little place, dusty and remorselessly concrete – and fortunately there's no real need to do so: most ferries arrive first thing and leave in the evening. If you are stuck you'll find just about every facility on the square right by the ferry dock: shops, a bank, a post office, a couple of bars and restaurants and two D-class hotels. Taxis also park up in the square – you may need one on arrival when buses can be swamped.

If you fly in, you'll find yourself at an **airport** which is tiny and offers absolutely no frills. About 15km out, in the middle of the Akrotíri peninsula, it doubles as a NATO air base – so no pictures. *Olympic* flights are met by a bus, and if you've arrived with a tour group you might be able to hitch a lift in their coach, otherwise there are plenty of taxis; official prices to most popular destinations are listed.

The **bus station** – if you've come from anywhere else in Crete – is on Odhós Kidhonías, easy walking distance from most of the action. There's a left luggage facility here if you want to leave your bags while you find a room. Turn right out of the entrance, then left down the side of Platía 1866, and you'll come to the major junction at the top of Hálidhon.

Orientation

This junction, as much as anywhere, marks the centre of town. East, to the right, Odhós **Yianári** leads past the market and, if you follow round, either to the main coast road or out onto the Akrotíri peninsula. **Skalídhi**, westwards, leads eventually out of town towards Kastélli Kisámou. North, straight ahead, **Hálidhon** descends to the harbour and into the heart of the old town. As you stand at this junction, everything in front and below you is basically the old, walled city – behind and to either side lie the newer parts.

Much of your **shopping** and other **business** will take place around this border of the old and new: down towards the market you'll find pharmacies, paper shops, banks. The market – of which more later – is amazing: **Tzanakáki** and **Konstantínou**, opposite, represent modern Haniá, full of clothes shops, car-hire places and more banks. At the bottom of Tzanakáki you'll find the post office and OTE. East along Skalídhi and back towards the bus station are more basic and old-fashioned shops, and at **Platía 1866** the terminus for most **city buses**, espe-

HANIÁ

Lighthouse

Firkas and Naval Museum

ANGELOU

AKTI KANARI

To the beach

APOSTOLIDHOU

METAHAKI

THEOTOKOPOULOU

Renieri Gate

AKTI KOUNDOURIOTOU

AKTI TOMBAZI

EOT

LITHINON

PLATIA SINDRIVANI

ZAMBELIU

SKUFON

KONDILAKI

Archeological Museum

KAPE...

PARDHALI

METAHAKI

HALIDHON

BOTOLO

SKRIDLOF

KIRILOU

Schiavo Bastion

SKALIDHI

PLATIA 1866

MANOUSOYANAKIDHOU

KIDHONIAS

Bus Station

ZIMYRAKAKIDON

SFAKIANAKI

LIMPUS

KISSAMOU

To Kastélli

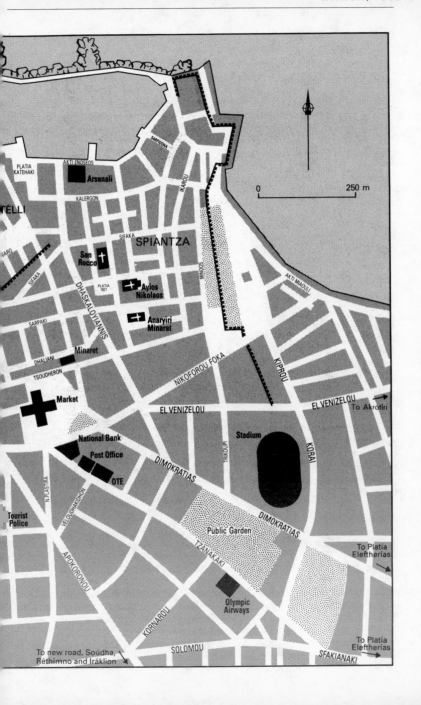

cially those heading west: for Sóudha and the eastern side of town you may find it easier to get on at one of the stops by the market.

Hálidhon is perhaps the most commercially touristic street in Haniá: walk down here and you pass the Cathedral square, about halfway down on the right, and the Archaeological Museum, just beyond on the left, before reaching at the bottom a square by the harbour called officially Platía Sindriváni but known by everyone simply as **Harbour Square**. To the left, Aktí Koundouriótou circles around the outer harbour, crowded with outdoor cafés. Straight ahead, in the strange, squat Mosque of the Janissaries, is the NTOG **tourist office** (Mon–Sat 8.30am–2pm & 3–8.30pm). On the little bluff which rises behind is the area known as **Kastélli**, site of the earliest habitation in Haniá.

Carry on past here and you'll curve round to the right to the **inner harbour**, where ruinous Venetian arsenals look out towards the breakwater. Behind is the most run-down, and in some ways the most atmospheric, part of the old town – alternatively approached by turning right off Hálidhon before reaching the harbour. To the left of Hálidhon, in the relatively narrow strip between the outer harbour and the wall, the alleys are narrower, the houses older and more attractive: here, though, they have been very much taken over by the tourist trade.

The telephone code for Haniá is ☎0821.

Accommodation

There must be thousands of **rooms to rent** in Haniá and, unusually, quite a few comfortable **hotels**. Though you may face a long search for a bed at the height of the season, eventually everyone does seem to find something.

Around the Harbour: west of Hálidhon

Perhaps the most desirable rooms of all are those **overlooking the harbour**, and, surprisingly, such rooms are sometimes available at quite reasonable rates: be warned that this is often because they're very noisy at night. Most are approached not direct from the harbourside itself but from the alley behind, Zambelíu, or other streets leading off the harbour further round (where you may get more peace). The nicest of the more expensive places are here too, usually set back a little so they're quieter, but often still with the views from upper storeys.

CHEAP ROOMS

Hotel Piraeus, Zambelíu 10 (☎54-154). One of the oldest in Haniá; basic and somewhat run-down but friendly, English-speaking and excellent value even for a room with a balcony over the harbour.

Rooms Antonis, Zambelíu next to *Piraeus*. Very plain rooms, not always too clean, but astonishingly cheap for the location.

Hotel Manos, Zambelíu 24 (☎52-152). More pricey, but worth checking as there are rooms at varying prices, including triples.

Rooms George, Zambelíu 30 (☎43-542). Old building with steep stairs and eccentric antique furniture – rooms vary in price according to position and size.

Pension Teris, Zambelíu 47 (☎53-120). Another of these old houses.

Artemis, Kondiláki 13 (☎21-196). One of many in this touristy street running inland from Zambelíu.

Pension Meltemi, Angelou 2 (☎40-192). First of a little row of possibilities in a great situation on the far side of the harbour; perhaps noisier than its neighbours, but ace views and a good café downstairs.

Rooms Stella, Angelou 10 (☎43-756). Creaky, eccentric old house with very plain, clean rooms.

Rooms Eleonora, Theotokópoulou 13 (☎50-011). One of several in the backstreets around the top of Angelou: prices are lower at nearby *Eugenia*.

HOTELS AND MORE EXPENSIVE ROOMS

Rooms Amarilis, Skufon, next to *Oleander Bar* (☎56-797). On a street running inland from Zambelíu, a lovely old house with tasteful antique decor, but not great value.

Pension Thereza, Angelou 8 (☎40-118). Beautiful old house in great position with stunning views from roof terrace and some rooms; classy decorations too. More expensive than its neighbours but deservedly so – unlikely to have room in season unless you book.

Hotel Lucia, Aktí Koundouriótou (☎21-821). C-class hotel right in the middle of the harbour-front. Less expensive than you might expect, probably because of total lack of character.

Hotel Amphora, Theotokópoulou 20 (☎43-132). Large, traditional building, beautifully renovated. Worth the expense if you get a view (around 6000drs), but probably not for the cheaper rooms with no view.

Hotel Porto del Colombo, Theofánous and Moschón (☎50-975). Similar to the *Amphora*, though slightly darker and more old-fashioned in feel. Occupies a building which they claim was once the French Embassy and later home of Eleftheríos Venizélos.

Hotel Contessa, Theofánous 15 (☎23-966). Another renovated old building, but more expensive and less attractive than the two above.

The Old Town: east of Hálidhon

In the eastern half of the old town rooms are far more scattered, and in the height of the season your chances are much better over here. **Kastélli**, immediately east of the harbour, has some lovely places with views from the height. Take one of the alleys leading left off Kaneváro if you want to try these, but don't be too hopeful – they are popular and often booked up. All of the below are standard rooms places in the usual price range.

Pension Kastelli, Kaneváro 39 (☎57-057). Not the prettiest location, but comfortable, modern, reasonably priced, and very quiet at the back. Alex, who runs the place, is exceptionally helpful and also has a few apartments and a beautiful house (for up to 5 people) to rent.

Stoa, Lithinon 5 (☎26-879). One of the cheapest of several on this street: rooms at the back look over the harbour from above.

Rooms 47, Kandanoléon 47 (☎53-243). Quiet, traditional rooms place on street leading up from Kaneváro into Kastélli.

Apartments Anastasia, Kandanoléon 41 (☎50-709). Worth a try for longer stays or if you want to self-cater.

Kydonia, Isódhion 15 (☎57-179). Between the Cathedral square and Platía Sindrívani, in first street parallel to Hálidhon. Rather dark, but good value for so central a position.

Pension Lito, Epískopou Dorothéou 15 (☎53-150). Very near the Cathedral; another street with several options.

Pension Fidias, Sarpáki 8 (☎52-494). Signed from the Cathedral. Favourite backpackers' meeting place: rather bizarrely run, but extremely friendly and has the real advantage of offering single rooms or fixing shares.

Pension Cleopatra, Botolo 51 (☎45-489). New place in lively but rather noisy area just north of Cathedral square.

Marina Ventikou, Sarpáki 40 (☎57-601). Small, personally run rooms place in quiet corner of old town. Others nearby include *Navarino*, on Sarpáki, and *Kinaret*, down a narrow alley beside Marina's rooms.

Stelios, Sífaka at corner of Karaolí. One of several on Sífaka.

Nikos, Dhaskaloyiánnis 58 (☎54-783). One of a few down here near the inner harbour; relatively modern rooms all with shower.

The modern city

There's really not much reason to stay in the **modern part of town**, and not many good places – the modern hotels are on the whole soulless business places, many of the rooms noisy and grimy. However, there might be advantages in staying near the bus station if you arrived late and couldn't face a long search for anywhere else, or if you were stopping over only to leave early the next morning. The other possibility is to stay in one of the streets leading back off the town beach; quieter and not unpleasant. But there are only a few scattered opportunities here and you'd probably be best finding somewhere to stay for the first night and then looking at your leisure over the next day.

Hotel Lato, Ionias 8 (☎56-944). Reasonably priced C-class hotel, with good rooms very handy for the bus station.

Manolis, Smirnis 23 (☎24-110). Ordinary rooms place near the bus station – others are signed as you come out, several on Milonoyiánni and Kareskáki near the tourist police, for example.

Hotel Tina, Boniali 3 (☎41-195). Backstreet location just off Tzanakáki near the Public Gardens. Quiet and comfortable, and may have rooms when everywhere else is full.

Helen Bambakaki, Moní Gonías, corner of Akti Papanikóli (☎53-572). Rooms right on the beachfront road, behind the town beach, which means some way from all the other action.

Hostel and campsites

Youth Hostel, Dhrakoniánou 33 (☎53-565). The youth hostel is a long way from anywhere you might otherwise visit and is not much of a place – four or five rooms with about eight metal bunks in each – but it is at least cheap and friendly, with a good view inland. You get here on the *Ay. Ioannis* bus (every 15min; last, they claim, at midnight) from the square opposite the market – ask for Platía Dhexamení. From the hostel they organise cheap guided tours to the Samarian Gorge and other places.

Camping Hania (☎31-686). Behind the beach some 4km west of Haniá, just about in walking distance if you follow the coast around, but much easier reached by taking the local bus (see "Beaches", below). There's a large sign to warn you where to get off; you walk down towards the sea for about five minutes through a patch of new development. The site itself is lovely, if rather basic in terms of facilities; small, shady, and just a short walk from a couple of the better beaches.

Camping Ayía Marína (☎48-555). A much bigger (and more expensive) site, 4km or so further west on an excellent beach at the far end of Ayía Marína village. This is beyond the range of Haniá city buses, so to get here by public transport you have to go from the main bus station. Check before turning up, because the site is earmarked for redevelopment.

The City

There is not a great deal specifically to do or see in Haniá, but it's a fascinating place simply to wander around, coming upon surviving fragments of city wall, holes in which ancient Kydonia is being excavated and odd segments of Venetian or Turkish masonry. Yet again, it's the harbour area which has most to offer.

The harbour

The **harbour** comes into its own at night, when the lights from bars and restaurants reflect in the water and animated crowds – locals every bit as much as tourists – parade in a ritualistic *voltá* of apparently perpetual motion. There are stalls set up on the waterside, and buskers serenading the passers-by. By day, especially in the hot, dozy mid-afternoon, it can be something of a letdown; deserted and with a distinct smell of decay from the rubbish washing up against the quayside. But you could always escape on a carriage ride round town behind one of the poor nags which stand waiting in the square all day, sweating beneath their straw hats.

Walk straight on from Platía Sindriváni, past the *Plaza Hotel*, and you reach the curious, domed shape of the **Mosque of the Janissaries**, restored to house the **tourist office**. The building has been rather spoilt by the café tacked onto the back, but it's an exemplary branch of the NTOG, with free maps and leaflets, unusually accurate timetables and excellent information sheets giving the latest information on, for example, walking the Samarian Gorge. When the office itself is closed, most essential information is displayed outside.

KASTÉLLI

The buildings on the height above the tourist office occupy the site of **Kastélli**, the oldest part of the city. Favoured from earliest times for its defensive qualities, this little hill takes its name from a fortress which dated, originally, from the Byzantine era. Later, it was the centre of the Venetian and of the Turkish towns (hence the proximity of the mosque) but very little survived a heavy bombardment during the war.

If you walk up Kaneváro from the harbour square you'll pass various remains, including – at the corner of Lithínon – the fenced-off site where a **Minoan house** is being excavated. Further up Lithínon, towards the top of the rise, are various Venetian doorways and inscriptions and, at the end of the street, a fine old archway. On the next corner, with Kandanoléon, is a larger area of excavation marked simply as "Minoan Kydonia". Neither of these digs is open to the public – though you can see a fair amount through the fence – and so far the archaeologists have revealed little of what they have found.

INNER HARBOUR

Back at the bottom of the hill the waterfront curls round to the right, into the **inner harbour**, where pleasure boats, private yachts and small fishing vessels tie up. Much of it, including the sixteenth-century Venetian arsenals and various traces of the ancient defensive bastions, has recently been refurbished, and in the evenings this is now a fashionable part of town among locals. Just on the corner past the tourist office is the local **handicraft co-operative**, with a permanent selling exhibition (Mon–Sat 9.30am–10.30pm) which can be interesting, though not everything is particularly good quality. In the line of old buildings facing the water beyond this, by the port police, are a couple of unusual antique shops, one full of wonderful old junk which unfortunately is mainly at tourist prices.

Beyond all this are the Venetian arsenals – which don't offer much to see – a cluster of restaurants and bars, and the modern *Porto Veneziana* hotel. From here you can follow the sea wall round as far as the minaret-style **lighthouse**, usually daubed in graffiti, from where there's an excellent view back over the city.

OUTER HARBOUR AND CITY WALLS

In the other direction from Platía Sindriváni the **outer harbour**, with its broad promenade, is entirely fronted by pavement restaurants and bars. The hefty bastion at the far end houses Crete's **Naval Museum** (Tues, Thurs and Sat 10am–2pm & 4–6pm). This is not of great interest unless you're heavily into naval warfare or seashells (one small room is full of them). It consists mainly of poorly labelled models and pictures of ships, diagrams of naval battles, and assorted memorabilia going back to the times of classical Greek triremes. Go through the main gate, however, into the compound of what is apparently a small naval garrison (open museum hours, but no need to pay the small fee) and you can climb onto the seaward fortifications of the **Fírkas**, as this part of the city defences is known. Here the modern Greek flag was first raised on Crete – in 1913 – and there are more fine views. Every Tuesday evening there's a Greek dancing display here.

Carrying on round the outside of the Fírkas, which has been well restored, you can peer through loopholes at the great vaulted chambers within. On the far side is the *Hotel Xenia*, itself raised up on part of the fortifications, and beyond this you can cut inland alongside the best preserved stretch of the **city walls**. Following the walls around on the inside is rather trickier, but worth a try for the chance to stumble on some of the most picturesque little alleyways and finest Venetian houses in Haniá. It's a quiet part of town – even were the streets wide enough to take much traffic, the steps which break up the roadways would keep it out. Yet again there's little to seek out specifically, but keep your eyes open for details on the houses – for old wooden balconies or stone coats of arms. The arch of the **Renieri Gate**, at the bottom of Moschón, is particularly elegant. There are, too, a number of good craft shops around here: a couple of the best, along with an expensive antiques store, are on Angelou just round from the Naval Museum entrance; several newer ones line Theotokopóulou, the delightfully old-fashioned street which runs behind.

The old city

South from the harbour square, up Hálidhon, lie the less picturesque but more lively parts of the old city. First, though, just a short way up on the right, is Haniá's **Archaeological Museum** (Mon–Fri 8.30am–3pm), housed in the Venetian-built church of San Francesco. Though it doesn't look much now, with its campanile gone and facade crumbled, this building was once one of the island's grandest: inside, where there has been substantial restoration, you get far more idea of its former importance. The Turks converted the church into a mosque from which a beautiful fountain and the base of a minaret have survived in the pungent flowery garden alongside.

Large quantities of Minoan pottery dominate the front part of the museum – clearly labelled and showing the usual stages of development: included here are a few of the huge Minoan storage jars, or *pithoi*. In the centre is a collection of *larnakes* (Minoan clay tombs), some wonderfully decorated, one still containing two small skeletons. The most important items as far as archaeologists are concerned, however – even if they don't look much to laymen – are the inscribed tablets excavated in Kastélli: this is the only place other than Knossós where examples of Linear A and Linear B script have been found together. Moving towards the back of the church, the collection moves on in time, with a large group of classical sculptures, a case full of Greco-Roman glassware and some recently discovered third-century Roman mosaics reassembled on the floor. These are really lovely, particularly those of Dionysos and Ariadne (one of two from the same house) and Poseidon and Amymone. Outside in the garden/ courtyard (often enlivened by classical music drifting over the wall from a café outside) are other assorted sculptures and architectural remnants, including a lovely one-legged, headless lion.

CATHEDRAL SQUARE AND "LEATHER STREET"

Just past the museum, on the other side of Hálidhon, the **Cathedral** sits at the back of a small square. Given Haniá's history and importance, you might expect this to be an impressive temple: in fact it's a singularly unattractive little building, dating only from the last century. Nor is the square, which must once have been at the heart of life in Haniá*, particularly lively any more except as a taxi rank – the action has moved down to the harbour or up to the newer plazas in the modern city (one boon of tourism is that some new cafés are now opening here). To one side, above a *períptero*, are the ramshackle domes of a former Turkish bath.

The street just above, **Odhós Skridhlóf**, is considerably more interesting and animated. Here traditional leathermakers still ply their trade, and although tourism may dominate nowadays, prices for leatherware remain the best in Crete and there are still a few shops which ignore sandals and bags in favour of traditional high Cretan boots and hefty work shoes.

As a final gesture to Hálidhon, take the last right before the top and walk down beside a high stretch of wall into the vicinity of the **Schiavo Bastion**. There's not a great deal to see here – apart from the high wall – but it's strange to find yourself so suddenly out of the crowds and among the scruffy yards and inquisitive dogs of the backstreets.

MARKET AND POINTS EAST

In the other direction, continuing to the end of Skridhlóf or up behind the Cathedral, you reach the back of the **market**. An imposing and rather beautiful cross-shaped building, this dates from the beginning of the century, when it was supposedly modelled on the market at Marseilles. At the back is a small shaded square where locals sit outside a couple of *kafenía*. As you wander round these streets there's a minaret which constantly appears above the rooftops only to disappear again as soon as you try to head towards it: its base is actually on Dhaliáni where it appears to be part of a carpenters' workshop. At any event it's fenced off and not open to visitors.

A second minaret (this one missing its top) adorns the church of Áyios Nikólaos in **Platía 1821**, further over to the east. Built by the Venetians, the church was converted to a mosque under Sultan Ibrahim and reconverted after Crete's reversion to Greek authority. It has been so often refurbished that there's nothing of great interest to see. The square itself, whose name recalls one of the larger rebellions against Turkish authority, after which an Orthodox bishop was hanged here, is another pleasantly shaded space set about with café chairs. Nearby are two more old churches: San Rocco, just a pace towards the harbour, is small and old-fashioned; Áyii Anáryiri, which retained its Orthodox status throughout the Turkish occupation, has some very ancient icons. Again the area as a whole – known as **Spiantza** – is full of unexpected architectural delights: carved wooden balconies, houses arching across the street at first-floor level. Many of the streets between here and the inner harbour have recently been re-cobbled and generally refurbished, and they're among the most atmospheric and tranquil in the old town.

Continue **eastwards**, past another section of ruinous wall stretching round from the inner harbour, and you'll hit the sea again. From here you could follow the coast round into the smarter areas of the modern city.

---

*The rebel Dhaskaloyiánnis (p.222) was tortured to death in the square around 1770.

The new town

Modern Haniá sprawls in every direction around the old. You can't hope, and nor would you want, to get to know all of these suburban areas, but with time on your hands there are parts of the centre which are worth the walk. Start in front of the market. Over to your right you could head towards **Platía 1866** and the bus station through areas which have an attractively old-fashioned commercialism about them, full of general stores stocking the essentials of village life. Ahead to the left, **Tzanakáki** leads to places of more specific interest.

First of these is the **Public Gardens**, a few hundred metres up on the left. Laid out by a Turkish Pasha in the nineteenth century, they include a few caged animals (not really enough to call a zoo, but there are *kri-kri*, ponies, loud monkeys and birds), a café where you can sit under the trees, a children's play area and an open-air auditorium. This latter, often used as a cinema, is also the setting for local ceremonies and folklore displays which can be really enjoyable – it's worth looking in to see what's on. Carry on down the street, then take the second left onto Sfakianáki (on a hot day, this is already beginning to feel like a major expedition) and you come to the **Historical Museum and Archives** (Mon–Fri 9am–1.30pm & 3–5.30pm) in a small, crumbling and not particularly distinguished grey building. It consists of a couple of gloomy rooms with poorly labelled photos, a few revolutionary arms and relics of Venizélos, and many more rooms filled with musty papers and books – but it's worth a look if you're passing this way anyway. Here, you are entering some of the wealthier residential districts.

At the end of Sfakianáki is **Platía Eleftherías**, with a statue of Venizélos in the centre and the imposing court building along the south side. This court house was originally the government building built for Prince George's short-lived administration; behind it rises an enormous new church. From here Dhimokratías leads back to the centre, running past the rear of the Public Gardens and ending (as Konstantínou) opposite the market again. Alternatively, follow **Iróon Politehníou**, which runs due north from Platía Eleftherías down to the sea. A broad avenue divided by trees and lined with large houses, this makes another interesting walk: there are several (expensive) garden restaurants and a number of fashionable café/bars where you can sit outdoors, and it's a very different city from the one you'll experience amid the tourist crowds on Hálidhon.

The beaches

Haniá's beaches all lie to the west of the city. There's a town beach within easy walk of the centre and from here you can follow the coast round almost indefinitely on foot. For the better stretches of sand, however, you really need to take the local bus along the coast road.

The **city beach** is about a ten-minute walk from the harbour: along Aktí Koundouriótou, round past the Fírkas and the *Hotel Xenia*, and on by the city's open-air swimming pools (often drained) and a small fishing-boat harbour. The beach starts in a very crowded section with showers, cafés and restaurants and a road running immediately behind. Offshore is a tiny islet with a sandy beach large enough for about five people at a time, but it's an unnervingly long swim – much further than it looks. Better to hire a pedalo or canoe if you want to explore.

If you continue west you can walk – for some twenty minutes – over a stony, scrubby stretch of sand where quite a few people camp or seek out isolation for nude sunbathing. It's not otherwise a pleasant place – a dirty and rather exposed length of gritty sand – though new blocks of apartments behind are beginning to provoke a clean-up. **Áyii Apóstoli**, at the end of this walk amid a clutch of restrained development, is much more agreeable: there's an excellent bungalow/hotel development (*Aptera Beach Bungalows*) with a beachside bar, a restaurant which serves a delicious lunchtime buffet, and a good long slather of yellow sand. The only drawback is the crashing breakers, which can become vicious at times. At the end of Apóstoli's beach a barbed-wire fence attempts to prevent you getting onto the next section, but if you want to continue on foot it's worth clambering over the rocks: going round to the road involves a long detour and something of a climb over a low hill. At the next section, known as **Hrissí Aktí** (Golden Beach), there's more good sand which again has attracted the apartment builders. But it's not overcrowded yet, it's popular with locals and there's a good taverna, and you're far enough off the main road to ensure that there aren't too many accidental visitors dropping in.

To get to either of these sections **from the road**, head down the track signed to the *Aptera Beach Bungalows* (for the beginning of the first beach) or past *Camping Hania* to approach from the other end. There's quite a bit of new development around, mostly apartments but also a number of restaurants – *Jetée*, to which you'll see signs, is good, if a little pricier than most.

At the far end, as the beach curves round to a little headland, a taverna is set out on stilts over the water. Beyond the headland lies a tiny sand cove, another small promontory, and then the long curve of **Oasis Beach** running on round to **Kalamáki**. This is crowded, and justly so – the swimming is probably the best you've yet encountered, with a gently shelving sandy bottom and a fossil-covered (and very sharp) rocky islet/reef which fends off the bigger waves. There's also a series of cafés and tavernas, and other facilities including windsurf hire or lessons.

Kalamáki is the furthest beach accessible by city bus and the only one, right by the road, which requires no walking at all once you've arrived. To have walked this far, non-stop, would probably have taken a little over an hour. If you're going to do it, though, it makes far more sense to dawdle and enjoy the empty beaches along the way, arriving at Kalamáki in time to get the bus back. The **bus for the beaches** leaves Haniá from the left-hand (east) side of Platía 1866, about halfway up, and runs along the main road towards Kastélli. This means that if you get off anywhere much before Kalamáki you face quite a walk down to the sea. It's easier to hang on, and get off either by the large Oasis Beach sign or, where everyone else does, at Kalamáki itself, the next stop. Buses run every twenty minutes or so throughout the day.

Food, drink and nightlife

Evenings in Haniá centre around the harbour, and you need not stray an inch from the waterfront walk to find a cocktail before dinner, a meal, a late-night bar and an all-night disco – numerous possibilities for all of these in fact. The most fashionable area these days, particularly with locals, is towards the far end of the inner harbour, around Sarpidóna. If you're on a tight budget, however, you'll need to steer clear of the waterfront.

Tavernas and restaurants

If finding a room can be hard in Haniá, finding something to eat never is. Yet again Platía Sindriváni is the focal point. Spanning out from here, in a circle round the **harbour**, is one restaurant, taverna or café after another: they all have their own character, but there seems little variation in price or what's on offer, although the inner harbour is a little less frantic. Places away from the water are generally a little cheaper: there are plenty of possibilities on Kondiláki, Kanaváro and most of the streets off Hálidhon.

Karnáyio, Platía Katecháki 8. Set back from the inner harbour near the port police. Not right on the water, but one of the best harbour restaurants nonetheless; touristy looks belie very good food, friendly atmosphere and prices certainly no higher than surrounding restaurants. *Faka*, on the other side of the square, is also good.

Dino's, inner harbour by bottom of Sarpidóna. One of the best choices for a pricey seafood meal with a harbour view; *Apostolis*, almost next door, is also good.

Tamam, Zambelíu just before Renieri Gate. Young, fashionable place with adventurous Greek menu including much vegetarian food. Unfortunately only a few cramped tables outside, and inside it's very hot. Slow service.

Kyttaro, Kondiláki. The first of numerous good places as you head up Kondiláki from Zambelíu. Again, some vegetarian food.

Emerald Bistro, Kondiláki 17. Irish-run place for the homesick, with Irish stew, Guinness, kids' menu of sausage, beans and chips, veggie food, as well as Greek staples. Friendly and fairly priced.

To Hani, Kondiláki 26. Claims to be a "garden restaurant" aren't strictly true, but there are tables at the back in a very quiet dead-end alley (as well as less inviting ones out front in Kondiláki). *Kali Kardia* is another standard Greek taverna nearby.

Taverna Ela, top of Kondiláki. With live Greek music to enliven your meal.

Pafsilipon, Sífaka 19. Good, standard taverna. Tables on the street and also on the raised pavement opposite.

To Dhiporto, Skridhlóf. Very long-established, very basic place amid all the leather shops whose multilingual menu still offers such delights as Pigs' Balls – or, more delicately, *Testicules de Porc*.

Le Saladier, Kanaváro just off Platía Sindriváni. French-run joint offering salads of every kind.

Pension Lito, Epískopou Dorothéou 15. Café/taverna with live music (usually Greek-style guitar), one of several in this street.

Hippopotamus Pizzeria, Sarpidóna. Surrounded by trendy bars and patronised by local youth; the pizza and pasta can make a welcome change.

Retro, Platía Venizélou in Halepa. Fashionable and fairly expensive place in former Russian embassy – beautiful setting, though food not always up to it. It's just off the road to Akrotíri but not easy to find, so consider a taxi.

Nikteridha, out of town in the village of Korakiés. Head for Akrotíri and at the top of the hill, after the Venizélos tombs, follow the signs to the left for the village. Beautiful garden setting for traditional taverna, especially worthwhile at weekends when there's often music and dancing. You'll pass a couple of other places with outdoor grills and views over Haniá – as well as more music and dancing – as you climb up the road out of town.

Cafés, bars and snacks

Yet again there are lots of cafés round the harbour – on the whole these now serve cocktails and fresh juices at exorbitant prices, though breakfast (especially "English") can be good value. There are more traditional places around the market (including a couple of *zaharoplastía*, one on Tsoudherón, the other on Mousoúron, down the steps from the side entrance) and along Dhaskaloyiánnis (*Singanaki* here is a good traditional bakery serving *tiropitta* and the like, with a cake shop next door). Fast food is also increasingly widespread, with numerous *souvláki* places and even a couple of burger joints (on Kalergón by the top of Sarpidóna).

Vasilis, Platía Sindriváni. Perhaps the least changed of the places here. Reasonably priced breakfasts.

Boúyatsa, Sífaka 4. Tiny place that serves little except the traditional creamy cheese pie – *boúyatsa* – to eat in or take away. A similar place is up in the new town on Apokoronóu, by the big junction on the corner of Veloudhákidhon.

Oblomov, Kondiláki. Trendy little cocktail bar/café with classical music, brown bread, and laid-back atmosphere.

Mitropolitikon, Cathedral square. Pleasant setting with tables out on the square in front of the Cathedral. Good juices.

Tasty Souvláki, Hálidhon 80. Seems always to have been here and is always packed despite being cramped and none-too-clean – which is a testimonial to the quality and value of the *souvláki*. Better to take away. A new rival further down the street, opposite the Cathedral, is rightly much less popular. Other *souvláki* places on Karaolí; round at the end of the outer harbour, near the naval museum; and around the corner of Plastíra and Yianári, across from the market.

Ideon Andron, in alleyway off Hálidhon next to the museum. Classy café/bar, rather slow and expensive, but in a delightful garden with piped classical or jazz music and, occasionally, something live.

Neorion, Sarpidóna. Place to sit and be seen in the evening; some tables overlook the harbour. Try an expensive but sublime lemon *granita*.

Oleander, Skufon. Smart piano/cocktail bar for an elegant drink before dinner.

Meltemi, Angelou 2. Slow, relaxed place for breakfast, and where locals (especially ex-pats) sit whiling the day away or playing *tavli*.

Late bars and discos

There are NATO air force and navy bases out on Akrotíri, and this means that there are some bars in Haniá that are a lot heavier than you'd expect, full of US and other servicemen. Over the last couple of years some of these places have been closed and others tamed, however, and the troops have been on their best behaviour in the face of local opposition to their presence: tourists and young locals predominate in most places. The smartest and newest places are on and around Sarpidóna.

Fraise, Sarpidóna. Just one of the bars in a street packed with them.

Berlin Rock Café, Radimanthus. Round the corner at the top of Sarpidóna, a late-night disco-bar.

Canale Club, Aktí Tobázi. Popular bar/disco, opens 11pm.

Disco Ariadni, inner harbour. The most central disco, just round the corner from above. Opens 11.30pm, but busy later.

Four Seasons, inner harbour. Very popular bar by the port police.

Fortetza, sea wall. Strange hybrid restaurant/café/nightclub on the far side of the harbour near the lighthouse. A ferry shuttle takes people across from outside the port police – a good gimmick though you could easily walk. Most popular late at night; there are queues for the boat at midnight.

Fagotto, Angelou 16. Very pleasant, laid-back jazz bar, often with live performers.

El Mondo, Kondiláki. Survivor from the days when this street was very rowdy, still popular with servicemen – further down the street *Notabene* is one of the less attractive dance bars.

Remember, outer harbour behind the *Plaza Hotel*. "English-style pub", quite pleasant if you like that sort of thing. *Scorpio*, nearby, is another survivor from the old days, now apparently on its last legs.

Agora Club, Tsoudherón behind the market. Big, bright disco. Not much happens before 2am – at midnight it's still deserted.

Traditional music and cinema

A couple of places which offer more traditional entertainment are the *Café Kriti* (Kalergón 22, at corner of Androgéo), basically an old-fashioned *kafen**íon* where there's **Greek music and dancing** virtually every night, and the Fírkas (the bastion by the naval museum), where there's Greek dancing at 9pm every Tuesday – pricey but authentic entertainment. It's also worth checking for events at the open-air auditorium in the park, and for performances in restaurants outside the city, which are the ones the locals will go to. Check for posters, especially in front of the market and in the little square across the road from there. On the new Iráklion road there's an enormous modern dance hall, *Haniá by Night*, which attracts many of Greece's best singers.

For **films**, you should also check the hoardings in front of the market. By far the most enjoyable place to go is the open-air *Attikon*, on El. Venizélou out towards Akrotíri, about 1km from the centre. The atmosphere here is great, and English-language films are usually subtitled, but be sure to sit near a speaker as no one else bothers too much about the soundtrack.

Listings

Airlines *Olympic*, the only people with scheduled flights to or from Haniá, have an office at Tzanakáki 88 (☎27-701; Mon–Fri 9am–4pm), opposite the Public Gardens. There's a bus from here connecting with their flights. For airport information phone ☎63-245.

Banks The main branch of the *National Bank of Greece* is directly opposite the market. Convenient smaller banks for exchange are next to the bus station, at the bottom of Kanenáro just off Harbour Square, or at the top of Hálidhon. There are also a couple of exchange places on Hálidhon, open long hours, and a post office van parked through the summer in Cathedral square.

Bike and car hire Possibilities everywhere, especially on Hálidhon though these are rarely the best value. For cars try *Hermes* (Tzanakáki 52; ☎54-418; 20% discount promised to readers), very friendly and efficient; for bikes and cars *Duke of Crete* (Sífaka 3, ☎21-651; Skalídhi 16, ☎57-821; and branches in Ayía Marína and Plataniás; 15% discount promised for cash). Others include *Summertime* (Dhaskaloyiánnis 7; ☎28-918), *Zeus* (Karaolí 38; ☎57-457) and *Cornaros* (Hálidhon 86; ☎73-131). *Hertz, Avis* and other big companies mostly have offices on Tzanakáki.

Boat trips Various boat trips are offered by travel agents around town, mostly round Soúdha Bay or out to beaches on the Rodhópou peninsula. *Domenico's* on Kanenáro offers some of the best of these, or for details of trips on a small yacht with an English skipper (1–3 days) call at the jewellery shop at Hálidhon 3 or at *E. Barbopoulos* (Tsoudherón 1; ☎22-244, 23-394).

Ferry tickets The agent for *Minoan* is at the bottom of Hálidhon (*Nanadakis Travel*, Hálidhon 8; ☎23-939); for *ANEK* on Venizélou right opposite the market (☎23-636). Several other travel agencies sell tickets.

Festivals The main annual event in Haniá is the commemoration of the Bàttle of Crete in the last week of May, with folklore and other events mostly in the Public Gardens. June 24, St John's Day, is also celebrated. Check with the tourist office for details of these and others in villages roundabout.

Launderette There are three, at Kanenáro 38 (9am–10pm), Epískopou Dorothéou 7 and Áyii Dhéka 18. All do service washes.

Left luggage The bus station has a left luggage office.

Mountain climbing The local EOS is at Mihelidháki 3 (☎24-647).

Newspapers and books English and other foreign newspapers are sold at two places on Odhós Yiánari, one right by the corner of Hálidhon, the other towards the market. There are two bookshops with a fair range of foreign material on Hálidhon, one (*Pelekanakis*) near the top, the other at the bottom in the square. For guides and maps you could also try the kiosk in the market or the one by the Cathedral square.

Pharmacies Several on Yiánari between the market and Platía 1866, more up Tzanakáki.

Post office The main post office is on Tzanakáki (open for stamps Mon–Sat 7am–8pm, exchange 8am–2pm). In summer there's a handy Portakabin branch set up in the Cathedral square.

Shopping Shops aimed at tourists are in the old town: jewellery and souvenirs on Hálidhon and all around the harbour. The leather goods on Skridhlóf are excellent value. If you want to buy food or get stuff together for a picnic, the market is the place to head. There are vast quantities of fresh fruit and vegetables as well as meat and fish, bakers, dairy stalls for milk, cheese and yoghurt, and general stores for cooked meats, tins and other standard provisions. One or two stallholders are none too friendly (particularly if you start prodding their fruit) but it's still a wonderful place to shop. When the market is closed there are several small stores down by the harbour square which sell cold drinks and a certain amount of food, but these are expensive (though they do open late): better to head for the shops in the new town where locals go. A couple of large supermarkets can be found on the main roads running out of town – particularly *CretaMarket* on the way to Akrotíri. There's a specialist cheese shop, with interesting mountain cheeses, on Potié, a narrow street running south from Karaolí where it becomes Sífaka. On the same street is a place selling nothing but chess and *tavli* sets in all shapes and sizes. Other interesting places to look include the handicraft centre and antique shops on the inner harbour, and various arty-crafty stores on Zambelíu, Kanecáro and Theotokopóulou.

Taxis The main taxi ranks are in the Cathedral square and, especially, Platía 1866. For radio taxis try ☎29-405 or ☎58-700.

Telephones OTE headquarters is on Tzanakáki just past the post office – open daily 6am–midnight. It's generally packed during the day, but often blissfully empty late at night. At a slightly higher rate you can also ring from any *períptero*. The one by the *Hotel Lucia* is quieter than that in the harbour square.

Tourist office The NTOG (Mon–Sat 8.30am–2pm & 3–8.30pm) is in the Mosque of the Janissaries on the harbour (Aktí Tobázi 6; ☎26-426).

Tourist police Kareskáki 44 (☎24-477). The town and harbour police are based on the inner harbour.

Travel agencies For cheap tickets home – *Magic Bus* and student/charter flights – *Bassias Travel* (Skridhlóf 46; ☎44-295) is the place, very helpful for regular tickets too. They also deal in standard excursions. Other travel agents for tours and day trips are everywhere – one of the biggest is *Interkreta* (Kanecáro 9; ☎52-552).

Work If you're looking for work picking oranges or on other harvests, join everyone else in *Costa's* on the harbour square first thing in the morning. Women wanting to earn money for hanging around in bars should either spend an evening doing it unpaid (you'll probably be approached) or make discreet enquiries through people already doing the job. But see the caveats at the beginning of this book.

Akrotíri and the Bay of Sóudha

The hilly peninsula of **Akrotíri** loops round to the east of Haniá, protecting the magnificent anchorages of the Bay of Sóudha. It's a somewhat strange amalgam, with a couple of developing resorts on the north coast; several ancient monasteries in the northeast; military installations and the airport dominating the centre and south. At the beginning the roads are good but as you progress the surfaces become worse and the signs more confusing: heading for the further monasteries you get onto a really narrow track and, eventually, are reduced to walking.

Following the Akrotíri signs east out of Haniá you embark on a long climb as you leave the city. At the top there's a sign to the **Venizélos Graves**, the simple stone slab tombs of Eleftheríos Venizélos, Crete's most famous statesman, and his son Sophocles. The setting, looking back over Haniá, is magnificent and also historic, the scene in 1897 of an illegal raising of the Greek flag in defiance of the Turks and the European Powers. The flagpole was smashed by a salvo from the European fleet, but the Cretans raised their standard by hand, keeping it flying even under fire. Two stories attach to this: one that the sailors were so impressed that they all stopped firing to applaud; the second that a Russian shell hit the little church of Profítis Elías (still here) and in divine revenge the Russian ship itself exploded the very next day.

The beaches: Stavrós

The road divides by the graves. Straight ahead takes you to the airport and to KORAKIÉS, very close by, where there's an excellent taverna, *Nikteridha*. For **beaches** follow the northern branch, to Horafákia and Stavrós. This is pleasant country to drive around, gently rolling and dotted with villages which are clearly quite wealthy – many city workers live out here or build themselves country villas. About 5km beyond the graves, past the village of KOUNOUPIDHIANÁ, the road suddenly plunges down and emerges by the beach at KALATHÁS, two little patches of sand, divided by a rocky promontory, and behind them a couple of tavernas on the road. The proximity of the road, in fact, is the only drawback – otherwise it would be a perfect place to spend a lazy day.

Carry on to the end of the road, another five kilometres, and you'll find a beach at **STAVRÓS** which is hard to fault in any respect: an almost completely enclosed circular bay, dead calm, with a gently shelving sandy bottom, ideal for kids. It's an extraordinary looking place, too, with a sheer, bare mountainside rising just a hundred yards away from you on the far side of the bay. This is where the cataclysmic climax of *Zorba the Greek* was filmed (the hill is known locally as Zorba's Mountain) and is also the site of a cave, whose entrance can just about be seen from the beach, in which there was an ancient sanctuary.

The beach is often crowded – it doesn't take many people to fill it up – but even so it's a pleasant place to bask for a few hours during a trip round the peninsula, and the one place here that's easily accessible by bus. There are tavernas behind the beach if you want to make it a meal break (*Mama's* rents rooms) and a lot of scattered building, mostly apartments. Nearby **Blue Beach**, with a tiny sand beach in a cove that is largely artificial (though you wouldn't know it), has one of the best apartment/rooms places, *Blue Beach* (☎64-140); pricey but worth it. Another good contact for apartments in Stavrós is in Haniá at the shop at Tsoudherón 1 (☎22-244).

The monasteries

For the **monasteries** the most direct approach is to branch right in Kounoupidhianá and follow the signs to Ayía Triádha, though there's also a road up from the airport and a dusty track which cuts across from the Stavrós road. If you follow the signs you should make it eventually.

Ayía Triádha

Ayía Triádha (sometimes known after its founder as *Moní Zangarólo*) was founded in the seventeenth century and built in Venetian style: today, while not exactly thriving, it is one of the few Cretan monasteries to preserve real monastic life to any degree. Its imposing ochre frontage is approached through carefully tended fields and olive groves – all the property of the monastery. Close up, though, the buildings themselves are distinctly dilapidated and at least half of the total space lies redundant and empty. Some of the halls at the back have been given over to the stabling of the monks' goats, and sleek, skinny cats wander seemingly at will.

You can wander right through the complex – though the cells themselves are locked – and sit on benches shaded by orange trees in the patio. The church, which feels strangely foreshortened, contains a beautiful old gilded altarpiece and, around the walls, ancient wooden stalls; it is built, like most of the monastery, from stone which seems to glow orange in the afternoon sun. By the entrance is a small museum with vestments, relics and ancient manuscripts, mostly dating from the eighteenth or nineteenth centuries, and a few icons which are considerably older. Above, you can climb up beside the campanile to look out over the monastery's fields and beyond. In the courtyard there's a water cooler, and if you're lucky the traditional hospitality will extend further, to a glass of raki and a piece of *loukoum* in the hall where you sign the visitors' book. Like many monasteries, both Ayía Triádha and Gouvernétou (below) close for an afternoon siesta, from 2 to 5pm.

Gouvernétou and Kathalikó

Outside Ayía Triádha a sign directs you towards **Gouvernétou** – about 4km away, first on dirt and then up a paved but twisting and rutted road through a rocky gully; a spectacular but not a particularly easy drive. The monastery itself is a simple square block of a building, older than Ayía Triádha, with the usual refreshingly shaded patio and ancient frescoes in the church. There's a tiny museum too. The few visitors here, and the stark surroundings, help to give a real sense of the isolation that the remaining monks must face for most of the year.

Beyond you can follow (on foot) a path which leads towards another monastery, Kathalikó, and the sea. After about ten minutes you reach a **cave** in which Saint John the Hermit is said to have lived and died – a large, low cavern, stark, dank and dripping, with hefty stalactites and stalagmites. Small outbuildings surround the entrance.

Thus far the walk has been easy, along an obvious path, but as you continue to descend the going gets steeper, rockier and sharper, and in places you have to look for the red paint daubed on the rocks to confirm that you are still on the right trail. In a further fifteen minutes you reach the amazing ruins of the **Monastery of Kathalikó**, built into the side of (and partly carved from) a craggy ravine of spectacular desolation. This is older still – it was abandoned over three hundred years ago when the monks, driven by repeated pirate raids, moved up to the comparative safety of Gouvernétou. The valley sides are dotted with caves which formed a centre of still earlier Christian worship, at least one of which (just before the buildings) you can explore if you have a torch.

Spanning the ravine by the ruins is a vast bridge leading nowhere. Cross it and you can scramble down to the bottom of the ravine and follow the stream bed all the way to the sea – about another fifteen minutes. There's a tiny natural

harbour, a fjord-like finger of water pushing up between the rocks, where remains of a port can still be made out. Hewn from the rock, and with part of its roof intact, is what appears to be an ancient boathouse or slipway. There's no beach, but it's easy enough, and delightfully welcome, to lower yourself from the rocks straight into the astonishingly clear green water.

The walk **back up** takes considerably longer – perhaps an hour in all – and is much more strenuous than it might have seemed on the way down.

Soúdha Bay

On the **south side of Akrotíri** there are beaches marked at STÉRNES, but in practice it's not worth the effort to get there. Almost all of this part of the peninsula is a military zone and the only coast you can reach is a small and rather scrubby stretch of sand. The one consolation is the view of the bay as you go down towards Miráthi: above all of the little island (NÉA SOÚDHA) bristling with Venetian and Turkish fortifications which, from a distance at least, appear miraculously well-preserved. It proved as impressive a defence as it looks, holding out as a Venetian stronghold for over thirty years after the rest of the island had fallen, before eventually being voluntarily abandoned.

For an alternative route back you can cut around the other side of the neck of the peninsula, following the road which curves round to SOÚDHA (the town). This again affords spectacular views of the bay (there are signs prohibiting photographs of the military secrets therein), down over the villas built into the hillside. Just before Soúdha, at the water's edge, you pass the **Allied war cemetery** (the only sign faces the other way, towards Soúdha, so keep an eye out). With its row upon row of immaculately kept white headstones, many of them to unknown soldiers, this looks hauntingly like one of the endless World War I graveyards and it brings home with some force the scale of the calamity of the Battle of Crete. From here the main Soúdha road heads back into town or you can join the highway and continue east.

East to Yeoryióupoli

Heading directly east out of Haniá you can either pick up the new road where it starts, on the south side of town, or follow the buses and most of the other traffic to Soúdha and join it there. As it climbs above the edge of the **Bay of Soúdha** the new road follows the former track of the old: if you pull over there are views over the shipping and naval installations below (no photographs) but from the road these are screened by an almost continuous line of high bushes. At the point of the bay stands an old fortress, originally the Turkish bastion of **Izzedin**, now pressed into service as a prison – though not a very secure one judging by the large breaches in the outer walls.

The new road is fast and extremely efficient, but following it you'll see little through the screen of trees and flowering shrubs until you emerge on the coast just past Yeoryióupoli. Once you set off down the hill past Izzedin there are a couple of barely marked turnoffs to villages but just one junction of any size, between Vrísses and Yeoryióupoli, signed to both of them. If you're in no hurry, or you simply want an attractive circular drive, then the minor roads that head inland or out onto the Dhrápano peninsula have much more to offer.

Áptera and inland

Shortly before the fort, roads lead off left and right: left is signed to KALÁMI (just a few hundred yards away, immediately below the prison) and Kalíves (which you can see on the coast way below); turn right and you climb to MEGÁLA HORÁFIA and, turning off again, **ÁPTERA**. Áptera occupies the table top of this mesa-like mountain, about 3km from – and a good climb above – the new road. From the fifth century BC well into early Christian times this was one of the island's most important cities: substantial ruins remain, although since their excavation early this century they have deteriorated considerably. Among the more obvious relics are the massive walls, almost 4km long, which predate everything else at the site; the large L-shaped Roman cisterns and other buildings scattered around the abandoned monastery which marks the centre of the site; and a classical Greek temple and theatre in the south. There is more, but since it all seems permanently locked behind its fences the excitement is limited, and the countryside is rough and barren (and hot) for exploring on foot. A much greater attraction of the setting is another crumbling Turkish fort – substantially shored up with reinforced concrete – on the lip of the hilltop, with the best of all the **views** across Sóudha and the Akrotíri.

Immediately below is the Izzedin fortress, and below that the three small islands, including heavily fortified Néa Sóudha, which protect the entrance to the anchorage. From here the superb strategic qualities of the bay are plain, with the deep water anchorages accessible only by running the gauntlet of these forts and fortified islands at the narrow entrance. In legend the islands were formed after a musical contest between the Muses and the Sirens on the height near the ancient city: defeated, the Sirens plucked off their wings and flung themselves into the bay to become the islands. Áptera, literally translated, can mean featherless or wingless – one derivation of the city's name.

Stílos and Samonás

From Áptera you can retrace your steps back to the main road, or you can continue inland to circle round via the Dhrápano peninsula, a very attractive drive. In Megála Horáfia, right opposite the Áptera turnoff, there's a large taverna which is frequently the venue of *bouzouki* nights – look out for posters advertising these.

The first place of any size south of here is **STÍLOS**, which is where the Australian and New Zealand rearguard made their final stand during the Battle of Crete (this was then the main road south), enabling the majority of Allied troops to be evacuated while they themselves were mostly stranded on the island. Many found refuge in the villages in the foothills around here and were later smuggled off the island – some of these villages were destroyed in retribution. Today Stílos is an unremarkable agricultural centre, and there are a couple of *kafenía* with shady tables beside the road where you can pull over for a drink.

Not far beyond comes the turning to **SAMONÁS**, a narrow road winding steeply up through 180° hairpins, with better views at every turn. The reason to take this detour is to visit the isolated Byzantine church of Áyios Nikólaos at KIRIAKOSÉLIA, which you'll see signed beyond Samonás. The church, which has recently been restored, contains fantastic **medieval frescoes**, as good as any on Crete. These have not been touched by the restorers – at least not recently – and are patchy and faded against their deep blue background, but parts still seem as vivid as the day they were created: in particular a *Madonna and Child*, at eye level on the left-hand side. To see them you have to have a car, because the keyholders (Kostas or Roussa) live in Samonás – you pick them up there and drive on to the church, a couple of hilly kilometres further (half on a bumpy dirt road). Head for the *kafenío* in Samonás – preferably in the afternoon – and they'll ring for someone to take you and cheerily overcharge for a drink while you wait. By contrast Kostas or Roussa (or one of their daughters) always seem to refuse money for their time.

The Dhrápano peninsula and Vrísses

A multitude of roads crisscross the **Dhrápano peninsula**, almost all of them scenic and well surfaced. This is rich agricultural land, a countryside of rolling green, wooded hills interrupted by immaculate white – and obviously wealthy – villages. Nowhere are there individual attractions to detain you long, but all these settlements have *kafenía* where you can sit awhile amazed at the rural tranquillity away from the main road traffic. Coming from Stílos you can either head through Néo Horío to Kalíves on the coast, or turn off later for Vámos at the centre of the peninsula. The direct approach, however, is from the new road below Áptera.

Kalíves, Almirídha and the coast

From Kalámi, the old road drops rapidly down to the coast at **KALÍVES**, an agricultural market centre of some size. Approaching, you pass a long sandy beach in the lee of Áptera's castle-topped bluff which looks attractive but is hard to reach. The town beach stretches west from the centre of the village, curving round at the far end by a small harbour where it's more sheltered – you're better off swimming at this end since at the other, just before the beach, what appears to be an open sewer flows past the public toilets and into the sea (a small river also empties at Kalíves). The village itself is still in the early stages of gearing up for tourism, with a scattering of apartments and studios and a few rooms. Empty apartments can be great value, but since they tend to be spread out at either end of the village it's easiest to start at one of the travel agencies in the centre – they should know where the vacancies are. You'll find several places to eat on the main road through, but the best spot is occupied by the *Mini-Golf Bar* (which really does have crazy golf), overlooking the western (town) end of the beach.

ALMIRÍDHA, the next village along the coast, is smaller, marginally more of a resort, and considerably more attractive. Again there are far more apartments than rooms (there's less chance of finding space here), and there's a row of tavernas behind a couple of small patches of sand in a sheltered little bay. It's a lovely beach – also a popular spot for windsurfing, with a fairly reliable breeze once you're slightly offshore – and like Kalíves is popular with local families who drive down to swim and enjoy a leisurely lunch. The best of the tavernas is the first, *Dimitri's*, with a sign advertising "fresh fishes".

Beyond Almirídha the coast becomes increasingly rocky, with cliffs almost all the way round to Yeoryioúpoli denying access to the sea. The roads also deteriorate if you go this way, but as you climb the views become increasingly worthwhile. There are more beaches below PLÁKA, a postcard-picturesque hamlet (with rooms) which, like KÓKKINO HORIÓ on the steep height above it, served as a set for the filming of parts of *Zorba the Greek*. KEFALÁS, with views over the sea on both sides, is a prettier village still.

Gavalohóri and Vámos

An excellent new road runs inland from Almirídha towards Vámos. Immediately inland you pass below ASPRÓ, a tiny, ancient hamlet looking down over the coast. This is the old Greek village as you've always imagined it: a couple of lucky foreigners have snapped up the only empty houses. GAVALOHÓRI, further on, offers something more tangible to stop for, namely a tiny museum in the town hall (daily 10am–1pm & 5–7pm; ask in the *kafeníon* if it's shut). This is an ancient settlement – there are Byzantine wells on the outskirts, and on the corner by the museum you can see the remains of a Turkish coffee shop with inscriptions and old jars – and the museum has gathered all sorts of ephemera found about the place. There's nothing really venerable (a few shards of broken Venetian pottery are the oldest pieces) but it's a wonderful old curiosity shop of junk, including nineteenth-century household goods – with labels such as "old sofa", "old bed" – antique and more recent embroidery, oil lamps, clocks, coins, banknotes, photos, shell cases, cannonballs: all of it muddled together and tremendous fun.

VÁMOS is the chief village of the region, complete with a big new health centre. Only size really distinguishes it from all the other villages, however, and the *kafenía* round the crossroads are as peaceful as any you'll find.

Vrísses

Almost whichever route you follow, you'll end up approaching VRÍSSES, a major junction of the old roads and still, though bypassed by the new, the crossroads for the route south to Sfakiá. Set on the banks of the Almirós (or *Tris Almiri*) river, Vrísses is a wonderfully shady little town, its streets lined with huge old plane trees. If you're travelling between Hóra Sfakíon and Réthimnon or anywhere else to the east you usually have to change buses here. On the riverside are a couple of tavernas by a bridge and a monument to the independence settlement of 1898; plenty of smaller cafés line the main street, many of them offering good local yoghurt and honey. There are also **rooms**, should you want one. If you're driving to Hóra Sfakíon, incidentally, it's a good idea to fill up with petrol here; it's available at a couple of villages en route but there's none in Hóra Sfakíon itself and only sparse, expensive supplies in other villages along the south coast. About 4km in this direction, and worth a look if you're passing, the village of ALÍKAMBOS lies just off the road – there are good fourteenth-century frescoes in its church of Panayía.

Continuing, the road cuts under the new highway once again, following the river valley down to Yeoryióupoli. This is another lovely stretch, through well-watered fields and woods. About halfway you can pull over to a picnic spot shaded by cypress trees, with a whitewashed chapel by the roadside, fresh spring water and huge picnic tables.

Yeoryióupoli

YEORYIÓUPOLI (or Georgioupolis) lies at the base of Cape Dhrápano where the Almirós flows into the sea. Like Vrísses it's a beautiful old place, with a tree-lined approach and ancient eucalyptus trees shading the huge square in the centre. Unlike Vrísses it's now an established resort, although on a small enough scale that it remains an extremely pleasant place to spend a few days.

The main course of the river runs into the Gulf of Almirós on the northern edge of Yeoryióupolis, by a small harbour protected by a long rocky breakwater, and there are numerous smaller streams running into the sea all around. The main town **beach** heads off to the south, curving round to join the continuous stretch which runs alongside the Réthimnon road for miles. Close to town it shelves very gently and enjoys the protection of the breakwater, further out it gets wilder, with sometimes vicious waves: there are new hotels and beach bars here, but there are also **dangerous currents** offshore – don't venture too far out, and take heed of any warning notices on the beach. The first part of this beach has showers and is popular with Greek families, and there are more showers further round, by *Mike's Oasis* (good ice cream and cocktails). Windsurfers can be hired still further on, by the *El Dorado* hotel. Streams crossing the beach create little quicksands in places (only knee-deep), but most of these now have wooden bridges to let you cross with dry feet.

A second, much more sheltered beach lies to the north of the river in a small bay. Swimming here is safer and there are generally fewer people, but the water can be extremely cold thanks to the rivers emptying at each end of the sand. There are a couple of simple bar/tavernas behind this beach. At the far end, beyond the smaller stream, you can follow a path over sharp rocks, past an old chapel and various caves, but in the end it leads only to more sharp rocks and eventually peters out above the cliffs.

Practical details

There are **rooms** to rent everywhere, it seems, and only at the height of season are you likely to have any trouble finding a vacancy; even then you should be all right if you arrive early in the day. If you arrive by bus you'll be dropped on the main road, just a couple of minutes' walk from the square and crossroads at the centre of town. Most of the better places to stay are to the right from here, down the lane which heads towards the beach: *Zorba's Taverna* and *Andy's Rooms* are both good possibilities, but further on are places where the views and sounds are of the sea rather than the street – *Rooms Irini* (☎61-278) and *Pension Cactus*, for example. If these are full, the town is small enough to wander around and check out everything on offer within half an hour. Another cluster of rooms places is to be found straight on from the square, where the road crosses the river: the appropriately named *The Bridge* on the near side, and *Anna* on the far side, for example. Mosquitoes can be a problem by the river, but the wildlife on the banks is some compensation. Kingfishers can often be seen here. If you do have trouble finding space, two E-class hotels right on the square, *Amfimala* (☎61-362) and *Penelope* (☎61-370), are often the last to fill, probably because of the noise at night. People **camp**, unofficially, at the far end of the small beach around the stream.

Restaurants are concentrated round the square too, and again there are plenty to choose from. The *Café Georgioupoli Pub* is a fine place for breakfast or simply to sit over a long drink, watching the world go by. One good alternative slightly away from the rush is *Arkadi*, on the point by the mouth of the river (on the far side). The *Hotel Gorgona*, on the town beach, also has a decent taverna looking out to sea. **Bars** again crowd round the square and out towards the main road – *Aetoma*, overlooking the square from the first floor, serves lousy cocktails but has good music and atmosphere. Alternative entertainment is on offer at the tiny, open-air **cinema**, where they show a different film every night, usually subtitled. Programme details are pinned to the tree in the square. There are also several travel agents and car hire places: *Georgioupolis Travel* (on the square; ☎61-206) is one of the best of these, with all services including exchange at decent rates. You can buy newspapers and attempt to make phone calls from the kiosk in the square: a couple of small shops here stock all the basics and there's a fruit stall set up in the centre most mornings.

Lake Kournás

Four kilometres inland from Yeoryióupoli, the island's only freshwater lake, **LAKE KOURNÁS**, shelters in a bowl of hills – an easy if unexciting walk. (If you want to walk for pleasure, there are more rewards in hiking up the Almirós valley towards Vrísses or tackling the steep climb to EXÓPOLIS on the road to Vámos.) The lake's uniqueness has given it a perhaps unfairly high profile (as lakes go, it's small and shallow), but it nevertheless makes for an interesting afternoon's excursion. On the bank where you arrive there's a taverna – a popular place for locals' outings, with lamb barbecued on spits – and a few pedaloes and canoes for hire. Upstairs the taverna has about six new **rooms**, overpriced and gnat-infested but immaculately sited, looking out over the water, and very comfortable if you have repellent coils to burn. The lake itself varies greatly according to when you visit. During the day its colours change remarkably as the sun shifts around the rim of the bowl: over the course of a year its size varies as well. In late summer the level drops to reveal sand (or dried mud) beaches all around and a number of popular camping spots – earlier in the year the water comes right up to the tidal ring of scrubby growth and it's much harder to find anywhere to camp or to swim from. The lake and the hills around it are also a good place to seek out some of the more unusual island wildlife (see p.275).

The village of KOURNÁS is another 4km beyond the lake, a stiff climb which reveals nothing very exciting – a tranquil, medium-sized village with a couple of sleepy cafés. From here you could follow the road, in poor condition, to rejoin the old Haniá–Réthimnon road somewhere before Episkopí. MOURÍ is closer to the lake, straight up from the junction with the path which leads down to the banks. If the lakeside taverna is full, you could try here for rooms.

Inland: walks and Venizélos country

The country behind Haniá, a small agricultural plain into which the foothills of the White Mountains intrude, is not the most thrilling in Crete, but with a day to spare it does deserve exploration – especially if you're prepared to embark on some serious hiking. For the most part they grow oranges here, oranges which are the best in Crete and hence, as any local will tell you, the finest in the world. Many of the villages are also associated with **Eleftheríos Venizélos**, the revered Cretan statesman who, as prime minister of Greece from 1910, finally brought Crete into the modern Greek nation.

Perhaps the most attractive journey is the 14km drive up to **THÉRISO**, home-town of Venizélos' mother and one of the cradles of Cretan independence. Here in 1905 was held the Revolutionary Assembly which ousted Prince George and did much to precipitate union with Greece – and pictures of which, all baggy black shirts and drooping moustaches, turn up so often in Cretan museums and exhibitions. The trip out to the little house, with its plaque commemorating the famous son, is an all but obligatory one for Cretans, and the village seems frequently to find itself crowded with coachloads of battling primary school kids. There's actually little to see apart from a traditional country village, but it's worth going anyway for the drive up **Thériso Gorge**. In terms of spectacle this can't, of course, compare with Samariá and in any case the bed of the ravine is given over to the (mostly paved) road. But it is exceedingly pretty in the lower reaches, gentle and winding with the stream crossed and recrossed on rickety bridges, and surprisingly craggy towards the top where the walls are cracked and pocked with caves.

If you want to continue and complete a circle round to Mesklá you face a heady climb into the foothills of the mountains and over what feels an impressively lofty ridge. This road is narrow, rocky and frequently blocked by gates to prevent livestock straying, and nor is it always obvious which way to go, but it's not too bad a drive. Alternatively, it makes a wonderful long hike, occasionally traversed by organised rambling groups and quite possible on your own as long as you check the route beforehand, ask frequently, and check bus times to get you home again. There are buses to both Thériso and Mesklá from Haniá, and the walk between the two takes less than three hours. Given the vagaries of the timetable, though, the trip is liable to take all day if you do it by bus.

Right at the top lies **SÓURVA**, a cluster of whitewashed houses with stupendous views over the surrounding valleys. There's nothing to do here – one *kafeníon* tended only by a menacing guard dog – but it is a hell of a setting. From Sóurva the way spirals slowly down to **MESKLÁ**, another beautiful village set on a swift-flowing brook and surrounded, as a result, by lush agricultural land and orange groves. There are several small café/tavernas. Under the Venetians Mesklá was a place of considerably more importance than it is now: for evidence, seek out the tiny chapel at the bottom of the village (a turn up to the left if you are approaching from the Fournés end) containing the remains of fourteenth-century **frescoes**. The chapel itself looks like nothing so much as a concrete Nissen hut and many of the paintings have been severely damaged by damp and mould, but parts remain clearly visible and it seems a remarkable place to find them. There's another chapel alleged to contain the remains of a fifth- or sixth-century Roman mosaic, alongside a modern church at the top end of the village. Since church and chapel both seem permanently locked, however, there's no way of knowing.

Mesklá was also the centre of one of the great legends of Cretan resistance, the **Kandanoleon revolt**. According to the story (which is certainly not historically accurate, though it must have some basis in fact), much of western Crete rose against the Venetians early in the sixteenth century. They elected as their leader one George Kandanoleon who established a base in Mesklá and from here ran a rebel administration, collecting taxes and effectively controlling much of the west. It was only by treachery that he was finally brought to heel. In order to legitimise his authority, Kandanoleon arranged for his son to marry the daughter of a Venetian aristocrat. The marriage took place and the celebrations began, with Kandanoleon and several hundred of his supporters eating and drinking themselves to a stuporous standstill. At which point, by pre-arranged signal, a Venetian army arrived and captured the Cretans as they slept; their leaders were hanged at villages around the countryside, and the revolt was over.

Continuing on foot you could climb steeply again to **LÁKKI** (see p.210) on the main road to Omalós and the Samarian Gorge. The road, however, and the direct route to Haniá, head down to **FOURNÉS** and join the main road there. Fournés is a very much larger place, with shops lining the road (good for stocking up if you're taking this circuit in reverse), heavily cultivated fields roundabout and a large producers' cooperative.

If you want to complete the round of Venizélos pilgrimages you should also visit **MOURNIÉS**, where the great man was born in 1864. Immediately south of Haniá, this is easiest reached by heading out towards the main Réthimnon highway. Mourniés is just a couple of kilometres from the end (or beginning) of the new stretch of road. Once there you can see the house in which Venizélos was born and little else – but it makes for another pleasant drive out of the city, along a road lined with ancient plane trees.

West of Haniá: the villa coast

West from Haniá the road follows the coastline more or less consistently all the way to the base of the Rodhópou peninsula. Occasionally it runs right above the water, more often a hundred metres or so inland, but never more than easy walking distance from the sea. In the early stages the various villages have merged into an almost continuous string of ribbon development – not exactly ugly, but not particularly attractive either. There are villas, hotels and sporadic pensions or rooms to rent all the way, though little that is particularly cheap or where you can really expect to find space in season without reservations. As you leave the city behind, this development thins, giving way between towns to orange groves protected from the *meltemi* by bamboo windbreaks, where only the occasional path penetrates down to the sea. There is **beach** of sorts almost all the way, though much is windswept, dirty and subject to crashing breakers; for secure swimming you're better off in the early parts, at the city beach of Kalamáki, at Ayía Marína, or at Plataniás.

This coastline was the scene of the fiercest fighting in the **Battle of Crete**, and the bridgehead from which the Germans established their domination. There's a reminder of this almost immediately you leave the city – an aggressive diving eagle beside the road, erected by the Germans as a memorial to their paratroops. Passing this, you're into the stretch of coast along which are ranged the town beaches (p.190), though the road here actually runs as far from the sea as it does anywhere. Frequent minor roads run either down to the beach or up into the hills, where there are some pleasant villas and small hotels looking down over the coastline, and a great deal of new development still going on. Villages like DHARÁTSOS, **GALATÁS** and places even less well-defined seem thoroughly unattractive as you drive along the main road, but in most cases there is a real village, up in the hills inland. Galatás turns out to be a fair-sized place, in whose village hall is a small Battle of Crete museum, basically a collection of rusty guns and helmets. Outside is a memorial to those who died here, including 145 New Zealand soldiers. *Uncle John's*, opposite, is a good place for a snack if you're passing.

Ayía Marína and Plataniás

KALAMÁKI, where the road finally comes in sight of the beach, marks the limit of the local bus service from Haniá and also the end of this strip of sand. Beyond, low hills drop straight to the sea round a couple of bends and then you emerge at KÁTO STALÓS, which runs into **AYÍA MARÍNA**, a village of considerably more size and character than anything which has preceded it. From here to Plataniás is the most developed strip in the west, with shops, restuarants, hotels, rooms for rent (though rarely any vacancies in summer), travel agents, tavernas, discos and bike hire places one after the other for miles. This is better than it sounds – it's all fairly low-rise, there's a decent beach almost all the way along (with facilities including jet-skis, windsurfers and parascending), and by resort standards it's all pretty quiet. Ayía Marína itself is distinguished by a small brick factory and, towards the end of the village, *Camping Ayia Marina* with its beautiful sector of beach. Curving round a little promontory, this has a fine view of the sunset and of **ÁYII THEÓDORI**, the island offshore which is now a sanctuary for *kri-kri* (you're not allowed to land on the island). From the west a great cave gapes like the jaws of a beast, and in legend the island was a sea-monster which, emerging from the depths to swallow Crete, was petrified by the gods in the very act. Remains found in the cave suggest that it was a place of worship in antiquity: more recently the Venetians turned the whole island into a fortress against the threat of piracy and a Turkish invasion.

West again, **PLATANIÁS** follows almost immediately (there's virtually no break in the development from Káto Stalós to beyond Plataniás to tell you when you leave one place and enter the next), another village of some substance with a delightful old quarter high on an almost sheer bluff above the road. There are a number of tavernas which attract evening and weekend trippers from Haniá, notably *O Milos* towards the west end of the village. Specialities here (and at others in the village) are *yíros* and *kokorétsi* – meat or offal cooked on huge spits over charcoal – but the *Milos* has extra attractions in the form of an old mill stream with ducks in it running through a walled garden at the back where you eat. *The Carop Tree*, halfway up the hill to the village, has a more varied menu and views way along the coast.

Yeráni to Tavronítis

Beyond Plataniás, things change little all the way to the Rodhópou peninsula, though signs of tourism get fewer the further you go. There are lots of isolated villas and one or two slightly more concentrated developments in places such as YERÁNI. These on the whole are pleasantly low-key, but the beach is rarely that great – very open to wind and waves and with rather gravelly, grey sand. Frequent paths and tracks lead down from the road to the sea.

MÁLEME is perhaps the place you're most likely to stop. Just beyond, the airfield which saw so much of the early fighting in the Battle of Crete, and whose loss in controversial circumstances was crucial to the German success, can have changed very little: more concrete perhaps, but otherwise a very simple, fenced-off military runway. Just before it, the giant *Crete Chandris* hotel lies to the right of the road, dominating the only bit of sandy beach around. If you're feeling brazen you can walk through to this: the hotel also has a pool and a couple of bars in its luxuriant grounds. Almost directly opposite, a narrow lane leads up to the **German war cemetery** on a hillside overlooking the battleground. This is, if anything, even more lovingly groomed and watered than the Allied one, and it certainly has a better position: in a piece of almost grotesque irony its keepers, until recently, were George Psychoundakis (author of *The Cretan Runner*, when offered the job, he was allegedly told "You looked after the Germans while they were alive, why not look after them now they're dead?") and Manoli Paterakis, who played a leading role in the capture of General Kreipe.

There's a final reminder of Máleme's significance as you cross the River Tavronítis, beyond the airstrip, on a long modern bridge. Beside it twin pontoon bridges survive from the war. **TAVRONÍTIS** itself is still a traditional farming centre with fruit for sale at stalls beside the road. It's here that you turn off to head across the island to Paleohóra (p.233). If you're not doing so, carry on to Kolimbári at the base of Rodhópou peninsula

Kolimbári and Moní Goniá

KOLIMBÁRI has far more appeal than anything that has preceded it along this coast. If there were a sandy beach it would be a perfect resort: as it is there's a long strip of pebbles and clear water looking back along all the coast towards Haniá, just about visible in the distance. Although you can see that tourists come here, it's little spoiled: there are about ten rooms to rent signs, and a few restaurants on the main street or around the crossroads. As a restful place to break your journey for a couple of hours, it's ideal.

Out onto the peninsula, it's only a few minutes' walk to the **Moní Goniá** (closed from 2–5pm). If this were a luxury hotel they could hardly have chosen the site better, with stupendous views and a scramble down to what appears to be a sandy cove (though I've never tried swimming here – it is apparently the monks' private beach). Founded at the beginning of the seventeenth century, the monastery perhaps has less to show than some, but as always there are stirring tales of resistance to the infidel Turk. Here they can point to the cannonballs still lodged in the walls to prove it – a relic they seem far more proud of than any icon. Which is not to say there are no worthwhile icons: the church has a series dating from the seventeenth and eighteenth centuries (plus a few modern ones), of which Áyios Nikólaos, in a side chapel, is particularly fine. More are kept in the small museum, along with assorted vestments and relics. Although there are (or were) only seven monks left, they remain very hospitable and there's even a "tourist monk" who has been pointing things out to visitors for years, often treating them to a glass of raki and a look at his treasured stamp collection (all contributions welcome).

The Rodhópou peninsula

The road which extends onto the **Rodhópou peninsula** goes nowhere in particular, petering out into a dirt track beyond Afráta and then circling back, but the first part at least is a superb drive. Just beyond the monastery is a modern Orthodox Academy and from here the road follows the coast for a short way and then begins to climb, hairpinning its way to a dizzy height above the sea before turning inland. The views are magnificent – not only back along the coast you have traversed but also down into the sea, a sea so clear and green you feel you can see through it like air.

AFRÁTA is a tiny place, little visited, with a few simple *kafenía*. Carry on down the hill past the first two of these and you'll come to *Roxani's* (identified simply by a blackboard saying "Taverna, Grills . . . "). Roxani speaks no English, but she serves good, simple food in a lovely setting. Below *Roxani's*, keep right on a rough track which drops steeply and after little more than 1km you'll reach a rocky cove, at the far end of the gorge you can see from the village. The exceptionally clear water here offers great swimming, often with no one else about, though you need to watch out for sea urchins and sharp rocks. In the other direction from Afráta, an unsurfaced road is signed to ASTRÁTIGOS and ASPRA NERA. This is not too bad a drive, and shortly after Aspra Nera you can rejoin the tarmacked Rodhopós road to head down to the base of the peninsula again.

THE GEOLOGY OF THE LEFKÁ ÓRI

The Lefká Óri take their name from the pale-coloured limestones of which they are formed. These limestones were laid down between 150 million and 40 million years ago. At that time the region which is now Greece and the Aegean Sea featured a different pattern of land and water, dominated by a large landmass called Apulia.

Material eroded from Apulia was transported southwards and deposited in the sea as a series of limestones which are now seen over much of Western Crete: they are known as the Plattenkalk or Ida limestones. The nature of the limestone varied according to the distance from the Apulian coast. Limestones deposited close to the coast were coarse and contained quite large pebbles. Those further away were much finer and were often in thin layers alternating with a flint-like rock called chert.

To understand how these limestones were formed into the mountains seen today it is necessary to understand something of the theory of "plate tectonics". This states that the earth's crust is composed of a number of large, very slowly moving plates, which are added to at "Mid Ocean Ridges" and destroyed again in ocean trenches at "subduction zones". About 35 million years ago the plate containing Africa began to move northwards relative to the plate containing Europe. (It was the collision between these two plates which caused the Alps to be formed.) In this area, the movement of the African plate caused the Plattenkalk limestones to be pushed up, and eventually caused slices of the Apulian rocks from the north to be pushed over them. This buried and deformed the Plattenkalk limestones – the results of which are now clearly seen in the walls of the Samarian Gorge where bands of light limestone and dark chert are intensely folded and deformed.

Eventually the movement of Africa caused some of the old sea floor to the south to be pushed under all these rocks and initiated a "subduction zone" running along the southern margin of Crete. Continued movement of the African plate has since been taken up by subduction of the sea floor. This process has caused continued slow uplift of Crete, particularly in the south close to the subduction zone. As the Lefká Óri have been pushed up in this manner the slices of Apulian rocks on top of them have been eroded away. (Although old Apulian rocks can still be seen to the north of the mountains where the uplift has been less.)

As the mountains move upwards only very slowly, streams flowing from the centre of Crete have been able to follow their original courses and cut through the mountains, causing the spectacular gorges now seen. This process has been going on for about the last 25 million years and is still continuing – hence gorges such as that at Samariá are getting deeper as the White Mountains continue to rise at about two metres every thousand years.

Towards the tip of the peninsula you'll find no more driveable roads, though there are a couple of sites you might consider getting to if you were prepared to undertake a major hike, or to go by boat. The latter is certainly the easier option – in summer the terrain is frighteningly hot, barren and shadeless for walking – especially as day-trip boats from Haniá quite often make for **Diktynna**, almost at the top of the peninsula above a little bay on the east side. An important Roman sanctuary to the goddess of the same name, this was probably built over more ancient centres of worship, and though it has never been properly excavated there's a surprising amount to be seen. The boats come here mainly because it's a sheltered spot to swim (when the sea is rough, fishing boats often shelter here too) but they allow plenty of time to explore.

On the other side of the peninsula, the isolated **Church of Ayío Ioánnis Giónis** can make a challenging hike. Here, on August 29 (Saint John the Baptist's Day), is held one of the most important festivals of the Cretan religious calendar: a major pilgrimage, and the mass baptism of boys named John. At this time the two- to three-hour walk (each way), among crowds of people, is definitely worth it. Although you can approach from Afráta, the main path up the spine of the island starts in RODHOPÓS, which you reach up the next turn off the main road after Kolimbári, and to where there is an occasional bus.

SFAKIÁ AND THE LEFKÁ ÓRI

South of Haniá loom the **White Mountains** – the Lefká Óri – a formidable barrier to progress. Just a couple of metres short of the Psilorítis range, these are in every other way more impressive mountains: barer, craggier and far less tamed. There is just one road into the heart of the mountains, climbing up to the cold, enclosed plateau of Omalós. From here any further progress southwards is on foot – most obviously the spectacular, and spectacularly popular, descent through the great cleft of the **Samarian Gorge**. Famous as it is, this is just the largest of a series of ravines by which streams make their escape to the coast. Far less beaten tracks lead, for example, down the **Ímbros Gorge** towards Hóra Sfakíon, or from Ayía Iríni to Sóuyia. With more preparation you could also go climbing among the peaks – there's a mountaineering hut above Omalós – or undertake an expedition right across the range.

Along the south coast, too, you can walk, although it's a great deal easier by boat. Regular summer services link **Ayía Rouméli**, at the bottom of the Samarian Gorge, with **Loutró** and Hóra Sfakíon, or in the other direction there are less frequent connections to Paleohóra and Sóuyia. **Hóra Sfakíon** is the capital of this region – **Sfakiá** – which for all its desolation and depopulation is perhaps the most famous, and certainly the most written about, in Crete. It is above all an area notorious for its fierceness: harsh living conditions; unrelenting weather; warlike people. Most men here, they claim, still carry a weapon of some kind concealed about their person.

Historically, the region was cut off and barbaric, almost a nation apart which, as occupying armies came and went, carried on with life – feuding, rustling, rearing sheep – pretty much regardless. Most of the great tales of Cretan resistance, of *pallikari* fighters and mountain guerrillas, originate in Sfakiá or in Sélinos, west of the mountains. The local version of the Creation reveals much of the Sfakiot spirit. As recounted in Adam Hopkins' book, it begins:

> with an account of all the gifts God had given to other parts of Crete – olives to Ierapetra, Ayios Vasilios and Selinou; wine to Malevisi and Kissamou; cherries to Mylopotamos and Amari. But when God got to Sfakia only rocks were left. So the Sfakiots appeared before Him armed to the teeth. "And us Lord, how are we going to live on these rocks?" and the Almighty, looking at them with sympathy, replied in their own dialect (naturally): "Haven't you got a scrap of brains in your head? Don't you see that the lowlanders are cultivating all these riches for you?"

Stealing was a way of life and so was feuding and revenge – with vendettas on a Sicilian scale continuing well into this century, and occasionally rumoured even now.

The Venetians had plans to pacify the region, but their castle on the coast at **Frangokástello** (still standing, by some excellent beaches) was rarely more than an isolated outpost. The Turks did more, imposing taxation on Sfakiá, for example, but they also provoked more violent revenge, notably in the revolt of Dhaskaloyiánnis (p.222), and many which succeeded it. The mountains were always a safe refuge in which bandits and rebels could conceal themselves while armies took revenge on the lowlands. In World War II Sfakiá resumed this traditional role: when the Germans invaded, King George was rushed across the island and down the Samarian Gorge to be evacuated, and it was from Hóra Sfakíon that the bulk of the Allied forces were taken off. Throughout the war, the mountain heights remained the realm of the resistance, and in the late Sixties two ex-Civil War guerrillas were found still hiding out here, twenty years on.

Nowadays all of this seems very distant: there are frequent buses to Hóra Sfakíon and Omalós and a constant stream of people trekking between the two. But you don't have to get far off this path to realise how the reputation grew, and why it is still so powerful.

Omalós and the heart of the mountains

The little plateau around Omalós lies pretty much at the heart of the Lefká Óri, surrounded by the highest peaks of the range. Several hundred people head up here daily to join the stampede down the Gorge of Samariá (on peak days as many as 2000), only a handful stop to see anything on the way, and very few indeed take any of the more adventuresome routes into the mountains. The gorge route is described in detail below, and while mountaineering doesn't really fall within the scope of this book, a few starter suggestions are also included. Bear in mind that this is a genuinely wild mountain zone – venture nowhere alone or without adequate equipment.

The **road up to Omalós** turns inland from Haniá's western outskirts, heading at first across a rich but rather dull countryside of orange groves and vineyards interrupted by large modern villages. Shortly before Alikianós (p.236), the large white building bristling with TV aerials is a prison with a fairly open regime (its inmates work in the fields). This is the building after which the Battle of Crete's "Prison Valley" was named, and at the Alikianós turnoff there's a large memorial to local members of the wartime resistance. Soon after FOURNÉS (p.204) you begin to climb in earnest to the Lefká Óri through a series of sweeping great loops with increasingly alarming drops. **LÁKKI**, the only village of any size you pass, is a bracingly green-and-white place looking back down over the plain. Delicious honey is sold here by local producers. It has a few rooms to rent (at prices better than those higher up) and a couple of tavernas which cater heartily for appetites generated by mountain air and whetted with the prospect of strenuous activity. In spring, especially, it's an attractive setting.

Omalós and the plateau

Leaving Lákki the road climbs on, past another memorial at the spot where Kapetan Vasilios (Sgt. Major Dan Perkins) and a Cretan colleague were ambushed (a story recounted in *The Cretan Runner* and elsewhere), to a pass at a little over 1200m, before dropping suddenly to the flat expanse of the **Omalós plain**. If you've caught the dawn bus up from Haniá it's only now that there's enough light properly to take in your surroundings (it is perhaps a mercy to have been spared the details of your bus's flirtations with the void at every curve of the ascent) and it's an eerily deserted, enclosed little world which is revealed. At over 1000m the Omalós is cold, its vegetation stunted, and the plain itself small enough to see, all around, the ring of stone which encloses it. There's just one small village on the road – **OMALÓS** itself. Here a couple of brand new hotels and several tavernas look very out of place alongside the chapel and few crude stone houses of the original settlement. The *Hotel Koutrouli*, in particular, is a large, modern building entirely out of keeping with its surroundings; the *Neos Omalos* is flash, too, though marginally less so, while relatively ordinary rooms are available at *Samaria*. Scattered about the plain are other settlements, but none have the air of permanent habitation. In winter everything is deep in snow and deserted. In spring the land is marshy and waterlogged – almost a lake if there's a sudden melt. Only in summer do people live here full time, moving up from Lákki and other villages on the lower slopes roundabout (Ayía Iríni, Zóurva, Prasés) to pasture sheep and goats or to cultivate, on a small scale, cereals and potatoes.

Walk out into the plain in almost any direction and within five minutes you'll have left all traces of modern life behind, with only the jingling of the occasional goat's bell or the deliberate piling of stones to remind you of human presence. If you spend the night, there are fabulous starry skies up here.

Scaling the peaks

If you need more of a reason to stay at the top, you could hike the one and a half hours up to the EOS (Greek Mountain Club) **Kallergi Hut** (☎54-560), at 1677m the base for climbing into the peaks. This is reached by following the road on from Omalós for about half an hour, then turning left onto the dirt track signed to the hut, a further hour's walking (or scary jeep ride; you can also take a path from the top of the gorge in about 1hr 15min). The hut itself – Austrian-run in summer, with no prizes for a friendly welcome – is probably the best source of information on tackling the peaks: it is open from May to October inclusive. Beds are cheap, but meals, served morning and evening, are not (and you're pretty much obliged to eat at least one). In winter it occasionally reopens, or can be opened by arrangement, for determined skiers.

For adventurous walkers, there's a two-day hike from here through the heart of the range to Anópoli and Hóra Sfakíon. This would take you right past **Páhnes**, the highest summit in the west and, at 2453m, just three metres short of Psilorítis for the title of loftiest in Crete: Haniot mountaineers regularly add stones to the cairn on the peak in an attempt to catch up. With less commitment you could follow the beginning of this trail for two or three hours for some scintillating views down into the gorge and across the seas to the south and west. The hut itself is perched high over the gorge, but it looks even more impressive from the isolation of these bare stone peaks, a slash of rich green in an otherwise unrelenting landscape of grey and brown.

You'll get more of a sense of achievement – and certainly impress others more – if you tackle the climb to the peak of **Mount Gíngilos** (2080m), beginning from the top of the gorge. Its north face, the one everyone sees, is a near vertical slope of solid rock – round the back, though, you can reach the summit with only a little scrambling. It's hard work and you need confidence with heights, especially if it's windy, but no special mountaineering skills are necessary. A large yellow sign points the way from the back of the Tourist Lodge at the top of the gorge and the path, though not marked with the usual paint splashes, should be easy enough to follow for the two and a half hours to the top. At first you track around to the west, climbing above the plain, before cutting south, downhill slightly, towards the back of the mountain. Here, almost exactly halfway, amid bizarre rock formations which include an arch across the path, there's a spring of ice-cold water. Beyond, you begin to climb in earnest until for the final half-hour the ascent is signalled with red paint – stick to the path as there are hidden hazards and even the official route needs hands as well as feet. The rewards are an all-round panorama from the summit and, with luck, the chance to sight some of the rarer animal life which crowds have driven from the gorge itself.

The Gorge of Samariá

The one trip that every visitor to Crete – even those eminently unsuited to it – feels compelled to make is the hike down the Samarian Gorge. So if you're expecting a wilderness experience, an opportunity to commune peacefully with nature, think again. On the other hand, this is not a Sunday afternoon stroll to be lightly undertaken; especially in spring when the river is roaring, or on a hot midsummer day, it can be a thoroughly gruelling test of fitness and stamina. Your body will know all about the walk next day. And the mules and helicopter standing by to rescue the injured are not mere talk – anyone who regularly leads tours through the gorge has a stack of horror stories (broken legs and heart attacks feature most frequently) to wheel out for inspection. To undertake the walk you should at least be reasonably fit and/or used to lengthy walks. And you should have comfortable, sturdy shoes that will stand up to hot, sharp rocks.

The gorge begins, startlingly sudden, on the far side of the plain. After the dull tranquillity of the plain you are faced with this great cleft opening beneath your feet and, across it – close enough to bounce stones off, it seems – the gaunt limestone face of Mount Gíngilos. It would be a daunting start were it not for the well-worn trail leading clearly down below you and the dozens of people hanging around ready to set off. Here **at the top** there's a large area where cars and coaches park, with a couple of mobile stalls doing a brisk trade in hot coffee (first thing, the air is breath-smokingly cold up here) and supplies for the journey. Just above perches the Tourist Lodge, and ahead a wooden railing marks the edge of the drop. This is a fine place to contemplate a while before heading down, allowing the crowds to disperse if you've arrived with the mob. There are maps showing the path and facilities en route, others with the vegetation zones marked, and lists of park regulations.

Heading down

The descent begins on the **Xilóskalon** (wooden stairway), a stepped path cut from the rock and augmented by log stairs and wooden handrails, which zigzags rapidly down to the base of the gorge, plunging 1000m in the first 2km or so of the walk. Near the bottom the chapel of Áyios Nikólaos stands on a little terrace of coniferous trees: there are benches from which to enjoy the view, and fresh water. Beyond, the path begins gradually to level out, following the stream bed amid softer vegetation which reflects the milder climate down here. In late spring it's

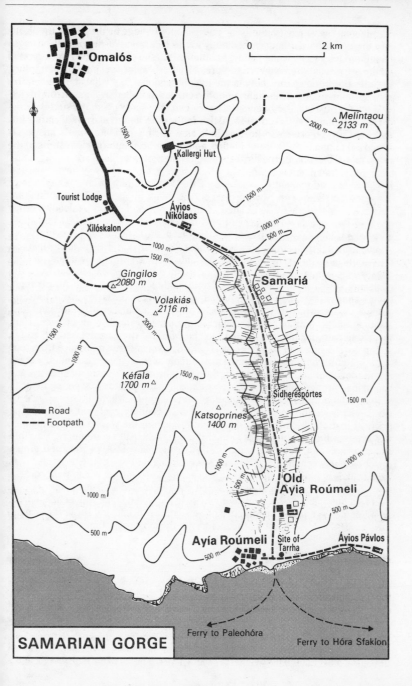

0   2 km

Omalós

Melíntaou
△ 2133 m
2000 m

1500 m

Kallergi Hut

1500 m

Tourist Lodge

Áyios
Nikólaos

Xilóskalon

1000 m

500 m

1000 m

1500 m

Gíngilos
△ 2080 m

Samariá

Volakiás
△ 2116 m

2000 m

1500 m

1000 m

Kéfala
1700 m △

1500 m

Sidherespórtes

1500 m

Katsoprínes
△ 1400 m

Road
Footpath

1000 m

1000 m

1000 m

Old
Ayia Roúmeli

500 m

1000 m

500 m

Ayía Roúmeli

Site of
Tarrha

500 m

Áyios Pávlos

Ferry to Paleohóra

Ferry to Hóra Sfakíon

SAMARIAN GORGE

magnificent, but at any time of year there should be wild flowers and rare plants easy enough to spot (though absolutely not to pick): one of the rarest and most endangered is a large white peony, *paeonia clusii*. The stream itself is less certain – there are places where you can be sure of icy fresh water, and pools to bathe sore feet, all year round (particularly in the middle sections), but what starts when the park opens as a fierce, even dangerous torrent has dwindled by autumn to a trickle between hot, dry boulders, disappearing beneath the surface for long stretches.

The abandoned village of **SAMARIÁ** lies a little under midway through the walk, shortly before the 7km marker. One of the buildings here has been converted to house the wardens' office, another pressed into (inadequate) service as a public toilet, but for the most part the remains of the village are quietly crumbling away. Its inhabitants, until they were relocated to make way for the park in 1962, were predominantly members of the Viglis family, who claimed direct descent from one of the twelve aristocratic clans implanted from Byzantium. Certainly this settlement, as isolated as any in Crete and cut off by floodwater for much of the year, is a very ancient one: the church of Óssia María, from which gorge and village take their name, was founded in the early fourteenth century.

After Samariá the path is more level, the walls of the gorge begin to close in and the path is often forced to cross from one side of the stream to the other, on stepping stones which at times may be submerged and slippery. Beside you, the contorted striations of the cliffs are increasingly spectacular. But the highlight comes shortly after the Christos resting point with the *Sidherespórtes* – the **iron gates** – where two rock walls rise sheer to within a whisker of a thousand feet: standing at the bottom one can reach out almost to touch both at once. Here there's no path, for the stream bed fills the whole of the narrow passage, and in spring the swirling waters can be a real hazard as you attempt to balance from rock to rock. But it's not for long. Almost as suddenly as you entered this mighty crack in the mountain you leave it again, the valley broadens, its sides fall away, and you're in a parched wilderness of rubble deposited here by the first spring melts.

Before long you reach the fringes of Ayía Rouméli where there's a gate by which you leave the park and a couple of stalls vending cool drinks at crippling prices. Frustratingly, however, this is not the end of the walk: old Ayía Rouméli has been all but deserted in favour of the new beachside community, a further excruciatingly hot, dull twenty minutes. Arriving finally in **Ayía Rouméli** proper the choice between plunging into the sea or diving into one of the tavernas for an iced drink is agonising – though in the event it takes a strong will to walk past the row upon row of enticingly dewdropped cans of chilled fruit juice and ice-cold beers set out to divert you from your course to the water. Once your senses adjust, Ayía Rouméli is a pretty unattractive place – but that drink, and the first plunge in the sea, are still likely to live in the memory as the most refreshing ever.

Samarian practicalities

The gorge is **open**, conditions permitting, from May to October inclusive (the hike is dangerous and often impossible through the winter*) and between the hours of 6am and sunset. If you enter after 3pm, you're only allowed into the first

---

*Early rains or a late spring melt may make conditions too hazardous – flash floods are a real possibility here. However, at the discretion of the wardens, you may be allowed through at other times if the weather is good. There will be very little transport though.

couple of kilometres from each end. There are a whole series of National Park rules (posted at the entrance), but the most important are **no camping**, no fires (or smoking), no hunting and no interference with the natural or wild life. There are wardens who patrol to ensure that these are obeyed, that no one wanders too far from the main path (another breach of regulations) and that no stragglers are overtaken by nightfall.

Buses and boats

The vast majority of people who walk through the gorge – several thousand a day in the height of the season – do so as part of a **day trip**: a very early bus to the top, walk down by early afternoon, boat from Ayía Rouméli to Hóra Sfakíon and coach from there back home. Most do this with one of the **guided tours** offered by every travel agent on the island – and certainly if you're staying in a hotel anywhere in the east of Crete this is much the simplest method, probably the only way of doing it in a single day. Most tours will include all bus and ferry connections, but not food or the entrance fee to the park itself. (If you're planning to stay on the south coast, the coach can save you the effort of carrying your bags; simply stow them underneath and retrieve them in Hóra Sfakíon. Do let them know your plan, though, both to avoid an unexpected switch of bus and to prevent search parties being sent out.) If, however, you are staying in Haniá, or marginally less straightforward in Iráklion or Réthimnon, you can save money and avoid having to walk in a large group going **by public bus**.

From Haniá there are four departures a day, at 6.15am, 7.30am, 8.30am and 4.30pm – arriving at the top about one and a half hours later. You'll normally be sold a round-trip ticket including the return leg from Hóra Sfakíon (which needn't necessarily be used the same day) so if you don't want this you'll have to make your intentions very clear: the bus station is in total chaos when the first buses leave. There's a lot to be said for taking the earliest bus. More of the walk can be completed while it's still relatively cool; there's no need to force your pace, and if you're planning to stop over anywhere at the bottom you've more chance of being among the first to arrive. On the other hand everyone now does this – there's often a procession of as many as five full buses leaving Haniá before dawn, the bus station is in turmoil, there are queues and confusion when you arrive, and you're unlikely to escape from crowds the whole way down. It may be hotter, but it's also quieter if you set out later. The first buses of the day **from Iráklion** (5.30am) **and Réthimnon** (6.15 and 7am) to Haniá continue direct to Omalós.

Heading back, at least seven boats a day leave Ayía Rouméli for Hóra Sfakíon through most of the summer (five of them call at Loutró), with a slightly reduced service from May to mid-June and from mid-September to the end of October, and hardly any boats from November to April when the gorge is closed. The boats take around an hour and you should check current times when you arrive: the first generally leaves around 9.15am, followed by one or two more in the morning, a gap around lunchtime, and several towards the end of the afternoon. You need to leave by 6pm to be sure of connecting with the last Haniá bus. **For Sóuyia and Paleohóra** there's a daily sailing at 5pm between July and September, three boats a week (Tues and Thurs mornings, Sat afternoons) in May and June. **Buses** from Hóra Sfakíon back to Haniá leave at 7am, 11am, 4.30pm, 6pm and 7pm – for Réthimnon there's one at 6.30pm (otherwise you change at Vrísses), and for Plakiás and Ayía Galíni at 4.30pm.

The walk

The gorge itself is some 16km long and **the walk** down takes about five hours if you're reasonably fit and take it at a comfortable pace with occasional halts to admire the scenery, bathe your feet and take refreshment. Go at it with determination and you could probably make it through in four hours; linger at every turn and this could easily stretch to six or seven. Be wary of the kilometre markers – these mark only distances within the park, and it can be extremely frustrating finally to arrive at kilometre 0 only to discover you face a further twenty minutes walk to the sea. At the park entrance, where there's a small fee to pay, you'll be given a date-stamped ticket which should be kept and handed in at the gate by which you leave; this is partly to make sure no one tries camping in the park, partly to check that nobody is lost inside. In practice little can be done if you lose your ticket, though you might be in trouble for handing in yesterday's.

Starting from the bottom, the hike up to Omalós is not as hard as some imagine, though it will take rather longer – six to seven hours at a reasonable, steady pace. Few people do it all the way which means that at the top you may well find the gorge almost empty; on the way up, however, you'll have had to pass all the hordes charging down. You could also walk a short way up and come back – an outing offered as a day trip known as "Samaria the Lazy Way". This will show you the Iron Gates, the most spectacular individual section, but it means a lot of walking in the dullest parts down by the coast and none of the almost alpine scenes you find nearer the top.

As for **supplies** for the walk, you want to carry the minimum possible. On a day trip you needn't necessarily carry anything, though a water bottle and something to munch on the way are probably worthwhile (there are springs at regular intervals and ice-cold water in the stream, but for long periods you'll find neither – especially over the last, hottest hour) as is some means of carrying clothes you discard en route (7am at the top feels close to freezing; 1pm at the bottom may hover around 100°F). If you plan to stay a day or two at the bottom you'd do better to leave your pack at Haniá's bus station for collection later, taking only what's essential (or make use of a day-trip bus as suggested earlier) – though people do struggle through carrying full packs. As far as **food** is concerned you needn't worry about starving: you can find enough for breakfast in the stalls at the top (or sit down properly for a meal in the Lodge) and Ayía Rouméli is more than equipped to feed everyone arriving at the bottom.

Wildlife

Gorge **wildlife** means most famously the *kri-kri* (variously the *agrimi, Capra Aegagrus*, the Cretan wild goat or ibex) for whose protection the park was primarily created. You are most unlikely to see one of these large, nimble animals with their long backswept horns – though you may well see ordinary mountain goats defying death on the cliff faces and convince yourself that you have. More likely candidates for nature spotters are the local birds and reptiles. Almost 400 varieties of birds are claimed to have been seen here, including owls, eagles, falcons and vultures. Bird-watchers after a coup should look out for the endangered *Lammergeier* (aka bearded vulture). On the ground lizards abound and there's also the odd snake, but the multifarious trees and the wild flowers and herbs are more rewarding finds. There are wild irises and orchids, thyme, sage, oregano and Cretan dittany.

Spending the night

If you want to make the gorge part of a longer excursion, there are several **accommodation options**. First of all you could **stay at the top**, at the Tourist Lodge (☎93-237; just seven rather pricey beds) or at one of the places in Omalós, or simply sleeping out (there are usually quite a few people trying to find a flat space for their sleeping bags around the entrance). This has few practical advantages – you'd have to be up very early to steal a march on the first arrivals from Haniá (for much of the year this would mean setting off before daylight) and from Omalós you face an extra 5km walk to reach the top of the trail – but it does make quite a change to stay up here and freeze for a night and of course it gives you the opportunity to explore more than just the gorge.

Staying **on the south coast** for a night or more after your exertions makes more sense: there are rooms at Ayía Rouméli, Loutró (p.218) and Hóra Sfakíon (p.225) or westwards in Sóuyia (p.237) and Paleohóra (p.233).

Ayía Rouméli

Once you've drunk and eaten your fill, plunged into the sea and out again, lain on the pebbles for a while and rested, **AYÍA ROUMÉLI**'s attractions soon begin to pall. It's a singularly unattractive example of over-rapid development, with a rash of concrete tavernas and rooms for rent spreading over a shingly beach. By local standards it's expensive too, although given the difficulties of transport this is perhaps not altogether surprising. Having said all this, Ayía Rouméli does have its good points – mainly the sheer number of places to eat and to stay plus most other essential facilities (money exchange at many of the tavernas) – and at night it's very peaceful. They're even attempting to be green: the pile of huge concrete tank traps behind the beach shields an experimental solar energy plant, converting sunlight directly to electric current. At night, or other times when this system can't cope, a diesel generator cuts in.

The kiosk which sells boat tickets is plainly marked down by the beach: if you're catching the bus back from Hóra Sfakíon get a ticket now for the last connecting boat, and spend the afternoon on the beach here; if you plan to stay elsewhere on this coast, take the first boat available for the best chance of finding a room. Given the choice, Ayía Rouméli is the least attractive of the places you could stay, though it does at least have a fair number of rooms and a surprisingly large beach if all you want to do is crash out on the pebbles (a couple of the tavernas have showers which they'll let you use if you eat there). Just to the east of the village (near the solar plant) is a clump of trees among which a few people are usually camped, and on the beach in this direction are some caves, also sometimes used to sleep out in.

Finding anything much to do apart from laze on the beach requires a deal of ingenuity, not to say desperation. For although there was an ancient settlement – *Tarra*, inhabited probably from the fifth century BC through to the fifth AD – and more or less constant later habitation, very little remains to be seen. The ruined Turkish fort, under which you pass as you emerge from the gorge onto the beach, doesn't really justify the scramble up to see it. Tarra straddled the stream where it ran into the sea, just to the east of the present village – the only obvious remains are the foundations of an early Christian basilica by the present church of Panayía, around which you may also spot a few tiny fragments of mosaic. This, supposedly, was the site of a much earlier Temple of Apollo.

THE FERRY BUSINESS

The ferry company operating along this part of the south coast is a spectacularly successful monopoly. When the gorge first started to attract tourists, several rival boats used to fight over passengers and race to be first in dock. Eventually they decided to combine forces and bought a couple of bigger boats, including the *Samaria*, a former car ferry which can be unloaded far quicker than the older vessels (it looks like a landing craft). The largest shareholder is now the owner of the new *Hotel Porto Loutro*.

When asked why no one sets up in rivalry, locals hint darkly at retribution and threats – suggesting that at least some of the old Sfakiot life is still alive and well. The ferry company is also said to be blocking the construction of the new road from Anópoli to Arádhena and Áyios Ioánnis (which would eventually be extended to Ayía Rouméli, allowing coaches to pick up passengers at the end of the gorge and destroying their business). In this, it has to be said, they have the support of most of the local people.

Loutró and south coast walks

Of all the south coast villages, **LOUTRÓ** perhaps best sums up what this coast ought to be all about. It's an incredibly soporific place, where there's absolutely nothing to do but eat, drink and laze – and where you fast lose any desire to do anything else. The big excitements of the day are the occasional arrivals and departures of the ferries. The days start bright and are soon lost in an overpowering heat shimmer; evening comes cool and darkness falls fast – by ten the place is virtually asleep. All this despite the fact that it has been entirely taken over by tourists. The waterfront consists of a row of perhaps six tavernas and a similar number of rooms places plus one new, but small, hotel; behind the waterfront the mountains rise immediately – there's no road in and everyone here has come on the boat or walked. Which helps keep things very low-key. Prices are reasonable, big groups rare, the people genuinely friendly.

Perhaps Loutró's main drawback is its lack of a real **beach**. There's a small stretch of pebbles in front of the eastern half of town with large signs asking bathers to remain respectable. Try lying topless here and you'll be told none too politely to cover up. But the sheltered little bay is otherwise ideal for swimming, clear and warm, and people bask nude on the rocks around the point, far enough out to avoid offence. You can also hire kayaks and snorkelling gear on the beach. The good news is that there are other beaches in walking distance (see below), with small boats ferrying visitors to the best of them, Sweetwater and Marmara.

Rooms in Loutró seem uniformly basic and comfortable, though to be sure of finding one you should arrive as early as possible – an increasing number seem to be pre-booked through enterprising travel agencies. Try for one with a balcony (a couple offer top-floor rooms with huge roof terraces), which here is really worthwhile; the quietest places are generally the furthest round to the east (such as *Keramos* – others are right above the tavernas) but nowhere is exactly loud or stays open late. The only place with more pretensions is the new C-class *Hotel Porto Loutro*, right in the middle of the village above the beach, whose white cubes fit in surprisingly well with the surroundings; it's lovely and not outrageously expensive (about 5000drs double), though since the rooms are pretty accurate reproductions of a simple Greek room you may question whether it's worth paying the extra. Even here you may find yourself showering in salt water if there's a shortage (as there is most summers these days). If you want to book, there is so far just one phone in Loutró, at *The Blue House* (☎0825/91127); they have pretty good rooms here and can also put you through to the hotel. If you can't find anywhere to stay then you could try the trek over to Fínix or Líkkos (or take a boat if you have luggage), or you can join others **camping** out on the point around the castle or on Sweetwater Beach.

The Blue House (identified by its blue-checked tablecloths rather than a sign) is also arguably the best **restaurant** in Loutró, and Vangelis who runs it one of the friendliest characters. There's usually a fair vegetarian selection here and at several of the others – it's part of the daily ritual to stroll up and down looking at what's on offer and deciding where to eat. The only place open late is the Café Bar Maistrali, the westernmost building in Loutró (alongside the concrete jetty) where everyone heads in the evening. Its cocktails and music – they also serve exotic breakfasts – may seem a bit slick in this setting, but it's relatively low-key, and certainly a pleasant way to wind up your day. The **practicalities** are easily taken care of: you can change money and buy supplies at the mini-market, and a second shop a little further on (immediately before the beach) has a good selection of second-hand books and also changes money.

Boat tickets are sold – only in the few minutes immediately before departure – from a table at the end of the dock. Try to have the right change. The smaller boats tie at this dock, but the *Samaria* sails straight up to the beach, lowering its bow onto the pebbles. (Occasionally it comes to the dock to unload supplies – a truck drives off onto the jetty, barely large enough to contain it, is unloaded and filled with empties and drives back onto the next ferry. There are no more than a few feet of space for it to drive up and down.)

The coast around Loutró: Sweetwater to Mármara

Anyone who spends any time at all in Loutró is eventually taken with the urge to explore – even if it's just climbing up to the ruins on the point. There are plenty of long, tough walks available (see the following section), but there are also easier hikes to nearby beaches. Some of these can also be reached by boat.

Sweetwater Beach

Sweetwater Beach lies approximately halfway between Loutró and Hóra Sfakíon, in the middle of a frighteningly barren coastline. From the sea, as you pass on one of the coastal boats, it appears as a long, extremely narrow slice of grey between sheer ochre cliffs and a dark, deep sea. Closer up, the beach seems much larger, but there's still a frightening sense of being isolated between unscalable mountains and an endless stretch of water.

The beach takes its name from the small springs which bubble up beneath the pebbles to provide fresh, cool drinking water. You can dig a hole almost anywhere to find water, but there are plenty already made – don't pollute these with soap. For years there was a little enclave of nudist campers here, their idyll interrupted only by the occasional intrepid cliff walker. Over the last couple of years, though, daily boat services have started from both Loutró and Hóra Sfakíon, bringing a lot more people. So far these have not spoilt the place – the beach is easily big enough to absorb everyone – and the campers are still here, for once doing a good job of keeping the place pristine: there are signs up warning against leaving rubbish and people who regularly make an effort to pick up any junk that is left. The long-term residents tend to monopolise the only shade, in the caves at the back of the beach, but you can always escape the sun at the small bar/taverna which sits on a lump of concrete just off the western end of the beach, reached by a rickety plank. You can get cold drinks and simple meals here and they also rent out sun umbrellas. There are no other facilities beyond the boats, which come once in the morning and again in the late afternoon. Walking is also a possibility, though very hot and shadeless: about 45 minutes to Loutró, an hour to Hóra Sfakíon (see following section); or on a calm day you can paddle a canoe over from Loutró. The path runs along behind all the houses in Loutró – to join it from there climb up behind the beachside kiosk and church.

Fínix

Immediately to the west of Loutró, in the little bay on the other side of the promontory, stood **ancient Fínikas** (now known as **FÍNIX** or Phoenix). This was a major town through the Roman and Byzantine periods, and a significant port long after that: it was the harbour at Fínix, a more comfortable place to wait out the winter storms than Kalí Liménes, which Saint Paul's ship was hoping to reach when it was swept away (p.95). A local story has the saint actually landing here and being beaten up by the locals he tried to convert: given the attitude to Cretans revealed in Paul's epistle to Titus, it is, as Michael Llewellyn Smith points out, "safe to say that if he *had* landed here they *would* have beaten him up".

Yet again there is very little to be seen. These days the bay, with its rocky beach, has just one taverna (an exceptionally languid place, with simple food and rooms) and no other development at all. It's hard to believe there could ever have been a population of any size. Up on the headland, though, there's certainly evidence of later occupation, principally in the form of the Venetian fortification on the point. Nearby are traces of a Byzantine basilica and other scattered remains; most curiously, however, there's a building, very much in the form of a Venetian church, sunk entirely below ground level. Its arched roof is intact, the interior entirely full of water. Nowadays it is deliberately flooded and used as a storage cistern, but its original purpose remains a mystery. It could always have been a cistern, of course, but it seems too elaborate for that: I prefer the explanation (no doubt equally wrong) that it was an underground arsenal attached to the castle.

To get to Fínix by the most direct route, join the path that runs behind Loutró, up behind the beachside kiosk and the church. This will lead you straight up, past the castle and directly over the point, in around ten minutes (if you're continuing beyond Fínix, you don't have to go down to the water as a path continues straight past the back of the bay – but it's only marginally shorter). It's also possible to get there by walking out past the last house in Loutró and simply following the rocky coast around. This is a much longer and tougher walk, but it does have the compensation of passing plenty of good rocks to swim from in wonderfully clear water, and extensive remains of old buildings which you can imagine are (and may indeed be) ancient Fínikas. Boats to Mármara also regularly call in at Fínix, bringing supplies.

Líkkos and Mármara

Beyond Fínix, the path continues to another, much longer bay, **LÍKKOS**. There are now three taverna/rooms places here, though quite why is a mystery since they rarely seem to have any custom. *Yioryio's*, the last of them, right in the middle of the beach, is very friendly and quiet (anywhere here is quiet), if a little bizarre: brand new, but with no electricity, so that the fridge full of bottles is just there for show, as are the light fittings in the rooms. Assuming the electricity is on by now it should be very comfortable – and there's plenty of fresh water here, which there may not be in Loutró. Unfortunately Líkkos is not a very attractive beach, with rock and pebbles and an ugly backdrop, and is awkward to swim from unless you wear shoes. Behind, you can look up and see the village of Livanianá and the Arádhena gorge (see below).

The gorge emerges at the sea in the next bay along, **Mármara** (or marble) **Beach**. This is another fairly small cove, with a sandy beach surrounded by interesting rock formations full of caves and slabs to dive from or sunbathe on. Unfortunately it also sees at least three boats a day from Loutró, which in summer bring more people than can comfortably be accommodated. So although out of season it might be more attractive than Sweetwater, at peak times it is far less so – and it has the additional disadvantages of no one to keep it clean and no fresh water (or anything else, so bring plenty to drink with you). Some people do camp here, but to do so you have to make a very long trek for supplies, or take the boats to and from Loutró. Walking to Mármara takes a little over an hour in all, and the second half, from the far end of the beach at Líkkos, is hot and exposed, climbing high onto the cliff.

More challenging hikes

Loutró lies close to the heart of the network of coastal paths linking Ayía Rouméli to Hóra Sfakíon in the absence of any road. Most real traffic nowadays goes by boat, of course, and the last inland hamlets have finally had a driveable track built to them. But the paths and tracks remain, to give a variety of possible hikes, even the easiest of which can be demanding in the heat of high summer. You'll need, at the very least, decent shoes to cope with rough, rocky terrain and a water bottle which you should fill at every opportunity. You should also have a companion, since some of these paths are pretty isolated, and outside help cannot be relied upon.

Ayía Rouméli to Hóra Sfakíon

The **coastal path** is the most obvious, the most frequently used by tourists, and in terms of not getting lost the simplest to follow. There's not a great deal to see en route, however, and nor is it altogether an easy walk – the path is often frighteningly narrow and uneven as it clings to the cliff face, and in summer it is very, very hot, offering no shelter at all from the sun.

From **Loutró to Hóra Sfakíon** this is barely a problem: it's the most heavily travelled part, the whole walk takes less than two hours, and there's a rest stop at Sweetwater Beach halfway. Loutró to Sweetwater is straightforward and fairly well beaten: beyond here the path clambers over a massive recent rockfall and then follows the cliffs until it eventually emerges on the Hóra Sfakíon–Anópoli road about half an hour's walk above Hóra. This is easy to find in the other direction too, the path leaving the road at the first hairpin bend.

In the other direction, **Loutró to Ayía Rouméli** is an altogether tougher proposition. For a start you can expect to be walking for four hours solid, and for seconds there's no chance of refreshment between the tavernas at Líkkos and

Ayía Rouméli. The path has already been described as far as Mármara Beach. Afterwards you climb again to track along the exposed cliff face for around an hour before reaching the first sign of civilisation, a solitary cottage and a few trees. In about another hour you'll arrive at the chapel of **Áyios Pávlos**, yet another site where Saint Paul is supposed to have landed. Here he allegedly christened locals in a nearby spring. The chapel itself is ancient and rather beautiful, set on a ledge above the water, surrounded by dunes. You could cool off in the sea here before setting out on the final hour to Ayía Rouméli.

Coming from Ayía Rouméli this path is well marked, heading east out of the village. Ten to fifteen minutes after Áyios Pávlos it splits, left to climb inland to Áyios Ioánnis and Anópoli, right to continue along the coast.

Anópoli

If you're hiking for pleasure, or for that matter if you want to take the easiest way from Ayía Rouméli to Hóra Sfakíon without necessarily calling at Loutró, then the **inland routes** centring on Anópoli have a great deal to be said for them.

ANÓPOLI itself is a quiet country town, not much used to visitors, dominating a small upland plain. There are a couple of *kafenía* and a small general store on the square, and if you want to stay away from all the hustle of the coast you should be able to find somewhere. There are several **rooms** places scattered along the road back towards Hóra Sfakíon; the rather tatty-looking one with green paint is actually quite comfortable (the more expensive new place opposite is more so, with showers), and serves fabulous home-made yoghurt.

Anópoli was the home of the first of the great Cretan rebels against the Turk, **Dhaskaloyiánnis** – the subject of a celebrated epic poem. To cut a very long story extremely short, Dhaskaloyiánnis, a wealthy ship-owner, was promised support by Russian agents if he raised a rebellion in Sfakiá, support which in the event never materialised. (The Russians hoped only to create a diversion for their campaigns against the Ottoman empire elsewhere.) The revolt, in 1770, was short-lived and disastrous for Sfakiá, which for the first time was brought well and truly under the Turkish heel: Dhaskaloyiánnis gave himself up and was executed. There's a statue of him in the square.

Getting to Anópoli, which is high above the coast, more or less directly above Loutró, is not always easy unless you have car. **From Hóra Sfakíon** it's 12km up a very steep, winding road – you wouldn't really want to walk this but you might not have much choice: the lone daily bus drives up at 4pm and down again at 6.30am. Hitching is likely to be better. The walk up from Loutró looks terrifying – you can see the path tracking back and forth across an almost vertical cliff – but is in fact far less bad than it seems: about an hour and a half, climbing steeply most of the way (this is best done very early, before the sun gets too powerful; at the top you're on the fringes of Anópoli – turn left for the centre).

Anópoli to Ayía Rouméli

Following this route in reverse is a much more pleasant way of getting from Ayía Rouméli to Hóra Sfakíon than the coast. Around Anópoli there's an attractive upland plain and a few vestiges of forest, all too rare on Crete these days.

Leaving Anópoli, follow the road through to the far end of town, where it becomes a little-used, dusty jeep track, signed to Arádhena. There may be shorter ways on the old paths than this track (ask in town if you're determined), but there's so little traffic that following the road makes little difference. It is just over an hour to the edge of the **Arádhena gorge**, on the far side of which is the virtually abandoned hamlet of ARÁDHENA*. Right on the opposite rim of the gorge here is a Byzantine church, with a strangely phallic dome standing proud against the Lefká Óri's heights. Inside, if you can find someone to show you, there are frescoes, and roundabout are a few traces of ancient *Aradin*, from whose stones the church is said to be built. A new bridge now takes the road across the gorge, with dizzy views down into it, and looking inland you can see the old path, negotiable on foot or by pack animals only, zigzagging down to the bottom and back up the other side. You still take this path if you want to follow the gorge down to the sea (see below).

The road now ends at ÁYIOS IOÁNNIS, another hour (or slightly more) beyond. A rather larger village, this goes so far as to have a taverna where you can rest up for a while. There are more Byzantine frescoes in the church here and several impressively large caves nearby. You'll have to ask to be put on the right path from here, as work on the road may have changed things. You have to head to the left, between two chapels, after which the path becomes hard to follow for a while until it emerges on top of the cliffs. From here it loops down a rough but obvious path to join the coast trail before the chapel of Áyios Pávlos. You should be able to complete the walk from Anópoli to Ayía Rouméli in about five hours, though with rest stops and wrong turnings it could well go some way above this: leave plenty of leeway if you need to catch a boat back. If you are undertaking this walk in reverse, start early so as to complete the climb of the cliffs before it becomes too hot.

The Arádhena Gorge

A round trip from Loutró, up to Anópoli and down to Mármara Beach (where you can get a boat back, last at 4pm) via the **Arádhena Gorge** makes a challenging excursion. You must be fit to tackle this, as the gorge involves some scrambling and climbing – there are ropes and rope-ladders to help you over the worst parts. Although this doesn't really need any special mountain-climbing skills, it can be pretty scary. You're not helped by the presence in places of the picked-clean skeletons of goats, which presumably have either fallen from the top or been washed away in spring floods.

The sense of achievement, however, is immense, and the gorge, though far smaller, of course, is in sheer physical terms almost as impressive as the Samarian one: there isn't much in the way of wildlife, but the rocky river bed is trapped into an extremely narrow gap between sheer walls almost all the way down – and there'll be hardly anyone else around. Allow six hours at least from Loutró to Mármara (two and a half to the top of the gorge, three and a half down) – eight may be more like it once you've stopped a few times.

You set off by turning off the road and onto the old path just before you reach the gorge, then following the stepped path down to the bottom (this is deteriorating fast now it's not used much, but this side is better than the other). This and

---

*Adam Hopkins claims that the people left to escape with their lives from a series of Sfakiot vendettas. He's probably right, but in the light of what is happening elsewhere, such depopulation seems commonplace. With the new road, one or two people have moved back and started to restore some of the crumbling buildings.

the first stretch, with a relatively flat bottom as you head under the bridge through an impressively deep section, conspire to lull you into a false sense of security: as it gets steeper further down you find yourself jumping from rock to rock or lowering yourself carefully down dry cascades. Look out as you go for the paint marks indicating the route – these often seem to take you over unnecessarily tricky terrain, but you usually discover the reason further on when you reach an impassable portion. Fill up with water at every opportunity, as there's none towards the end of the gorge or at the beach.

If all this sounds too tough there is an **easier alternative**, though not tested personally. Head out past Fínix (follow the upper path, bypassing the cove) and you'll come to a fork in the path: the lower one goes to Líkkos, the upper to LIVANIANÁ, which you can see above you. From here a path leads down into the gorge, emerging fairly near the bottom having bypassed all the really difficult bits. The Ímbros Ravine (see below) is another slightly softer option, with more wildlife but less dramatic terrain.

The road south: Hóra Sfakíon and Frangokástello

The easy way **into Sfakiá** is by a good road which cuts south from Vrísses (p.201), almost immediately beginning to spiral up into the mountains, towards the Plateau of Askífou. The climb seems straightforward from a bus or car, but the country you drive through has a history as bloody as any in Crete: you pass first through a little ravine where two Turkish armies were massacred, the first during the 1821 uprising, the second in 1866 after the heroic events at Arkádhi (p.154); the road itself is the one along which the Allied troops retreated at such cost in the final stages of the Battle of Crete. This chaotic flight has been described in detail in just about all the books covering the battle (and also in Evelyn Waugh's *Officers and Gentlemen*) – it makes for strange reading from the comfort of a modern journey.

The **Plateau of Askífou** offers the relief of level ground for a while, now as it did then. The plain is dominated by a ruined castle on a hill to the left of the road – a hill so small and perfectly conical it looks fake, put there simply to raise the castle above its surroundings. There are several small villages up here, chief of them AMOUDHÁRI, with a couple of small tavernas and the chance of a room if you wanted to stay (one place, over the bakery, tends to be noisy in the morning; the only other disturbance to the peace here is the twice-daily convoy of buses, arriving empty and returning with sated gorge-walkers). For keen walkers, a path leads from Amoudhári to Anópoli, a long day's hike through the mountains via the hamlet of Kalí Láki, which is not terribly easy to follow. You should attempt to get thorough directions locally before trying this, though this may not be easy unless you speak fluent Greek: some readers who tried the walk found themselves instead circling back, via the deserted village of Lákki, to Ímbros.

The Ímbros Ravine

On the far side of the Askífou plateau lies ÍMBROS. Beyond, the road climbs briefly again out of the plain and then begins gradually to descend to the south coast. This stretch is lovely: an excellent, winding track which follows dramatically one side of the **Ímbros Ravine**, tracking high through conifer-clad slopes with the cleft always dizzily below. As you approach the coast, still high above it, you begin to glimpse distant sparkles of water until finally the road breaks out of its confinement, way above the sea, with a broad plain to the east (and Frangokástello hazy in the distance), steeper drops to the west, and immense vistas out towards Africa ahead. Hóra Sfakíon is out of sight until you are almost upon it, an alarming plunge down through hairpin bend after hairpin bend. Driving, you need to watch out for buses: it can be alarming in the evening meeting the vast convoy coming the other way on these relatively narrow curves, and in the afternoon you'll pass them parked in every available spot since they can't all squeeze into Hóra Sfakíon.

It is also possible to **walk down the Ímbros ravine**, following a track which until the completion of the new road was the district's main thoroughfare. This is easily enough done – in less than three hours – and it's a wonderfully solitary walk, a spectacular contrast to the crowds at Samariá. The only problem is that in doing this you miss the wonderful views from above. In its own way the ravine is as interesting as its better-known rival, albeit on a smaller scale: narrow and stiflingly confined in places, speckled with caves in others and at one point passing under a monumental natural stone archway. The path starts from the southern fringe of Ímbros village, close by a green shrine, where a well-trodden trail leads down to the stream bed. Through the ravine you simply follow the stream until, emerging at the lower end, an obvious track leads away again towards the village of KOMITÁDHES. This is about 5km east of Hóra Sfakíon, a distance you might well be able to hitch, especially if you walk the first kilometre or so to the junction of the main road. If you can't hitch a lift, this last section makes a hot, boring anticlimax to your walk. It's also easy to walk the gorge as a half-day trip from Hóra Sfakíon (or Loutró, by getting the first boat from there): simply take the early bus to Haniá, and get off at Ímbros.

Hóra Sfakíon

Squeezed between the sea and the mountains, **HÓRA SFAKÍON** couldn't grow even if it wanted to. Nevertheless it's a surprise to find the capital of Sfakiá quite so small. It is, too, a thoroughly commercial centre these days: restaurants cram the seafront promenade between the square where the buses stop and the pier where the boats dock, and every house in town seems to display a large "Rooms" sign. Though it is cheap and pleasant enough if you do decide to stay, and relatively quiet by the end of the day, there's not a great deal of point in doing so. The beach is small and pebbly (desperately uncomfortable if you're trying to sleep on it, as it's also immediately beneath the noise and bright lights of the waterfront tavernas) and there is little else to do. Still, Hóra is convenient and comfortable enough as a short-term base.

There are a couple of good supermarkets selling all possible supplies (including new and second-hand books in English), and some excellent restaurants showing off their wares along the promenade. Unusually, there's a good array of vegetarian food here, often including *boureki* and vegetable-stuffed aubergines. **Rooms** are better and cheaper if you avoid the obvious places right on the front or the main road (though these may also have cheaper rooms at the back): try the street which runs behind all the tavernas.

This backstreet is also where almost all the other facilities are. Practically the first building is an excellent bakery, and there's also a big supermarket with better prices than those on the front, a dairy shop for local cheese, yoghurt and honey, several exchange places, the post office and the OTE (open 7am–3pm).

Supposedly, Hóra once had as many as a hundred churches and chapels, built for one reason or another by devout Sfakiots: I doubt this was ever true, but in any event few survived the wartime bombardments. There are a couple of ancient-looking examples on the road as you curve down into Hóra, but all seem permanently locked. As for other monuments, a plaque on the waterfront, between the restaurants, commemorates the Dunkirk-style wartime evacuation when some 10,000 men were taken off the island: almost as many were left behind to be bombed as they waited to be taken prisoner or to escape as best they could.

If you have time to kill you're probably best off getting out, to **Sweetwater Beach** an hour along the coast path west (or by twice-daily boat), or to Frangokástello, 14km east. It's also possible to visit the **Cave of Dhaskaloyiánnis**, one of several large caves in the cliffs to the west of Hóra. Always a hideout in times of trouble, this was where the rebel leader (p.222) set up a mint to produce revolutionary coinage. Ask locally how to find it.

Leaving, **boat tickets** are sold from a hut at the bottom of the jetty: check which boat you'll be getting as the *Samaria* is too big for the dock and comes in instead right on the other side of town, quite a long way to run if you're waiting in the wrong place. **Bus tickets** are sold from a wooden hut on the square: for Haniá, most people already have tickets and the important thing is to get on the bus in order to secure a seat*. The south coast bus to Plakiás leaves at 4.30pm, and this is often even more crowded.

Frangokástello

Eastwards from Hóra, the coast road runs some way from the sea through a series of small, little-visited villages. KOMITÁDHES has a couple of tavernas and even a few rooms (also expensive petrol if you're running low), VRASKÁS and VOÚVAS can offer no more than a *kafeníon* and a general store each.

FRANGOKÁSTELLO lies 3km off the main road, just under 10km from the junction with the Hóra–Vríses road (buses divert along the new road through the village): the castle makes an easy target to aim for. If you take the first turning you'll head straight down to the sea and then turn left along the shore, a route which will take you past just about all the places which offer **rooms**. There seem more of these every year, and there's even a rock bar/disco (though who goes there remains a mystery) but so far Frangokástello remains in the early stages of

---

* Theoretically, everyone who turns up on time with a ticket will get back to Haniá. I wouldn't go out of your way to try it, but being stranded can be rather wonderful. I was one of half a dozen passengers from Loutró who saw the bus leave (early) as our boat docked. After an hour of phone calls a bus was eventually tracked down in some nearby village where it and its driver had been enjoying a well-earned retirement – the ride back, in a rattling old wreck propelled at breakneck pace by a moustachioed maniac in traditional Cretan dress, was legendary. Along the way our driver kept up an incomprehensible running commentary on everything we passed, and in Haniá he insisted on all his passengers joining him in a drink to celebrate their safe arrival.

development. If you don't want a room – or can't find one – there's good **camping** among the dunes, both right by the castle and along the longer beach to the west, with plenty of ruined walls and bamboo groves for shelter.

For peaceful lassitude on the beach Frangokástello is still among the best spots in Crete, with fine sand, luminescently clear water and very little effort required either to get here or to find food and drink once you've arrived. There's good snorkelling too, though the water is so clear you barely need to bother with the mask. If you want company you'll find it around the castle where the best part of the sand is, sheltered and slowly shelving; for solitude head westwards along the shoreline – less soft sand and more wind, but still very pleasant. There are beaches to the east, too: follow the coastal path for ten to fifteen minutes and you'll arrive at the top of a low cliff overlooking perhaps three-quarters of a mile of beautiful, deserted sand and rocks. Lying in the sun here the only thing to disturb the afternoon tranquility is the occasional muffled crump of an explosion offshore. This is not, as you might expect, US warplanes practicing for the big attack on Libya but the home-made depth charges of local fishermen going about their business in the time-honoured and highly illegal way. Watch closely and you'll see the sudden spout of water near the boat before the noise of the explosion reaches you.

The **castle**, so impressively four-square from a distance, turns out close up to be a mere shell. Nothing but the bare walls survive, with a tower in each corner, and over the seaward entrance an escutcheon which can just be made out as the Venetian Lion of Saint Mark. Inside it's overgrown, with litter scattered about and worse in the towers. Still, it's some shell. The fortress was originally built in 1371 to deter pirates and in an attempt to impose some order on Sfakiá: a garrison was maintained here throughout the Venetian and Turkish occupations, controlling the plain as surely as it failed to tame the mountains (even today, the orange-pink walls look frighteningly puny when you see them with the grey bulk of the mountains towering behind). In 1828, Frangokástello was occupied by Hadzimihali Daliani, a Greek adventurer attempting to spread the War of Independence from the mainland to Crete. Instead of taking to the hills as all sensible rebels before and since have done, he and his tiny force attempted to make a stand in the castle. Predictably, they were massacred and their martyrdom became the fuel for yet more heroic legends of the *pallikari*. Locals will claim that to this day, on or around the May 17, the ghosts of Daliani and his army march from the castle: they are known as *dhrossoulítes*, or dewy ones, because they appear in the mists around dawn.

Just below the castle, before the beach, there's a patch of greenery which shades a taverna and a tiny freshwater creek with thoroughly incongruous ducks on it: between the road and sea to the west are more little streams and marshy patches like this – terrapins and some type of water snake or eel live here. More tavernas can be found around the beach to the right, on the point, and others out along the road. None are particularly sophisticated but they're friendly and reasonably priced. There are also a couple of mini-markets, selling most things you're likely to want. There are a few **rooms** right on the beach below the castle, well placed but subject to mosquitoes, lots more possibilities along the road westwards. An early morning bus (at 6.30am) runs to Hóra Sfakíon to connect with the first bus from there, and buses running between Plakiás and Hóra Sfakíon also pass through.

For a description of the road **east to Plakiás**, see p.174.

THE FAR WEST

Crete's far west has to date attracted surprisingly little attention from tourists or developers, though inevitably that is beginning to change. The one town of any size west of Haniá is **Kastélli Kisámou**, a port with a twice-weekly ferry service to the Peloponnese, very regular buses to Haniá, and little else to attract visitors. Beyond, Crete's west-facing coast remains remote. West of a line between Kastélli and Paleohóra there's little public transport, no more than a handful of rooms to rent, and absolutely nothing in the way of facilities for more luxurious tourism. Yet here you'll find two of the finest beaches on the island – **Falásarna** and **Elafonísi** – both of them, sadly, beginning to suffer from overexploitation. For longer stays in this part of Crete it's important to take all the money and most of the supplies you'll need – there are some facilities at the beaches, but they're a long way from any villages and even these have only the most basic of shops.

On the **south coast**, good roads, and several buses a day, run to **Paleohóra** and, now, to **Sóuyia**. The former is already a resort of some size – surprisingly large given its isolation, but far from totally despoiled – the latter is smaller and less attractive but still cheap and friendly. Regular boats connect the two places, or there's a footpath by way of the ruins of ancient **Lissós**, on the coast just west of Soúyia. Moving between them by road is rough and sometimes impossible unless you're prepared to backtrack most of the way to the north coast: the only properly paved roads are those which run north–south. Along the way there's spectacular mountain scenery in which frescoed medieval churches are liberally scattered.

Kastélli and the north coast

Kastélli lies some 20km beyond the crossroads at Kolimbári (p.207). A brand new road being built across the bottom of the Rodhópou peninsula and along the coast towards Kastélli should cut journey times greatly. When it's completed it should also leave the **old road** – always a beautiful drive – as a delightful backwater. Going this way you wind steeply up a rocky spur thrown back by the peninsula and emerge through a cleft in the hills to a magnificent view of the Gulf of Kisámou, with Kastélli in the middle distance. With the sun setting behind the craggy heights of Cape Voúxa at the far west of Crete, this is a memorable panorama. There's a roadside taverna from which you can enjoy the view, and a number of quite large, entirely unvisited villages, such as NOCHIÁ, where you could stop for a drink.

Leaving the height, the road loops back out of the hills on to the fertile plain of Kastélli. Almost as soon as you hit level ground there's a sign to a **campsite**, *Camping Mithymna*, on the coast about a kilometre from the road. It's well equipped, reasonably priced and generally fairly empty (though this is an obvious first stop for people who bring cars or campers across on the ferry from Yíthio), and it's quite a pleasant setting, on a sand and stone beach with excellent wind-surfing. Nearby are a couple of tavernas, and you can also get details of local rooms to rent from the campsite. The new road runs very close, however, which may change things here somewhat. The site is named after the ancient town of *Mithymna*, thought to have stood approximately where the tiny modern settlement of NOPÍYIA now stands. Further along there's a turn-off at the village of KALOUDHIANÁ for the inland route to Topólia and on to Elafonísi.

Kastélli Kisámou

Heading for the west coast, you'll pass through **KASTÉLLI**, which at first sight seems to offer little to get excited about. It's a busy little town with a rather rocky beach. But this very ordinariness has a real charm once you get over your initial reaction: it's a working town full of shops that the locals use and café's not entirely geared to outsiders, and yet it has just about every facility you could hope to find.

The strip of highway heads straight through the northern fringe of town, bypassing the centre: parallel to it, towards the sea, runs Kastélli's main street – with shops and banks – and just off this lies the central square where **buses** pull in. You'll see signs for rooms and restaurants all around – the C-class *Castelli Hotel* (☎22-140) on the square is a good place to eat, with **rooms** considerably cheaper than its rating might suggest. Other facilities are mostly found nearby: the E-class *Hotel Morpheus* (☎22-475) between the highway and the main street; **ferry tickets** and motorbike hire right on the main square from *Ksirouksakis* (☎22-655); and shops, more places to eat, travel agents and rooms along the main street. While you're here, try to taste some of the local red wine, as good as any produced in Crete.

There's a second cluster of development down by the **waterfront**, with several tavernas (*Makedonas* is good) and rooms places facing the concrete quay directly down from the main square, and a couple of newer hotels to the east out along the beach – try the *Galini Beach* (☎23-288). The small **folklore museum**, with an interesting collection of household miscellany, has recently been moved to a brand new building down here on the front. The **ferry** dock is some 2km west of town – a significant walk if you're heavily laden, or a cheap taxi ride.

Polirinía

Kastélli is known as Kastélli Kisámou (and sometimes simply as Kisámou or Kísamos) to distinguish it from the other Kastéllis scattered around Crete. The name is taken from ancient *Kíssamos* which stood here, port for the sizeable ancient city of **POLIRINÍA**. This lies about 7km inland, above the village of PALEÓKASTRO (also known as Polirinía), and can still be seen. There are buses up from Kastélli (Mon, Wed & Fri 7am & 2pm; returning 30min later), but the walk is a perfectly feasible one (better still, take a bus or taxi up, and walk back down). It's something of a climb from the village to the hilltop site, where ruins are scattered about two horns of high ground which seem to reach out to enclose the Gulf of Kisámou. The most obvious is the Acropolis, which is in fact almost entirely a Venetian defensive structure, but there are all sorts of foundations and obscure remains, including Roman and Greek masonry clearly incorporated into the church which now stands on the site. Founded around the eighth century BC, Polirinía survived as one of the island's more important cities at least into the late Roman era. On the way back from the site, the taverna in the village has views almost as good.

The west coast: Falásarna

Leaving Kastélli for the west, the road climbs back into the hills again, cutting south across the base of the Gramvoúsa peninsula. The paved road, and the buses, used to stop at the village of PLÁTANOS, but it's a sign of the changing times that tarmac now continues all the way down to the beautiful beach at **FALÁSARNA**, with two buses a day direct from Haniá (the signs in Plátanos seem designed to confuse – you should turn right fairly early, and the road should be good and new). The last part snakes down a spectacular series of hairpin bends before turning north onto the narrow coastal plain, where farmers have discovered the benefits of plastic greenhouses for force cultivating tomatoes, melons and the like.

The end of the asphalt is marked by two tavernas just above a sublime beach, a broad crescent of yellow sand edged by turquoise waters. There are an increasing number of **rooms** places here, some of them quite good, but many of the people who stay here **camp** at the back of the beach, either in a couple of small caves or beneath makeshift shelters slung between a few stumpy trees. Unfortunately this can mean that the beach is filthy, since some of these people just leave all their rubbish behind, and at times there's also a good deal of oil and tar washed up. Still, this can't really detract from the overall beauty of the place, and if it does get crowded there are two more beaches within easy walking distance, and others further south which can be reached along rough tracks.

Ancient Falásarna and Gramvoúsa

The **ancient city** – and port – of Falásarna lay somewhere just to the north of the beach. If you follow the main dirt track past the tavernas you should find the large stone "throne" half-hidden under bushes a kilometre or so away. Much of the site is similarly disguised by the spiny undergrowth spreading all over it: with luck some of this will have been cleared by the excavators currently working here. What you see, if you can find them, are the scattered remains of a city built around a large depression (its inner harbour) and the bed of a canal which once joined this to the sea. All of it is now high and dry, the site offering conclusive proof that Crete's western extremities have risen at least 8 metres over the last 24 centuries or so.

Continue on the best of the roads past the throne and you pass under Cyclopean walls to emerge above another small bay. This is too sharp and rocky for you to be able to get to the sea – tempting as it is – but it does give you views to the north, over **Cape Voúxa**, which are shielded from Falásarna itself. Towards the top you can see the island of **Gramvoúsa** (not to be confused with the uninhabitable rock of Pontikonísi, a more distant islet which can sometimes be seen from the beach at Falásarna) on which the Venetians built an important castle. Along with the fortified islands of Néa Sóudha and Spinalónga, this was one of the points which held out against the Turks long after the Cretan mainland had fallen. When the Venetians left, the fort was allowed to fall into disrepair until it was taken over by Greek refugees from other Turkish occupied islands (notably Kásos) who used it as a base for piracy. It took a major Turkish campaign to wrest the fortress back, and thereafter they maintained a garrison here. In the Wars of Independence it became a base for the Turkish ships attempting to maintain a blockade of the coastline. Another slightly larger and wilder island, Agría Gramvoúsa, lies to the north just off the cape.

It would be possible to visit these islands if you hired a boat in Kastélli (or Haniá for a cruise of several days), and I've also heard claims that you can wade across to one of them if you hike up the peninsula. This seems unlikely, but certainly if you fancy some wild and lonesome walking **the peninsula** fits the bill – it's extraordinarily barren and quite unpopulated. A path of sorts runs up the eastern side from the village of KALIVIANÍ and about three hours walk will take you to a really spectacular white sand beach (unfortunately with an even worse tar problem than Falásarna) more or less opposite Gramvoúsa.

Hrissoskalítissa and Elafonísi

Heading for the southwest, the normal route is to turn off the north coast highway at KALOUDHIANÁ, before Kastélli. This is a lovely rural drive, up the valley of the Tiflós, and a reasonably good road as far as VÁTHI. The coast road, however, is even more spectacular and although there are still large sections unpaved between Kefáli and Sfinári, it's a perfectly easy drive. If you have your own transport, try to take one route in each direction.

On the **inland route**, after some ten climbing kilometres, you come to TOPÓLIA, just beyond which is the cave of **Ayía Sofia**: this has been known since Neolithic times and now shelters a small chapel along with the usual stalactites and stalagmites. As you proceed, the valley gradually becomes a ravine and the road begins to run, above it, through magnificent stands of chestnut and other deciduous trees. Chestnuts, in fact are the main local crop and ÉLOS, with a lovely chestnut-shaded square, the centre of this industry: it has a chestnut festival in late October. Here you are really quite high – the mountains immediately to the south rise to about 1200m – and the road beyond starts slowly to descend. At KEFÁLI (a village with a frescoed church) there's a turning left for VÁTHI (with another) and Hrissoskalítissa.

If you were to carry straight on in Kefáli, you'd be on the **coast road** back around to PLÁTANOS. This very soon emerges to views and alarming drops over the Mediterranean, making for a spectacular drive, particularly in the evening when the setting sun in your eyes contributes not only to the scenery but also to the dramatic possibilities of plunging off the edge. Around you, olives ripen on the terraced hillsides and the villages seem to cling desperately to the high mountainsides, as if saved miraculously from some calamitous slide to the sea, glittering far below. By **KÁMBOS** you've descended enough for there to be a beach, albeit a considerable trek below the village, and perhaps the odd room. **SFINÁRI** is more developed, with several houses offering rooms for rent, some good tavernas, and a quiet pebble beach no more than ten minutes' walk below.

Hrissoskalítissa

HRISSOSKALÍTISSA is some 10km from Váthi, on a road which deteriorates rapidly. There are numerous tavernas here, but otherwise little beyond the nunnery, beautifully sited but today barely functioning, reduced from some 200 residents to just one nun and one monk, whose main task seems to be keeping the place acceptable for tourists. The present church dates only from the last century, but the nunnery is an ancient foundation – the first church was built in a cave here in the thirteenth century. Look out for the ninety steps which lead to the top of the crag around which the place is built: one of them appears golden (*Hrissí skála*) to those who are pure in spirit – a fact which I can't, personally, verify.

Elafonísi

For **ELAFONÍSI** you've another five kilometres of very dusty, bumpy road to traverse, but it's worth it. The almost tropical lagoon of white sand beaches tinged pink by shells, aquamarine waters, salt-encrusted rock pools and bright red starfish is still, despite increasing exploitation, as idyllic a spot as any in Crete. The water is incredibly warm, calm and shallow and Elafonísi itself (it's actually the island just offshore) is a short wade across the sandbar. There are more beaches on its far side (with waves), along with the odd ruined wall, seashells, and a monument to Australian sailors shipwrecked here in 1907. A couple of simple cafés stand on the road as you arrive, and you could camp just about anywhere. The best spots are behind the beach where there are trees for shade and usually a couple of vans parked up.

Not surprisingly, this has not gone undiscovered, and there are now two boats a day from Paleohóra, a daily bus from Haniá, and often at least one coach tour. The chief result of this is that there are often piles of rubbish on the mainland beach, but for now the water, and the island, remain pristine, and there are rarely so many people that the island can't absorb them.

Continuing south from Elafonísi is no easy matter, though you could catch the boat if you were heading for Paleohóra. There's a coastal path, reasonably well marked, along which you should be able to reach Paleohóra in about six hours. Be sure to get some accurate directions before setting out, however, as this coastline is barely inhabited and a wrong turn could lead you a very long way astray. Note, also, that things may be changing around here: apparently much of this corner of the island has been sold to a German consortium and undoubtedly they plan to develop it.

If you're driving, there is a road which turns off the inland route between Élos and Topólia, cutting down to Paleohóra. This soon becomes dirt track and splits: the easiest way is to keep left, through ALIGÍ and DRÍS, to meet the main road at the village of PLEMENIANÁ. This is rough, but not too bad, while the routes that bear directly south are really atrocious in places: if you're feeling adventurous, though, it is a very rewarding effort. Along the way scores of little streams cascade beside, under or sometimes across the road. Hardly any traffic passes, certainly few tourists, and the rare villages are ancient and rustic, their inhabitants standing to stare as you drive through, extremely welcoming if you stop. You may have begun to doubt that this could lead anywhere, and by the time you finally come in sight of Paleohóra, it's a welcome vision.

The southwest

The direct route to Paleohóra has to negotiate the same mountains, but it's a well-surfaced road and takes the line of least resistance: it feels a great deal less intimidating. From the turning at Tavronítis the road traces a long valley fingering its way beneath the hills as far as VOUKOLIÉS, a large village with a crowded Saturday morning market (all over by about 10am). Hereafter you begin to climb in earnest, through several much smaller villages, towards the eparchy of Sélinos.

Sélinos, the southwestern corner of Crete, is famous these days mainly for its Byzantine churches, of which every village seems to offer at least one example. FLÓRIA, almost exactly halfway across the island, has two – Áyios Yióryios and, in the upper village, Áyii Patéres, each with remains of frescoes – as well as a café and two war memorials facing each other across the road, one German, one Greek. If you take the short detour from Kándhanos up to ANISARÁKI you'll find more fresco traces in the churches of Ayía Ánna, Panayía and Ayía Paraskeví.

The next two villages on the main road are also worth a look: Áyios Yióryios in PLEMENIANÁ has paintings dating from the fifteenth century, while KAKODHÍKI, known for its curative springs, has several churches nearby. These include the very ancient chapel of Mihaíl Arhángelos, probably early thirteenth-century, beside the modern church of Ayía Triádha, and the hilltop Áyios Isidhóros, with magnificent views and frescoes which were deliberately defaced by the Turks. Many more small churches can be found throughout the area, particularly if you get off the road into the smaller villages. Few, if any, of them will be open when you arrive – but express an interest at the nearest *kafenío* or to a local passer-by and it rarely takes long to hunt out the priest or someone else with a key.

KÁNDANOS, though it's a great deal smaller than Paleohóra these days, is the chief village of the eparchy and makes a pleasant, quiet place to stop for a coffee. Its buildings are almost entirely new, for the place was razed to the ground by the Germans for its role in the wartime resistance. The original sign erected then is today preserved on a war memorial in the square. In German and Greek it reads "Here stood Kándanos, destroyed in retribution for the murder of 25 German soldiers".

Paleohóra

PALEOHÓRA was known originally as Kastél Selínou – the castle of Sélinos – and for much of its history was no more than that, a castle. Built by the Venetians in 1279, the fort was destroyed by Barbarossa in 1539 and never properly reconstructed even when the small port grew up beneath it. Its ruins still occupy the bulbous end of the headland across which Paleohóra is spread; at its narrowest a bare four blocks across from the harbour on one side to the beach on the other.

The village is rapidly growing and increasingly upmarket, and its facilities can barely cope with the ever-increasing volume of visitors. For the time being, though, it retains an enjoyably laid-back, end-of-the-line feel, helped out by superb and extensive sands. Out of season the town reverts to the backwater it so recently was: warm right through the winter and an excellent place to rent an apartment long-term for virtually nothing, or to look for work.

A eucalyptus-lined avenue leads into the single main street, Venizélos, lined with taverna after café after bar. The heart of life in every way, this is not particularly attractive by day, but in the evening fills to overflowing as the restaurants spill their tables across the pavement and into the road, creating total chaos when the bus arrives or an oil tanker tries to squeeze its load through, as it invariably does. Chaos tends to reign anyway, as the waiters and cooks keep up voluble arguments with each other and their customers, or vie to outdo the sales pitches of their rivals. It's an enjoyable madness as long as you're in no hurry to eat or go anywhere.

Not that you're likely to have far to go, since nothing here is more than five minutes' walk away. The better **beach**, magnificently broad and sandy, lined with tamarisks and supplied with showers, is on the west side of town, facing a bay with excellent easy windsurfing (good boards for hire) but incredibly cold water. People still camp all along here under the trees, although there's an official campsite and more (much less attractive) beach, pebbly at first but sandy further out, at the base of the peninsula on the east side. The oldest parts of town, if you want to explore, are on the east side around the harbour: from here you can clamber up into the **castle**, for the views back over town, or walk right around the end of the promontory to return to the beach on the other side. Neither of these options are as appealing as they might be, since the fortress itself is little more than a hillock ringed with broken walls, while a new marina being built on the far side is at present little more than a building site. There are some very much more attractive walks to be had inland, or along the coast in either direction.

Practicalities

Apart from the beach, entertainment in Paleohóra is confined mainly to the **tavernas** and **bars**. These hardly need pointing out – they're on every street in the centre of town and make their presence obvious. In addition to the numerous choices along Venizélos – *Dionisos* here is a straightforward taverna where you choose from the kitchen, usually with some vegetarian options, *Savas* has good swordfish, and there are a couple of old-fashioned café/ouzeris for good value drinks – there are others strung out along both shores and the streets leading down to them. *Nike*, on the main street down to the western beach, has excellent pizzas cooked in a wood-fired oven; nearby are a couple of popular *souvláki* and *tiropitta* places, where you can sit or take-away. Places looking over the sandy beach enjoy particularly good sunsets, and there are numerous quite fancy bars here, like *Jetée*, where you can linger over a sundowner. Facing east there's much more choice, with a solid line of places that are especially popular for breakfast (there'd be a great sunrise here if you were up in time, and a beautiful view of the mountains even if you miss it), though breakfast is a severe rip-off in most of them. (For some reason almost everywhere in Paleohóra offers muesli for breakfast – you won't see it anywhere else in Crete – but you're better off with a coffee and something from the baker.) *Caravela*, just south of the dock, is good in the evening, as is *Stavros Souridakis* in the other direcion, the last of the main group on this side, easily identified by the "Souvlaki" sign by it's grill – grilled meats a speciality. The *Port* bar, though expensive, is a pleasant place to sit and watch.

There's also a **disco** in Paleohóra – *Paleohóra Club*, open-air, on the east side just before the campsite – and nightly showings at the open-air **cinema**, signed behind the sand beach.

Finding **somewhere to stay** is unlikely to be a major problem, though it can take a while. Arriving by bus or ferry you'll probably be inundated with offers the moment your feet hit the street, and if not it's simply a question of wandering around until you strike lucky, with the campsite or beach as insurance in the unlikely event that nothing at all is available. The cheaper rooms are mostly in the backstreets, but you'll see signs to them everywhere. Good possibilities include *Dionisos*, right on Venizélos; *Blue Sky*, in the first right off the road leading down to the beach (and many others off this road); *Hotel Rea* (☎41-307; C-class but not unreasonable), signed off Venizélos; *Pension Lissos* (☎41-266), on Venizélos; and *Oasis* (☎41-328), a rooms place to the west of Venizélos. The official **campsite**, *Paleohóra Club Camping*, is about 1km beyond the eastern edge of town; not a very attractive setting.

The **tourist office** (daily 9.30am–1pm & 5.30–9pm), in the town hall on Venizélos right in the centre of town, is very helpful and hands out a small map to identify most local landmarks – though this is hardly necessary. There are two **banks** on Venizélos just north of the town hall, and the **OTE** (Mon–Fri 7.30am–3.10pm) is immediately south. There are also phones next door, at the nearby kiosk, and at the kiosk down by the sandy beach. The **post office** (Mon–Fri

7.30am–2pm, Sat 8am–3pm; July & Aug only Sun 9am–1.30pm) is out on the road behind the sandy beach, a short way north by the *Galaxy* restaurant. There's a **health centre** in the street parallel to Venizélos to the west (daily 8.30am–2pm & 5–8pm). There are several **travel agents** and bike hire places: *Reiseladen* and *Interkreta* on the road down to the beach, for example. *Paleohóra Moto Rent* (☎41-542), just round the corner, may be better value for bikes. These places also have details of and tickets for the local **ferries** – to Elafonísi (at 9am, 11am and 4pm), Gávdhos (every Thurs, and, in July and Aug Mon, at 8.30am) and along the coast to Sóuyia and Ayía Rouméli (daily at 8.30am) – or the ferry company offices are on the road down to the jetty, opposite the *Pelican Restaurant*.

Around Paleohóra

Follow the coast either way from Paleohóra and you'll find more beaches. To the **west** it's not a terribly pretty coastline, marred as ever by plastic greenhouses, but there are some excellent beaches along the way and a paved road leads some 7km – past the odd villa and rooms-to-rent place – to the hamlet of YIALÓS. This continues on dirt to several shingly, deserted bays, where some people camp beside incredibly clear water. In theory you can continue on foot right around this coast to Elafonísi (p.232) but check first for the exact route and what is happening along the way.

East, things are simpler: a footpath traces the shore for miles beyond the campsite, passing a succession of grey pebble strips with fewer people in fewer clothes the further you venture. This path continues to Lissós (3hr) and Sóuyia (four and a half hours), and if you time it right you can return to Paleohóra by boat. Again, you should carefully check out both the route and the boats beforehand. The path is waymarked, but it doesn't simply follow the coast all the way, and there are one or two steep scrambles. Nor do the boats run every day except at peak season. Since the most scenic section is through the gorge between Lissós and Sóuyia, it might be easier to do it from there.

An alternative, easier walk would take you down from PRODHRÓMI, inland, but this presents the problem of getting into the hills in the first place. You could take a taxi or it might even be possible to hitch, but this is risky – almost anyone who passes will stop but vehicles are often as much as an hour apart on these back roads, and no one is going far. The village of ÁNIDHRI, en route, is particularly beautiful, with a fourteenth-century church, Ayios Yióryios, which has an unusual double altar and frescoes by Ioánnis Pagoménos (John the Frozen), the most prolific of several painters whose signatures appear frequently around Sélinos.

Azoyirés

Other villages in **the interior** are equally unspoilt, and if you have transport almost any of the tracks into the hills are fascinating. Heading north out of Paleohóra on the main road you'll soon reach a couple signs to **AZOYIRÉS**: one official, the other extolling the virtues of "Azoyires, Paradise Village", with its museum and caves. The road up there is a very rough eight kilometres. Head straight for the centre of the village (ignoring the sign for the museum, which will almost certainly be closed), where there are two taverna/rooms places, *Mihailis* and *Alpha*. At the latter, with good, cheap food, they speak very good English, and the menu has a little map of the village and surrounding attractions. Tony and Harriet, who run the place, are relentless self-publicists (and publicists for the village) who used to live in the States – ads for and reviews of the restaurants they used to run are plastered all over the walls. The village itself is a quiet retreat from the coast, a pleasant place to spend a night if you want to escape, but it's not that special; it is really only the publicity that draws people here. And you may find your tranquil evening somewhat spoiled if a coach party comes up from Paleohóra to enjoy a "traditional Cretan evening"

The **museum** is a single-room record of the Turkish occupation, full of fascinating old stuff, which is officially open weekends only from 9am to 2pm. However if you ask at *Alpha* the curator can usually be found to open it up for you. It's right at the bottom of the village, by a chapel built into a cliff and the old olive-oil factory: a pretty path leads down there, above a lovely tree-filled ravine where pine, cypress, olive, maple and others grow. The **cave** is in the other direction, on a road which sets off opposite Mihailis and winds steeply upwards for nearly 2km (keep climbing and turning where there's any doubt about the way). At the top you have to park and there's an obvious path leading on – look up and you'll see a cross, which is where you're heading. Approaching the cave, some 200m above, you may disturb quail (they're on the menu at *Alpha*) – the eerie sounds emanating from the cave itself are more birds, mostly pigeons, bizarrely amplified by the cave. Going down, there's a steep metal stair and rock-cut steps descending 50m or so to a little shrine lit from above by dim, reflected light. If you have a powerful torch you can continue a fair way, although there's no proper path here: frankly, it's not that impressive.

Beyond Azoyirés you can continue for a further 10km or so – on a road no worse than you've already endured – to TEMÉNIA, where there's another medieval frescoed church and on a nearby hilltop scant remains of the ancient city of Yrtakína. As you leave Azoyirés look out for the *River Bar*, with a wooden terrace overlooking a small waterfall. At Teménia you rejoin a good, newly surfaced road which cuts through from Kandános to the Soúyia road at Rodováni; in this directin, MÁZA is a particularly attractive village.

Towards Sóuyia: Alikiános

Although you can cut through by the route outlined above, the main road to Sóuyia is the one which runs right **across the island from Haniá**. This follows the route to Omalós for about 13km before turning off through **ALIKIANÓS** to skirt west of the highest mountains. Beside this turning there's a large war memorial. The Cretans it remembers were mostly local members of the irregular forces which defended the area known as Prison Valley in the Battle of Crete (you've already passed the prison, see p.210). Cut off from any other Allied units – who indeed believed that resistance here collapsed on the first day of the battle – the Greeks fought on even as everyone else was in full retreat. By doing so they prevented the Germans getting around the mountains to cut the road and guaranteed that the evacuation from Hóra Sfakíon could go ahead. In much earlier history, Alikianós was also the site of the wedding massacre which ended the Kándanoleon revolt (p.204).

In Alikiánós itself, the fourteenth-century church of Áyios Yióryios has well preserved fifteenth-century frescoes. After SKINÉS, a large village with several tavernas and *kafenía*, set among extensive orange groves, the road starts to climb out of the valley into the outriders of the Lefká Óri. Here the citrus trees give way to leafier, deciduous varieties – chestnuts and planes especially – and the villages are a great deal smaller. Just over halfway across the island, near AYÍA IRÍNI, there's a road signed to Omalós: the asphalt lasts only a few hundred yards – though gradually being extended – and beyond that becomes just another track. But it's an exhilarating drive over extremely high mountains, with wonderful views and plenty of vegetation. Ayía Iríni itself is also a very green village, with lots of old chestnut trees. Continuing south, you start gradually to descend, looping down to occasional views of the Libyan Sea and in the last few kilometres tracing a gorge with Sóuyia framed at the far end. Beyond RODHOVÁNI are the remains of ancient **Elyrós**, the most important city in southwest Crete in Roman times and earlier, now offering very little to see. In MONÍ, the last village before the coast, the fourteenth-century church of Áyios Nikólaos has a fresco of Saint Nicholas by Ioánnis Pagoménos.

Koustoyérako

Only about 5km short of Sóuyia, a road cuts back to the ancient Selinos villages of Livadás and Koustoyérako, some eight and a half kilometres away at the end of the road. **KOUSTOYÉRAKO** is a very ancient village that was, and still is, the home of the Paterakis family whose names are famous in the annals of resistance to German occupation. Manoli Paterakis was one of those who took part in the capture of General Kreipe. He died not long ago, at the age of 73, when he fell while chasing a wild goat through the mountains.

The village, like so many, has a long history of resistance to foreign occupation, and was destroyed by Venetians, Turks and Germans alike. In 1943, German troops entered the village, which the men had deserted, and rounded the women and children up in the village square:

> They lined them all up, and, as they refused to speak, prepared to execute the lot. But, before they could press the trigger of their heavy machine-gun, ten Germans fell dead. For some of the village men – about ten – had taken up position along the top of a sheer cliff above the village, from where they could watch every detail, and, at just the right moment, had opened fire. Not a bullet went wide. Terrified, the Germans took to their heels. . . .
>
> George Psychoundakis, *The Cretan Runner*

Next day the Germans returned, but by then the village was deserted – they blew up the empty houses. Costas Paterakis, who fired the first shot and killed the machine-gunner (Patrick Leigh Fermor has described this as one of the most spectacular moments of the war), still lives here.

While the villagers have no desire to become tourist attractions, the village itself is a lovely and very friendly one, set beneath the heights of the White Mountains looking out over the Libyan Sea. At the entrance to the village there's a striking modern war memorial, and then a simple taverna, next to the school and village playground. Continuing, you reach the square, with a couple of *kafenía*. The famous shot was fired from the rocky cliffs above, to your right as you face inland. At the top of the village, to your left from the square, is a tiny Byzantine chapel, Áyios Yióryios, inside which are some beautiful remains of frescoes – with sixteenth-century graffiti carved into them. The chapel itself may in origin be as early as tenth-century: the inscription inside the door dates from sixteenth-century restorations and records various generations of the Kandanoleon family – the last named is one Maria Theotokopoulos. From this they claim that El Greco (Domenico Theotokopoulos) came originally from Koustoyérako.

In summer French groups frequently camp by the school, and from here climb – with a guide – to Omalós and the gorge. If you ask permission, and take your meals at the taverna, you'd probably be allowed to camp here too.

Sóuyia

SÓUYIA is a small village on its way to becoming a big resort. For the moment though, there are no big hotels, no major tour operators, just lots of rooms, simple restaurants and bars, and general stores which double as travel agents, phone office and bank. In front there's an enormous swathe of bay and sparklingly clean, clear sea, and a long pebbly beach. None of it is particularly attractive – the village has an untidy, half-built feel to it, the beach is not always especially clean – but it is a very welcoming place, with plenty of room to spread out. Although increasing numbers have already brought discos in their wake, this is hardly the big time. You could camp here under a few scraggly trees if you wanted (assuming that a scenic spot is not too high a priority), and around at the east end of the bay there's a bit of a nudist community – known locally as the Bay of Pigs.

The village church, down by the beach, seems symptomatic of the local lack of concern about the beauty of the environment. The story goes that it was built after a villager slept here and dreamt that an ancient church lay beneath him and that he was being summoned to erect a new one on the site. Sure enough the ancient church was found and the new one built. Unfortunately the new building was far smaller than the old and at a different angle: as a result the sixth-century Byzantine mosaic which formed the floor of the original stuck out beyond the walls of the new one, with bits of it to be seen all around and more inside. (Much of this mosaic has been taken away for "restoration" and seems unlikely to return – you can still see where it was, however). The original church was a part of ancient *Syía*, a port for Elyrós which flourished through the Roman and early Christian eras: other remains can be seen in the village and around to the east of the bay, where a broken fence allows people to camp among the ancient walls.

Practicalities

Rooms are everywhere in Sóuyia, and the place is small enough to discover them all in a few minutes. Some of the best are to the left of the main street as you come in, overlooking where the gorge* opens out on the coast. In the same street on the edge of town are *Paradisos* (☎51-358), *Lissos* (☎51-244) and *Filoxenia*, all with very pleasant rooms. *Zorba's*, on the seafront to the right from the bottom of the main road, is German-run and rather more expensive, but a great position. *Paradisos* is also the home of a good café/pizzeria, and of the local **travel agent** (*Syia Travel*; exchange daily 8.30am–12.30pm & 4.45–8.45pm). Other **places to eat** include the *Hotel Pikilassos*, just off the main street, with more regular taverna fare served on a little terrace where a tame pelican lives, and several along the front: *Liviko* is one of the most popular, a bar/restaurant which is as much a place to hang out as to eat. At night, there's a **disco bar** among the trees on the far side of the stream from *Paradisos*, or the *Stekkie* cocktail bar, on the road as you enter Sóuyia, has music till the early hours. There's a **phone** in the mini-market on the main road.

---

* There's said to be a good walk down this gorge from Ayía Iríni, but you'd need to check locally whether it's really possible. Don't, incidentally, attempt to walk the coast from here to Ayía Rouméli – at least not without a guide. There is no path.

Lissós

The archaeological site of **LISSÓS** is a great deal more rewarding than anything you'll see in Sóuyia itself. The walk there, a little over an hour, is part of the pleasure: you set out on the road which heads west, behind the beach, and at the harbour turn right on to a track leading slightly inland. The route is well marked once you're on it, leading up a beautiful echoing gorge, which you follow until you've been going for about half an hour, and then climbing steeply out of it towards the sea. After a short distance on the level the sea comes into view, followed almost immediately by Lissós, below you at the back of the little bay of Áyios Kiriákos.

Originally a Dorian city, Lissós grew through the Hellenistic and Roman eras and continued to thrive, along with its neighbours Syía and Elyrós, right up to the Saracen invasion in the ninth century, when they were all abandoned. These places have little history, although it is known that they joined together around 300 BC – along with Yrtakína in the hills behind, Pikilássos on the inaccessible coast between here and Ayía Rouméli, and Tarra, at modern Ayía Rouméli – to form the *Confederation of Oreioi*, later joined by Górtys and Cyrenaica (in North Africa). The remains at Lissós are mostly classical Greek and Roman. The most important survival is an **Asklipion**, or temple of healing, built beside a curative spring against the cliffs on the east side of the site. The temple probably dates from the the third century BC, although the mosaic floor which is its most obvious feature was added later, in the first century AD: notice also the marble altar-base which would have supported a statue, and the "snake pit" (or hole to place sacrifices) next to it. On the gentler, western slope of the valley, opposite, are a group of tombs that look like small stone huts, with barrel-vaulted roofs – hardly the best advertisement for the healing temple. You'll also find a small ruined theatre and two thirteenth-century churches, Áyios Kiriákos and Panayía, which reused older material from the site.

Having explored Lissós, there's a small pebble **beach** for a swim, and a hut, occupied by the site's guardian, where you can get a drink. Ask here if you find the site locked or if you need directing onto the path towards Paleohóra.

Gávdhos – southernmost point of Europe

Gávdhos is the largest of the offshore islands which are "part of" Crete and the only one with any significant population. Plain and somewhat barren, its attraction lies in its enduring isolation. The fifty kilometres of rough sea separating it from the coast of Crete frequently prove too much for the caiques, and the ports from which these leave have themselves only begun to see tourists in the last few years. Consequently – and despite the fact that it's now possible to get a very basic package tour based on Gávdhos – the trip to the island remains one more talked about than done. Not that you can expect complete solitude, since through the summer there's a semi-permanent community of campers (mostly German) spread around the beaches. They often outnumber the local population of little over fifty.

As you approach, the island looks totally uninhabited – the harbour is hidden behind a headland – and only with the aid of binoculars might you pick out one or two isolated homes. In the north and east, the coast is low with a number of deserted beaches; in the southwest the island rises to 384m, its shoreline rocky and difficult of access. The interior, with four distinct settlements, is much greener – carpeted with squat pines and scrub and rich with the scent of wild thyme – but it can still be a pretty inhospitable environment, with summer temperatures which frequently go well beyond 100°F.

The island

The port at **KARABÉ** is minute. Lost in a drab expanse of rock and scrub, two *kafenía* sit side by side by a stubby concrete breakwater, a few ramshackle houses and a church squatting behind in silent support. It's normally possible to find a boat here if you want to get to one of the **beaches** the easy way, or you could take one of the vehicles (tractors with trailers or minibuses) that usually meet the ferry. Forty minutes' stiff walk will take you north across the headland, past the pretty little church of Áyios Yioryios, to SARAKINÍKOS, one of the best of the strands, a broad strip of golden sand where there are eight or nine very basic tavernas. It's a fair size track which leads here, but the only real road – a dirt track built in 1980 for the benefit of Gávdhos' four vehicle owners – runs inland from Karabé. You could also head south, a similar distance, to Kórfos beach, the second most popular.

KASTRÍ, the island capital, is an hour's walk along this steadily climbing dirt track – a ghostly sort of place where only a handful of houses remain inhabited while the majority gradually crumble away to become one with the weathered and fissured rock on which they stand. Depopulation here has been acute and constant. In the Middle Ages Gávdhos is said to have had 8000 residents and had a bishop of its own: as recently as 1914 there were 1400 souls living here. Given the isolation and the stark severity of island life the drain is hardly surprising, but it has undoubtedly made conditions harder for the members of the six families who remain. Not far from the village there is a minor archaeological site (nothing momentous but, if you can find it, unfenced and worth a wander) from which some claim proof that the island was settled as far back as Neolithic times. What is certain is that Gávdhos was inhabited in the Classical Greek era (some claim that this was the island of *Calypso* visited by Odysseus) and well known to the Romans, who christened the place Clauda or Kaudos – Saint Paul was blown past Clauda in the storm which carried him off from Kalí Liménes (p.95).

In Kastrí you'll find the island post office (incorporating the telephone office, shop and occasional taxi service) which along with a number of other very basic shops also serves as a café and meeting place. On the outskirts stands a substantial two-storey building where between the wars political prisoners were incarcerated: there have been attempts since to convert it to a hotel and a sanatorium but currently it stands empty.

Climbing out of Kastrí the track reaches the ridgeline and divides. Close to this junction is the island school with its one pupil and one teacher – a facility jealously guarded by the islanders. The left branch leads to the tiny settlement of **VATSIANÁ**, the right to the equally sparse hamlet of **ÁMBELOS**. From the latter there's a particularly fine view towards North Africa, a sealane ploughed constantly by enormous supertankers. From either village you can continue by narrow paths to some great beaches: north from Ámbelos to POTÁMOS, behind which you can explore a couple of spectacular ravines; east from Vatsianá to KÓRFOS where there's a good beach, a taverna and maybe even a few rooms. South from Vatsianá it's a rather longer hike to the promontory of **TRIPITÍ**, which can legitimately claim to be the very southernmost spot in Europe. There's another fine, sheltered beach in the lee of the point.

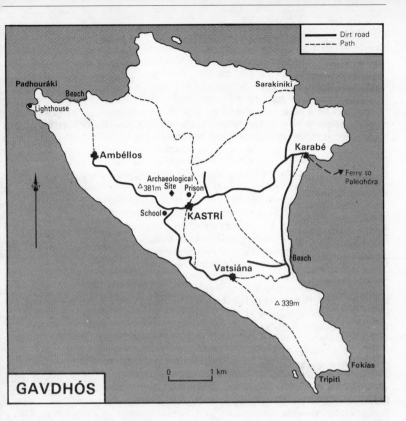

GAVDHÓS

Gávdhos practicalities

The most obvious sign of the hardship of Gávdhos life is the paucity of **food** available. With the exception of a few basic vegetables, and the occasional feast when someone slaughters a sheep or goat, almost everything has to be imported from the mainland and there is little choice in any of the island's shops or eating places. (Karabé and Sarakiníkos have the best options, with a chance at least of fresh fish). It makes sense to bring some supplies with you, especially fresh bread and fruit, although visitors who fail to spend anything at all not surprisingly irritate locals somewhat. The local honey is wonderful, and watch out for the island wine, which is vicious.

Water is also in short supply. There is very little springwater and most fresh water has to be drawn from wells or collected in rainwater cisterns; check with locals before drinking from any of them. Don't expect to find showers or modern plumbing, and don't join those thoughtless visitors who insist on contaminating the limited fresh water supply with soap. There is no mains electricity either, though generators are fairly widespread as can be seen from the number of TV aerials.

Rooms are most obviously available in Karabé, though they can also be had in Kastrí and elsewhere if you ask around, and there are now a couple on each of the main beaches. For reassurance, it's even possible to book ahead from Paleohóra. If you're prepared to **camp** you can pick your spot just about anywhere, on the beaches or in any number of sheltered spots inland. In **emergencies** there should be a doctor in Kastrí during the summer and there's also a telephone line to the mainland (with a phone in each of the four main settlements). The best advice, however, is not to need either. At least a few words of **Greek** would be extremely useful, though locals try their best with all their visitors.

Getting there

Ferry connections aren't bad in summer: from Paleohóra via Sóuyia (July & Aug leaves Paleohóra 8.30am Mon & Thurs, Sóuyia 9.30am, returns 4pm; June & Sept Thurs only, weather permitting); and from Hóra Sfakíon from mid-June to the end of September (leaves Hóra Sfakíon 9am Sat & Sun, returns 5pm). Out of season things are much less certain – there are occasional sailings all year round taking essential supplies across (mostly from Paleohóra) but these are dependent on weather and circumstances. The only accurate information can be had on the spot. Whatever time of year, this crossing can be rough, so take some pills if your seaworthiness is in doubt.

To the northwest of Gávdhos (and passed en route from Paleohóra) lies the flat little islet of **GAVDHOPOÚLO**, inhabited only in summer by the occasional shepherd taking advantage of the grazing. If you wanted to visit you'd have to arrange a trip with one of the local fishermen.

travel details

Buses

Haniá–Réthimnon/Iráklion (1hr 30min/3hr) 27 daily, 5.30am–8.30pm, a couple via the old road (2hr/5hr).

Haniá–Kastélli (1hr 30min) 13 daily, 6am–8pm.

Haniá–Ay. Marína/Máleme at least every half hour, 6am–10pm.

Haniá–Kolimbári (1hr) 27 daily, 6am–10pm

Haniá–Omalós (90min) 4 daily.

Haniá–Hóra Sfakíon (2hr) 3 daily, 8.30am, 11am & 2pm.

Haniá–Paleohóra (2hr) 5 daily, 8.30am–5pm.

Haniá–Sóuyia (2hr) 2 daily, 8.30am & 1.30pm.

Haniá–Foúrnes (30min) 7 daily, 6.45am–8pm.

Haniá–Skalóti (Frangokástello) (2hr 30min) daily at 2pm.

Haniá–Hórafakia/Stavrós (30min) 4 daily, 7am–6pm.

Haniá–Vámos/Kalíves (30min/45min) 5 daily, 7am–7.30pm.

Haniá–Gavalohóri (45min) daily at 2.15pm.

Haniá–Falásarna (2hr) daily at 8.30am & 3.30pm.

Haniá–Elafonísi (3hr) daily at 8.15am.

Kastélli–Elafonísi (1hr 30min) daily at 9.30am.

Kastélli–Omalós (3hr) daily at 5am.

Hóra Sfakíon–Plakiás/Ayía Galíni (1hr 30min–3hr) daily at 4.30pm.

Ferries

Sóudha–Pireás *ANEK Line* daily at 7pm; *Minoan* at 6.30pm Tues, Thurs & Sat.

Kastélli–Peloponnese 8am Tues to Kíthira & Neápoli, 8am Fri to Kíthira, Yíthio, Monemvassía & Pireás.

Paleohóra–Gávdhos July–Aug Mon and Thurs 8.30am, returning 4pm; rest of year Thurs only, weather permitting.

Hóra Sfakíon–Gávdhos Mid-June to end Sept Sat & Sun 9am, returning 5pm.

Kaíkia also run along the south coast, daily from Paleóhora to Sóuyia and Ayía Rouméli (depart 8.30am, return 4.30pm); at least 5 times a day from Ayía Rouméli to Loutró and Hóra Sfakíon.

Planes
Haniá–Athens (45min) 5 daily.

Haniá–Thessaloníki (1hr 15min) Tues at 8.40pm.

ΑΓ ΜΑΡΙΝΑ	Αγ Μαρίνα	Ay. Marína
ΑΓ ΡΟΥΜΕΛΗ	Αγ Ρουμέλη	Ay. Rouméli
ΑΚΡΩΤΗΡΙ	Ακρωτήρι	Akrotíri
ΑΛΙΚΙΑΝΟΣ	Αλικιανός	Alikianós
ΑΠΤΕΡΑ	Απτερα	Áptera
ΑΛΜΥΡΙΔΑ	Αλμυρίδα	Almirídha
ΑΝΟΠΟΛΗ	Ανόπολη	Anópoli
ΒΑΜΟΣ	Βάμος	Vámos
ΒΡΥΣΕΣ	Βρύσες	Vrísses
ΓΑΥΔΟΣ	Γαύδος	Gávdhos
ΓΕΩΡΓΙΟΥΠΟΛΗ	Γεωργιόυπολη	Yeoryióupoli
ΕΛΑΦΟΝΗΣΗ	Ελαφονήση	Elafonísi
ΕΛΟΣ	Ελος	Élos
ΘΕΡΙΣΟ	Θέρισο	Thériso
ΚΑΛΑΜΙ	Καλάμι	Kalámi
ΚΑΛΥΒΕΣ	Καλύβες	Kalíves
ΚΑΝΤΑΝΟΣ	Κάντανος	Kándanos
ΚΑΣΤΕΛΛΙ	Καστέλλι	Kastélli
ΚΟΛΥΜΒΑΡΙ	Κολυμβάρι	Kolimbári
ΚΟΥΡΝΑΣ	Κουρνάς	Kournás
ΛΑΚΚΟΙ	Λάκκοι	Lákki
ΛΟΥΤΡΟ	Λουτρό	Loutró
ΜΑΛΕΜΕ	Μάλεμε	Máleme
ΜΕΣΚΛΑ	Μεσκλά	Mesklá
ΜΟΥΡΝΙΕΣ	Μουρνιές	Mourniés
ΟΜΑΛΟΣ	Ομαλός	Omalós
ΠΑΛΑΙΟΧΩΡΑ	Παλαιοχώρα	Paleohóra
ΠΕΡΙΒΟΛΙΑ	Περιβόλια	Perivólia
ΠΛΑΤΑΝΟΣ	Πλάτανος	Plátanos
ΠΟΛΥΡΡΗΝΙΑ	Πολυρρηνία	Polirinía
ΡΟΔΩΠΟΣ	Ροδωπός	Rodhopós
ΣΑΜΑΡΙΑ	Σαμαριά	Samariá
ΣΟΥΓΙΑ	Σούγια	Sóuyia
ΣΟΥΔΑ	Σούδα	Sóudha
ΣΤΑΥΡΟΣ	Σταυρός	Stavrós
ΣΦΑΚΙΑ	Σφακιά	Sfakiá
ΣΦΗΝΑΡΙΟ	Σφηνάριο	Sfinári
ΦΑΛΑΣΑΡΝΑ	Φαλάσαρνα	Falásarna
ΦΟΥΡΝΕΣ	Φουρνές	Fournés
ΦΡΑΓΚΟΚΑΣΤΕΛΛΟ	Φραγκοκάστελλο	Frangokástello
ΧΑΝΙΑ	Χανιά	Haniá
ΧΡΥΣΟΣΚΑΛΙΤΙΣΣΑΣ	Χρυσοσκαλίτισσας	Hrisoskalítissa
ΧΩΡΑ ΣΦΑΚΙΩΝ	Χώρα Σφακίων	Hóra Sfakíon
ΧΩΡΑΦΑΚΙΑ	Χωραφάκια	Horafákia

PART THREE

THE

CONTEXTS

THE HISTORICAL FRAMEWORK

The people of Crete unfortunately make more history than they can consume locally.

Saki

The discovery of the Minoan civilisation has tended to overshadow every other aspect of Cretan history. And indeed it would be hard for any other period to rival what was, in effect, the first truly European civilisation. It was in Crete that the developed societies of the east met influences from the west and north, and here that "western culture", as synthesised in Classical Greece and Rome, first developed.

Yet this was no accident or one-off freak: Crete's position as a meeting place of east and west, and its strategic setting in the middle of the Mediterranean, has thrust the island to the centre-stage of world history more often than seems comfortable. Long before Arthur Evans arrived to unearth Knossós, and for some time after, the island's struggle for freedom, and the great powers' inactivity, was the subject of Europe-wide scandal. The battle for the island when the Turks arrived had similarly aroused worldwide interest, and represented at the time a significant change in the balance of power between Islam and Christianity. In fact from Minoan times to World War II, there has rarely been a sustained period when Crete didn't have some role to play in world affairs.

THE STONE AGE

Crete's first inhabitants, **Neolithic cave dwellers**, apparently reached the island around 6000 BC. They came, probably, from Asia Minor, or perhaps from Syria, Palestine or North Africa, bringing with them the basics of Stone Age culture – tools of wood, stone and bone; crude pottery; and simple cloth. A possible clue to the origins of these peoples may lie in the importance of bull cults at certain centres in Neolithic Anatolia (see below).

Development over the next 3000 years was almost imperceptibly slow but gradually, whether through new migrations and influences or internal dynamics, advances were made. Elementary agriculture was practised, with domestic animals and basic crops. Pottery became more sophisticated, with better made domestic utensils and clay figurines of humans, animals and especially of a fat mother goddess or fertility figure. Obsidian imported from the island of Mílos was used too. And though caves continued to be inhabited, simple rectangular huts of mud bricks were also built, with increasing skill and complexity as the era wore on. One of the most important of the Neolithic settlements was at Knossós, and there is abundant evidence that many other sites of later habitation were used at this time – Mália, Festós, Ayía Triádha, the Haniá area – as were most of the caves later to assume religious significance.

THE BRONZE AGE: MINOAN CRETE

Minoan Crete has been the subject of intense and constant study by archaeologists since its emergence from myth to archaeological reality at the beginning of the century. Yet there is still enormous controversy even over such fundamental details as who the Minoans were and what language they spoke. No written historical records from the time survive (or if they do, they have not yet been deciphered) so almost everything we know is deduced from physical remains, fleshed out somewhat by writings from classical Greece, almost 1000 years after the destruction of Knossós. Nevertheless it is not hard to forge some kind of consensus from the theories about the Minoans, and this is what is set out below: fresh discoveries may yet radically change this view.

One of the central arguments is over **dating**. The original system, conceived by Sir Arthur Evans, divided the period into Early, Middle and Late Minoan (see p.265), with each of these again divided into three sub-periods – a sequence that has become extremely complicated and cumbersome as it has been further qualified and sub-divided. Arcane distinctions between the pottery styles of Early Minoan IIa and IIb have no place in a brief history and I've therefore used a simpler system of four periods: **pre-palatial**, proto-palatial or **First Palace**, neo-palatial or **New Palace**, and **post-palatial**. This has the additional advantage of avoiding many of the niceties of exact dating and of uneven development across the island. However, as many archaeological texts and guides, as well as some museums on the island use the Evans system, the approximate corresponding periods – Early, Middle and Late Minoan – are given in brackets below.

PRE-PALATIAL: 3000–1900 BC (EMI–MMI)

Among the more important puzzles of Minoan society is its comparatively sudden emergence. During the centuries before 2600 BC there were important changes on the island, and thereafter very rapid progress in almost every area of life. Villages and towns grew up where previously there had been only isolated settlements, and with them came craft specialists: potters, metalworkers, weavers. Many of these new settlements were in the east and south of the island, and there was for the first time significant habitation on the coast and near natural harbours.

It seems safe to assume that these changes were wrought by a new migration of people from the east, bringing with them new technologies, methods of agriculture and styles of pottery, but most importantly, perhaps, a knowledge of seafaring and trade. The olive and the vine – which need little tending and

CRETE IN MYTH

Crete is intimately associated with much of ancient Greek mythology, and in particular with Zeus, who was not only brought up on the island, but according to some ancient Cretans was buried here as well.

Zeus was the third generation of rulers of the gods. The original ruler, Uranus, was overthrown by his youngest son Kronos. In order to prevent such a fate overtaking him, too, Kronos ate his first five children at birth. When she was bearing the sixth, his wife, Rhea, took refuge in a Cretan cavern (a site much argued over, but most commonly assigned to the Dhiktean cave, p.105). Here Zeus was born, and in his place Rhea presented Kronos with a rock wrapped in blankets, which he duly devoured. Zeus was brought up secretly in the cave, his cries drowned by the *Kouretes*, who kept up a continuous clashing of shields and spears outside. The baby fed on milk from a mountain goat, Amalthea, one of whose horns he later made into a miraculous gift which a wish would fill with whatever was desired (hence the horn of plenty).

Having grown to manhood on Crete, Zeus declared war on Kronos and the Titans, a war which lasted ten years. Eventually, however, Zeus emerged as supreme ruler of the gods, and Kronos was banished to the Underworld.

The god's most famous return to the island of his birth was with **Europa**, the daughter of king Phoenix (after whom Phoenicia was named). Zeus saw her gathering flowers by the shore, came to her in the shape of a white bull, ravished her and carried her off across the sea to Crete. They landed at Mátala, travelled to Górtys (where in a plane tree they are said to have dallied in the shape of eagles) and were married at the Dhiktean cave. One of the presents of Zeus to his bride was **Talos**, a bronze giant who strode round the island hurling boulders at approaching strangers. Jason and the Argonauts were greeted by a hail of stones from Talos when they approached Crete: their companion, the magician Medea, brought about the giant's fall when he induced him to graze his one vulnerable spot – his ankle – against the rocks.

The Zeus of the Europa tale, taking the form of a **bull**, is almost certainly mixed up with earlier, native Cretan gods. The sun god of Crete also took the form of a bull, and the animal is a recurrent motif in the island's mythology. In the story of Minos, a bull once again has a prominent role. Europa bore Zeus three sons – Minos, Rhadamanthys and Sarpedon – before eventually being deserted. Later she married the king of Crete, Asterios, who adopted her children. At his death both **Minos** and Sarpedon claimed the throne (Rhadamanthys, known as a law-maker, appears in some tales as ruler at Festós, and in therefore help free a labour force – began to be produced alongside cereal crops. Copper tools replaced stone ones and were themselves later refined with the introduction of bronze. Art developed rapidly, with characteristic Vasíliki ware and other pottery styles; gold jewellery; and stone jars of exceptional quality, based originally on Egyptian styles. Significantly, large quantities of seal stones have been found too, almost certainly the mark of a mercantile people. They were used to sign letters and documents, but especially to seal packets, boxes or doors as proof that they had not been opened: the designs – scorpions or poisonous spiders – were often meant as a further deterrent to robbery.

At the same time new methods of burial appear – *Thólos* and chamber tombs in which riches were buried wih the dead. These appear to have been communal, as, probably, was daily life, based perhaps on clan or kinship groupings.

THE FIRST PALACES: 1900–1700 BC (MMI–MMII)

Shortly before 1900 BC the first of the palaces were built, at **Knossós**, **Festós** and **Mália**. They represent another significant and apparently abrupt change: a shift of power back to the centre of the island and the emergence of a much more hierarchical, ordered society. Knossós was perhaps originally as much a religious centre as a base of secular power: certainly at this time religion took on a new importance, with the widespread use of mountain-top peak sanctuaries and caves as cult centres. At the same time much larger towns were growing up, especially around the palaces, and in the countryside substantial "villas" appeared.

The palaces themselves are proof of the island's great prosperity at this period, and the artefacts found within offer further evidence. Advances were made in almost every field of artistic and craft endeavour. From the first

others is exiled by his jealous brothers). Minos prayed to Poseidon (or perhaps his father Zeus) for a bull to offer as sacrifice, and as proof that he was favoured by the gods. When the radiant bull emerged from the sea Minos was accepted as the chosen candidate. So beautiful was the bull, however, that he determined to keep it, sacrificing in its place another from his herds.

Punishment for such hubris was inevitable, and in this case the gods chose to inflame Minos's wife, Pasiphae (a moon goddess in her own right – again the bull symbolises the sun), with intense desire for the animal. She had Daedalos construct her an artificial cow, in which she hid and induced the bull to couple with her: the result was the **Minotaur**, a beast half man and half bull (probably human with a bull's head). To hide his shame, Minos had Daedalos construct the labyrinth in which to imprison the monster.

Meanwhile Minos had waged war on Athens, and part of the settlement was that an annual tribute of seven young men and women be provided as sport or sacrfice for the monster. The third time the tribute was due, **Theseus**, the son of king Aegeus of Athens, resolved to end the slaughter and himself went as one of the victims. In Crete he met Minos's daughter Ariadne, who fell in love with him and resolved to help him in his task. She provided him with a ball of thread which he could unwind and, if he succeeded in killing the Minotaur, follow to find his way out of the maze.

So far everything went to plan, and Theseus killed the beast and escaped from the island with Ariadne and the others. On the way home, though, things were less successful. Ariadne was abandoned on a beach in Náxos, and approaching Athens Theseus forgot to change his black sails for white – a pre-arranged signal that the mission had succeeded. Thinking his son dead, king Aegeus threw himself into the sea and drowned.

Back on Crete, Minos imprisoned Daedalos in his own labyrinth, furious at Ariadne's desertion, at the failure of the maze and, perhaps, having discovered the truth about the Minotaur's conception. Locked up with Daedalos was his son Ikaros. They escaped by making wings of feathers held together with wax. Daedalos finally reached Sicily: Ikaros, though, flew too close to the sun, the wax melted and he plunged to his death in the sea. Still set on revenge, Minos tracked Daedalos down by setting a puzzle so fiendishly difficult that only he could have solved it. In Sicily in pursuit of the fugitive, however, Minos met an undignified end when he was scalded to death in his bath by the daughters of the king.

The postscript to all this concerns Zeus's death. According to the Cretans he was buried beneath Mount Yioúhtas, in whose outline his profile can still be seen. It was a purely local claim, however. For everyone else the idea that the immortal god could die was further proof of the unreliability of the island.

palace era came the famous **Kamáres Ware** pottery – actually two distinct styles, one eggshell thin and delicate, the other sturdier with bold-coloured designs. The true potter's wheel (as against the turntable) was introduced for the first time, along with a simple form of hieroglyphic writing. Elaborate jewellery, seals and bronzework were also being produced.

Cretan bronze was used throughout the Mediterranean, and its production and distribution were dependent on a wide-ranging **maritime economy**. For though Crete may have produced some copper at this time, it never yielded tin, the nearest significant sources of which were as distant as Iran to the east, Central Europe in the north, Spain, Brittany and even Britain in the west. While some claim that Minoan ships actually sailed as far afield as the Atlantic, it seems more likely that the more exotic goods were obtained through middlemen. Nevertheless, in the Mediterranean, Crete controlled the trade routes, importing tin, copper, gold, silver and precious stones of every kind, exporting timber, olive oil, wine and bronze goods. Minoan **colonies** were established on many Cycladic islands and there were regular trade links above all with Egypt and the east.

Around 1700 BC, the palaces were destroyed for the first time, probably by earthquake.

THE NEW PALACES: 1700–1450 BC (MMIII–LMI)

Though the destruction must have been a setback, Minoan culture continued to flourish, and with the palaces reconstructed on a still grander scale the society entered its Golden Age. It is the **new palaces** which provide most of our picture of Minoan life and most of what is seen at the great sites – Knossós, Festós, Mália, Zákros – dates from this period.

The **architecture** of the new palaces was of an unprecedented sophistication: complex, multi-storey structures in which the use of space and light was as luxurious as the construction materials. Grand stairways, colonnaded porticoes and courtyards, brightly frescoed walls, elaborate plumbing and drainage, and great magazines in which to store the society's accumulation of wealth, were all integral, as were workshops for the technicians and craftsmen, and areas set aside for ritual and worship.

Obviously it was only an elite which enjoyed these comforts, but conditions for the ordinary people who kept Minos* and his attendants in such style appear to have improved too: **towns** around the palaces and at sites such as Goúrnia and Palékastro were growing as well.

Very little is known of how the **society** was organised, or indeed whether it was a single entity ruled from Knossós or simply several city states with a common cultural heritage. However, in an intriguing reference to Crete in his *Politics* Aristotle implied that a caste system had operated in the times of Minos. Clearly, though, it was a society in which **religion** played an important part. The great Corridor of the Procession fresco at Knossós depicted an annual delivery of tribute, apparently to a Mother Goddess; bull leaping had a religious significance too; and in all the palaces substantial chambers are set aside for ritual purposes. Secular leaders were also religious leaders.

That Minoan society was a very open one is apparent too. There are virtually no **defences**, internal or external, at any Minoan site, and apparently the rulers felt no threat either from within or without. As far as internal dissent goes it seems safe to assume that the wealth of the island filtered down, to some extent at least, to all its inhabitants: the lot of a Minoan peasant may have been little different to that of a Cretan villager as little as fifty years ago.

Externally, maritime supremacy was further extended: objects of Cretan manufacture turn up all over the Mediterranean and have even been claimed as far afield as Britain and Scandinavia (amber from the Baltic certainly found its way to Crete). Behind their seapower the Minoans clearly felt safe, and the threat of attack or piracy was further reduced by the network of colonies or close allies throughout the Cycladic islands – Thíra most famously but also at Mílos, Náxos, Páros, Mikonós, Ándhros and Dílos – and in Rhodes, Cyprus, Syria and North Africa. Nevertheless this remained a trading empire rather than a military one.

Cultural advances

If the New Palace period was a high point of Minoan power, it also marked the apogee of

---

*Arthur Evans named Minoan society after the legendary King Minos, but there is little doubt that Minos was in fact the title of a dynasty of priest/kings, a word rather like Pharaoh.

arts and crafts in the island: again, the bulk of the objects you'll admire in the museums date from this era. The **frescoes** – startling in their freshness and vitality – are the most famous and obviously visible demonstration of this florescence. But they were just the highly visible tip of an artistic iceberg. It was in intricate small-scale work that the Minoans excelled above all. Naturalistic **sculpted figures** of humans and animals include the superb ivory bull-leaper, the leopard-head axe and the famous snake goddesses or priestesses, all of them on show in the Iráklion museum. The carvings on seal stones of this era are of exceptional delicacy – a skill carried over into beautifully delicate gold jewellery. Examples of **stone vessels** include the bull's head rhyton from Knossós and the three black vases from Ayía Triádha which are among the museum's most valuable possessions. And **pottery** broke out into an enormous variety of new shapes and design motifs, drawing their inspiration especially from scenes of nature and marine life.

The other great advance was in **writing**. A new form of script, Linear A, had appeared at the end of the first palace period, but in the new palaces its use became widespread. Still undeciphered, Linear A must record the original, unknown language of the Minoans: it seems to have been used in written form almost exclusively for administrative records – stock lists, records of transactions and tax payments. Even were it understood, therefore, it seems unlikely that the language would reveal much in the way of history. The pieces which have survived were never intended as permanent records, and have been found intact only where the clay tablets used were baked solid in the fires which destroyed the palaces. It is possible that a more formal record, an abstract of the annual accounts, was kept on a more valuable but also more perishable material such as imported papyrus or even a paper produced from native date palm leaves.

The end

Around 1600 the island again saw minor earthquake damage, though this was swiftly repaired. But about 1450 BC came **destruction** on a calamitous scale: the palaces were smashed and (with the exception of Knossós itself) burned, and smaller settlements across the island devastated. The cause of this disaster is still the most controversial of all Minoan riddles, but the most convincing theory links it with the explosion of the **volcano of Thíra** about 1500 BC: a blast which may have been five times as powerful as that of Krakatoa. The explosion threw up great clouds of black ash and a huge tidal wave, or waves. Coastal settlements would have been directly smashed by the wave, and perhaps further burnt by the overturn of lamps lighted on a day made unnaturally dark by the clouds of ash. Blast, panic and accompanying earth tremors would have contributed to the wreck. And then, as the ash fell, it apparently coated the centre and east of the island in a poisonous blanket under which nothing could grow, or would grow again, for as much as fifty years.

Only at Knossós was there any real continuity of habitation, and here it was with **Mycenaean Greeks** in control, bringing with them new styles of art, a greater number of weapons, and above all keeping records in a form of writing known as **Linear B**, an adaptation of Linear A now used to write in an early Greek dialect. In about 1370 BC, Knossós was itself burnt, whether by rebellious Cretans, a new wave of Mycenaeans, or perhaps as a result of another natural disaster on a smaller scale.

Such at least is the prevailing theory. But it has its problems – why, for example, should Festós have been burnt when it was safe from waves and blast on the south side of the island? And why should the eruption that vulcanologists now date to 1500 BC have had such a dramatic effect only fifty years later – indeed there are signs that away from the worst effects of the devastation many areas on Crete experienced comparative prosperity after it. As the debate continues the best that can be said currently is that the volcano theory fits the available evidence better than most of its rivals. But many scholars still claim that the facts are more consistent with destruction by human rather than natural causes. The main counter-theory assumes an invasion by the Mycenaeans, and points to some evidence that Linear B was in use at Knossós *before* 1450 BC. But if the Mycenaeans came to conquer, they would have gained nothing by destroying the society already flourishing on Crete; nor would they have subsequently left the former population centres deserted for a generation or more.

A third theory attempts to answer these inconsistencies suggesting that an internal revolt by the populace against its rulers (possibly in the wake of the chaos caused by the Thíra eruption) could provide an explanation. This theory would fit the evidence from sites such as Mírtos Pírgos on the south coast, where a villa dominating the site was burned down whilst the surrounding settlement remained untouched. Needless to say this theory does not find favour with those who see Minoan civilisation as a haven of tranquil splendour, but it does fit with the later Greek tradition of a tyrannical Minos oppressing not only his own people but those abroad as well. Further archaeological investigation both on Crete and other islands in the Aegean may ultimately resolve this Minoan mystery.

POST-PALATIAL: 1450–1100 BC (LMII–LMIII)

From their bridgehead at Knossós, the Mycenaeans gradually spread their influence across the island as it became habitable again. By the early fourteenth century BC they controlled much of Crete, and some of the earlier sites, including Goúrnia, Ayía Triádha, Tílissos and Palékastro, were reoccupied. It is a period which is still little-known and which by the early Minoan scholars was written off almost entirely. More recent excavations are revealing, though, that the island remained productive, albeit in a role peripheral to the mainland.

In particular **western Crete** now came into its own, as the area least affected by the volcano. **Kydonia** became the chief city of the island, still with a considerable international trade and continuing, in its art and architecture, very much in the Minoan style. But Kydonia lies beneath modern Haniá and has never been (nor is ever likely to be) properly excavated – another reason that far less is known about this period than those which preceded it. In **central Crete** the main change was a retreat from the coasts, a sign of the island's decline in international affairs and trade and perhaps of an increase in piracy. Even here, however, despite the presence of new influences, much of the art is recognisably Minoan. Most of the famous clay and stone *larnakes* (sarcophagi) – which was a distinctly new method of burial – date from this final Minoan era.

More direct evidence of the survival of Crete comes in Homer's account of the **Trojan War**, when he talks of a Cretan contingent taking part under King Idomeneus (according to him, the grandson of Minos). The war and its aftermath – a period of widespread change – also affected Crete. In the north of Greece the Mycenaeans were being overrun by peoples moving down from the Balkans, in particular the **Dorians**. Around 1200 BC the relative peace was disrupted again: many sites were abandoned for the last time, others burnt. Briefly, Mycenaean influence became yet more widespread, as refugees arrived on the island. But by the end of the twelfth century BC Minoan culture was in terminal decline, and Crete was entering into the period of confusion which engulfed most of the Greek world. Some of the original population of the island, later known as **Eteo-Cretans** (true Cretans), retreated at this time to mountain fastnesses at sites such as Présos and Karfí where they survived along with elements of Minoan culture and language for almost another millenium.

THE IRON AGE: DORIAN AND CLASSICAL CRETE

The bulk of the island, however, was taken over by the Dorians: there may have been an invasion, but it seems more probable that the process was a gradual one, by settlement. At any event over the succeeding centuries the Dorians came to dominate the central lowlands, with substantial new cities such as Láto.

Dorian Crete was not in any real sense a unified society: its cities warred with each other and there may, as well as the Dorians and Eteo-Cretans, have been other cultural groupings in the west, at Kydonia and sites such as Falásarna and Polirínia. Nevertheless the island saw another minor artistic renaissance, with styles now mostly shared with the rest of the Greek world, and in tools and weapons iron gradually came to replace bronze.

Much the most important survival of this period, however, is the celebrated **law code from Górtys**. The code (p.83) was set down around 450 BC, but it reflects laws which had already been in force for hundreds of years: the society described is a strictly hierarchical one, clearly divided into a ruling class, free men, serfs and slaves. For the rulers, life followed a harsh, militaristic regime similar to that of

Sparta: the original population, presumably, had been reduced to the level of serfs.

As mainland Greece approached its **Classical Age**, Crete advanced little. It remained a populous island, but one where a multitude of small city-states were constantly vying for power. Towns of this period are characterised by their heavy defences, and most reflected the Górtys laws (Górtys remained among the most powerful of them) in tough oligarchical or aristocratic regimes. At best Crete was a minor player in Greek affairs, increasingly known as the den of pirates and as a valuable source of mercenaries unrivalled in guerrilla tactics. The island must have retained influence, though, for it was still regarded by classical Athenians as the source of much of their culture, and its strict institutions were admired by many philosophers. In addition, many Cretan shrines and caves show unbroken use from Minoan through to Roman times, and those associated with the birth and early life of Zeus (the Dhiktean and Idean Caves especially) were important centres of pilgrimage.

The multitude of small, independent city-states is well illustrated by the Confederation of Oreii, an accord formed around 300 BC between Élyros, Lissós, Írtakina, Tarra, Syía and Pikílassos: six towns in a now barely populated area of the southwest. They were later joined in the Confederation by Gortys and Cyrenaica (in North Africa). Meanwhile Roman power was growing in the Mediterranean, and Crete's strategic position and turbulent reputation drew her inexorably into the struggle.

ROME AND BYZANTIUM

From the second century BC on, **Rome** was drawn into wars in mainland Greece and the involvement of Cretan troops on one or often both sides became an increasing irritation. Hannibal was staying at Górtys at the time of one Roman attempt to quiet the island, around 188 BC. More than a century passed with only minor interventions, however, before Rome could turn her full attention to Crete – the last important part of the Greek world not under her sway.

In 71 BC Marcus Antonius (father of the famous Mark Antony) attempted to invade but was heavily defeated by the Kydonians. In 69 BC a fresh attempt was made under **Quintus Metellus**. This time a bridgehead was successfully established by exploiting divisions among the Cretans: Metellus was supported in his initial campaign against Kydonia by its rivals at Polirinia. The tactic of setting Cretan against Cretan served him well, but even so it took almost three years of bitter and brutal warfare before the island was subdued in 67 BC. It was a campaign marked by infighting not only among the Cretans – Górtys was among those to take Metellus's side – but also between Romans, with further forces sent from Rome in an unsuccessful bid to curb Metellus's excesses and his growing power.

With the conquest complete, peace came quickly and was barely disturbed even in the turbulent years of Julius Caesar's rise and fall. Perhaps in part this was because there was little immediate change in local administration, which was simply placed under Roman supervision. At the same time, the end of the civil wars brought much greater prosperity: Crete was combined with Cyrenaica (in North Africa) as a single province whose capital was at **Górtys**, and though there was little contact between the two halves of the province, both were important sources of grain and agricultural produce for Rome.

Through the first and second centuries AD important **public works** were undertaken throughout Crete: roads, aqueducts and irrigation systems; important cities at Knossós, Áptera, Lyttos and others as well as considerable grandeur at Górtys. **Christianity** arrived with Saint Paul's visit around 50 AD – soon after, he appointed Titus as the island's first bishop to begin the conversion in earnest. Around 250 AD, the Holy Ten – *Áyii Dhéka* – were martyred at Górtys.

With the split of the Roman empire at the end of the fourth century, Crete found itself part of the eastern empire under **Byzantium**. The island continued to prosper – as the churches which were now built everywhere would testify – but in international terms it was not important and Byzantine rule, here as everywhere, imposed a stiflingly ordered society, hierarchical and bureaucratic in the extreme. Of the earliest churches only traces survive, in particular of mosaic floors like those at Soúyia or Thrónos, though there are more substantial remains at Górtys, of the basilica of Áyios Titos.

Then in 824 Crete was invaded by a band of **Arabs** under Abu Hafs Omar. Essentially a piratical group who had been driven first from Spain and then Alexandria, they nevertheless managed to keep control of the island for well over a century. There was not much in the way of progress at this time – for its new masters the island was primarily a base from which to raid shipping and launch attacks on the Greek mainland and other islands – but there was a fortress founded at al-Khandak, a site which later developed into Iráklion. At the same time Górtys and other Byzantine cities were sacked and destroyed.

After several failed attempts, the Byzantine general **Niceforas Fokas** reconquered Crete in 961, following a siege at Khandak in which he catapulted the heads of his Arab prisoners over the walls. For a while the island revived, boosted by an influx of colonists from the mainland and from Constantinople itself, including a number of aristocratic families (the *Archontopouli*) whose power survived throughout the medieval era. By now, however, the entire empire was embattled by Islam and losing out in trade to the Venetians and Genoese. Frescoed churches continued to be built, but most were small and parochial.

Ironically enough it was not Muslims who brought about the final end of Byzantium, but Crusaders. The **fourth Crusade** turned on Constantinople in 1204 (perhaps at the instigation of the Venetians) sacking and burning the city. The leader of the Crusade, Prince Boniface of Montferrat, ceded Crete to the Venetians for a nominal sum.

VENETIAN CRETE

Before Venice could claim her new territory, she had to drive out her chief commercial rivals, the **Genoese**, who had taken control in 1206 with considerable local support. By 1210 the island had been secured, though for more than a century thereafter the Genoese pursued their claim, repeatedly siding with local rebels when it looked like there was a chance of establishing a presence on the island.

The **Venetians**, however, were not going to surrender the prize lightly. Crete for them was a vital resource, both for the control of eastern Mediterranean trade routes which the island's ports commanded, and for the natural wealth of the agricultural land and the timber for ship-building. The Venetian system was rapidly and stringently imposed, with Venetian overlords, directly appointed from Venice, administering what were effectively a series of feudal fiefdoms.

It was a system designed to exploit Crete's resources as efficiently as possible, and not surprisingly it stirred up deep resentments from the beginning. There were constant **rebellions** throughout the thirteenth century, led as often as not by one or other of the aristocratic Byzantine families from an earlier wave of colonisation. Certainly the wealthy had most to lose: it was their land which was confiscated to be granted to military colonists from Venice (along with the service of the people who lived on it) and their rights and privileges which were taken over by the new overlords. The rebellions were in general strictly noble affairs, ended by concessions of land or power to their Cretan leaders. But there were more fundamental resentments too. Heavy taxes and demands for feudal service were widely opposed – by the established colonists almost as much as by the natives. And the **Orthodox church** was replaced by the Roman as the "official" religion, the senior clergy expelled and much church property seized. Local priests and monasteries which survived helped fuel antagonism: even from this early date the monasteries were becoming known as centres of dissent.

In the mid-fourteenth century, one of the most serious revolts yet saw Cretans and second generation Venetian colonists fighting alongside each other, in protest at the low fixed prices for their produce, steep taxes, and the continued privileges granted to "real" Venetians. Although on this occasion the revolt was put down in a particularly fierce repression, the end result of this and the other rebellions was a gradual relaxation of the regime and integration of the two communities – or at least their leaders. The **Middle Ages** were perhaps the most productive in Crete's history, with exports of corn, wine, oil and salt, the ports busy with transhipment business, the wooded hillsides being stripped for timber.

After 1453, and the final fall of Constantinople, Crete saw a spectacular **cultural renaissance** as a stream of refugees arrived from the east. **Candy** – as the island and its capital were known to the Venetians – became the centre of Byzantine art and scholarship. From this later period, and the meeting of the traditions of Byzantium and the Italian renaissance, come the vast majority of the works of art and architecture now associated with the Venetian era. The great icon painter Dhamaskinos studied alongside El Greco in the school of Ayía Ekaterini in Iráklion; the Orthodox monasteries flourished; and in literature the island produced, among others, what is now regarded as its greatest work – the *Erotokritos*.

But it was the growing **external threat** which stimulated the most enduring of the Venetian public works – the island defences. Venice's bastions in the mainland Middle East had fallen alongside Constantinople, and in 1573 Cyprus too was taken by the Turks, leaving Crete well and truly in the front line. Large scale pirate raids had already been common: in 1538 Barbarossa had destroyed Réthimnon and almost taken Haniá, and in the 1560s there were further attacks. Across the island, cities were strengthened and the fortified islets defending the seaways were repaired and rebuilt. As the seventeenth century wore in, however, Venice herself was in severe decline: weakened by the Thirty Years War; her Mediterranean trade overshadowed by a preoccupation with the New World, a business dominated by the Spanish, English and Dutch.

Finally in 1645 an attack on an Ottoman convoy provided the excuse for an all-out **Turkish assault** on Crete. Haniá fell after a siege which cost 40,000 Turkish lives, and Réthimnon rapidly followed. By 1648 the Turks controlled the whole island except **Iráklion**, and they settled down to a long siege. For twenty-one years the city resisted, supplied from the sea and with moral support at least from most of Europe. The end was inevitable, though, and from the Turkish point of view there was no hurry: they controlled the island's produce, they were well supplied, and they enjoyed a fair degree of local support, having relaxed the Venetian rules in, for example, allowing Orthodox bishops back into Crete. By 1669 the city was virtually reduced, and in a final effort the Pope managed to persuade the French to send a small army. After a couple of fruitless sorties involving heavy losses, the French withdrew in an argument over the command. On September 5, the city surrendered, leaving only the three fortified islets of Soúdha, Spinalónga and Gramvoúsa in Venetian

hands, where they remained until surrendered by treaty in 1715.

TURKISH CRETE

It is arguable whether the **Turkish occupation** was ever as stringent or arduous as the Venetian had been, but its reputation is far worse. In part this may simply be that its memory is more recent, but Turkish rule was complicated too by the religious differences involved, and by the fact that it survived into the era of resurgent Greek nationalism and Great Power politics.

If on their arrival the Turks had been welcomed, it was not a long-lived honeymoon. Once again Crete was divided, now between powerful Pashas, and once again it was regarded merely as a resource to be exploited. The Ottoman Empire was less strictly ordered than the Venetian, but it demanded no less: rather than attempt to take control of trade themselves, the Turks simply imposed crippling **taxes**. There were fewer colonists than in the Venetian era, and they took far less interest in their conquest so long as the money continued to come in. Very little was re-invested: outside the cities there was hardly any building at all, and roads and even defences fell into gradual disrepair. As far as local administration went, it was left to local landlords and the mercenary *Janissaries* they controlled to impose. At the local level, then, there was a further level of exploitation as these men too took their cut. Stultified by heavy taxes and tarriffs, slowed by neglect, the island economy stagnated.

One way to avoid the worst of the burden was to become a Muslim and, gradually, the majority of the Christian population was **converted to Islam** – at least nominally. Conversion brought with it substantial material advantages in taxation and rights to own property, and it helped avoid the worst of the repression which inevitably followed any Christian rebellion. These Greek Muslims were not particularly religious: even among the Turks on the island, Islamic law seems to have been loosely interpreted and many continued to worship as Christians in secret, but the mass apostasies served to further divide the island. For those who remained openly Christian the burden became increasingly heavy as there were fewer to bear it. Many took to the mountains, where Turkish authority barely spread.

As the occupation continued, the Turks strengthened their hold on the cities and the fertile plains around them, while the mountains became the stronghold of the Christian *pallikares*. The first major **rebellion** came in 1770, and inevitably it was centred in Sfakiá. Under **Dhaskaloyiánnis** (p.222) the Cretans had been drawn into Great Power politics; drawn in and abandoned, for the promised aid from Russia never came. With the failure of this struggle, Sfakiá was itself brought under Turkish control for a while. But a pattern had been set, and the nineteenth century was one of almost constant struggle for independence.

The beginning of the century saw the Ottoman Empire under severe pressure on the Greek mainland, and in 1821 full scale revolution, the **War of Greek Independence**, broke out. Part of the Turkish response was to call on the Pasha of Egypt, **Mehmet Ali**, for assistance: his price was control of Crete. By 1824, in a campaign which even by Cretan standards was brutal on both sides, he had crushed the island's resistance. When in 1832 an independent Greek state was finally established with the support of Britain, France and Russia, Crete was left in the hands of the Egyptians whence it reverted to Turkish control within ten years.

From now on guerrilla warfare in support of union with Greece (*Enosis*) was almost constant, flaring occasionally into wider revolts but mostly taking the form of incessant raids and irritations. The Cretans enjoyed widespread support, not only on the Greek mainland but throughout western Europe and especially among expatriate Greek communities. But the Greeks alone were no match for the Ottoman armies, and the Great Powers, wary more than anything of each other, consistently failed to intervene. There was a major rising in 1841, bloodily suppressed, and in 1858 another which ended relatively peacefully in the recall of the Turkish governor and some minor concessions to the Christian population.

In 1866 a Cretan Assembly meeting in Sfakiá declared independence and union with Greece, and Egyptian troops were recalled to put down a further wave of revolts bolstered by Greek volunteers. Again the Egyptians proved ruthlessly effective, but this campaign ended in the explosion at **Arkádhi** (p.154), an act of defiance which aroused Europe-wide sympathy. The Powers – Britain above all – still refused to involve themselves, but privately the supply of arms and volunteers to the insurgents was redoubled. From now on some kind of solution seemed inevitable, but even in 1878 the Congress of Berlin left Crete under Turkish dominion, demanding only further reforms in the government. In 1889 and 1896 there were further violent encounters, and in 1897 a Greek force landed to annexe the island. Finally, the Powers were forced into action, occupying Crete with an international force and dividing the island into areas controlled by the British, French, Russians and Italians.

INDEPENDENCE AND UNION WITH GREECE

The outrage which finally brought about the expulsion of Turkish troops from Crete in 1898 was a minor skirmish in Iráklion which led to the death of the British vice-Consul. A **national government** was set up, still nominally under Ottoman suzerainty, with Prince George, younger son of King George of Greece, as High Commissioner: under him was a joint Muslim-Christian assembly, part elected, part appointed.

Euphoria at independence was muted, however, for full union with Greece remained the goal of most Cretans. A new leader of this movement rapidly emerged – **Eleftheríos Venizélos**. Born at Mourniés, outside Haniá, Venizélos had fought in the earlier independence struggles and become a member of the Cretan Assembly and Minister of Justice to Prince George. Politically, however, he had little in common with his new master, and in 1905 he summoned an illegal Revolutionary Assembly at Thériso. Though the attempt to take up arms was summarily crushed, the strength of support for Venizélos was enough to force the resignation of Prince George. In 1908, the Cretan Assembly unilaterally declared *Enosis* – much to the embarassment of the Greek government. For meantime the "Young Turk" revolution looked set to revitalise the Ottoman Empire, and the Great Powers remained solidly opposed to anything which might upset the delicate balance of power in the Balkans.

The failure of the Greek government to act decisively in favour of Crete was one of the factors which led to the *Military League* of young officers forcing political reform on the mainland. With their backing, Venizélos became

Premier of Greece in 1910. In 1912 Greece, Serbia and Bulgaria declared war on the Ottoman Empire, making spectacular advances into Turkish territory. By the peace of 1913, Crete finally and officially became **part of the Greek nation**.

Though Greece was politically riven by World War I, and succeeding decades saw frequent, sometimes violent changes of power between Venizelist and Royalist forces, Crete was little affected. On just one further occasion did the island play a significant role in Greek affairs before the outbreak of war in 1940: in July 1938 there was a popular uprising against the dictator Metáxas and in favour of Venizélos. But it was swiftly put down.

The island was, however, hit hard by the aftermath of the disastrous Greek attempt to conquer Istanbul in pursuit of the "Great Idea" of rebuilding the Byzantine Empire. As part of the peace settlement which followed this military debacle, there was a forced **exchange of populations** in 1923: Muslims were expelled from Greece, Orthodox Christians from Turkey. In Crete many of these "Turks" were in fact Muslim Cretans, descendants of the mass apostasies of the eighteenth century. Nevertheless they left — some 30,000 in all — and a similar number of Christian refugees from Turkey took their place.

WAR AND OCCUPATION

In the winter of 1940 Italian troops invaded northern Greece, only to be thrown back across the Albanian border by the Greek army. Mussolini's humiliation, however, only served to draw the Germans into the fight, and although an Allied army was sent to Greece, the **mainland** was rapidly overrun.

The Allied campaign was marked from the start by suspicion, confusion and lack of communication between the two commands. On the Greek side Metáxas had died in January, and his successor as Premier committed suicide, leaving a Cretan — **Emanuel Tsouderos** to organise the retreat of king and government to his native island. They were rapidly followed by thousands of evacuees, including the bulk of the Allied army, a force made up in large part of Australian and New Zealand soldiers. Most of the native Cretan troops, a division of the Greek army, had been wiped out in defence of the mainland.

According to the Allied plan, Crete should by now have been an impregnable fortress. In practice, though, virtually nothing had been done to improve the island defences, there were hardly any serviceable planes or other heavy equipment, and the arriving troops found little in the way of a plan for their deployment.

On May 20, 1941 the **invasion** of the island began, as German troops poured in by glider and parachute. It was at first a horrible slaughter, with the invaders easily picked off as they drifted slowly down. Few of the first wave of parachutists reached the ground alive and many of the gliders crashed. The main German force was smashed before it ever reached the ground. In the far west, however, beyond the main battle zone, they succeeded in taking the airfield at Máleme. Whether through incompetence (as much of the literature on the Battle of Crete suggests*) or breakdown of communications, no attempt to recapture the field was made until the Germans had had time to defend it and, with a secure landing site, reinforcements and equipment began to pour in. From now on the battle, which had seemed won, was lost, and the Allied troops, already under constant air attack, found themselves outgunned on land too.

Casualties of the **Battle of Crete** were horrendous on both sides — the cemeteries are reminiscent of the burial grounds of World War I victims in northern France — and the crack German airborne division was effectively wiped out. No one ever attempted a similar assault again. But once they were established with a secure bridgehead, the Germans advanced rapidly, and a week after the first landings the Allied army was in full retreat across the mountains towards Hóra Sfakíon, whence most were evacuated by ship to Egypt. On the May 30, the battle was over, leaving behind several thousand Allied soldiers (and all the Cretans who had fought alongside them) to surrender or take to the mountains.

*Recent theories stress the importance of intelligence. Not long before the Battle, the German codes had been cracked, and General Freyberg therefore knew in detail exactly where and how the attacks would come. Whether because he didn't trust the info, however, or because of the need to keep secret the intelligence breakthrough, he did not redeploy his troops.

THE RESISTANCE

One of the first tasks of **the resistance** was to get these stranded soldiers off the island, and in this they had remarkable success, organising the fugitives into groups and arranging their collection by ship or submarine from isolated beaches on the south coast. Many were hidden and fed by monks while they waited to escape, especially at the monastery of Préveli. In this and many other ways the German occupation closely mirrored earlier ones; opposition was constant, reprisals brutal. The north coast and the lowlands were, as in the past, easily and firmly controlled, but the mountains, and Sfakiá above all, remained the haunt of rebel and resistance groups throughout the war.

With the boats which took the battle survivors away from Crete were landed intelligence officers whose job it was to organise and arm the resistance: throughout the war there were a dozen or so on the island, living in mountain shelters or caves, attempting to organise parachute drops of arms and reporting on troop movements on and around the island.

How effective the sporadic efforts of the resistance were is hard to gauge: they had one spectacular success when in 1944 they kidnapped **General Kreipe**, the German commander, outside Iráklion, and succeeded in smuggling him across to the south coast and off the island to Egypt. Among this group were the author Patrick Leigh Fermor and Stanley Moss (whose *Ill Met by Moonlight* describes the incident in detail). The immediate result of this propaganda coup, however, was a terrible vengeance against the Cretan population, in which a string of villages around the Amári Valley were destroyed and such menfolk as could be found slaughtered. Harsh **retribution** on Cretan civilians, indeed, was the standard reaction to any success the resistance had.

At the end of 1944, the German forces withdrew to a heavily fortified perimeter around Haniá, where they held out for a final seven months before surrendering. In the rest of the island, this left a **power vacuum** which several of the resistance groups rushed to fill. Allied intelligence would no doubt claim that one of the achievements of their agents in Crete was the virtual avoidance of the Civil War which wracked the rest of Greece. On the mainland the organisation of the resistance had been very largely the work of Greek communists, who emerged at the end of the war as much the best organised and armed group. On Crete, groups in favour with the Allies had been the best armed and organised, and certainly in the latter stages of the war, communist-dominated organisations had been deliberately starved of equipment. There were only a few, minor incidents of violence on the island, and these were swiftly suppressed.

MODERN CRETE

In avoiding the Civil War, Crete was able to set about **reconstruction** some way in advance of the rest of Greece, and since 1945 it has become one of the most prosperous and productive regions of the nation. The really spectacular changes, however, date from the last twenty years, fuelled above all by a tidal wave of tourism.

Politically, post-war Crete remains a place deeply mistrustful of outside control, even from Athens. At the local level above all, loyalties are divided along clan and patronage lines rather than party political ones, and leaders are judged on how well they provide for their areas and their followers. Kostas Mitzotakis, head of the right-wing Néa Dhimokratía (ND) party and currently prime minister after a narrow election victory in 1990, is a Cretan, respected for his ability to get things done on the island even if his party is not much liked.

Cretan politicians at the local level (there is no overall island government, only a regional administration controlled by appointees from Athens) continue to take an almost universal joy in standing up to central authority. In one famous incident the mayor of Iráklion organised a sit-in at the Archaeological Museum to prevent artworks being taken abroad for an exhibition: 50,000 turned out to support him, and though President Karamanlis ordered his arrest, the national government was eventually forced to back down.

Rivalries within Crete are fierce, too, most notably between Haniá, the traditional capital, and upstart Iráklion which nowadays is richer and politically more important. This factionalism results in all sorts of anomalies and compromises: symptomatic was the thoroughly impractical decision to spread the University of Crete across three campuses, at Iráklion, Réthimnon (which has always considered itself the most cultured town in Crete) and Haniá.

In **national politics**, the island presents a more unified front as the upholder of Venizélos liberal tradition. After the overthrow of the Colonels, Crete voted heavily against a restoration of the monarchy and for a republican system; in the presidential election which followed, support for the right-winger Karamanlis was less than half as strong on Crete as it was in the rest of Greece. This has been an abiding pattern. Pasok (the socialist party) has consistently polled twice as many Cretan votes as ND, despite the local connections of the latter's leader.

Increasingly, however, the hold of the powerful old families (Mitzotakis is a member of one such long-established clan) and traditional loyalties are crumbling as their power-broking becomes less effective. The day-to-day reality of control from Athens cannot be denied even by the most fervent Cretan nationalist. It first flexed its muscles under the Colonels, when the major tourist developments were got underway, brushing aside local qualms over planning or the desirability of mass tourism. Nowadays the EC has also started to affect Crete, above all her farmers. But central power – and the increasing importance of issues over personalities – perhaps manifests itself most clearly over **NATO**.

Crete is home to numerous American and NATO bases, a couple of which are believed by local activists to store atomic weapons. The missile base on Akrotíri is the chief suspect – its missiles (you can see them test firing most Wednesdays) are certainly capable of carrying nuclear warheads. At Soúdha, as well as extensive naval installations, the US marine corps has its Mediterranean ammunition store in submarine pens. Also based on Crete is the most advanced listening station in the Mediterranean, monitoring transmissions from the Middle East. On a slightly crazier level, Crete is earmarked as a potential emergency landing site for the space shuttle. None of this is popular locally, and again the extent of it is a legacy of the Colonels: the Americans are singled out as the butt of most protests because of their part in the '67 coup and their role (or lack of one) in the Cyprus affair. Crete's all too recent past of military occupation does nothing to make the presence of foreign troops easier.

In June 1981 a massive demonstration, supported among others by Iráklion's mayor and bishop, blockaded Soúdha with people and slow-moving vehicles. Andhreas Papandhreou's Pasok, which won 60 percent of the total Cretan vote in 1985, promised that all US bases in Greece would be closed by 1988. But it didn't happen, and there seems little prospect of it happening now or in the near future: too much has been invested. Around $1000 million annually in rent and military aid is hard to give up, to say nothing of the other pressures applied. Above all is the fear that if they were thrown out, both bases and aid would simply be transferred to Turkey. But at least plans for expansion seem to have been shelved: there was to have been another base on the Méssara plain, possibly at Timbáki where the Germans had a big wartime base and where new barracks have been built but never occupied.

Meantime, Crete is currently enjoying a period of peace and prosperity unrivalled in its modern history.

MONUMENTAL CHRONOLOGY

STONE AGE 6000 BC	First inhabitants arrive from east.	Neolithic habitation of caves, and later more settled centres at Knossós and elsewhere.
PRE-PALATIAL 2600 BC	New migration brings more sophisticated culture and larger settlements: first Minoans.	Settlements especially in the south: Vasíliki, Móhlos and Mírtos among the best-known.
PROTO-PALATIAL 2000 BC	Emergence of a more formally structured society.	First palaces built at most of the famous sites.
1700 BC	Earthquake destroys the palaces.	
NEO-PALATIAL 1700 BC onwards	The Minoan Golden Age.	Great palaces at Knossós, Festós, Mália, Zakrós; thriving towns at Goúrnia, Palékastro. Most of the Minoan remains date from this era.
1450 BC	Final destruction of the palaces.	Many earlier sites reoccupied. Kydonia the island's chief city.
POST-PALATIAL	Gradual revival under Mycenaean influence.	Eteo-Cretans keep Minoan culture alive at Présos and Karfí.
1100 BC	Mycenaean control giving way to Dorian.	
DORIAN	Island divided between rival groups, gradually emerging as constantly warring city-states.	Hundreds of small towns: Láto, Falásarna, along the south coast, Knossós and, above all, Górtys.
300 BC	Cities on south coast form Confederation of Oreii.	
71 BC	Failed Roman invasion.	
69–67 BC	Romans subjugate the island.	
ROMAN		Górtys the chief Roman city. Others include Lyttos, Áptera, Knossós. Public works across the island.
325 AD	Empire split, Crete ruled from Byzantium.	
BYZANTINE		Traces of early churches at Górtys, Sóuyia, Thrónos.

824	Arab invasion.	
ARAB		Górtys sacked. El Khandak, later Iráklion, the Arab base.
961	Liberation by Nikiforas Fokas.	
BYZANTINE		Small churches throughout Crete.
1204	Fourth Crusade, Byzantium sacked, Crete sold to Venice.	
VENETIAN		Very extensive building. Early remains are mostly in the form of churches and monasteries.
1453	Fall of Constantinople, renaissance of Byzantine art on Crete.	Later works include the shape of most major towns and defences all over the island. The cities of Iráklion, Réthimnon and Haniá owe much to the Venetians; castles include Frangokástello and the fortified islets; other reminders in the shape of saltpans (eg Olóus) and deforested hillsides.
1645	Turks capture Haniá.	
1669	Iráklion surrenders.	
TURKISH		Mosques and fountains in the cities, especially Haniá and Réthimnon, but few public works undertaken in the rest of the island.
1770	Revolt of Dhaskaloyiánnis.	
1821	Greek War of Independence.	
1866	Explosion at Arkádhi.	
1897	Great Powers occupy Crete.	
1898	Independence under Prince George.	
INDEPENDENT		New government buildings at Haniá.
1905	Revolutionary Assembly at Thériso, prince abdicates.	
1908	Crete declares *Enosis*.	
1913	Union of Greece and Crete formally declared.	
1941	German invasion.	Cemeteries and war memorials.
1945	Liberation.	
1960s		Tourist boom starts.

THE DISCOVERY OF BRONZE AGE CRETE

The story of the discovery of Bronze Age Crete – dominated by two larger than life characters in Heinrich Schliemann and Arthur Evans – is almost as fascinating as that of the Minoans themselves. Long before the appearance of these two giants, however, others had taken soundings and laid the foundations for their discoveries.

Already in antiquity ancient Crete had disappeared into the mists of Greek mythology and Homeric legend, and it was only during the Venetian period that curiosity about the island's illustrious past was re-awoken. In 1422 a Florentine, **Buondelmonte**, visited Crete and reported that he had seen over 2000 columns and statues at Górtys. More monuments and inscriptions were recorded by **Honorio de Belli** in 1596. In 1675, the Dutchman **Johann Meursius**, in his book *Creta*, sifted through the classical references relating to the island.

In the eighteenth century a French explorer and botanist, **Joseph Tournefort**, described Crete in his *Voyage au Levant* of 1717; and the English navigator **Richard Pococke** also took an interest, documenting his findings in the second volume of his *Description of the East* published in 1745. But these were largely superficial observations and early in the nineteenth century it fell to another Dutchman, **Karl Hoeck** (who never actually visited the island) to write the first scholarly account of ancient Crete.

THE NINETEENTH CENTURY: TRAVELLERS AND TRADITION

A more genuinely first-hand record, and the best description of Crete's monuments and sites so far was provided by Cambridge scholar **Robert Pashley** who, in the early 1830s, travelled extensively throughout the island in what can only have been a rugged journey. Pashley allied a classical education to a keen eye and seems to have had an uncanny knack when it came to identifying ancient sites, written up in his entertaining *Travels in Crete*

(1837). A century later, Pendlebury, the eminent Cretan archaeologist, paid Pashley fulsome tribute when he credited the traveller-scholar with identifying most of the important Cretan sites, including Knossós.

It was probably as well for those who were to come after him that it never occurred to Pashley to take up the spade. That he came near to doing so is borne out by his prophetic comments on Knossós: "The mythological celebrity and historical importance of Cnossus, demand a more careful and minute attention than can be bestowed on them in a mere book of travels".

During the years 1851–3 **Captain (later Admiral) Spratt** surveyed the Cretan coastline for the British admiralty. Taking an interest in the island's archaeological remains, Spratt imperiously shipped quite a few of these back to the British Museum – often against the wishes of the local population. In an attempt to move a stone sarcophagus on board ship at Ierápetra he describes how one of his officers had to sleep in the sculptured coffin on the beach overnight " . . . to prevent it being injured wantonly or by local enemies (there were a party there who were opposed to our removal of the relic) . . . yet it did not wholly escape mischief, for some wanton hand destroyed what remained of the face of Hector".

Spratt also studied the island's natural history and geology, and it was the latter pursuit which earned him a footnote in Cretan archaeology. His work for the British navy enabled him to demonstrate that, as a result of a geological convulsion in the sixth century AD*, the whole island had been tilted upwards at its western end by as much as 26 feet while the eastern end had sunk down: something clearly visible in the marshy swamps at the eastern site of Zakrós.

THE AGE OF SCHLIEMANN

None of these early visitors to Crete, however, were concerned with pre-classical history. The discovery of the great **Bronze Age** Minoan civilisation was the almost single-handed achievement of Arthur Evans.

An important clue had been found as early as 1878. Digging at Knossós a Cretan

---

*Spratt was probably wrong about the cause, but his observations remain valid.

merchant, with the appropriate name of **Minos Kalokairinos**, had uncovered some large storage jars mixed in with Mycenaean pottery fragments – something that was to confuse later investigators. This find attracted the attention of **Heinrich Schliemann**, who had already excited world interest by his excavations of ancient **Troy** in northwest Turkey, followed by the fortresses at **Mycenae** and **Tiryns** in the Greek Peloponnese. The son of a poor German pastor who filled his son's head with the fabulous tales of Homeric Greece, Schliemann left school without completing his studies to set up in business. In the course of a highly successful commercial career in which he amassed a fortune based on military contracts in the Crimean war and participation in the California gold rush, Schliemann never lost sight of the goal that he had set himself as a boy: to prove that the world of Homer was not a mere myth as the majority of scholars then believed and to discover the fabulous places mentioned in the *Iliad* and the *Odyssey*.

When he finally embarked on this quest in his late forties, Schliemann taught himself Latin and Greek which he used to dissect his Homer before setting out for Turkey and then Greece. To the chagrin of the professional classicists, he was later to claim that it was a thorough reading of Homer which had led him to his discoveries. In fact Schliemann became so besotted with his Hellenic vision that he not only took a Greek wife but did so only after a public competition in which the celebrated archaeologist offered his hand in marriage to the first Greek girl who was able to render a faultless recitation of the entire *Iliad* from memory. Given Schliemann's luck it was inevitable that the first woman to achieve this was also an outstanding beauty and **Sofia Schliemann** became as enthusiastic as her husband in the pursuit of Greece's Bronze Age past.

Schliemann arrived in Crete in 1887, made a visit to the site at Knossós, and became convinced that a substantial palace, equivalent to those he had discovered on the mainland, lay waiting to be unearthed. But Crete was still under the subjection of Turkey and the authorities were often indolent and obstructive. In addition, when Schliemann attempted to negotiate the purchase of some land at Knossós, the Turkish owners proved impossible to deal with and finally, with his patience exhausted and his

health declining, Schliemann departed. A chill, caught after an ear operation in Naples, led to his sudden death in 1890. It was this twist of fortune which was destined to make Arthur Evans the discoverer of Knossós and Minoan Crete.

THE FIRST EXCAVATIONS

Meanwhile, others had also begun to take an interest in the island's past. During the twilight period of Turkish rule there was some relaxation of the iron grip, and the Sultan gave permission to a Cretan archaeologist, **Joseph Hadzidhakis**, to set up the **Cretan Archaeological Society**, the forerunner of the Iráklion museum. In 1884 an Italian scholar arrived in Crete, became friends with Hadzidhakis, and the two men began to search for ancient sites.

The scholar was **Federico Halbherr**, whose name was also destined to become prominent in Cretan archaeology. It was on one of their expeditions in 1885 that the **first recorded discovery of Bronze Age artefacts** was made at the **Psihró Cave** above the Lasíthi Plateau. The following year the chance unearthing of a tomb near **Festós** gave Halbherr the idea that there was probably a settlement nearby. Preliminary excavations revealed substantial buildings as well as prehistoric pottery, but the political turmoil leading up to the end of Turkish rule postponed further progress.

Another important clue to what was to come had also been found on the volcanic island of **Thíra** in the 1860s. During quarrying operations for the enormous amounts of pumice needed to make cement for the construction of the Suez canal, a buried settlement was revealed. Here whole rooms had been preserved intact, their walls covered with remarkable fresco paintings. Although it's now understood to be a colony or outpost of Minoan civilisation, this was long before any comparable Minoan remains had been discovered on Crete itself.

ARTHUR EVANS

In 1882 a meeting occurred at one of Athens' most elegant mansions which was to have an enormous importance for Cretan archaeology. The host was the famous archaeologist Heinrich Schliemann, his guest a young scholar and journalist – **Arthur Evans**. Born in 1851, the son of a wealthy and distinguished numismatist, Evans's upbringing could hardly have differed more from that of the self-made German businessman. Educated at Harrow and then Oxford, Evans was always to have the time and financial security to pursue his interests wherever they might lead him.

Schliemann was digging again at Troy and regaled his guest with the story of his excavations both there and at Mycenae. But Evans displayed more interest in Schliemann's extensive collection of ancient artefacts, particularly some **engraved seals** bearing an octopus design which he felt must be of Aegean, possibly Cretan, origin. Schliemann then announced to Evans that his next project was to be the excavation of another Mycenaean fortress at Tiryns following which he would dig at the site in Crete from where, as Homer put it in the *Iliad*, "came forth the men from Knossós". Little can he have realised the frustration of the goal that lay ahead, or that his attentive guest would himself be the recipient of this great archaeological prize.

For the time being, Evans returned to England to take up a post as keeper of the Ashmolean Museum at Oxford, although he continued to pay visits to the Balkans and Greece. Evans's studies during this period, allied to the discovery of more seal stones bearing **pre-alphabetical writing**, led him to the proposition that Crete had been an important centre of Mycenaean culture, possibly even its birthplace. When, in 1893, a great horde of **painted pottery** was discovered by Italian archaeologists at the **Kamáres Cave** on Mount Ida (Psilorítis), Evans's mind was made up: he would visit Crete to search for more seal stones and, if circumstances allowed, make a fresh attempt to carry out the excavations at Knossós which had been denied to Schliemann.

Evans arrived in Crete for the first time on March 15, 1894. Typically, in spite of an horrendously rough voyage from Pireás lasting twenty-four hours, no sooner had he set foot on the island than he records in his diary that he has toured the Candia bazaar and purchased "twenty-two early Cretan stones at about one and a half piastres apiece". Evans had started out as he meant to continue, and once the initial obstacles had been overcome the pace

was hardly to slacken over the next thirty years.

With the assistance of Joseph Hadzidhakis, now curator as well as president of the Cretan Archaeological Society, Evans began to negotiate for the purchase of the land at Knossós with its Turkish owners. He became bogged down in the same protracted wrangles that had forced Schliemann to despair. But Evans was a man who usually got what he wanted. Even so it took five years, some valiant efforts from Hadzidhakis, and a stroke of the kind of luck that some people seem to attract. In this case it was the **lifting in 1898 of the Turkish yoke** which had burdened Crete for 230 years. Evans, possessing a Liberal political outlook, had worked with Hadzidhakis to raise funds in Britain and Crete for the victims of the insurrections during this period. But finally the major obstacle to starting excavations at Knossós had been removed.

KNOSSÓS: THE EARLY YEARS

In 1899 the new government changed the law and most of the restrictions on foreign excavators were cleared away. Evans's purchase of the land at **Knossós** went through and work started on March 23, 1900. Interestingly for the future, the team that Evans assembled for the dig included an architect, **Theodore Fyfe**, from the British School at Athens. As the excavations progressed Evans soon realised that he was dealing with a site far older than the Roman, Greek or even Mycenaean periods. Then out of the earth came **frescoes**, **pottery** and what came to be known as **Linear B** tablets bearing the ancient Minoan script. On April 10 the throne room was discovered with its elegant **gypsum throne** – named at first the "throne of Ariadne" by Evans who thought it too dainty to hold the manly posterior of Minos himself – flanked by stone benches and frescoed walls.

During the first five years of the excavations, in which most of the palace was revealed, Evans made a number of innovations. In his magisterial style he named the new civilisation "**Minoan**" after the legendary Cretan king. He then went on to delineate his division of the island's Bronze Age into **Early**, **Middle** and **Late Minoan** based on pottery styles found at Knossós (see box).

EVANS'S DATING SYSTEM

Early Minoan 3000–2000 BC
Middle Minoan I & II 2000–1700 BC
Middle Minoan III + Late Minoan I & II
1700–1400 BC
Late Minoan III 1400–1100 BC

In spite of problems later encountered with this system – for example, not all contemporary sites went through the same artistic developments in similar timescales – Evans's system remains the one used by archaeologists and scholars if only because no one has yet bettered it.

RESTORATION AND CONTROVERSY

Another of Evans's early decisions was to prove far more controversial: he determined that he would not only reveal the palace of Minos but that he would also **restore** large parts of it (he insisted on the word "reconstitute") to the splendour prior to its final destruction around 1400 BC. That Evans was able autocratically to decide this rested on his personal ownership of one of the major sites of antiquity, something that would be unthinkable today. "I must have sole control of what I am personally undertaking . . . my way may not be the best but it is the only way I can work," he said revealingly about this decision in a letter to his father.

What Evans had now embarked upon was one of the most expensive enterprises in the history of archaeology, and in the early years funds were often stretched. But fortunately or otherwise for Knossós – depending on your viewpoint – two large legacies fell into Evans's lap eight years into the mammoth task, as a result of the deaths of both his father and his uncle (John Dickinson the paper millionaire) within months of each other in 1908. Evans's plans for Knossós, destined to last for a further 23 years, were now financially secure.

With the assistance of Theodore Fyfe and later **Piet de Jong**, the architects, Evans first roofed the throne room and then reconstructed the **grand staircase**, replacing the **tapered columns** with his imaginary reconstructions (none of the wooden originals was ever found). Two French artists then began to repaint the reconstructed walls with **copies of the**

frescoes now in the museum. In 1930 the almost entirely conjectural upper storey (or **Piano Nobile** as Evans termed it) was added using reinforced concrete. Next the **Central Court** was completely restored as the archaeological site became a building site. Evans attempted to deflect criticism of his methods as he imposed his own grand design on the work of architects and artists by saying that he wanted to recreate the "spirit" of the Palace structure and decor rather than create a literal reconstruction. This was where many scholars parted company with him. Pendlebury, who was to be Evans's successor at Knossós (see over), put aside earlier reservations and defended Evans in a guidebook to the site stating that "without restoration the Palace would be a meaningless heap of ruins". Others furiously disagreed and the debate is no less heated today. One thing, however, is certain: no professional archaeologist would be allowed or would expect to carry out such a work again.

In his views on Minoan scholarship Evans could be equally autocratic and blinkered. When **Alan Wace**, director of the British School at Athens, excavated a number of tombs on the site of Mycenae in the Greek Peloponnese in the early 1920s, his findings led him to conclude that Mycenae had not only been a culture independent from that of Crete – Evans stated that it had been a colony of Crete ruled by Cretan overlords – but that in the later period Mycenaeans had been in control at Knossós. For Evans this was heresy and he used his considerable influence to attack Wace, get him sacked, and stop him carrying out any further work at Mycenae. Evans went to his grave believing he was right, but in the light of the decipherment of Linear B and later investigation, it is Wace's views that are generally accepted today.

THE END OF AN ERA

During the long periods that Evans spent working at Knossós he lived in some style at the villa he had constructed for himself overlooking the palace site. The **Villa Ariadne**, as he typically named it, became the focus of scholarly life of a slightly stuffy, Victorian kind. Evans revelled in the stream of distinguished visitors to Knossós – who were met at the harbour by his chauffeur-driven limousine – and the house's servants would ply them with French champagne following a guided tour of the site. His relationship with the Greeks, not to say the native Cretans, seems to have been scratchy by comparison. A crusty, aloof man by nature, he seems never to have been able to relax with them and certainly would never be seen around a table at the *kafenío*, as Pendlebury later was. Evans's lack of fluency in modern Greek – in spite of the time he spent on the island – was also taken by many as a sign of his disdain for the degenerate latterday occupants of such ancient lands.

In 1924 Evans donated the Knossós site and the Villa Ariadne to the British School at Athens – it was only in 1952 that the site was to become the property of the Greek government – and in the early Thirties, approaching his eightieth year, he handed over the reins at Knossós to a young English archaeologist, **John Pendlebury**, and retired to his home near Oxford to complete the final volumes of his monumental work *The Palace of Minos*. It was the end of an era. Sir Arthur Evans (as he was now titled) paid his last visit to the site with which his name remains inextricably linked in 1935, when he attended the festivities surrounding the unveiling of his **bronze bust** in the palace grounds. He died six years later, in 1941.

CONTEMPORARIES AND SUCCESSORS

Although Evans stole the headlines for forty years, much important work was meanwhile being carried out elsewhere. Above all, Federico Halbherr was excavating **Festós** and later **Ayía Triádha.** In the same year that Evans began digging at Knossós, 1900, Halbherr started work on the beautifully situated palace at Festós. He soon acquired legendary status among the country people, thanks to his custom of riding around on a coal-black Arab mare. The bulk of the palace – including a dramatic **staircase** – was laid bare in three seasons of work. Although some restoration was done on the site, it was nothing resembling Evans's efforts at Knossós – in fact Halbherr and his colleagues pursued a far more **rigorously scientific excavation**: the first carried out on Crete. The Italian School has continued its work both at Festós and Ayía Triádha throughout the century.

In the east **British teams** worked at **Zakrós** (where Hogarth narrowly failed to uncover the palace) and the Minoan settlements at **Paleókastro** and **Présos**. An English archaeologist who made a great impression in this period was **John Pendlebury**. A man with great affection both for Crete and the Cretans, he covered vast tracts of the island on foot in his search for evidence of ancient sites. He found countless numbers of these and made many friends along the way. Besides his work at Knossós he also excavated the late Minoan refuge at **Karfí** above the Lasíthi Plateau. Pendlebury was killed in the early years of World War II, fighting alongside the Cretans during the German attack on Iráklion in 1941. Work by the British School has continued at Knossós as well as more remote sites such as the Minoan settlements at **Mírtos Pírgos** and **Mírtos Foúrnou Korifí**.

The **Americans** were also active in eastern Crete from the earliest days of exploration. A woman – in a field dominated by men – staked out her claim at **Goúrnia** on the Gulf of Mirabéllo. **Harriet Boyd** (later Mrs Boyd-Hawes), a young classics scholar from Massachusetts, visited Athens in 1900 and was gripped by the excitement surrounding the archaeological excavations then getting under way. She visited Crete, received the almost obligatory encouragement from Evans, and the following year set off by donkey for the east with her foreman, the Zorba-like Aristides, and his mother, her constant companions. After a number of false starts she alighted on Goúrnia and to her own, and the world's, surprise there uncovered the **workers' village**. The telegram she sent to the American Exploration Society, after three days' digging, says it all: "Discovered Goúrnia Mycenaean site, streets, houses, pottery, bronzes, stone jars". It was, of course, a Minoan site, but the archaeologists were still feeling their way back into a much more ancient past than anyone then realised.

Another skilled American archaeologist working in the east was **Richard Seager**. In the early 1900s he excavated the important early Minoan settlement at **Vasilikí**, with its famous pottery, before moving on to the islands of **Psíra** and then **Móhlos** where substantial settlements were found. Seager was a good friend of Evans, who attended the funeral following Seager's sudden death at Iráklion in

1925. "He was the most English American I have ever known" was Evans's quintessential epitaph. The north American contribution continues at Móhlos as well as at **Kómmos**, where Joseph Shaw is excavating the impressive Minoan port to the north of Mátala.

The **French** have also contributed some excellent work at **Mália**. After initial investigations by Joseph Hadzidhakis during the years of World War I from 1915 on, the French School at Athens were awarded the site in 1922. Having excavated the **Minoan palace** they are now at work on unearthing the extensive settlement which surrounded it.

RECENT DEVELOPMENTS: ZAKRÓS

The discovery of ancient Crete has continued steadily throughout this century – barring wartime interruptions – if not always as spectacularly as it began. The outstanding exception was **Nikolaos Platon's** excavations at **Zakrós** which, from 1962 onwards, finally revealed the palace long suspected to have been there. Sixty years earlier Hogarth had missed the palace by a few yards, and in one of his treks around eastern Crete in 1938 the voracious Pendlebury, accompanied by his archaeologist wife Hilda, had combed the area. "We must have been sitting on the very site – and we saw nothing" said Hilda Pendlebury later. Fittingly, one of Crete's greatest archaeological prizes of all fell to a Greek.

Prior to Hogarth and Pendlebury, Zakrós had also been visited by Captain Spratt in 1852, as well as Halbherr, and Evans himself. **Hogarth** did expose parts of the surrounding settlement, with houses containing rich pottery, clay seals and bronze tools. The site then lay dormant until after World War II. Nikolaos Platon became convinced that because of the submerged but excellent harbour – in a prime position for trade with the Near East – there had to be a palace here. With funds from the Greek Archaeological Society and two wealthy American backers, he started work in 1962 where Hogarth had left off. The **unlooted palace**, never reoccupied after its destruction by fire around 1450 BC, was now revealed, together with a rich yield of artefacts, including over 3000 vases. Platon continues to supervise the excavations at Zakrós which in recent years have uncovered much of the town surrounding the palace.

In the recent work, Greek and Cretan archaeologists have finally been able to play a more equal role than in the early days, when foreign archaeological teams often treated them with patronising high-handedness. Some, like Hadzidhakis and Marinatos, were there from the start but unable to compete with the wealthy foreigners in what was very much a private enterprise affair. Now, with mainly academic funding, Greek archaeologists such as **Yannis and Efi Sakellarakis** (at Arhánes and Anemóspilia), **Davaras** (Móhlos and Psíra), **Tzedakis** (Arméni) and **Papadakis** (Koufonísi) are contributing greatly to the island's archaeological discoveries. These continue to be added to as each season passes and although it is unlikely that another Knossós will come to light there are indications – such as those in the work continuing at **Haniá** – that many more sites, particularly in the west, lie awaiting the spade.

A once neglected area of Cretan archaeology – the post-Bronze Age, Dorian and Roman – is also now being given more attention than ever before at sites across the island. These Minoan and post-Minoan sites today stand as a tribute not only to the dedicated archaeologists who discovered and exposed them, but also to the work of the nameless thousands of Cretans who laboured with spade, trowel and barrow to uncover the past of their illustrious island ancestors.

Geoff Garvey

WILDLIFE

Although the south coast of Crete is closer to Libya than it is to Athens, the island's wildlife owes much more to mainland Greece than it does to Africa. This is because Crete lies at the end of the long range of drowned limestone mountains which make up most of the Balkan peninsula: the range peters out in Libya and Egypt, and you need to go a long way south into the Sahara before you again find mountains as high as the Cretan ones. Crete, then, has typically northern Mediterranean fauna and flora.

Islands tend to be short on wildlife because of their isolation from the main bulk of species on the mainland. Not so Crete – it's big in all three dimensions, and provides the full range of Mediterranean habitats. In fact, there are over 2000 species of **plants** in Crete, nearly a third of the Greek flora, and about as many as in the whole of Britain; richer partly because it went relatively unscathed through the Ice Ages, and partly because botanical variety tends to increase the nearer you go to the equator. With the wealth of plant life come far more **insects** than you get further north. The survival of Cretan wildlife has also been helped by the fact that agriculture remains fairly "undeveloped" – much of the land is steep and rocky with only a thin capping of soil, and you'll see modern intensive agriculture only on the lowland plains. You won't find many birds or wild flowers amongst the hectares of plytunnels around Timbáki, but you will in the mountains where such methods remain uneconomic.

The only feature really lacking, as elsewhere in Greece, is **trees**. The Minoan civilisation was a seafaring one, so as early as the Bronze Age there was a high demand for timber for shipbuilding. Some of the lower hills were perhaps cut down 4000 years ago, a deforestation process completed by the Venetians. Today, native forests exist only in remote uplands and gorges.

Crete's chief drawback, at least if you hope to combine nature with the rest of the island's sights and life, is the pattern of its **climate**. Because it's so far south, the summers are long and dry, and that period equates to our northern winters, when many plants shut down or die, with a corresponding decline in activity from all other wildlife. Trying to see wild flowers or birds in lowland Crete in August is a bit like going out for a nature ramble in Britain in January. For flowers, the best time to go is March: the season continues through to late June in the mountains, while around the coasts many plants keep flowering right through the winter.

MAJOR HABITATS

Rarely in Europe do you find such a wide range of habitats so tightly packed, or real "wilderness" areas so close to modern towns and resorts, as in Crete. Broadly speaking, you can divide the island into four major **habitats** : the coast; cultivated land; low hillsides less than 1000m; and mountains above 1000m. Crete is the only Greek island which is mountainous enough to have all four of these habitats.

Along **the coast** sandy beaches and low rocky cliffs are the norm. Marshy river deltas or estuaries are rare (simply because Crete is a dry country and there aren't too many rivers) but where you can find them, these wetland habitats are among the best places to look for birds.

Cultivated land is very variable in its wildlife interest. Huge wheatfields, or huge olive groves for that matter, have little to offer, but where the pattern is smaller in scale and more varied, it can be very good. This is especially true of the small market gardens – *perivólio* – often found on the edge of towns and villages, which are particularly good for small birds. Small hayfields can be a colourful mass of annual flowers, and attendant insects, in spring and early summer.

Low hillsides to 1000 metres includes much of Crete. Scrubby hillsides, loosely grazed by goats and sometimes sheep, are the most typical Mediterranean habitat, extremely rich in flowers, insects and reptiles. Botanically, they divide into two distinct types: the first is *phrígana*, the Greek word for the French *garigue*, and consists of scattered scrubby bushes, always on limestone, especially rich in aromatic herbs and wild flowers. You can often find *phrígana* by looking for beehives: Cretan beekeepers know where to find the thyme and rosemary that gives the local honey its wonderful flavour. The other hillside habitat is *maquis*, a dense, very prickly scrub with scattered trees. Of these two hillside habitats, *phrígana* is better for flowers, *maquis* for birds.

Mountains over 1000 metres are surprisingly common: three separate ranges go over 2000m, and they are responsible for much of the climate, creating rain and retaining it as snow for a large part of the year. The small upland plateaux amongst the mountains – Omalós or Lasíthi most famously – are a very special feature, with their own distinctive flora and fauna. Although the Cretan mountains don't, by and large, have the exciting mammals of the mainland, they are very good for large and spectacular birds of prey.

FLOWERS

What you will see, obviously, depends on where and when you go. The best time is **spring**, which generally starts in mid-February in the southeast corner of the island, is at its peak during March over most of the lowlands (but continues well into April), and in the mountains comes later, starting in late April and going on through to June. In **early summer**, the spring anemones, orchids and rockroses are replaced by plants like brooms and chrysanthemums; this ranges from mid-April in southern Crete to late July in the high mountains. These timings vary from year to year, too, exceptionally by as much as a month – in early April 1986 it was too hot to lie on the beach at Yeoryióupoli at midday, but at the same time in 1987 there was snow on the beach at Réthimnon, just 30km away.

Things are pretty much burnt out over all the lowlands from July through to the end of September, though there are still some flowers in the mountains. Once the hot summer is over,

blooming starts all over again. Some of the **autumn** flowering species, such as cyclamens and autumn crocus, flower from October in the mountains into December in the south. And by then you might as well stay on for the first of the spring bulbs in January.

Year-round, the best insurance policy is to be prepared to move up and down the hills until you find flowers – from the beginning of March to the end of June you are almost guaranteed to find the classic displays of flowers somewhere on the island, and you'll see the less spectacular but still worthwhile displays of autumn flowering species from October to early December. If you have to go in July, August or September, then be prepared to see a restricted range, and also to go high up the mountains.

The four habitats all have their own flowers, though some, of course, overlap.

On **the coast** you might find the spectacular **yellow horned poppy** growing on shingled banks, and **sea stocks** and **Virginia stocks** growing amongst the rocks behind the beach. A small pink **campion**, *Silene colorata* is often colourfully present. Sand dunes are rare but sometimes there is a flat grazed area behind the beach; these are often good for **orchids**. **Tamarisk trees** often grow down to the shore, and there are frequent groves of Europe's largest grass, the **giant reed**, which can reach 4m high. In the autumn, look for the very large white flowers of the **sea daffodil**, as well as **autumn crocuses** on the banks behind the shore. The **sea squill** also blooms in autumn, with very tall spikes of white flowers rising from huge bulbs.

On **cultivated land** avoid large fields and plantations, but look for small hay meadows. These are often brilliant with annual "weeds" in late spring – various **crysanthemum** species, **wild gladiolus**, **blue and purple vetches**, and in general a mass of colour such as you rarely see in northern Europe. This is partly because herbicides are used less, but mostly because the hot summers force plants into flowering at the same time.

The trees and shrubs on **low hillsides** are varied and beautiful, with colourful brooms flowering in early summer, preceded by bushy **rockroses** – *Cistaceae* – which are a mass of pink or white flowers in spring. Dotted amongst the shrubs is the occasional tree; the **Judas**

tree flowers on bare wood in spring, making a blaze of pink against green hillsides which stands out for miles. Lower than the shrubs are the **aromatic herbs** – sage, rosemary, thyme and lavender – with perhaps some spiny species of **Euphorbia**. My favourite of these is *Euphorbia acanthothamnos*, a rock-hugging species which forms low humps with small green leaves and delicate golden flowers. Because Crete is dry and hot for much of the year, you also get a high proportion of **xerophytes** – plants that are adapted to drought by having fleshy leaves and thick skins.

Below the herbs is the ground layer; peer around the edges and between the shrubs and you'll find a wealth of **orchids**, **anemones**, **grape hyacinths**, **irises**, and perhaps **fritillaries** if you are lucky. The orchids are extraordinary; some kinds – the *Ophrys* species – have especially fascinating and unusual flowers. Each *Ophrys* species is pollinated by a particular insect species, which they attract by sight and smell: sight by having a flower which imitates the female insect and so deludes the male into "mating" with it; smell by imitating the particular sex pheromone which the insect uses. They're much smaller and altogether more dignified than the big blowsy tropical orchids you see in florists' shops. But beware of orchids – they are addictive, and you can easily become an orchid freak and spend your entire holiday face down on a hillside, to the extreme boredom of your non-botanical friends!

I like the **irises** too; one of them, a small blue species called *Iris sisyrinchium*, only flowers in the afternoon, and you can actually sit and watch them open at around midday. Once spring is over, these plants give way to the early summer flowering of the brooms and aromatic herbs, as well as a final fling from the annuals which sense the coming of the heat and their own death. When the heat of the summer is over, the autumn bulbs appear, with species of **crocus** and their relatives, the **colchicums** and the **sternbergias**, and finally the **autumn cyclamens** through into early December.

Mountains are good to visit later in the year. The rocky mountain gorges are the home of many familiar garden rock plants, such as the **aubretias**, **saxifrages** and **alyssums**, as well as **dwarf bellflowers** and **anemones**. Look for dwarf **tulips** in fields on the upland plateaux in spring. The mountains are also the

place to see the remaining Greek native **pine forests**, and in the woodland glades you will find **gentians**, **cyclamens**, and **violets**. Above 1500m or so the forests begin to thin out, and in these upland meadows glorious **crocuses** flower almost before the snow has melted in spring – a very fine form of *Crocus seiberi* is a particularly early one. Autumn flowering species of crocus and cyclamen should reward a visit later in the year.

BIRDS

There are less speciality **bird species** in Crete than there are flowers, because birds can move around. However, Greece has a good range of the resident Mediterranean species, plus one or two very rare ones such as the **Ruppell's Warbler** or the **Lammergeier vulture**, which have their European breeding strongholds in Greece. The great thing about birdwatching in Crete is that, if you pick your time right, you can see both resident and migratory species. Crete is on one of the main flypast routes for species that have wintered in East Africa, but breed in northern Europe. They migrate every spring up the Nile valley, and then move across the eastern Med, often in huge numbers. This happens from mid-March to mid-May, depending on the species, the weather, and where you are. The return migration in autumn is less spectacular because it is less concentrated, but still worth watching out for.

One drawback is that until recently the "sport" of shooting songbirds was common, and although things have improved, the birds remain understandably cautious. Some are still caught for the cagebird trade, as you will realise from looking at the goldfinches and others hung in cages from the front of houses and flats. Birds of prey get a rough deal, too, as witness the dusty cases of badly stuffed eagles in many tavernas and *kafenía*.

A general point about watching birds is that they're active at a pretty antisocial time – just after dawn is the peak activity time for most small birds. A walk before breakfast can produce heaps of birds, yet you can walk the same area a few hours later and see almost nothing. Exceptions to this are water birds and wading birds, which are often visible all day, and big birds of prey, which frequently use the rising thermals of early evening to soar and gain height.

On the **outskirts of towns** and in the **fields** there are some colourful residents. Small predatory birds such as **woodchat shrikes**, **kestrels** and migrating **red-footed falcons** can be seen perched on telegraph wires, and **lesser kestrels** nest communally and noisily in many small towns and villages. The dramatic pink, black and white **hoopoe** and the striking yellow and black **golden oriole** are sometimes to be found in woodland and olive groves, and **Scops owls** (Europe's smallest owl) can often be heard calling around towns at night. They monotonously repeat a single "poo", sometimes in mournful vocal duets.

Look closely at the **swifts** and **swallows**, and you will find a few species not found in northern Europe; **crag martins** replace house martins in the **mountain gorges**, for example, and you may see the large **alpine swift**, which has a white belly. The **Sardinian warbler** dominates the rough scrubby **hillsides** – the male with a glossy black cap and an obvious red eye. These hillsides are also the home of the **chukar**, a species of partridge similar to the red-legged partridge found in Britain.

Wetlands and coastal lagoons are excellent for bird spotting, especially at spring and autumn migration, although this habitat is hard to find. There's a wide variety of **herons** and **egrets**, as well as smaller waders such as the **avocet** and the **black-winged stilt**, which has ridiculously long pink legs. **Marsh harriers** are common too, drifting over the reedbeds on characteristic raised wings. Scrubby woodland around coastal wetlands is a good place to see migrating smaller birds such as **warblers**, **wagtails** and the like. They usually migrate up the coast, navigating by the stars; a thick mist or heavy cloud will force them to land, and you can sometimes see spectacular "falls" of migrants.

The **mountains** hold some of the most exciting birds in Crete. Smaller birds like **blue rock thrush**, **alpine chough** and **rock nuthatch** are pretty common, and there is a good chance of seeing large and dramatic birds of prey. The **buzzards** and smaller **eagles** are confusingly similar, but there are also **golden eagles** and **vultures**. One very rare species of vulture, the **Lammergeier**, is more common in Crete than anywhere else in Europe and you may be lucky and see it soaring above the

Lasíthi or Omalós plateaux. It's a huge bird, with a wingspan of nearly 3m, and with narrower wings and a longer wedge-shaped tail than the other vulture you are likely to see, the **Griffon vulture**.

MAMMALS

Cretan mammals are like most others – elusive, generally nocturnal, and very hard to see. Islands tend to have less mammal species than the mainland, because mammals can't swim or fly to get there, and in this Crete is no exception, with about half the species that you could expect to see on mainland Greece. Even such common animals as red squirrel and fox have never made it across the water, nor will you find large exciting mammals like wolves or lynxes in the mountains, as you might (although very rarely) on the mainland.

However, there are some compensations. Islands often have their own endemic species, and the one in Crete is the **Cretan spiny mouse**, which is found nowhere else. So if you happen to be on a rocky hillside at dusk and you see a largish mouse with very big ears and a spiny back fossicking around – then you might have seen it! The other compensation in Crete is the ancestral **wild goat** or *Kri-Kri*, a small population still exists in the White Mountains around the Samarian gorge, and also on some offshore islands – but you'll be very lucky if you see one outside the zoos. Apart from those, Crete has quite a few **bat** species, as well as **weasels**, **badgers**, **hares** and **beech martens**.

REPTILES AND AMPHIBIANS

The hot, rocky terrain of Crete suits reptiles well, with plenty of sun to bask in and plenty of rocks to hide under, but the island's isolation has severely restricted the number of species occurring: less than a third of those that are found on the mainland. Identification is therefore rather easy. If you sit and watch a dry stone wall almost anywhere you're bound to see the small local wall lizard, **Erhard's wall lizard**. A rustle in the rocks by the side of the road might be an **ocellated skink** – a bit like a lizard, but with a thicker body and a stubbier neck. In the bushes of the *maquis* and *phrígana* you may see the **Balkan green lizard**, a truly splendid bright green animal up to half a metre long, most of which is tail; usually seen as it runs like the clappers on its hind legs from one bush to another!

At night, **geckoes** replace the lizards. Geckoes are small (less than 10cms), have big eyes and round adhesive pads on their toes which enable them to walk upside down on the ceiling. Sometimes they come into houses – in which case welcome them, for they will keep down the mosquitoes and other biting insects. Crete has three out of four European species. The island is also one of only a handful of places where the **chameleon** occurs in Europe, although it is nowhere common. It lives in bushes and low trees, and hunts by day; colour is greenish but variable, for obvious reasons.

Tortoises, sadly, don't occur in Crete, but the stripe-necked **terrapin** does. Look out for these in any freshwater habitat – Lake Kóurnas for example. There are also **sea turtles** in the Med: you might be lucky and see one while you're swimming or on a boat, since they sometimes bask on the surface of the water. The one you're most likely to see is the **loggerhead turtle**, which can grow up to a metre long.

The final group of reptiles are the snakes, represented by four species, only one of which is poisonous – the **cat snake**: even this is back fanged and therefore extremely unlikely to be able to bite anything as big as a human. So you can relax a bit when strolling round the hillsides – though most snakes are very timid and easily frightened anyway. One species worth looking out for is the beautiful **leopard snake**, which is grey with red blotches edged in black. It's fond of basking on the sides of roads and paths.

Only three species of amphibian occur in Crete. The **green toad** is smaller than the common toad, with an obvious marbled green and grey back. The **marsh frog** is a large frog, greenish but variable in colour, and very noisy in spring. And **tree frogs** are small, live in trees, and call very loudly at night. They have a stripe down the flank, and vary in colour from bright green to golden brown, depending on where they are sitting – they can change colour like a chameleon.

INSECTS

Insects are a much-neglected group of animals, which is a shame because many of them are beautiful, most lead fascinating lives, and they are numerous and easy to observe. You need to adjust your eyes to their scale to see them best: sit down for half an hour in the countryside by a bit of grazed turf, a patch of long grass, or a shrubby bush, and think small. You'll be surprised at the variety of shapes and colours of insects that will slowly come into focus.

There are around a million different species of insects in the world, and even in Crete there are probably a few hundred which have yet to be scientifically described or labelled. About a third of all insect species are **beetles**, and these are very obvious wherever you go. You might see one of the **dung beetles** rolling a ball of dung along a path like the mythological Sisyphus, and I watched a **rhinoceros-horned beetle** digging a hole in a Cretan sand dune for hours – every time the hole was complete it collapsed, and the beetle had to start all over again.

If you have time to look closely at bushes and small trees, you might be rewarded with a **stick insect** or a **praying mantis**, creatures that are rarely seen because of their excellent camouflage.

The **grasshopper** and **cricket** family are well represented, and most patches of grass will hold a few. Grasshoppers produce their chirping noise by rubbing a wing against a leg, but crickets do it by rubbing both wings together. **Cicadas**, which most people think of as a night-calling grasshopper, aren't actually related at all – they're more of a large leaf hopper. Their continuous whirring call is one of the characteristic sounds of the Mediterranean night, and is produced by the rapid vibration of two cavities, called tymbals, on either side of the body.

Perhaps the most obvious insects are the **butterflies**, because they're large, brightly coloured, and fly by day. Any time from spring through most of summer is good for butterflies, and there's a second flight of adults of many species in the autumn. Dramatic varieties in Crete include two species of **swallowtail**, easily told by their large size, yellow and black colouring, and long spurs at the back of the hind wings. **Cleopatras** are large, brilliant yellow butterflies, related to the brimstone of northern Europe, but bigger and more colourful. Look out for **green hairstreaks** – a small green jewel of a butterfly that is particularly attracted to the flowers of the asphodel, a widespread plant of overgrazed pastures and hillsides. One final species typical of Crete is the **southern festoon** – an unusual butterfly with tropical colours, covered in yellow, red and black zig-zags. It flies in the spring, its caterpillars feeding on *Aristolochia* (birthwort) plants.

SITES

You don't need to go that far to see Cretan wildlife – even in Iráklion, patches of waste-land hold interesting and colourful flowers, and nearby Knossós is good for flowers, insects and reptiles. In general, though, people and wildlife don't go together too well, so it's best to get away from the towns and into the villages.

The places described in the following pages are a very personal selection. I've mostly been to them in spring; but in general, a good site is a good site at any time of the year, except in high summer when everything is burnt out anyway. It's also usually true that a good flower site will yield plenty of other wildlife, and vice versa: a wide variety of plants leads to a wide variety of insects, which in turn implies that birds and reptiles will be numerous. So you can often use a blaze of plants as an indicator for a spot that would be worth exploring.

One possible exception to this is birds. Birds are mobile and fickle, often choosing to congregate in unprepossessing places such as windswept estuaries or smelly sewage farms. Birds adapt well to small scale agriculture, too, even though the native plants may have been outcompeted by olives, artichokes or melons.

Any information on alternative or better sites would be more than welcome.

LASÍTHI

The **eastern end** of Crete is the driest part, and also the part where spring comes first. So it would be good to base yourself here if you were planning a trip **early in the year**, say February. The extreme eastern coast is dry and rocky, although Vaí boasts a much photographed grove of the Cretan date palm – one of only two native European palm species. Further west, the scenery is dominated by the Dhíkti mountains and the big bay of Áyios Nikólaos: even close by the development here, some good sites for flowers and birds survive.

The nearest of these is **Láto**, overlooking plains of olives and fruit trees that run down to the sea. It's a mass of colour with flowers in the spring, and, in common with other ancient sites, its old walls and ruins are a perfect habitat for lizards. **Mália**, similarly, has good flowers in spring and early summer, and the added advantage of being close to seacliffs where you can find many of the typical Mediterranean seashore flowers. Between the ancient site and the shore are the remains of a marsh, which is likely to hold interesting birds including herons, harriers, and migrating small warblers. **Goúrnia** is also worth a trip for its flowers: they're particularly good at all of these sites because goats are excluded. Look for anemones in the spring. Although there's only one spring species, *Anemone coronaria*, it comes in a bewildering range of colours from white to purple and scarlet. An asiatic buttercup species which grows round here (*Ranunculus asiaticus*, a common plant over much of Crete) is quite unlike the buttercups of northern Europe, being much larger and with colours including white, pink and yellow. Around the walls of Goúrnia you'll also find a large yellow and white daisy, *Chrysanthemum coronarium*, a species which is attractive to butterflies.

Just north of Áyios Nikólaos is the island of **Spinalónga**, and nearby, the disused saltpans at **Eloúnda**. The island is good for flowers, and the saltpans are always worth checking out for birds, especially during spring and autumn migration time.

Later in the year, the uplands of **Mount Dhíkti** and the **Lasíthi plateau** come into their own. The plateau is at 850m, so its spring flowers come later than those in the lowlands – April or early May would be a good time, with the summer flowers going on into June. The plateau itself is well cultivated, but the areas round the edge are rich in flowers including many orchids. Try exploring a bit off the well worn track from Psihró to the Dhiktean cave. Here you may find two varieties in particular: *Ophrys tenthredenifera*, one of the largest and most dramatic of the insect-imitating orchids, with beautiful pink sepals and a brown lower lip fringed with pale yellow; and the butterfly orchid *Orchis papilionacea*, which has a compact spike of pink florets, each with a large lip spotted and streaked with darker pink. Keep your eyes on the skies, too, since you are close to the mountains: sightings of eagles and vultures, including Lammergeiers, are always possible.

Mount Dhíkti goes up to over 2000m, and boasts most of the dramatic flowers of the Cretan mountains. Look for early flowering crocus species on the edge of the melting snowfields in April and May, and maybe you'll find cyclamens and paeonies under the mountain woodland as well. Rocky gullies amongst the mountains are rich in specially adapted plants called chasmophytes, including endemic Cretan species.

IRÁKLION

Although Iráklion is the only one of the four Cretan provinces that doesn't have a major mountain range, it includes the foothills of both the Dhíkti range to the east and the Psilorítis massif in the west.

The ancient Minoan site of **Festós** is an excellent start. The ruins are only average for wildlife, but the hills around are excellent for flowers, insects, and reptiles, and the river running through Ayía Triádha is always worth checking out for birds. The site of Festós itself is also a good place to look for bird migration; since it's high up, you stand a good chance of seeing migrating birds of prey coming over the plain and up into the hills.

If you walk from the car park heading north, you find yourself on a lovely hillside. There are scrubby bushes of rockroses – *Cistus* species – and round these a wonderful display of anemones, irises, orchids and the whole panoply of Cretan spring flowers. *Anemone heldreichii*, a delicate blue and white variety, is one of Crete's 130 or so endemic species. Another plant with a very restricted distribution is *Ophrys cretica*, one of the insect-imitating orchids with distinctive white markings on its maroon lip. In spring, *Orchis italica* is the most obvious orchid – tall shaggy spikes of small pink florets, each looking like a small man with a cap. I say "man" advisedly, as you will realise if you look closely at the plant! One final flower to look out for is familiar as an annual garden flower, love-in-a-mist *Nigella arvensis*. With blooms varying from deep blue to pale pink, it's best known for its extraordinary inflated fruit, surrounded by a crown of deeply dissected bracts.

There are butterflies here too, attracted by the nectar. Scarce swallowtail was much in evidence when I was there, and many others. Keep your eyes open, too, for Balkan green lizards in the bushes. Further on towards Ayía Triádha the river holds passage migrants including herons, terns and sandpipers – and the bushes are often full of migrating passerines, hotfoot, from Africa. As always, a careful scrutiny of bushes and grasses will produce a horde of beetles, spiders and other invertebrates – with a chance of a praying mantis to brighten things up.

RÉTHIMNON

The two areas selected in this province are both on the south coast. That doesn't mean that you should ignore the rest: three other extremely promising sites are the Nídha plateau above Anóyia, the foothills of Mount Kédhros, above Spíli, and the Amári Valley.

Ayía Galíni, for all its summer crowds, is a great spot in spring, with some excellent walks on the headlands and hills roundabout, small scale hayfields and olive groves, and a river bed with some marshy areas. In other words, a really good range of the typical Cretan lowland habitats, and all within easy walking distance.

The river flows in to the east of the village. On the far side is a range of hills, worth exploring for spring flowers, and the caves and cliffs overlooking the river have breeding colonies of lesser kestrels and Alpine swifts. The small reedbeds and marshy areas around the river have warblers and nightingales, too, and there are hoopoes in the olive groves.

A series of tracks lead away to the north and along the cliffs to the west. Any of these go through typical *phrígana* habitat, in which are scattered small meadows with wild gladioli and tassel hyacinths. The latter species is related to the grape hyacinth which is often used in boring clumps by British gardeners, but is far more attractive growing wild. Look for Jerusalem sage *Phlomis fruticosa*, a downy shrub whose golden flowers are attractive to bees. Another plant that grows around here (and many other places in Crete) is the unmistakable giant fennel, a huge plant over two metres tall. Its scientific name is *Ferula communis*, which implies to me that it was once used as a walking stick, and, seeing the size of the stems, you can see why. There are orchids growing on the hillsides, including a Cretan speciality that rejoices in the name of *Ophrys fuciflora maxima*; a large orchid, it has a "face" on its lower lip that looks exactly like a Minoan bull. But maybe I have an overactive imagination.

Further along the coast to the west, **Moní Préveli** has a similar range of habitats and less people. Again, there is a river valley that repays exploration for migratory birds, open hillsides with all the flowers and aromatic herbs, and some rugged coastal scenery. If you see a small scrub warbler around here with a black cap and throat, a red eye, and a white "moustache" then you may have seen Ruppell's warbler, probably the rarest warbler in Europe. The whole coastline from Préveli to Ayía Rouméli, some 75kms to the west, is wild and rugged, punctuated by gorges, and a good place to look for large eagles and vultures.

HANIÁ

The western end of Crete contains some of the wildest and least developed scenery in the whole of the Med. I've chosen Yeoryióupoli on the north coast and the famous Samariá gorge to describe in detail – but there are lots of other opportunities.

Yeoryióupoli has a wide range of habitats within easy reach – a marsh, a river with reedbeds, dry hillsides along the coast to the north, Crete's only freshwater lake – and an excellent beach as well. Between the main road and the sea are low sand dunes, often a good place for colourful flowers like Virginia stocks, sea stocks, and the yellow horned poppy. Close to the east of the village is a marshy area, with birds like reed (and other) warblers, and marsh harriers floating overhead. There's a very pleasant walk along the Almirós river, branching up through olive groves and scrubby slopes to the hilltop village above. Here you'll find numerous small birds, attracted by unusually dense and lush woodland. Inland a bit is the small lake at **Koúrnas**; a solitary Squacco heron was the only bird I saw when I was there, but a paddle round the lake revealed loads of stripe-necked terrapins poking their heads out of the water.

The **Samarian gorge** is rightly famous for wildlife as well as scenery, but remember that you'll find very similar flora and fauna at Imbrós and the other less known ravines. The best flowers and other wildlife all come in the higher reaches, where you have the marvellous combination of rocky cliffs coming down into upland woods.

Still better, if you have time, is to take more than a day over this trip and spend some time on the **Omalós plateau** before heading down. This is especially rewarding later in the year, when the plateau and the slopes around it will have spring and summer flowers long after all is burnt out on the coast. The plateau is renowned for its mountain flowers, including the very variable *Tulipa saxatalis*, a small pink or purple tulip endemic to Crete. Other endemic species found here include Cretan dittany *Origanum dictamnus*, a low shrub with furry rounded leaves and pink flowers, regarded by locals as a medical panacea (you may be offered it as a tea) and *Daphne sericea*, an evergreen shrub, with very unusual two-tone flowers of pink and yellow. There are also rare birds and mammals – watch the sky for golden eagles, griffon vultures, lammergeiers and falcons, and the distant cliffs and surrounding mountains for wild goats.

The start of the gorge takes you down the wooden staircase through light woodland. There are rock thrushes on the cliffs – the male has a striking orange breast, blue head and white rump. Rock plants like *Aubretia* grow on the cliffs, along with *Linum arboreum*, a low perennial flax with brilliant yellow flowers. Two endemic cliff plants to watch for are the Cretan rock lettuce *Petromarula pinnata*, which looks nothing like a lettuce and isn't even related, with long spikes of deep blue flowers, and *Ebenus cretica*, a bushy pea with grey foliage and pink flowers.

Under the trees at the sides of the paths are orchids, including the handsome yellow *Orchis provincialis*, with a tight flowerhead of spiked yellow florets. Cyclamens and anemones grow here, and you may find a fritillary *Fritillaria messanensis*, with a drooping purple and green bell-shaped flower. Perhaps the most stunning flower is a white paeony with huge, yellow-centred flowers: called *Paeoni clusii* , it grows in profusion around a ruined chapel about 3kms down the gorge. There are more lovely flower meadows round the village of Samariá, about halfway down, but as you drop lower the cliffs tower above you until it is hard to see anything else, and once you are through the famous gates at the end, the walk is less interesting in every sense. Around the base of the cliffs at the bottom of the gorge are colonies of crag martins – a drab-looking bird, but a dramatic flier.

Pete Raine

BOOKS

ARCHAEOLOGY AND ANCIENT HISTORY

There is a vast body of literature on ancient Crete, especially on the Minoans, but a lot of it is very heavy going. Below are some of the more widely available, accessible and useful books. Other names to look out for include **Nicolas Platon** and **Stylianos Alexiou**, whose books you may find available in local translations.

Arthur Evans *The Palace of Minos* (Macmillan 1921). The seminal work, still worth a look if you can find it in a library.

Gerald Cadogan *Palaces of Minoan Crete* (Methuen £5.95). Complete guide to all the major sites, with much more history and general information than the name implies.

R. F. Willetts *The civilization of Ancient Crete* (Batsford £29.95), *Cretan Cults and Festivals* (Greenwood £32.50), *Aristocratic Society in Ancient Crete* (Greenwood £32.50). Rather heavy, scholarly accounts of the social structure of ancient Crete.

Peter Warren *The Aegean Civilizations* (Phaidon £9.95). Illustrated introduction by one of the leading modern experts, a coffee-table book, but informative and easy on the eye. Warren's other publications tend to the technical.

Leonard Cottrell *The Bull of Minos* (Efstathiadis, widely sold on Crete). Breathless and somewhat dated account of the discoveries of Schliemann and Evans; easy reading.

J. D. S. Pendlebury *The Archaeology of Crete* (Methuen 1939, Methuen reprint £37.50). Still the most comprehensive handbook, detailing virtually every archaeological site on the island.

John Chadwick *Linear B and related scripts* (British Museum £4.95). A short version of the decipherment of Linear B by one of those closely responsible – the author of other heavy tomes.

Ian F. Sanders *Roman Crete* (Aris & Phillips £32) Very dry, and hard to come by, but a total record of all Roman remains on Crete.

H. G. Wunderlich *The secret of Crete* (Efstadhiadis, widely sold on Crete). The secret is that the palaces were really elaborate tombs or necropoli. Sensationalist nonsense.

FICTION, TRAVEL AND GENERAL

By contast with the proliferation of ancient history, there is no book in English devoted to modern Cretan history: good general accounts are included in Hopkins's and Smith's books on the island, otherwise you're forced to wade through Greek or Ottoman history, selecting the relevant portions.

Níkos Kazantzakís. Something by the great Cretan novelist and man of letters is essential reading. The novels are all great and easily available in paperback (Faber in Britain, local editions in Crete). Try *Freedom and Death* or *Report to Greco* before *Zorba the Greek*.

Vitzentzos Kornaros *Erotokritos* (tr. Theodore Stefanides; Merlin £16). Beautifully produced English translation of the massive sixteenth-century Cretan epic poem.

Adam Hopkins *Crete, its past, present and people* (Faber £4.99). Excellent general introduction to Cretan history and society.

Michael Llewellyn Smith *The Great Island* (Longman 1965). Covers much of the same as the above, but with more emphasis on folk traditions, and a lengthy analysis of Cretan song.

Robert Pashley *Travels in Crete* (Murray 1837, reprint 1970). The original nineteenth-century British traveller, full of interesting anecdote and outrageous attitude. Very expensive, so try the library.

Edward Lear *The Cretan Journal* (Denise Harvey £14.50). Diary of Lear's trip to Crete in 1864, illustrated with his sketches and watercolours. He didn't enjoy himself much.

Capt. T. A. B. Spratt *Travels and researches in Crete* (1865, reprinted 1965). Another nineteenth-century Briton.

J. E. Hilary Skinner *Roughing it in Crete* (1868). Great title for account of another Englishman's adventures, this time with a band of rebels. Interesting on the less glamorous side of the independence struggle, since he spent the whole time searching for food or dodging Turkish patrols.

Pandelis Prevelakis *Tale of a Town* (Doric Publications, Athens 1977). Rare English translation of a native's description of life in Réthimnon.

Dilys Powell *The Villa Ariadne* (Michael Haag £5.95; also Efstadhiadis, Athens). The story of the British in Crete, from Arthur Evans to Paddy Leigh Fermor, through the villa at Knossós which saw all of them. Good at bringing the excitement of the early archaeological work to life, but rather cloying in style.

David MacNeill Doren *Winds of Crete* (John Murray 1974). An American and his Swedish wife find enlightenment on Crete – between times, quite an amusing travelogue.

Jackson Webb *The Last Lemon Grove* (Weidenfeld 1977). An American surviving alone in Paleohóra. Wonderfully atmospheric.

WORLD WAR II

There is a substantial literature on the Battle of Crete and the resistance, only a part of which is set out below. Several of these were brought out in new editions for the fiftieth anniversary celebrations.

George Psychoundákis *The Cretan Runner* (John Murray £7.95). Account of the invasion and resistance by a Cretan participant; Psychoundakis was a guide and message-runner for all the leading English-speaking protagonists. Great.

I. McD. G. Stewart *Struggle for Crete: a story of lost opportunity* (OUP £7.95). New edition, with authoritative detail on the battle from someone who was there. Critical of the command but a rather dry, military historian's approach.

Antony Beevor *Crete: The Battle and the Resistance* (John Murray £17.95). Published in 1991. Rather shorter, with more on the characters involved. Beevor looks at recent evidence to conclude that defeat was at least in part due to the need to conceal Allied intelligence successes.

Alan Clark *The Fall of Crete*. Very widely available in Crete (in a terrible Efstadhiadis edition) this is a racy and sensational military history. Detailed on the battles, and more critical of the command than you might expect from a Tory cabinet minister.

Tony Simpson *The Battle for Crete, 1941* (Hodder & Stoughton 1971). A very different way of looking at the subject, putting the campaign into an international context and relying heavily on oral history for details of combat. Uncompromisingly critical of the command, and far more interesting than straight military history.

W. Stanley Moss *Ill Met by Moonlight* (Buchan & Enright £5.95). An account of the capture of General Kreipe by one of the participants, largely taken from his diaries of the time. Good Boys' Own adventure stuff. Moss also translated **Baron von der Heydte**'s *Daedalus returned* (Hutchinson 1958) which gives something of the other side of the story.

Evelyn Waugh *Officers and Gentlemen* (Penguin £4.99), *Diaries* (Penguin £9.99). Both include accounts of the battle, and particularly of the horrors of the flight and evacuation.

HIKING AND WILDLIFE

In addition to those below, local shops in Crete have a number of poorly produced guides, especially to wild flowers. There are also local guide booklets on all the major museums and sites, often with nice pictures, but usually very poor text.

Jonnie Godfrey and Elizabeth Karslake *Landscapes of Eastern/Western Crete* (Sunflower £6.95 each). Full of hiking and touring suggestions which make a useful adjunct to this guide.

Marc Dubin *Greece on Foot* (Cordee £6.95). Not much on Crete, but slightly dated details of the south coast paths around the Samarian gorge. New edition due shortly.

Anthony Huxley and Taylor *Flowers of Greece* (Chatto & Windus). The best book for identifying flowers in Crete.

Paul and Jenne Davies and Anthony Huxley *The Wild Orchids of Britain and Europe* (Chatto & Windus). Ideal for orchid freaks, with a good section on where to look for orchids, including some sites in Crete.

Stephanie Coghlan *Birdwatching in Crete* (Self-published £3.50: ISBN 0 9513772 0 5 if you want to order). Slim booklet detailing the best birdwatching sites and what you may see there, with checklists. No pictures for identification, though, so you'll need a guide too.

Peterson, Mountfort and Hollom *Field Guide to the Birds of Britain and Europe* (Collins £9.95). There's no complete guide to Cretan birds, but this is probably the best general tome, ageing but excellent.

Christopher Perrins *Collins New Generation Guide to Birds of Britain and Europe* (Collins £7.95). A newer alternative, which looks at bird ecology as well as pure identification.

Corbet and Ovenden *Collins Guide to the Mammals of Britain and Europe* (Collins £5.95). As good as they come.

Arnold, Burton and Ovenden *Reptiles and Amphibians of Britain and Europe* (Collins £8.95). Again, the Collins guide is the best one.

Michael Chinerey *Collins Guide to the Insects of Britain and Western Europe* (Collins £7.95). This doesn't specifically include Greece (there's no comprehensive guide to Greek insects) but it gives a good general background and identification to the main families of insects that you're likely to see.

BOOKSHOPS

The Travellers' Bookshop (25 Cecil Court, London WC2N 4EZ; ☎071/836 9132), **The Travel Bookshop** (12 Blenheim Crescent, London W11; ☎071/229 5260) and **Daunt's Books for Travellers** (83 Marylebone Hige Street, London W1M 4AL; ☎071/224 2295) are all excellent for travel books of every kind – including second-hand. Specialist titles might be more easily found at the **Hellenic Bookservice** (91 Fortess Road, London NW5, near Kentish Town tube; ☎071/267 9499) or **Zeno's Greek Bookshop** (6 Denmark Street, London WC2, close to Foyles; ☎071/836 2522). Many of the more popular titles are available in Crete, but local editions tend to be shabby and expensive.

LANGUAGE

So many Cretans have been compelled by poverty and other circumstances to work abroad, especially in the English-speaking world, that you'll find someone who speaks some English in almost any village. Add to that the thousands attending language schools or working in the tourist industry – English is the lingua franca of the north coast – and it's easy to see how so many visitors come back having learnt only half a dozen restaurant words between them. You can certainly get by this way, but in quite out of the way places, but it isn't very satisfying.

Greek is not an easy language for English-speakers, but it is a beautiful one and even a brief aquaintance will give you some idea of the debt western European languages owe to it. More important than that, the willingness and ability to say even a few words will transform your status from that of dumb *touristas* to the honourable one of *ksénos*, a word which can mean stranger, traveller and guest all rolled into one.

On top of the usual difficulties of learning a new language, Greek presents the added problem of an entirely separate **alphabet**. Despite initial appearances, this is in practice fairly easily mastered; a skill that will help you enormously if you are going to get around independently (see the *Alphabet and transliteration* section below). In addition, certain combinations of letters have unexpected results. This book's transliteration system should help you make intelligible noises but you have to remember that the correct **stress** (marked in the book with a ´) is absolutely crucial. With the right sounds but the wrong stress people will either fail to understand you, or else understand something quite different from what you intended.

Greek **grammar** is more complicated still: nouns are divided into three genders, all with different case endings in the singular and in the plural, and all adjectives and articles have to agree with these in gender, number and case. (All adjectives are arbitrarily cited in the neuter form in the following lists.) Verbs are even worse. To begin with at least, the best thing is simply to say what you know the way you know it, and never mind the niceties. "Eat meat hungry" should get a result, however grammatically incorrect. If you worry about your mistakes, you'll never say anything.

LANGUAGE BOOKS

TEACH YOURSELF GREEK COURSES

Breakthrough Greece (Pan; book and two cassettes). Excellent, basic teach-yourself course – completely outclasses the competition.

Greek Language and People (BBC Publications; book and cassette available). More limited in scope but good for acquiring the essentials, and the confidence to try them.

PHRASEBOOKS

Harrap's Greek Phrasebook (Harrap; £1.95). Good standard phrasebook.

Greek Travelmate (Drew; £2.25). Functional pocket phrasebook, with contemporary phrases laid out in dictionary form.

Tom Stone *Greek Handbook* (Lycabettus Press, Athens). A cross between a cultural guide, phrasebook and dictionary; excellent emergency manual.

DICTIONARIES

The Oxford Dictionary of Modern Greek (Oxford University Press; £9.95). Considered the best Greek-English, English-Greek dictionary.

Collins Pocket Greek Dictionary (Collins, £4.95). Very nearly as complete as the Oxford and probably better value for the money.

Langenscheidt Pocket Greek Dictionary (Harrap £4.95). Also good, and more genuinely pocket-size.

GREEK WORDS AND PHRASES

Essentials

Yes	Néh	Now	Tóra	Small	Mikró
No	Óhi	Later	Argótera	More	Perisótero
Please	Parakaló	Open	Aniktó	Less	Ligótero
Okay, agreed	Endáksi	Closed	Klistó	A little	Lígo
Thank you (very much)	Efharistó (polí)	Day	Méra	A lot	Polí
		Night	Níkhta	Cheap	Ftinó
I (don't) understand	(dhen) Katalavéno	In the morning	To proí	Expensive	Akrivó
		In the afternoon	To apóyevma	Hot	Zestó
Excuse me, do you speak English?	Parakaló, mípos miláte angliká	In the evening	To vrádhi	Cold	Krío
		Here	Edhó	With	Mazí
		There	Ekí	Without	Horís
Sorry/excuse me	Signómi	This one	Aftó	Quickly	Grígora
		That one	Ekíno	Slowly	Sigá
Today	Símera	Good	Kaló	Mr	Kírios
Tomorrow	Ávrio	Bad	Kakó	Mrs	Kiría
Yesterday	Khthés	Big	Megálo	Miss	Dhespinís

Other Needs

I eat	Trógo	Stamps	Gramatósima	Toilet	Toualéta
I drink	Píno	Petrol station	Venzinádhiko	Police	Astinomía
Bakery	Foúrnos, psomádhiko	Bank	Trápeza	Doctor	Iatrós
Pharmacy	Farmakío	Money	Leftá/Hrímata	Hospital	Nosokomío
Post office	Tahidhromío				

Questions and Requests

To ask a question, its simplest to start with *parakaló*, then name the thing you want in an interrogative tone

Where is the bakery?	Parakaló, o foúrnos?	How many/How much?	Pósi/Póso?
Can you show me the road to . . . ?	Parakaló, o dhrómos ya . . ?	When?	Póte?
		Why?	Yatí?
We'd like a room for two	Parakaló, éna dhomátio ya dhío átoma?	(At what time . . . ?	Ti óra . . . ?
		What is/Which is . . . ?	Ti íneh/pió íneh
May I have a kilo of oranges?	Parakaló, éna kiló portokália?	How much (does it cost)?	Póso káni?
		What time does it open?	Tí óra aníyi?
Where?	Pou?	What time does it close?	Tí óra klíni?
How?	Pos?		

Talking to People

Greek makes the distinction between the informal (*esí*) and formal (*esís*) second person as French does, though only the urban middle class tend to speak this way. Young people, older people and country people nearly always use *esí* even with total strangers. In any event, no one will be that bothered if you get it wrong. By far the most common greeting, on meeting and parting, is *yá sou/yá sas* – literally 'health to you'.

Hello	Hérete	My name is. . .	Meh léne. . .
Good morning	Kalí méra	Speak slower, please	Parakaló, miláte pió sigá
Good evening	Kalí spéra	How do you say it in Greek?	Pos léyete sta Eliniká?
Good night	Kalí níkhta		
Goodbye	Adío	I don't know	Dhen kséro
How are you?	Ti kánis/Ti kánete?	See you tomorrow	Tha se dho ávrio
I'm fine	Kalá ímeh	See you soon	Tha se dho se lígo
And you?	Keh esís?	Let's go	Páme
What's your name?	Pos se léne?	Please help me	Parakaló, na me voithíste

Greek's Greek

There are numerous words and phrases which you will hear constantly, even if you rarely have the chance to use them. These are a few of the most common.

Éla	Come (literally) but also Speak to me! You don't say! etc.	*Po-po-po!*	Dismay! Concern! Surprise! (like French 'O la la')
Oríste	What can I do for you? At your service	*Pedhí mou*	My boy/girl, sonny, friend, etc.
Ti néa?	What's new?	*Maláka(s)*	Literally 'wanker', but often used as an informal way of
Ti yíneteh?	What's going on (here)?		addressing someone.
Étsi k'étsi	So-so	*Sigá sigá*	Take your time, slow down
Opá!	Whoops! Watch it!	*Kaló taxídhi*	Bon voyage

Accommodation

Hotel	*Ksenodhohío*	Cold water	*krío neró*
A room. . .	*Éna dhomátio . . .*	Can I see it?	*Boró na to dho?*
for one/two/three people	*ya éna/dhío/tría átoma*	Can we camp here?	*Boróume na váloumeh ti skiní edhó?*
for one/two/three nights	*ya mía/dhío/trís vradhies*		
with a double bed	*meh megálo kreváti*	Campsite	*Kamping/Kataskínosi*
with a shower	*meh doús*	Tent	*Skiní*
hot water	*zestó neró*	Youth hostel	*Ksenodhohío neótitos*

On the Move

Aeroplane	*Aeropláno*	I'm going to. . .	*Páo sto. . .*
Bus	*Leoforío*	I want to get off at. . .	*Thélo na katévo sto. . .*
Car	*Aftokínito*	The road to. . .	*O dhrómos ya. . .*
Motorbike, moped	*Mihanáki*	Near	*Kondá*
Taxi	*Taksí*	Far	*Makriá*
Ship	*Plío/Vapóri/Karávi*	Left	*Aristerá*
Bicycle	*Podhílato*	Right	*Dheksiá*
Hitching	*Otostóp*	Straight ahead. . .	*Katefthía*
On foot	*Meh ta pódhia*	A ticket to. . .	*Éna isistírio ya. . .*
Bus station	*Praktorío leoforíon*	A return ticket	*Éna isistírio me epistrofí*
Bus stop	*Stási*	Beach	*Paralía*
Harbour	*Limáni*	Cave	*Spiliá*
What time does it leave?	*Ti óra févyi?*	Centre (of town)	*Kéndro*
What time does it arrive?	*Ti óra ftháni?*	Church	*Eklisía*
How many kilometres?	*Pósa hiliómetra?*	Sea	*Thálasa*
How many hours?	*Póses óres?*	Village	*Horió*
Where are you going?	*Pou pas?*	Crossroads	*Dhiastávrosi*

Numbers

1	*éna/mía*	12	*dhódheka*	90	*enenínda*
2	*dhío*	13	*dhekatrís*	100	*ekató*
3	*trís/tría*	14	*dhekatéseres*	150	*ekatón penínda*
4	*téseres/tésera*	20	*íkosi*	200	*dhiakósies/ia*
5	*pénde*	21	*íkosi éna*	500	*pendakósies/ia*
6	*éksi*	30	*triánda*	1000	*hílies/ia*
7	*eftá*	40	*saránda*	2000	*dhío hiliádhes*
8	*okhtó*	50	*penínda*	1,000,000	*éna ekatomírio*
9	*enyá*	60	*eksínda*	first	*próto*
10	*dhéka*	70	*evdhomínda*	second	*dhéftero*
11	*éndheka*	80	*ogdhónda*	third	*tríto*

The time and days of the week

Sunday	*Kiriakí*	Saturday	*Sávato*	Five minutes past seven	*Eftá keh pénde*
Monday	*Dheftéra*	What time is it?	*Ti óra íneh?*	Half past eleven	*Éndheka keh misí*
Tuesday	*Tríti*	One, two, three o'clock	*Mía, dhío, trís*	Half hour	*misí óra*
Wednesday	*Tetárti*			Quarter hour	*éna tétarto*
Thursday	*Pémpti*	Twenty minutes to four	*Tésseres pará íkosi*		
Friday	*Paraskeví*				

THE GREEK ALPHABET: TRANSLITERATION

Set out below is the Greek alphabet, the system of transliteration used in this book, and a brief aid to pronunciation:

Greek	Transliteration	Pronounced
Α, α	a	a as in cat
Β, β	v	v as in vet
Γ, γ	y/g	y as in yes, except before consonants and a, o or long i, when it's a breathy, throaty version of the g in gap.
Δ, δ	dh	th as in then
Ε, ε	e	e as in get
Ζ, ζ	z	z sound
Η, η	i	ee sound as in feet
Θ, θ	th	th as in theme
Ι, ι	i	i as in bit
Κ, κ	k	k sound
Λ, λ	l	l sound
Μ, μ	m	m sound
Ν, ν	n	n sound
Ξ, ξ	ks	ks sound
Ο, ο	o	o as in hot
Π, π	p	p sound
Ρ, ϱ	r	rolled r sound
Σ, σ, ς	s	s sound
Τ, τ	t	t sound
Υ, υ	i	long i, indistinguishable from η
Φ, φ	f	f sound
Χ, χ	h	harsh h sound, like the ch in loch
Ψ, ψ	ps	ps as in lips
Ω, ω	o	o as in hot, indistinguishable from o

Combinations and dipthongs

ΑΙ, αι	e	e as in get
ΑΥ, αυ	av/af	av or af depending on following consonant
ΕΙ, οι	i	long i, exactly like η
ΟΙ, οι	i	long i, identical again
ΕΥ, ευ	ev/ef	ev or ef depending on following consonant
ΟΥ, ου	ou	ou as in tourist
ΓΓ, γγ	ng	ng as in angle
ΓΥ, γυ	g/ng	g as in goat at the beginning of a word; ng in the middle
ΜΠ, μπ	b	b as in bar
ΝΤ, ντ	d/nd	d at the beginning of a word; nd in the middle
ΤΣ, τσ	ts	ts as in hits

GREEK TERMS AND ACRONYMS: A GLOSSARY

ACROPOLIS Ancient, fortified hilltop.

ÁYIOS/AYÍA/ÁYII Saint or holy (m/f/pl), common place name prefix (abbrev. Ag. or Ay.): Áyios Nikólaos, St. Nicholas; Ayía Triádha, Holy Trinity.

AGORA Market and meeting place of an ancient city.

AMPHORA Tall, narrow-necked jar for oil or wine.

ÁNO Upper; as in Ano Zákros.

APSE Curved recess at the altar end of a church.

ARCHAIC PERIOD Late Iron Age from around 750 BC to the start of the Classical Period in the fifth century BC.

ARSENALI Arsenals – a term used rather loosely for many Venetian defensive and harbour works.

ATRIUM Central altar-court of a Roman house.

BASILICA Colonnaded "hall-type" church.

BYZANTINE EMPIRE Created by the division of the Roman Empire in 395 AD, this was the eastern half, ruled from Byzantium or Constantinople (modern Istanbul). On Crete Byzantine churches of the fifth to the twelfth century are almost commonplace, and Byzantine art flourished again after the fall of Constantinople in 1453, under Venetian rule, when many artists and scholars fled to the island.

CENTRAL COURT Paved area at the heart of a Minoan palace.

CLASSICAL PERIOD Essentially from the end of the Persian Wars in the fifth century BC to the unification of Greece under Philip II of Macedon (338 BC).

DHIMARHÍO Town hall (modern usage).

DORIAN Civilisation which overran the Mycenaeans from the north and became their successors through most of Greece, including Crete.

EPARHÍA Greek Orthodox diocese, also the smallest subdivision of a modern province.

ETEO-CRETAN Literally true Cretan, the Eteo-Cretans are believed to have been remnants of the Minoan people who kept a degree of their language and culture alive in isolated centres in eastern Crete as late as the third century BC.

GEOMETRIC PERIOD Post-Mycenaean Iron Age named for the style of its pottery: beginnings are in the early eleventh century BC with the arrival of Dorian peoples – by the eighth, with the development of representational styles, it becomes known as the ARCHAIC period.

HELLENISTIC PERIOD The last and most unified Greek Empire, created by Philip II and Alexander the Great, finally collapsing with the fall of Corinth to the Romans in 146 BC.

HÓRA Main town of a region; literally it means "the place".

IKONOSTÁSI Screen between the nave of a church and the altar, often covered in icons.

JANISSARY Member of the Turkish Imperial Guard: in Crete under the Turks a much feared mercenary force, often forcibly recruited from the local population.

KAFENÍON Coffeehouse/café: in a small village the centre of communal life and probably the bus stop too.

KAÍKI A caique, or medium-sized boat, traditionally wooden. Now used for just about any coast-hopping or excursion boat.

KAPETÁNIOS Widely used term of honour for a man of local power – originally for guerrilla leaders who earned the title through acts of particular bravado.

KÁSTRO Medieval castle or any fortified hill.

KÁTO Lower; as in Káto Zákros.

KERNOS Ancient cult vessel or altar with a number of receptacles for offerings.

KRATER Large, two-handled wine bowl.

LARNAKES Minoan clay coffins.

LUSTRAL BASIN A small sunken chamber in Minoan palaces reached by steps: perhaps actually some kind of bath but more likely for purely ritual purification.

MEGARON Principal hall of a Mycenaean palace.

MELTÉMI North wind that blows across the Aegean in summer and can be vicious in Crete. Its force is gauged by what it knocks over – "tableweather", "chairweather" etc.

MINOAN Crete's great Bronze Age Civilisation which dominated the Aegean from about 2500–1400 BC.

MONÍ Monastery or convent.

MYCENAEAN Mainland civilisation centred on Mycenae c.1700–1100 BC: some claim they were responsible for the destruction of the Minoans, and certainly Mycenaean influence pervaded Crete in the late and post-Minoan periods.

NÉOS, NÉA, NÉO New

NEOLITHIC The earliest era of settlement in Crete, characterised by the use of stone tools and weapons together with basic agriculture.

NOMÓS Modern Greek province: Crete is divided into four.

PALEÓS, PALEÁ, PALEÓ Old.

PALLIKÁRI Literally "brave man': in Crete a guerrilla fighter, particularly in the struggle for independence from the Turks, also a general term for a tough young man.

PANAYÍA The Virgin Mary.

PANIYÍRI Festival or feast – the local celebration of a holy day.

PANTOCRATOR Literally "The Almighty", a stern figure of God the Father frescoed or in mosaic on the dome of many Byzantine churches.

PARALÍA Seafront promenade.

PEAK SANCTUARY Mountain-top shrine, often in or associated with a cave, sometimes in continuous use from ·Neolithic through to Roman times.

PERÍPTERO Street kiosk.

PERISTYLE Colonnade or area surrounded by colonnade, used especially of Minoan halls or courtyards.

PÍTHOS (pl. PÍTHOI) Large ceramic jar for storing oil, grain etc very common in the Minoan palaces and used in almost identical form in modern Cretan homes.

PLATÍA Square or plaza. KENTRIKÍ PLATÍA is the main square.

PROPILEA Portico or entrance to an ancient building.

RHYTON Vessel, often horn-shaped, for pouring libations or offerings.

STELE Upright stone slab or column, usually inscribed.

STOA Colonnaded walkway in classical era marketplace.

THEATRAL AREA Open area found in most of the Minoan palaces with seat-like steps around. May have been a type of theatre or ritual area, but not conclusively proved.

THÓLOS Conical or beehive-shaped building, especially a Mycenaean tomb.

ACRONYMS

EA Greek Left (*Ellenikí Aristerá*), formerly the Euro-communists (*KKE-Esoterikóu*).

EOS Acronym for the Greek Mountaineers' Club.

EOT *Ellinikós Organismós Tourismóu* – the official Greek tourist organisation.

EPEN Fascist party, consisting mostly of adherents to the imprisoned Papadopoulos.

KKE Greek Communist Party.

KTEL The bus company (actually a national syndicate of small companies). Often used to refer to bus stations.

ND Conservative *Néa Dhimokratía* party, led by Konstantine Mitsotakis and currently holding power by a narrow majority.

NTOG National Tourist Organisation of Greece (English version of EOT).

OTE Greek telephone company.

PASOK Pan-Hellenic Socialist Movement, currently led by Andreas Papandreou and the main opposition party.

INDEX

THE ROUGH GUIDES

The complete series of Rough Guides are available from all good bookshops but can be obtained directly from Penguin by writing to: *Penguin Direct, Penguin Books Ltd, Bath Road, Harmondsworth, West Drayton, Middlesex UB7 0DA; or telephone our credit line on 081 899 4036 (9am - 5pm)* and ask for Penguin Direct. Visa, Access and Amex accepted. Delivery will normally be within 14 working days.

Title	ISBN	Price	Mediterranean Wildlife	0747100993	£7.95
Amsterdam	1858280184	£6.99	Mexico	0747101493	£6.95
Barcelona and Catalunya	0747102716	£7.99	Morocco	1858280648	£7.99
Berlin	1858280338	£8.99	Nepal	0747102562	£6.95
Brazil	0747101272	£7.95	New York	1858280737	£6.99
Brittany & Normandy	1858280192	£7.99	Nothing Ventured	0747102082	£7.99
Bulgaria	1858280478	£8.99	Paris	1858280389	£7.99
California	1858280575	£9.99	Peru	0747102546	£7.95
Canada	185828001X	£10.99	Portugal	1858280222	£7.99
Crete	1858280494	£6.99	Prague	185828015X	£7.99
Cyprus	185828032X	£8.99	Provence/Cote d'Azur	1858280230	£8.99
Czech and Slovak Republics	185828029X	£8.99	Pyrenees	1858280524	£7.99
Egypt	1858280028	£9.99	San Francisco	0747102589	£5.99
Europe	1858280273	£12.99	Scandinavia	1858280397	£10.99
Florida	1858280109	£7.99	Sicily	1858280370	£8.99
France	1858280508	£9.99	Spain	1858280079	£8.99
Germany	1858280257	£11.99	Thailand	1858280168	£8.99
Greece	1858280206	£9.99	Tunisia	074710249X	£8.99
Guatemala & Belize	1858280117	£7.99	Turkey	1858280133	£8.99
Holland, Belgium, Luxembourg	1858280036	£8.99	Tuscany and Umbria	1858280559	£8.99
Hong Kong & Macau	1858280761	£6.99	U.S.A.	1858280281	£12.99
Hungary	1858280214	£7.99	Venice	1858280362	£8.99
Ireland	1858280516	£8.99	West Africa	1858280141	£12.99
Italy	1858280311	£12.99	Women Travel	1858280710	£7.99
Kenya	185828063X	£7.99	Zimbabwe & Botswana	1858280060	£8.99

The availability and published prices quoted are correct at the time of going to press but are subject to alteration without prior notice.
Penguin Direct ordering facilities are only available in the UK.

You are A STUDENT

You travel THE WORLD

You want TO SAVE MONEY

Here's how

The International Student Identity Card

Available at Student Travel Offices Worldwide.

Entitles you to discounts and special services worldwide.

BEFORE YOU TRAVEL THE WORLD, TALK TO AN EXPERIENCED STAMP COLLECTOR.

At STA Travel we're all seasoned travellers so we should know a thing or two about where you're headed. We can offer you the best deals on fares with the flexibility to change your mind as you go – without having to pay over the top for the privilege. We operate from 120 offices worldwide. So call in soon.

74 and 86 Old Brompton Road, SW7, 117 Euston Road, NW1. London.
Manchester. Leeds. Oxford. Cambridge. Bristol.
North America **071-937 9971**. Europe **071-937 9921**. Rest of World **071-937 9962**
(incl. Sundays 10am-2pm). **OR 061-834 0668 (Manchester)**

WHEREVER YOU'RE BOUND, WE'RE BOUND TO HAVE BEEN. **STA**

STA TRAVEL